THIS DAY IN VANCOUVER

ACKNOWLEDGEMENTS

This project would not have been remotely possible without access to the Vancouver Archives' extensive and invaluable collection, including Early Vancouver, and the hundreds of public domain photographs of the city and its history that they have collected. I also owe a huge debt of thanks to a number of folks far cleverer than myself, for their help throughout the research process—in particular Sean Kheraj for his help with the finer details of Stanley Park, Vaughn Palmer for his reminiscences of The Clash, Aaron Chapman for setting me straight on Howard Hughes, Rosanne Sia for her insight into the racial politics of Chinatown cafés, Gordon Price for his knowledge of the West End, and Pierre Coupey for his assistance with the early days of the *Georgia Straight*.

A special thanks to Brian Kaufman and Karen Green at Anvil Press, for taking a chance on a first-time author, and for being such generally swell individuals; and to Derek von Essen for both his saintly patience and stellar design work. And one final word of thanks to Jillian Povarchook at the Museum of Vancouver, Ann Dreolini at the Vancouver Aquarium, Sandra Boutilier with Pacific Newspaper Group, Sophie Brodovitch at Equinox Gallery, and Fred Herzog for being so incredible and accommodating when it came to image licensing. Also, Jeannie Hounslow at CVA, and Weiyan Yan and Chelsea Shriver at UBC Rare Books and Special Collections for their diligence and assistance.

You are gods and goddesses all.

—JESSE DONALDSON, VANCOUVER

THIS DAY IN VANCOUVER
JESSE DONALDSON

ANVIL PRESS | VANCOUVER | 2013

2nd printing: December 2013

Library and Archives Canada Cataloguing in Publication

Donaldson, Jesse, 1982-
    This day in Vancouver / Jesse Donaldson.

Includes bibliographical references and index.
ISBN 978-1-927380-42-0

    1. Vancouver (B.C.)--History. I. Title.

FC3847.4.D65 2013   971.1'33   C2013-901602-3

Book design by Derek von Essen

Anvil Press gratefully acknowledges the support of the Government of Canada through the Canada Book Fund, the Canada Council for the Arts, and the Province of British Columbia through the British Columbia Arts Council and the Book Publishing Tax Credit.

 Canada Council **Conseil des Arts**
for the Arts **du Canada**

 BRITISH COLUMBIA ARTS COUNCIL
Supported by the Province of British Columbia

Canadä

Anvil Press Publishers
P.O. Box 3008, Main Post Office
Vancouver, B.C. Canada
V6B 3X5
www.anvilpress.com

Printed and bound in Canada

To Mom and Dad
And to Nettie, Who Got Everything Started

JANUARY 1, 1929

AFTER YEARS OF CIVIC PLEBISCITES, and petitioning of the provincial government, the city establishes for the first time the boundaries of modern-day Vancouver.

"With the advent of 1929, the city further expands by amalgamating with the municipalities of South Vancouver and Point Grey," declares Mayor William Malkin in his inaugural address, "an undertaking which I consider will prove more beneficial to the three districts than even the most optimistic can at present predict."

The merger, made official by a provincial statute approved in 1928, brings Vancouver's total population to almost 229,000. Its total land area now covers 114 square kilometres—a far cry from its humble beginnings as a one-street logging village.

"With amalgamation has come a new vision," Malkin continues. "I trust we shall not disappoint the hope which this new vision has developed . . . We are entering an era of permanent development and I feel certain the citizens expect us to show courage, initiative and foresight, adopting a progressive program for the building and development of the new greater city on modern and up-to-date lines."

This merger is not the first time Vancouver has chosen to amalgamate with a nearby district. Before 1911, the Greater Vancouver area was a smattering of small, spread-out municipalities, each with its own services, finances, and government, and the boundaries of Vancouver itself extended only as far as Nanaimo Street to the east, Alma to the west, and 16th Avenue to the south. However, in early 1911, a merger with both Hastings Townsite and District Lot 301 (also known as "No Man's Land") expanded the city's boundaries and saw its population increase by a half. Attempts to annex even more territory were discussed (with the residents of working-class South Vancouver avidly supporting the idea), but those plans were ultimately halted by an unwilling provincial government.

The amalgamation will proceed remarkably quickly, mostly because the municipalities already share sewage, water, and transit systems. The monumental task of drafting a new civic budget, and combining the police and the fire departments, will still take a number of months.

The boundaries set by the 1929 amalgamation will remain unchanged into the next century.

Granville Street, circa 1920.
IMAGE COURTESY OF THE VANCOUVER ARCHIVES (STR N187)

JANUARY 2, 1943

FOLLOWING A SPIKE IN HOLIDAY LIQUOR SALES, and as a result of wartime restrictions on commodities, Vancouver experiences an acute beer shortage.

"The stocks of bottled beer are 'very lean' and may continue to be so for some time," reports the *Vancouver Sun*. "The breweries may not be able to supply the stores for a time."

"The cut ordered by Ottawa to 70 percent of supplies from the distilleries will inevitably mean that stocks of some brands will go short," Liquor Control Board chairman W.F. Kennedy tells associates at a conference that afternoon. "But if the public is reasonable in its drinking there should be little trouble."

With World War II at its height, wartime restrictions are in full effect in Vancouver, with "dimouts" required overnight, federal orders to simplify clothing (thus reducing demand for materials), and rations on tea, coffee, butter, and gasoline. Some commodities, such as condensed milk (particularly the 16-ounce containers) are entirely withheld from the public.

Luckily, while beer may be in short supply, decent stockpiles of other types of alcohol are still available, with the local dailies reporting a reasonable supply of imported scotch, rum, and other hard alcohol. However, as the *Sun* cautions, "The 40-oz bottles of rye, which practically disappeared for days before Christmas and again at New Year's, will be in the stores again but in a limited quantity. Other provinces have discontinued selling the large bottles altogether and BC may follow suit before long."

As a result of the shortage, the Liquor Control Board issues an order stating that no citizen may purchase more than a dozen bottles of malt liquor from any government liquor store, with beer parlours receiving only "10 percent of the former supply of bottled beer."

People lined up outside the government liquor store on Beatty Street, 1943.
IMAGE COURTESY OF THE VANCOUVER ARCHIVES (CVA 1184-637, PHOTOGRAPHER JACK LINDSAY)

JANUARY 3, 1922

AFTER TWO DAYS WITH FEW PROBLEMS AND—surprisingly—no accidents, the *Vancouver Province* reports on the biggest change to city traffic since the introduction of the automobile: switching to the right side of the road.

"With the customary adaptability of the West and its attitude of studied calm in the presence of an approved reform or of anything which it does not understand, the City of Vancouver kept to the right at 6 a.m. on Sunday," reports the paper, "and has been there ever since, just as if it had been doing it for centuries."

The change, which has been in effect since January 1, comes as the result of a desire to unify with the US and other Canadian provinces, including Alberta, Saskatchewan, and Quebec, whose citizens have driven on the right-hand side of the road for years.

"It was supposed and prophesied by croakers that there would be a scene of wild confusion at all the great nerve centres of the traffic system, that there would be innumerable accidents," the article continues, "that people would be killed every ten minutes and the gods of all old customs would rise up and demand a continuous stream of human sacrifices. But there were no sacrifices and no confusion."

Shortly thereafter, many of the maritime provinces will follow suit—though Newfoundland (not officially part of Canada until the late 1940s) will resist the change for a further 25 years, keeping its drivers on the left side of the road until 1947.

"One of the most noticeable features of the change is the air of uncertainty that seems to pervade the minds of pedestrians while they are still safe on the sidewalk," the paper concludes. "You will see a man going quietly about his business till a street car approaches him on the new side of the road and then just for a moment there passes over his face a look of indecision and he peers furtively over his shoulder to make sure that he isn't walking backwards."

Car on its side after an accident, circa 1940.
IMAGE COURTESY OF THE VANCOUVER ARCHIVES (CVA 1184-3226, PHOTOGRAPHER JACK LINDSAY)

JANUARY 4, 1889

"ANOTHER EPOCH IN THE HISTORY OF VANCOUVER," declares the *Vancouver Daily World*, as Mayor David Oppenheimer and a "little knot of citizens" gather at exactly noon to witness a momentous event in the history of downtown traffic: the opening of the Granville Street Bridge.

"Those present asserted that never before had they beheld so perfect a piece of work," the paper reports, "all of which reflects credit on the mechanical skill and ability of those connected with the Vancouver Foundry."

The as-yet-unnamed timber-and-ironwork bridge (the *Vancouver Daily News-Advertiser* refers to it as the "North Arm Road Bridge") measures 2,400 feet in length, cost roughly $16,000 to construct, and contains a "swing" section in the middle to allow for the passage of boats. Construction took a total of 16 months, and, with the span's official opening (the switch is thrown by Oppenheimer's young son), Vancouverites are given their first built crossing of False Creek.

"Just at twelve o'clock the order was given to open," reports the *News-Advertiser*, "and in answer to the lever the bridge swung gradually round with an ease that bore evidence to the skill which had been expended on its construction, and fitted to its place with such exactness that it was impossible to detect the slightest lowering or rising . . . After the bridge had been opened and closed several times, and every person had expressed his admiration at the manner in which it worked, the Mayor congratulated Engineer Lawson on the successful completion of his labor."

"When given a coat of paint," the *World* concludes, "this bridge will be a credit to the city, one which will last for many years to come."

The original Granville Street Bridge will last for exactly 20 years, before being replaced in 1909 by a two-lane, $500,000 swing-span made of solid steel. The two bridges will exist side by side until the original is demolished in 1910. Following years of discussion, and concerns over increasing auto traffic, a third bridge will be erected in 1954, at a cost of $16.4 million.

The original Granville Street Bridge, 1909.
IMAGE COURTESY OF THE VANCOUVER ARCHIVES (M-11-21)

JANUARY 5, 1912

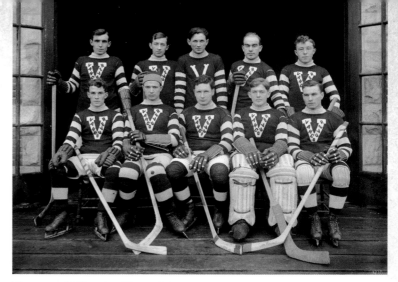

Vancouver Millionaires Team, 1914.
Image Courtesy of the Vancouver Archives (CVA 99-126, photographer Stuart Thomson)

Vancouverites flock to the arena on Georgia Street for a chance to see the Vancouver Millionaires play against the New Westminster Royals, as the two teams compete in the city's first game of ice hockey.

"Real hockey has never been seen here before, so if the good people of the city who have sport at heart fail to be present at the exact minute of 8:30 p.m., they will miss an epochal minute in the sporting life of the province," reports the morning edition of the *Vancouver Sun*.

"Only a small percentage of the city's population has been privileged to see the game played in other parts of Canada," agrees the *Vancouver Province*, "and to over fifty per cent of the attendance this evening the game will be very much of a novelty."

Since the appearance of the first club teams in Montreal more than 30 years earlier, ice hockey has become wildly popular throughout eastern and central Canada. The Pacific Coast Hockey League on the other hand, is a relatively new addition to the game, featuring only three teams, and having been formed just one year earlier by brothers Frank and Lester Patrick. At first, the arena's 5,000 spectators (half of its 10,000 seat capacity) are lukewarm in their response to the game; however, it takes only minutes before the athletes (referred to by the *Province* as "hockeyists") have whipped the crowd into a cheering frenzy. Of particular note to attendees are the game's speed (compared favourably by some to lacrosse), the dazzling athleticism of one "Si" Griffis, and a hitherto unseen technological marvel: the "monster" electric clock used to keep time.

"One feature of hockey which makes it so popular everywhere is its simplicity," explains the *Province*, detailing the rules of the thrilling new sport. "The game is played with teams of seven men a side and victory is decided by the number of goals scored by each. The players line up on side as in rugby football and the puck, a flat rubber disc is faced in the centre of the ice, which measures 85 feet by 210."

Despite their rookie status, the fledgling Millionaires manage to defeat the Royals by a margin of 8 to 3.

"It was not Stanley Cup hockey by any means. It was simply individual brilliance in play which took the hearts of the fans on a toboggan, and for that reason, it was a good hockey match," reports the *Province*. "Vancouver has yet to be educated up to the hockey game. When it is, there will be better games played than that witnessed last night, because the people will demand them."

The Millionaires will go on to win the Stanley Cup in 1915, the only time the trophy has been awarded to a Vancouver hockey team.

JANUARY 6, 1908

ALL THE SEATS IN THE HOUSE ARE FILLED (twice over), and Vancouver buzzes with excitement as Alexander Pantages opens the first of his Canadian vaudeville houses at 152 E. Hastings Street, setting the stage for the beginning of an international empire.

"When the orchestra at Pantages' new vaudeville theatre sounded its first note last night, an audience that filled every seat in the splendid house vouchsafed its appreciation of the opening of the theatre by applause that only subsided with the raising of the curtain upon the first act," reports the *Vancouver Province*. "Long before the performance opened every seat in the house was taken and even when the second performance was ready for the stage the house was again filled to capacity."

Pantages—who began his career in Skagway, Alaska, entertaining prospectors for the exorbitant price of $12.50 a ticket—has already gained a reputation as a shrewd and ruthless businessman, keeping his vaudeville shows brief and gearing them toward a working-class audience. The evening features seven acts in its program, including "Wallace, the Untameable Lion," "Bunth and Rudd, dancers, burlesquers and comedians," and "Mr. and Mrs. John Chick in their sketch, A Matrimonial Mix-up."

"There were seven feature acts upon the programme," the paper gushes, "and to pick out one as the premier would be doing an injustice to the others."

Pantages will continue to expand his theatre empire, eventually incorporating motion pictures, fighting off numerous takeover bids from rival RKO, and, at the height of his power, owning more than 70 theatres in the US and Canada. The Vancouver Pantages will go on to feature such acts as Charlie Chaplin, Stan Laurel, Jack Dempsey, and even Babe Ruth.

By the late 1920s, however, the theatre mogul will have fallen on hard times: charged with the rape of a 17-year-old chorus girl, Pantages will be sentenced to 50 years in prison. Although an appeal will grant him a new trial and an eventual acquittal, the exhausted Pantages will choose to retire from the business, selling his empire to RKO in 1929 for $24 million—much below his initial asking price.

The Vancouver Pantages will continue to provide live entertainment until 1974, at which point it will become exclusively a movie theatre, showing low-quality foreign-language films for close to 20 years. It will then remain vacant for decades, despite the efforts of a number of local organizations (such as Heritage Vancouver) to preserve the building.

In 2007, after years of negotiations, public consultation, and numerous proposals, city council will vote to demolish the Pantages Theatre, thus destroying the oldest surviving vaudeville stage in the country.

JANUARY 7, 1925

"John Bruce Kills Sea Monster 90 Feet Under Water!" exclaims the front-page headline of the *Vancouver Daily Province* as a city diver spends 15 minutes in the waters of the Second Narrows locked in mortal combat with a shark.

The burly, square-jawed Bruce, a 17-year veteran diver, who has worked all over the world, including for the British, French, and Italian governments, and who has called the waters of Burrard Inlet his home for the past three years, was inspecting water mains when he encountered the creature.

"It was early in the afternoon while I was surveying the pipes for possible leaks that the shark appeared," Bruce explains, "and I saw the dark shadow of his form coming for me. It made three attacks and for fifteen minutes I had to watch my step and an opening for an uppercut. On the second I hit him on the nose with an iron bar I had for warding off any prowling octopus. I have killed two of those chaps within the past week. I was not prepared for a shark."

Luckily, Bruce managed to keep his wits about him, and over the course of the battle, succeeded in gaining the upper hand, finally killing the shark with three powerful blows to the head. Following Bruce's victory, the creature is hauled up onto a nearby dock, where it will be displayed for the remainder of the day, drawing a sizable crowd before the carcass is finally destroyed. This is not the first time a Vancouverite has been attacked by a shark in local waters. In 1905, 8-year-old Harry Menzies was nearly devoured in False Creek by an 1,100-pound shark of the "genuine man-eating Hawaiian variety."

"I have had tussles with sharks in many waters, but never before one in these, nor anywhere at that depth," Bruce concludes. "The next time Mr. Shark will find me well armed, believe me."

Diver inspecting a broken water main in the First Narrows, 1890.
Image courtesy of the Vancouver Archives (Port P162, photographer Bailey & Neelands)

JANUARY 8, 1886

Water Street circa 1890.
IMAGE COURTESY OF THE VANCOUVER ARCHIVES (STR P266)

FOLLOWING AN IMPROMPTU PUBLIC MEETING and address by MLA John Robson, citizens of the tiny logging community of Granville elect a committee for the express purpose of petitioning the provincial government to allow them to incorporate as an official city.

"The attendance was large, very large, considering the shortness and inefficiency of the notice," the *New Westminster British Columbian* will report the following week. "Before sitting down, the speaker suggested whether it would not be as well that the present meeting should appoint a committee for the purpose of preparing a bill for incorporation and taking the necessary steps towards the attainment of that object."

Robson, a former journalist and MLA for New Westminster, has more than a passing interest in the future of the rough-and-tumble town. In addition to being the owner of the *British Columbian*, Robson is a wealthy land speculator with CPR affiliations and a considerable investment in the land surrounding the Coal Harbour terminus. His speech to the crowd is as much public address as it is CPR sales pitch, extolling "the bright prospects opening up before the people of Granville" and warning residents to act "in harmony with the Canadian Pacific Railway Company and others largely interested in the great city of the future." (The railway is already notorious for bullying governments and private citizens into giving up their land, which is then sold at a profit.) Minutes after Robson's address, a committee will be elected to draft the petition for Granville's incorporation, with one additional request: that its name be changed (at the suggestion of CPR general manager W.C. Van Horne) to "Vancouver."

A little over a month later, the petition will be received by the legislature, though few MLAs will be enthusiastic about the name change.

"I did not suppose anyone would say the selected name had been a wise one," MLA John Grant will say, adding grudgingly that he "thought it to be an extremely injudicious one, but many maps had been draughted, and other matters affecting the place had dealt with it under this name, which now being pretty well known, it would be better to retain."

MLA R.L. Galbraith will be even less supportive, stating that "the selection of the present name was not a matter of local option at all but was forced on the citizens of that place by an agent of the CPR."

Nonetheless, the City of Vancouver will be officially incorporated less than two months later. Robson (along with several other prominent CPR associates) will become an instant millionaire and will go on to serve as the ninth premier of British Columbia.

JANUARY 9, 1972

AFTER NEARLY A DECADE OF CONSULTATION, Mayor Tom Campbell cuts the ribbon on the newly completed Georgia Viaduct before a crowd of more than 250—virtually all of them present to protest the project.

"Mayor Tom Campbell completed the official opening of the new Georgia Viaduct Sunday by driving across in his official limousine," reports the *Vancouver Sun*, "but he needed the help of four motorcycle police to get through jeering demonstrators."

The viaduct—the first part of a proposed freeway system that would see large portions of Strathcona and Chinatown bulldozed—has drawn considerable fire from locals and community activists. The crowd heckles speakers, waves signs, drowns out Archbishop James Carney with a chorus of boos as he attempts to pray for the $11.2 million structure, and manages to block traffic for close to an hour.

"The demonstrators strung their own ribbon and blocked the west end of the new north span immediately after the official ribbon-cutting," the *Sun* continues. "The mayor's car was dented and had its aerials damaged as demonstrators kicked the sides, spat at the windows and jumped on the hood."

Police on motorcycles manage to push through the crowd, but not before several firecrackers are thrown at the mayor's car, and a woman with a cap gun is wrestled to the ground by a nearby constable. According to an offhand comment in the paper, some demonstrators in the crowd (which includes a number of children) are also "knocked down by the motorcycles," though no injuries are reported.

The demolition of the original Georgia Viaduct, 1971.
IMAGE COURTESY OF THE CITY OF VANCOUVER ARCHIVES (CVA 216-14, PHOTOGRAPHER A.J. INGRAM)

"The ratepayers approved this viaduct," Campbell tells reporters. "We're a growing, developing city and if we were to listen to the knockers we'd never get anything done. As long as I am in office we'll pay no attention to these vocal minorities."

Campbell's tenure as mayor has been a tumultuous one. Hated by the city's youth and counterculture figures, he has also been regularly accused of being in bed with big development (a former property developer himself), and many of his proposals (including a plan to build a hotel at the entrance to Stanley Park) have met with widespread opposition.

In the face of community protest, and with civic, federal, and provincial governments unwilling to foot the bill, the freeway project will fall apart. At the end of 1972, when Campbell's term as mayor is up, he will not seek re-election.

JANUARY 10, 1978

WITH THE HOLIDAY SEASON OFFICIALLY ENDED, the *Vancouver Province* reports on the curious case of a Christmas card delivered to a Kitsilano address . . . 40 years late.

"We have some strange ones from time to time," says post office spokesperson Betty Amos. "We would certainly like to see the card. There could be a thousand reasons as to why this occurred. It's like buying a pig in a poke to guess at the reason."

The card, postmarked December 22, 1937, and addressed to a Mrs. S. Cousins (now deceased), has been in transit for 14,610 days before arriving at its designated address, now the home of John Johnson, a 52-year-old foreman at Vancouver General Hospital.

"The post office may be slow—but they're thorough," Johnson quips. "Mail gets there in the end."

The card, printed in 1927, was discovered by Johnson's 19-year-old daughter Julie, while she sorted through the morning mail. It carries little more than a simple holiday greeting addressed to Mrs. Cousins—who, as Johnson discovered after a phone call to the city archives, did indeed live at his address back in 1937. Following some consideration, the family will later decide to mail the card back to the post office.

"Obviously this was an accident," Johnson says. "But it does draw attention to the more serious question of what the post office is doing with a lot of regular mail which takes ages to be delivered."

Postal employees sorting mail, Dec. 23, 1943.
IMAGE COURTESY OF THE VANCOUVER ARCHIVES (CVA 1184-191, PHOTOGRAPHER JACK LINDSAY)

JANUARY 11, 1949

"It costs the average industrial worker here, as in Vancouver, practically every cent he makes to live," remarks the *Vancouver Sun,* reporting on working conditions and the high cost of postwar living in Seattle and Vancouver.

"The Seattle man makes $1.54 an hour against a Vancouver equivalent of $1.37," writes the paper, "and both work a 40-hour week. Each spends his entire income on straight living costs and in each case, thrifty wives make a good portion of their own and the children's clothing. Each family has the same scale of living, though the Seattle steelworker drives a 10-year-old car and his wife has a $300 fur coat. The Vancouver family feels it cannot afford either."

The paper goes on to detail the case of Arnold Mosley, a 35-year-old "bender machine operator" at Dominion Bridge. Mosley has 12 years as a steelworker and already owns his own home, but, as the paper explains morosely, he is barely able to provide for his wife and two daughters.

"It costs them the complete $55 a week Arnold earns to live," the paper laments, "despite the fact that Jean makes 40 percent of the children's clothes and 50 percent of her own, and that they raise all their vegetables and fruit, canning for winter use."

The paper goes on to outline the Mosley family's weekly budget in grim detail—a budget that includes income tax payments, house insurance, maintenance, utilities, food, and $5 for entertainment.

"Arnold owns two suits," the paper says, "one good, one worn, buys one about every two years. Jean has no fur coat."

Portrait of the Reventlow family, circa 1940.
Image Courtesy of the Vancouver Archives (CVA 1184-1135, Jack Lindsay, photographer)

JANUARY 12, 2009

AFTER LEARNING THAT Millennium Development Group has been refused additional funds from its lender, and bound by a completion guarantee made by the previous NPA administration, city council passes a motion allowing it to bypass the civic referendum required by its charter and request a $458 million loan from the province to finish the Olympic Village.

"The Olympic Village is a billion-dollar project, and the City's on the hook for all of it," reads a statement from the mayor's office dated January 9. "To my great frustration, we can't turn back the clock on the actions of the last Mayor and Council. We are financially and legally committed to complete this project. The 2010 Olympic Winter Games will be held here in Vancouver. We will meet this challenge, and we will excel as proud hosts to the world's greatest athletes. And we'll be doing it in the most difficult economic environment we've seen in more than a generation."

Ordinarily, the *Vancouver Charter* requires a civic plebiscite to approve loans from the provincial government, with the issue placed on the ballot at election time. However, finding itself in the midst of what Robertson terms "urgent and difficult" circumstances (whereby the city, bound by the completion guarantee, has ostensibly become a property developer itself), and following a $100 million bailout already advanced by the city, council requests an emergency sitting of the legislature to deal with the problem.

"We now know why the previous city government didn't want to talk about the deal they'd made," Robertson's statement continues. "The arrangements were not in the public's interest. The decisions taken by the previous city government have put the city at enormous financial risk, even as we were told in 2006 by our elected leaders that the Olympic Village would be developed at no risk to the taxpayers . . . We know we've been dealt a very tough hand, but I believe we can meet our obligations. We're working very closely with our partners—VANOC, the province and the federal government—to maintain the financing for the Olympic Village project and deliver it in time for the Games."

On January 15, the deputy city manager overseeing the project will resign. Three days later, the provincial government will agree to amend the city's charter and to advance nearly unlimited funds to complete the project. Following the 2010 Games, the Olympic Village will be converted into residential housing. Despite an extensive publicity push by real estate marketer Bob Rennie, many of the 737 units will remain vacant, and a number of others will be sold at a deep discount.

Millennium will default on its loan repayments in January 2011.

JANUARY 13, 1965

"STUDENT CAMPAIGN TOPPLES BUS FARE" exclaims a headline in the *Vancouver Sun* as, after nearly two weeks of campaigning, high school and university students force BC Hydro into a 20 percent reduction in student bus fares.

"Militant students have won the battle of bus fares, forcing a 20-per-cent reduction by beleaguered BC Hydro," reports the *Vancouver Sun*. "Hydro co-chairman Dr. Gordon Shrum conceded victory to high school and university students late Tuesday when he announced directors of the huge government agency will cut fares to 10 rides for $1 during school hours."

Protest action included demonstrations, petitions, and a number of students paying their 15-cent fare entirely in pennies, after the student rate was increased by 300 percent on January 1. Following the fare reduction, students are exuberant.

"This shows that even a group of students can do battle with a big company and win," beams Doug Costain, head of the fare protest committee at Lester Pearson High School.

Hydro, meanwhile, is less than pleased, estimating that the fare cut will cost $125,000 a year, in addition to its current million dollar deficit, prompting fears that the company may "dump" the bus franchise on local municipalities.

"The directors took a second look at the fares and agreed there was some hardship particularly in the case of families with several children attending school," Shrum explains. "You might say it is our contribution to education."

BC Electric Bus, 1946.
IMAGE COURTESY OF THE VANCOUVER ARCHIVES
(CVA 586-4378, PHOTOGRAPHER DON COLTMAN, STEFFENS COLMER)

JANUARY 14, 1982

IN AN UNEXPECTED AND DRAMATIC REVERSAL (even to his lawyers) in the Supreme Court of British Columbia, Clifford Robert Olson recants his original plea and pleads guilty to the murder of 11 BC children and teens, cementing his place as one of the province's most notorious serial killers.

"I do not have the words to adequately describe the enormity of your crimes and the heartbreak and anguish you have brought to so many people," Justice Harry McKay says, sentencing the 42-year-old former construction worker to 11 consecutive life sentences in front of a court packed with spectators. "No punishment a civilized country could give you could come close to being adequate."

Olson, dubbed "The Butcher of BC," is a high school dropout and habitual criminal who has spent the better part of his life behind bars for a variety of offences, including theft, break and enter, armed robbery, indecent assault, rape, and buggery—a life of crime culminating in the string of stabbing, beating, and strangulation deaths that terrorized the Lower Mainland throughout 1981. Olson's history of aggressive, criminal, and erratic behaviour dates back to his early childhood and includes numerous instances of sexual assault and sodomy (even while he was in prison), as well as a number of highly publicized escape attempts.

"It's a very unusual case," explains Dr. Guy Richmond in an interview with the *Vancouver Sun*. "Normally people like Olson come out of the blue like the Yorkshire Ripper did. But ever since 1957 Olson has been under professional surveillance and no one has spotted the degree of violence of which he's capable."

The sudden change in Olson's original not guilty plea comes on the heels of a controversial agreement between Olson and Attorney General Allan Williams, whereby Olson agreed to provide police with the location of 10 of his victims—all between the ages of 9 and 18—in exchange for $10,000 a body.

"Olson entered the court this morning wearing the same cocky expression he has worn since the case started Monday," the *Sun* reports. "But three times, as he pleaded guilty to charges of murdering the 10 children, he took a white handkerchief from the jacket pocket of his grey suit and wiped his eyes."

In addition to his agreement with the statement of facts prepared by Crown and defence counsel, Olson pleads guilty to an additional murder with which he was never charged, that of 16-year-old Sandra Wolfsteiner.

The jury will deliberate for less than half an hour before sentencing Olson to life in prison.

JANUARY 15, 1953

"SKELETONS HINT MURDER OF GIRL, BOY" reads the front-page headline in the *Vancouver Province*, as the discovery of two skeletons in Stanley Park touches off what will become one of the city's most infamous unsolved murder investigations.

"Murder is suspected by police after the skeletons of a boy and girl—about 10 and 12 years of age—were found today buried under leaves and an oilskin coat in dense bush in Stanley Park," reports the paper. "Police said foul play was a definite factor as a hole was found in the head of one of the skeletons. Both skeletons were weather worn."

Discovered by Park Board forestry worker Albert Tong, the skeletons—quickly dubbed the "Babes in the Wood" by local media—were found lying side by side, less than 300 yards from Park Drive, one wearing a leather aviator cap. A woman's shoe and a rusty hatchet (the murder weapon) are also found nearby, and the decay of the bodies leads examiners to believe that they have been hidden in the park since at least 1947.

"I was working over there clearing the bush for tree planting," Tong explains. "On Tuesday I walked over the spot and heard a loud crack as my foot went on a bundle of leaves. I went back and told my friends: 'It looks as if there is someone buried there.' But I did nothing about it as I was too busy. Then this morning I went over and raked at the leaves. I saw a skull with a boy's cap on it, so I went for the police."

The initial coroner's examination concludes that the skeletons belong to a boy and a girl, between 7 and 10 years of age, both killed by blunt force trauma to the skull. Because of the coroner's findings, police discount eyewitness testimony from a logger who,

The "Babes in the Wood" crime scene, January 15, 1953 (note the skull on the left).
IMAGE COURTESY OF THE VANCOUVER POLICE MUSEUM

in 1947, dropped a female hitchhiker and her two sons in Stanley Park, both of whom were wearing aviator caps.

DNA testing in the 1990s will prove that the children are, in fact, two brothers.

The case will never be solved, despite the *Sun* offering a $500 reward into the 1980s, a number of leads that will appear well into the late 1990s, and the tireless work of retired Detective Sergeant Brian Honeyburn, who will investigate the murders for the better part of 40 years.

JANUARY 16, 1953

AFTER LEARNING THAT THE CAST has defied a city order to clean up "lewd" and "obscene" material, Vancouver police storm the stage at the Avon Theatre and arrest five members of Everyman Theatre Company's staging of *Tobacco Road*—in the middle of a performance.

"Seven big city detectives joined the cast of 'Tobacco Road' at the Avon Theatre Friday night," reports the *Vancouver Province*, "and five members of the regular cast were taken to jail, charged with taking part in an indecent performance. But the show went on after a 1.5 hour delay in which the actors were bailed out and returned to take up their lines where they were forced to break off."

The arrests draw a chorus of boos and cries of "Gestapo!" from the 850-person, sellout crowd.

Tobacco Road—based on Erskine Caldwell's novel about life, love, and poverty in the American South—has been a phenomenal success on Broadway, going on to become the second-longest-running nonmusical in Broadway history. In Vancouver, it has been drawing large crowds since its opening two weeks earlier. However, it has also attracted attention from the Vancouver Police Department, with two separate teams of detectives sent to investigate the performance, submitting reports claiming the show is "lewd and filthy" and "full of blasphemy." Resultant orders from City Prosecutor Gordon Scott to remove any offensive material were ignored by the cast.

Following the arrests, the entire audience will remain in their seats, chanting "We'll wait." They are treated to a cappella singalongs with the cast (which includes Bruno Gerussi). The audience will consume 39 gallons of coffee in the hour and a half to follow. When the cast members are finally released, they will re-enter a theatre "rocked with cheers" and pick up exactly where they left off.

"Everything went on as usual," the *Province* reports, "except that the constabulary kept 'Ellie May's' share-cropper dress, described as somewhat longer than a sweater. They said they wanted it for evidence."

The next day, Everyman Theatre Company will file an injunction against the VPD, barring the police from further interference with the production.

"The theatre has announced the show will go ahead tonight and all next week," the *Province* reports, "without a line changed from the original. The house is sold out tonight."

A Theatre Under the Stars production of "Brigadoon", 1948.
IMAGE COURTESY OF THE VANCOUVER PUBLIC LIBRARY (ART JONES, PHOTOGRAPHER)

JANUARY 17, 1913

"SARAH BERNHARDT, greatest of actresses, considers Vancouver the most beautifully situated city in the world," gushes the *Vancouver Sun* as, for the first time in 22 years, the 19th-century's most famous performer visits the city.

"I adore your city and the Canadian Rockies," she enthuses in Parisian French. "What is more beautiful? They seem to be the only friendly landmarks all the way from Calgary. I have kept my eyes glued to the window revelling in the fleeing landscape. But I can scarcely believe my eyes when I see all the magnificent improvements that have taken place in and around Vancouver."

Bernhardt, the highest-paid performer in vaudeville and a presence on the international stage for more than half a century, is one of the most colourful show business personalities of her time. Her early life is shrouded in mystery, due to her propensity for exaggeration. Among the rumours, it is said that she sleeps in a coffin, once worked as a courtesan in Paris, and had an affair with a Belgian nobleman. Giving an interview with the *Sun* aboard her private railcar, en route to Victoria (where she will give two performances), the actress says "many nice things" about the city's geography.

Recalling her previous visit to Vancouver in 1891 (when she played the Vancouver Opera House), Bernhardt fondly remembers a trip up Burrard Inlet with a "well-known CPR official." They were in search of ducks, she says, "which were plentiful then, and I bagged one."

"Madame laughed girlishly at her triumph," reports the paper. Bernhardt does not make a Vancouver appearance.

Sarah Bernhardt, circa 1878.
PAUL NADAR, PHOTOGRAPHER

JANUARY 18, 1956

"LAMONT GIVEN CASH, CONSTABLE TESTIFIES" reads the front page of the *Vancouver Sun* as the Tupper Inquiry—the largest police corruption investigation in city history—enters its 34th day.

Early in the afternoon, Constable Lorne Tompkins takes the stand, testifying that he saw, on a number of occasions, envelopes being exchanged between identified underworld figures and police.

"There were quite a number of bills," Tompkins testifies. "I would say the bills would be an inch or more thick in the man's hand."

Tompkins also testifies to seeing officers (including the aforementioned Lamont) accept envelopes of money from underworld figures on other occasions. The Tupper Inquiry was convened in late December of 1955 after allegations that Police Chief Walter Mulligan, as well as several detectives, sergeants, and constables, regularly accepted money in exchange for police protection. One officer implicated in the scandal has already committed suicide, and another, Detective Sergeant Len Cuthbert, shot himself but survived.

Tompkins's testimony comes on the heels of explosive revelations by Cuthbert himself that he had, on orders from Mulligan, approached a number of underworld types to offer police protection in exchange for money, including bootlegger Joe Celona, who intimated "he would be willing to pay $200 a month to police for protection."

The inquiry, which has been receiving national attention and drawing record crowds to the courtroom, is of particular embarrassment to City Hall. Mulligan, the youngest and longest-serving police chief in city history, was hand-picked by then mayor Gerry Mc-

Geer in response to years of lax enforcement during the L.D. Taylor administration. Mulligan's appointment was initially lauded as one that would make the VPD tougher on crime.

Six days later the Tupper Inquiry will end. It will reveal that Mulligan and officers at all levels of the department were indeed accepting bribes of $200 to $300 a month from dozens of underworld figures, among them Celona and West End gambling kingpin Bruce Snider. But by this point, Mulligan has already fled the country after being replaced as chief of police by George Archer.

Though no police officer involved in the graft racket will ever be charged, Walter Mulligan will spend the remainder of his life working as a limousine driver at Los Angeles International Airport.

Walter Mulligan, circa 1950.
IMAGE COURTESY OF THE VANCOUVER ARCHIVES
(PORT P1200, DON COLTMAN, PHOTOGRAPHER
IMAGE COPYRIGHT: CITY OF VANCOUVER

JANUARY 19, 1869

IN A MEETING ROOM originally known as Bummer's Hall, Captain James Raymur, manager of the Hastings Mill, opens the New London Institute, a reading room that will serve as Vancouver's first public library.

An accomplished seaman, Raymur took over management of Edward Stamp's lumber mill after the latter went bankrupt and returned to Europe. The captain is an intelligent, well-dressed man, with a keen interest in establishing decorum and education on the uncivilized shores of Burrard Inlet.

"He had the pallor of ascetic which could be mistaken for intellect," early settler Joe Mannion, owner of the Granville Hotel, will say of Raymur. "Nobody would believe that he had sailed the seven seas—well educated, well dressed, with a ready business manner."

The institute has just a few books, the first of which was likely received on January 9, some 10 days before they had anywhere to store it. Three months later, Admiral George Fowler Hastings will donate the majority of his ship's library (including George Eliot's *Middlemarch*, Byron's *Works*, and a book known as *The Wonders of Optics*) to the reading room, on the occasion of his return to Europe. In honour of this gesture, New London will be renamed the Hastings Institute and will remain the repository for the city's books until the Great Fire of 1886.

"After Vancouver got started the boarding house at the Hastings Sawmill was discontinued," city pioneer H.P. McCraney will later explain. "There was no further use for the library there and the books were collected into a pile and lay unused. Mr. Alexander (the manager of the sawmill) mentioned the matter to the Rev. Henry G. Fiennes-Clinton and asked if he could make use of them. Clinton spoke to Mr. Carter Cotton who lived at the same house with me. So the three of us got together and appointed ourselves a library committee and took over the books."

In December 1887, the Vancouver Reading Room will be established as the city's first official library in rented space above Thomas Dunn's hardware store at 136 Cordova Street, with a subscription fee of 50 cents a month. All members of the Hastings Institute will be made lifetime members of the new reading room, though the service will be available only to men until 1888. Fees will later be abolished, and by 1892, the city's new Free Library and Reading Room will feature new facilities and a full-time librarian, with free access for all.

A number of the New London Institute's original books will remain in the possession of the Vancouver Public Library.

Granville and Hastings, 1868. IMAGE COURTESY OF THE VANCOUVER ARCHIVES

JANUARY 20, 1972

"Revolution has hit *The Georgia Straight*" reads the front page of the *Ubyssey* as, following failed negotiations with owner Dan McLeod, the alternative paper's staff members take over its Powell Street offices.

"Staff members of the Vancouver alternative weekly Wednesday morning occupied the paper's publishing office at 56-A Powell Street in an attempt to give the *Straight* legal status as a co-operative," the *Ubyssey* explains, reporting that the occupation, which began at 6:30 in the morning, is expected to last "indefinitely."

A "negotiation committee" was formed in December 1971 to convince McLeod to forfeit ownership of the paper. McLeod, who owns all legal rights to the company, was uninterested in discussing the issue. His counter-offer of allowing the staff to use *Straight* offices and equipment to start their own enterprise was flatly refused.

"The basis was economic," former music editor Rick McGrath will claim in a 2010 interview. "Basically, we wanted to get paid. For the last eight or nine months I was there, I didn't see a nickel. But McLeod, at the same time, had a distribution company. And he was making all this money distributing these American magazines and rock newspapers, and he was also distributing pornography. Well, of course, it finally dawned on some people that the money from the *Straight* was being siphoned off into this distribution company, and at the same time we weren't getting paid. It didn't bother me so much, because I was making money as a teaching assistant, but the other guys, it was killing them. And, they finally said: 'Okay, enough of this.'"

In response to the occupation, McLeod (who, according to the *Ubyssey*, owes staff members more than $2,000) will cut off mail and phone service and file a number of injunctions—one to repossess the office and equipment, and another to prevent the collective from distributing an alternative *Straight*, known as the *Georgia Grape*.

"The paper and the community it serves are more important than the staff," McLeod argues in a *Straight* interview published later that month, "and if that paper folds, it is the community which will suffer most. I believe it is quite possible the paper will fail under collective ownership, and this must not happen. I never wanted to own the *Straight*, but I've always felt very strongly that the *Straight*, or a paper like it, *must* survive. I have never found, though I wish I could find one, an alternative to single ownership which would ensure the survival of some kind of free press in Vancouver."

After two weeks, the collective will be removed from the *Straight*'s offices, taking with them the only piece of equipment they officially own (a typewriter). Shortly thereafter the *Georgia Grape* will cease publication.

The exterior of the Straight office during the staff occupation, January 1972.
Image Courtesy of The Ubyssey

JANUARY 21, 1935

An alley near Beatty and Pender, February 1916.
IMAGE COURTESY OF THE VANCOUVER ARCHIVES (CVA 789-89)

"PROVINCE IN THE GRIP OF WILD BLIZZARD" exclaims the front page of the *Vancouver News-Herald* as the city digs itself out from under the heaviest one-day snowfall ever recorded: 17.5 inches (about 45 centimetres).

"Old Man Winter dealt Vancouver a knockout blow early this morning," reports the *Vancouver Province*. "After the low temperatures of Saturday and Sunday he dished out a blizzard which tied up street car traffic, snowed in automobiles, closed up businesses and generally indulged in a climatic caper which will be the talk of this city for years."

As could be expected in a city as unfamiliar with heavy snowfall as Vancouver (which averages one day of snowfall above five centimetres in a typical January), the local dailies are crammed with dramatic, weather-related stories, bearing headlines such as "Transportation in Chaos," "Workers Battle to Reach Offices," "Girl Heroines of Storm," and "Many Injured in Sleighing Mishaps."

"Held in the grip of one of the worst blizzards in its recorded history, the coastal area of British Columbia shivered under driving snowstorms and a biting southeasterly gale Sunday night," the *News-Herald* writes. "And as it continued late into the night, it threatened complete disruption of all transportation systems and brought added hardships to thousands of already suffering residents in many parts of the Lower Mainland, islands in the Gulf of Georgia, and Vancouver Island. During the weekend Vancouver experienced a 'famine of sawdust.' Many residents left fuelless were forced to abandon their homes and take up quarters in hotels."

"Hundreds of homes are facing a minor famine due to failure of delivery trucks," the *Province* adds, with horror.

The city's previous record for snowfall in a single day was set in February 1916, when 26 inches (about 66 centimetres) were recorded on the ground. However, as the *Sun* helpfully notes, that total "was the accumulation of continued snowfalls and in no way comparable to today's condition." The inclement weather has halted bread deliveries, stranded employees overnight in their office buildings, and caused dozens of roofs to collapse, including that of the Hastings Park Forum. By early the next afternoon, the snow will have turned to rain, a downpour that will cause widespread flooding in the outlying areas of the city and throughout the Fraser Valley. While flooding and washouts in the valley will continue for the better part of a week, Vancouver will return to normal operations within a few days.

As of 2012, this blizzard will remain the heaviest 24-hour snowfall in the city's history.

JANUARY 22, 1974

SPECTATORS GATHER, CARS ARE DETOURED, teenagers jaywalk, and Mayor Art Phillips begins tearing up portions of concrete with a backhoe as, after four years of planning and consultation, the six blocks of Granville Street between Nelson and Hastings are closed to begin its transformation into a $3.25 million pedestrian mall.

"Phillips closed Granville to traffic by digging up a ceremonial chunk of pavement at Granville and Hastings with a huge backhoe after a few minutes' instruction from the operator," the *Vancouver Sun* will explain, the following day. "Work on ripping up the pavement started in earnest a short while later. The mall will feature a meandering two-lane bus route, with the rest of the street covered with beige concrete, for pedestrians."

"It's going to be the best mall in the world," beams Ed Martin, chairman of the Granville Street merchant association advising the city on the mall's development.

The plan, modelled in part on the Nicollet Tramway in Minneapolis, is intended to revitalize and transform the character of the downtown core, calling for Granville's six lanes of traffic to be reduced to two in favour of expanded sidewalks, new street furniture, a crackdown on drugs and prostitution, and a permanent ban on cars. And, for the first time, liquor licences will be granted to "the better quality" of establishments wishing to serve alcohol on their patios—provided the drinks are served with a meal.

"You won't be allowed to just have a beer though," Alderman Jack Volrich assures the public.

Closing Granville Street to vehicle traffic has been proposed before, as part of "Concept Five," a plan drafted in 1971 to re-imagine downtown as an "executive city," complete with street trees, sidewalk cafés, mixed land-use, pedestrian walkways, and eventually a rapid transit system. In April 1971, SFU commerce students proposed the closure of Granville Street between Robson and Nelson on a trial basis. Their plan even gained traction in city council; however, concerns about traffic problems shelved the project until 1973.

"We want to encourage as much people activity, pedestrian activity, as we can and make downtown a really pleasant place," grins Mayor Phillips.

By 1981, the Granville Mall will be known to police as the drug capital of Vancouver, with 40 percent of all narcotics cases before the courts originating from the area.

JANUARY 23, 1931

"BAND COURT, PROMENADE, GLASS DOME, Cafe and Ballroom Designed; Decision Expected to Be Reached in Week," exclaims a headline in the *Vancouver Sun* as plans are unveiled for the construction of a new $500,000 English Bay Pier.

"It is proposed that the pier shall be approximately 900 feet in length," the paper explains, breathlessly. "The top deck will contain 170,000 square feet and will be available for amusements. The lower deck, also 170,000 square feet, will be used for parking autos and have a capacity equal to three and a half miles of street curb parking."

"More than half the top deck area will be glassed in completely and heated—for year-round operation," explains the proposal submitted to the Parks Board by engineer T.H. Eslick. "This glassed and heated area will include a band court with seating, promenades and a palm court, Winter Garden with amber glass sunburst roof and sides, a tropical cafe, recreation hall and promenade, and a grand Ballroom-Auditorium on ultra luxurious lines."

The attached blueprint is extreme in its opulence, featuring cafés, magnificent gables and arches, an entryway adorned with a flaming torch, and, of course, the glass-domed dance hall (labelled a *Palais de Danse* in the official blueprint). Though the proposal will cause quite a stir in both the *Sun* and the *Province*, it turns out the Parks Board doesn't share the newspapers' enthusiasm.

"The Commission feels that the press reports can scarcely represent the intentions of the Parks Board when it is suggested that a project of this magnitude, the bare outlines of which were presented at a meeting last Thursday or Friday, could be thoroughly digested by the Parks Board Staff and a possible favourable decision reached

English Bay Pier, circa 1910.
IMAGE COURTESY OF THE VANCOUVER ARCHIVES (CVA 677-95, PHOTOGRAPHER FRANK GOWEN)

and a contract entered into during the present week," an internal board memo will read, several days later.

On March 31, the board will vote against the pier proposal, categorically rejecting the notion of further built structures dominating English Bay.

"The Committee does not feel that the proposed pier is an appropriate development for English Bay," Superintendent W.S. Rawlings will write. "It believes that the English Bay foreshore should be preserved as nearly as possible as part of a natural park and parkway for the general beautification of the city and the preservation of the amenity of the West End during its development as a high class Apartment District and that any development should be confined to what is necessary for the use of the beach by the whole body of citizens for bathing, boating, and similar recreation purposes unaccompanied by noise and commercialism."

JANUARY 24, 1918

PROVINCIAL ELECTORAL HISTORY IS MADE for the second time in a week as female voters (exercising their franchise for the first time) and their male counterparts grant a landslide victory to Mary Ellen Smith, BC's first female MLA.

"Not only did the women of my fair city stand behind me . . . but the men were there too," Smith says in her victory speech.

Smith, who ran as an independent with the slogan "Women and Children First" and who took up politics after the death of her MLA husband, wins a decisive victory of 3,500 votes over her opponent, returning soldier Sergeant Walter Drinnan—much to the chagrin of the *Province*. The paper does little to disguise its bitterness over the win, running several full columns on the outrage of voters of both sexes, with colourful subheadings such as "How Did It Happen?"

"Why that's horrid of you awful men," a female voter is quoted as saying. "Now I hope that you will all have to wear petticoats. I am sorry that I am a voter in Vancouver when the people will defeat a returned soldier."

"The returned soldiers waged a good, clean and able campaign," the *Province* concludes, attempting at last to hide its rancour. "They can take comfort that no one could have headed off Mrs. Ralph Smith. The truth is that she, as a leader of her newly-franchised sex and a fitting successor to her late husband, was certain of election on the day she announced her candidature. Against any male candidate in a campaign fought under regular conditions, the returned soldier would probably have won in a walk. Now that the ladies have tasted blood, there is, of course, no telling how far they will go."

Mary Ellen Smith will go on to have a lengthy career in politics, spearheading a number of initiatives, including a minimum wage for women and girls, laws regarding juvenile courts, and social welfare for mothers. She will become the first female cabinet minister in the country and be appointed in 1928 as the first female Speaker of the House in the British Empire.

Mary Ellen Smith, circa 1920.
IMAGE COURTESY OF THE VANCOUVER ARCHIVES (PORT N31, PHOTOGRAPHER WALTER H. CALDER)

JANUARY 25, 1971

"Representatives of Vancouver's poor people marched on City Hall Monday to declare council 'null and void' and to establish a shadow civic government," reports the *Vancouver Province* as members of the BC chapter of the National Coordinating Committee of Poor People join a national protest movement and occupy City Hall.

"The 200 participants had hoped to take over the council chamber, but found the doors locked and guarded by two dozen policemen," the paper reports. "They camped for an hour outside the mayor's office, decrying their plight and demanding change."

Establishing a "provisional council" in the building's foyer, the committee protests the province's high unemployment rate and outlines a number of demands, among them rent control, cash assistance for welfare applicants, and that "lands owned by the city shall be used for low-cost housing and not for private developers' profit."

Alderman Harry Rankin, an outspoken supporter of many of the committee's goals, is named "Honorary Mayor of Vancouver," though when he attempts to make a speech, he is greeted with "a chorus of boos."

Mayor Tom Campbell—a former property developer and an outspoken enemy of the city's poor, youth, and alternative voices—is characteristically unsympathetic to the protesters' demands, staying in his office during the entirety of the occupation, and stating: "I think it was rather childish. They're just playing games now . . . They're not doing their cause any good."

A protest march across the Granville Street Bridge, circa 1970.
Image Courtesy of UBC Rare Books and Special Collections, Georgia Straight Collection

The protest, part of a nationwide movement that included direct action in Toronto, Ottawa, Kingston, Halifax, Saskatoon, and Calgary, is largely composed of young people, the *Province* notes, "but all ages were represented."

Following the occupation, a small group marches on the Canada Manpower Agency, protesting British Columbia's high unemployment rate and demanding jobs. They vow to meet each Monday, Wednesday, and Friday, in an attempt to "mobilize the poor."

"We are in a position of having to tell the present council that it has failed at its job," claims a statement by the group, "and that it is now time to move over and give someone else a try."

JANUARY 26, 1946

"Occupation of the old Hotel Vancouver was accomplished swiftly Saturday afternoon without casualties or even an argument," reports the *Vancouver Sun* as, at 2:30 in the afternoon, an "occupying force" of World War II veterans descends on the Hotel Vancouver, determined to solve the problem of acute city-wide housing shortages.

"We're taking over the Hotel Vancouver—so sit tight," says group leader Bob McEwen, calmly, to the single army guard posted at the door as the 35 members of the "army of occupation" take up residence in the lobby.

The protest itself comes as a result of two years of popular agitation over housing shortages. Although the city has responded with the construction of additional units, eviction freezes, and rent control, it has been unable to keep up with the demand brought about by the roughly 44,000 new arrivals, 30,000 returning soldiers, and 2,600 war brides who have flooded into the city since 1939.

"The lobby took on the tone of a camping expedition en route three hours after the siege Saturday," the paper continues. "Each vet shouldered bed springs, mattresses and blankets, borrowed from ordnance division of local army headquarters, and carried them upstairs to individual suites. Six women vets obtained doubledeck army cots. One of the CWACs established herself as a room clerk in the lobby, registering each occupant according to room number. Squares of cardboard with names scribbled on them in pencil were tacked to the door of each suite."

The building itself seems the perfect choice for protesters. CPR property, it is slated for demolition if it remains unsold by the end of 1946, despite the work of local groups trying to have

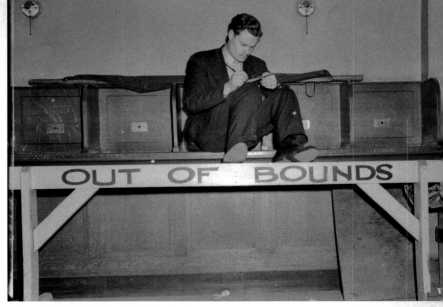

The Hotel Vancouver, occupied by the army, January 1946.
PHOTOGRAPH BY THE PROVINCE NEWSPAPER (VPL 42378)

it preserved as an auditorium, library, or government building. Transforming the hotel into a servicemen's hostel has already been discussed at both the local level and the federal level throughout 1945; however, because of confusion about funding the project, no agreement could be reached.

Despite a police presence at the scene, no attempt will be made to remove the protesters. In fact, the occupation will quickly garner support from the BC Provincial Command of the Canadian Legion and several prominent MPs. Local cafés will donate food, and a banner will be hung outside the lobby which reads "Action At Last! Veterans! Rooms for You. Come and Get Them."

The veterans will remain in the building for only a week, and their action will spawn the creation of a veterans' hostel, with financial support from the civic, provincial, and federal governments. The hostel will operate until 1948.

Other city measures brought about by local unrest, such as rent control and eviction freezes, will not last.

JANUARY 27, 1960

Just in time for the opening of Western Canada's first High Fidelity Music Show, the *Vancouver Sun* attempts to make sense of the latest technological and "cultural revolution": hi-fi.

"Painting, the book industry, sculpture—none of the arts has had anywhere near such benefits from an invention," raves the paper, "nor can they even begin to approach great music in popular dissemination."

News of the benefits of hi-fi, which, by no coincidence, shares two full pages with advertisements for the upcoming trade show, explains the intricacies of woofers and tweeters, and the "electronic cop" known as a crossover frequency, as well as innovations such as stereophonic sound.

"Stereo recordings use two microphones or two sets of mikes in a studio or concert setting," the paper explains, helpfully. "Each set of mikes is aimed at a particular section of the orchestra or opera, but picks up the entire sound as a background . . . When the sounds are played back on stereo equipment, the sound from the right of the orchestra comes out of the right-hand speaker."

"The LP record does for music what the invention of printing had done to literature," the *Sun* quotes a University of Michigan professor as saying. "Because of the extent of coverage of all types of music by LPs I'll wager the music of the 14th and 15th centuries is more familiar to our students than the literary works of the period."

Among the paper's predictions for the future are that records will one day be "trinaural" and speakers will "work by cosmic rays."

Man in control room of CKWX Radio, circa 1940.
Image courtesy of the Vancouver Archives (CVA 1184-2382 photographer Jack Lindsay)

JANUARY 28, 1978

TERROR DESCENDS ON NEW WESTMINSTER as, shortly after 10:30 a.m., following a botched escape attempt, five inmates of the maximum-security BC Penitentiary smash through the glass of the visitors' area and take 13 people captive, beginning the lengthiest prison-hostage incident in British Columbia history.

"New Westminster police initially said eight inmates armed with knives grabbed eight hostages," reports the *Vancouver Sun*. "But a man identifying himself only as one of the convicts telephoned radio station CKNW to claim six convicts, armed with several .38 calibre revolvers, were holding a total of 13 hostages."

The inmates—all with lengthy lists of convictions ranging from armed robbery to attempted murder to buggery—stab guard Roy Yasuda four times in the throat before being thwarted in their escape attempt by a quick-thinking guard who blocks their access to the waiting getaway vehicle. Among their initial demands are food, Demerol, a press conference, and the transfer of two inmates to a facility in Quebec.

"The demands we are going to make are not negotiable," the convicts claim on the phone with CKNW. "We want immediate attention, like somebody in authority."

The BC Penitentiary, which opened in 1898, has become notorious for its use of solitary confinement, leading to hunger strikes and a legal challenge by prisoners to have solitary declared "cruel and unusual." In addition (and perhaps as a result of its conditions), the Pen has gained a reputation for riots and violent hostage situations throughout the 1970s, including two in 1970, one in 1972, one in 1973, four in 1975, and five in 1976. The most dramatic of these incidents involved snipers and the Canadian Army, and saw prisoners destroy 275 cells, many with their bare hands. Two of the current hostage takers, Andy Bruce and Stephen Albert Hall, already have a lengthy history of prison violence. Bruce had been involved in two previous hostage situations, including one in summer 1975 which ended with the death by friendly fire of prison classification officer Mary Steinhauser. Hall had attempted an escape in 1971 by stabbing himself in the stomach and subsequently using the knife to hijack the ambulance while en route to the hospital.

Negotiations between the Correctional Service and the hostage takers will continue for a week, during which time several hostages will be released in exchange for food and drugs, and two of the inmates will surrender to authorities. The surrender of the remaining three prisoners will take place on February 4, after an agreement is reached that includes transfer for all the inmates involved (with the exception of Bruce) to Millhaven Institution in Ontario. Miraculously, there will be no fatalities.

Conditions of solitary confinement at the BC Penitentiary will later be ruled a violation of the *Canadian Bill of Rights*, and the facility will officially close in 1980.

JANUARY 29, 1912

Police on the scene of a Free Speech Demonstration on Powell Street, 1912.
IMAGE COURTESY OF THE VANCOUVER ARCHIVES (CVA 371-971)

"PETTIPIECE WAS DRAGGED from Soap Box to Police Station" declares a headline in the *Vancouver Daily Province*, reporting on a vocal demonstration that took place on Powell Street the day before—one that quickly degenerated into the city's last major "free speech" riot.

"Twenty-four men were placed under arrest and many more were injured by policemen's batons and Mounted officers' whips yesterday," the paper explains, "as the result of the most riotous events that have been witnessed in Vancouver since the stormy day of the anti-Oriental riots several years ago."

Free speech rallies have been held regularly in Vancouver since 1909, organized by a group known as the Industrial Workers of the World (founded in Chicago in 1905 and nicknamed the "Wobblies"). Although these rallies are billed as being in support of free speech (in a clever piece of public-relations tweaking), the IWW's true goal is the proliferation of industrial unionism, as a vocal part of the early 20th-century's burgeoning labour movement. The Powell Street riot began as a public demonstration spearheaded by "well-known socialist" Richard "Parm" Pettipiece, and was intended to protest a recent city council ban on public meetings, a ban instituted by newly elected mayor James Findlay in a misguided attempt to curb a series of recent IWW demonstrations.

"Shortly after the crowd had assembled on the Powell Street grounds, Deputy Chief of Police Mulhern appeared on the scene with a large force of constables," the *Daily News-Advertiser* reports. "Mr. R. Parm Pettipiece was at this time proclaiming the right of every man to freedom of speech. The deputy chief forced his way through the crowd to the impromptu rostrum, and asked Mr. Pettipiece to stop speaking while he read a copy of the street traffic bylaw. The deputy then called upon the crowd to disperse, but in spite of this warning Mr. Pettipiece again mounted on the box, and the crowd commenced to boo and hoot at the police."

Within moments, Pettipiece was arrested and the crowd dispersed by dozens of police officers, charging on all sides and brandishing weapons.

"Heavy whips and batons were freely used, and more than one man went down before the onslaught," the *News-Advertiser* continues, "although the weapons used did not inflict any very serious injuries."

The crowd then surged through the streets of Vancouver, stopping several more times in an attempt to assemble, each time being dispersed by police. By the time the story goes to press, a number of the participants (Pettipiece included) have been released on bail. And, although there will be rumours of a retaliatory IWW "invasion," the Wobblies will quickly be abandoned by their less radical labour partners. Despite successful protest action in a number of American cities, they will effectively vanish from Vancouver's labour landscape.

Pettipiece will go on to become an NPA alderman.

JANUARY 30, 1946

Techno-savvy Vancouverites swoon, and the city prepares to plunge headfirst into the future with the news that it will soon be home to its very own FM radio station.

"A 250-watt frequency modulation broadcasting system, latest radio development, will be established in Vancouver as soon as equipment is available," reports the *Vancouver Sun*. "Frequency modulation, or 'FM' as it is familiarly known in radio language, reduces static to almost nothing and permits truer reproduction of broadcasting, including reception of musical overtones and other notes not now available in transmissions."

The 250-watt stations, which will be installed by the CBC in Toronto, Vancouver, and Montreal, are expected to open "new vistas in broadcasting," according to an address by CBC chairman A.D. Dunton, speaking to a luncheon meeting at the Hotel Vancouver. Unfortunately, as of Dunton's address, not a single FM radio set is available in retail outlets in Vancouver, and due to technological limitations, it is likely that the new CBC frequency won't be available to all areas of the city. AM radio has been available in Vancouver since the early 1920s, when the *Vancouver Province*—followed shortly by the *Sun* and the *World*—established a station of its own, broadcasting news and music.

"It is expected [FM sets] will be manufactured and ready for sale on the retail market in Canada this fall," the *Sun* reassures its readers.

CBC Radio Broadcasters, circa 1940.
Image Courtesy of the Vancouver Archives (CVA 1184-3201, Jack Lindsay, photographer)

JANUARY 31, 1979

"THERE ARE ROCK AND ROLL BANDS on every street corner in the world, and then there is The Clash," claims an article in the *Vancouver Express* as "The Only Band That Matters" plays its first-ever North American show at the Commodore Ballroom.

"The Clash is a band of four Britons whose angry young music is exceeded only by their vision: nothing less than a world in flames," notes the paper in an article by budding rock journalist Vaughn Palmer. "The Clash came to North America this week playing their first concert ever on this continent at the Commodore Wednesday night. If the boys like it as little here as they have elsewhere, we can expect some bad notices when they get back home—perhaps in the form of a scathing song or two."

The show starts with local all-girl punk band The Dishrags, followed by rock 'n' roll legend Bo Diddley—less enthusiastically received by fans who force him offstage with abuse and catcalls before he can complete his set. The Clash then turns in a solid performance, opening with "Complete Control" (described by Palmer as "a blistering attack on the sins of their own record company that is also a statement of brazen artistic freedom") and playing songs such as "Drug Stabbing Time," "I'm So Bored with the USA," and "Tommy Gun."

Though the show is well received by Vancouverites—who show their appreciation by hurling beer cans at the band, allegedly prompting Joe Strummer to jeer, "If anyone had any fucking balls, they'd be throwing wine bottles!"— it ends prematurely as The Clash, irritated by fans' treatment of Diddley, cut the performance short, ending with a jam on "I Fought the Law."

Interior of the Commodore Ballroom, 1930.
IMAGE COURTESY OF THE VANCOUVER ARCHIVES (CVA 99-3855, PHOTOGRAPHER STUART THOMSON)

Following the successful conclusion of its first North American tour, the band will return to England to record "London Calling," an album that will go on to sell more than five million copies and be ranked at Number 8 on *Rolling Stone*'s list of the best albums of all time.

"The Clash are unbeatable at anything that can be done with three electric guitars and a drumkit," Palmer concludes. "As for Wednesday night, we heard you boys, and it sounded mighty fine. But was anyone really listening?"

FEBRUARY 1, 1955

Maclean's magazine gives the nation its first look at the seedy underbelly of the Downtown Eastside, in a sensationalist feature entitled "The Dope Craze That's Terrorizing Vancouver."

"Since the end of the Second World War the number of known drug addicts in Canada has risen from two thousand to five thousand," the article declares. "Of these, three thousand live in British Columbia, and two thousand of them inhabit or frequent a down-at-the-heel business section in Vancouver's east end near the waterfront, bordered by Chinatown, and crisscrossed by such streets as Hastings, Main, Pender, Powell, and Cordova."

The piece, written by journalist and war hero McKenzie Porter (later infamous for inflammatory editorials calling for, among other things, an end to workplace bathroom usage and for the resignation of all gay politicians), explores the intricacies of the area known as "Skid Row," and the crime and vice that have "set new records for lawbreaking in varieties ranging all the way from the 'one-way ride' of gangsterdom to ordinary brutal murder."

According to the article, Vancouver has the highest rate of drug addiction in the western hemisphere (at one in every 250 citizens), and, according to *Transition*, a newspaper published by prisoners in the BC Penitentiary, dealers have followed the migration of their clients, leading to widespread "gangsterism" in the local drug trade.

"The characters in the east, especially in Montreal and New York, have lately shown a keen interest in Vancouver's large drug population," *Transition* alleges. "Profits from illegal drugs have for the past few years been divided between about a dozen local men who have operated without molestation from the big operators in the east. Now these big operators in the east have decided they want to move in and reap all the profit so they have sent their gunmen to take over à la Prohibition."

Porter's article also contains helpful descriptions of cocaine and heroin, as well as the practices of addicts determined to score "a fix."

"The capsules are wrapped in silver foil," the article explains. "This is always contained in a small rubber balloon. Whenever they venture out to meet an addict they carry the separate capsules or bargain balloons in their mouths. If they are approached by police they immediately swallow the capsules and balloons and recover them later. When addicts have made a purchase they too pop the drugs into their mouths. Police who nab addicts or peddlers always thrust their fingers into the suspect's mouth to try and grab the drugs before they are swallowed."

"Addiction nearly always begins in a criminal environment," says Detective Mead of the VPD Drug Squad. "The youngsters get to know thieves and prostitutes and begin to regard them as heroes and heroines. Then they start imitating them. When they first take drugs it's rather like a boy taking his first cigarette. They do it to show off."

FEBRUARY 2, 1969

POLICE ARE BAFFLED AND VANCOUVERITES REEL following the discovery that the city's famous Nine O'Clock Gun has been kidnapped from its emplacement in Stanley Park.

"It was all done with somebody who had expert knowledge of this kind of thing," explains Park Board chairman Andy Livingstone in an interview with the *Vancouver Sun*. "It wasn't somebody going down there and casually taking it."

Because of the precision of the theft—and because it's Engineering Week—UBC engineering students are the prime suspects, but concrete leads are scarce. The following morning, a ransom note will arrive at City Hall which reads:

"Dear Sir: As you are probably aware, the nine o'clock gun has been kidnapped. If the city of Vancouver wants it back, a photo of our mayor Tom Campbell or a reasonable substitute should appear in the *Vancouver Sun* on Tuesday, donating $100 to the Children's Hospital."

Campbell—a public figure despised by the city's youth—will not respond to the ransom note, given that he is in the hospital for stomach surgery. And unfortunately, his replacement, Acting Mayor Hugh Bird, will also not be in a charitable mood.

"The city certainly is not going to start to pay ransoms to people who carry out irresponsible actions," Bird will claim. "It's not the policy of the city to make grants to worthwhile causes because of a ransom note."

Despite the city's refusal to pay the ransom, the Engineering Undergraduate Society will raise more than $1,500 in public donations to return the 1,500-pound gun—all of which will be immediately donated to Children's Hospital. The gun will be "found" by UBC engineering students four days later, with EUS Chairman Fraser Hodge denying any knowledge of the incident.

City police are unable to say whether charges will be laid.

"But," says Inspector Victor Lake, "a pretty dim view will be taken of the incident."

The Nine O'Clock Gun, 1943.
IMAGE COURTESY OF THE VANCOUVER ARCHIVES (CVA 586-1645, DON COLTMAN, STEFFENS COLMER)

FEBRUARY 3, 1972

CITIZENS AND DEVELOPERS ABRUPTLY FIND THEMSELVES seeing eye to eye, as Marathon Realty's Phil Boname speaks out on the latest issue to arouse civic outrage: a proposal to build a tunnel under the First Narrows.

The proposed $177 million crossing has been poorly received by the public, business owners, and the media, who accuse the NPA council of being out of touch with public opinion. The crossing is the latest civic undertaking by rabidly pro-development Mayor Tom Campbell (others include the Pacific Centre project, turning the entrance to Stanley Park into a Four Seasons Hotel, and bulldozing large portions of Chinatown for an expressway). It has already gained several high-profile opponents, such as *Vancouver Sun* columnist Allan Fotheringham.

"If we [Marathon] are to make money over the long run, as opposed to the quick buck tomorrow, then I can't see any advantage in providing greater access to the downtown by the private automobile," Boname complains. "To turn over substantial acres of land for parking and roads and other automobile-related services is not good for the big developers, and it's not good for the taxpayers."

In the days to come, city council will announce that no plebiscite will be conducted on the crossing (likely a tunnel connecting the North Shore with Brockton Point). In response, critics will step up their efforts, circulating petitions against the development. However, neither Campbell nor Port Authority chairman Bill Rathie will be able to drum up sufficient civic or financial support for the project. With Campbell's retirement from office in late 1972, the project will fizzle.

Mayor Tom Campbell, circa 1972.
IMAGE COURTESY OF UBC RARE BOOKS AND SPECIAL COLLECTIONS, GEORGIA STRAIGHT COLLECTION

"Mayor Tom Campbell, the Pushmi-Pullyu of local politics, puffed up his pigeon breast and announced that there would be no plebiscite held on the question of the third crossing," Fotheringham will write in the *Sun* several days later. "'Those who want to oppose it, ignore them,' he advised, in a memorable statement that will be well remembered when the NPA asks for endorsement in the December elections. The pertinent fact is that the NPA is no longer representative of the feeling of this city. The people who live in this city know it and the NPA, within itself, knows it."

FEBRUARY 4, 1922

THE CITY MOURNS AS JOSEPH SERAPHIM FORTES—English Bay's first lifeguard—passes away at Vancouver General Hospital.

"Joe Fortes is dead" reads the *Vancouver Province*. "For more than a quarter of a century in the employ of the city as a lifeguard at English Bay pier, the popular coloured man passed away at the Vancouver General Hospital this afternoon from a paralytic stroke. He was taken ill three weeks ago with pneumonia, which was succeeded by mumps. He showed signs of recovering but this morning took a turn for the worse."

The Trinidad-born Fortes, who arrived in Vancouver in 1885 and who worked a number of odd jobs including porter, shoeshine boy, and bartender (he was also known to help local chain gangs with clearing work), made a name for himself early in life when he began acting as English Bay's unofficial lifeguard. While the position was originally a volunteer one, undertaken by Fortes of his own initiative, his drive and skill later convinced the city to put him on its payroll. Having been a swimmer of some note in his youth, Fortes was officially credited with 29 rescues, though the unofficial total is thought to be more than 100. He also taught hundreds of children to swim, and made his home in a "creeper-clad cottage" near the waterfront. (In his early years, Fortes lived in a tent on the beach.)

"Joe was officially appointed to the beach patrol twenty-five years ago and held authority as a special constable," the article continues. "He was very jealous of his authority and would not tolerate any invasion of the bathing area by people in boats or canoes . . . He was immensely popular with Vancouver people and with visitors, and the fact that he was such a vigilant guard at the beach made English Bay a favorite spot for children. In his rowboat Joe kept watch over the rising generation and daily in the season he saw the little ones did not come to harm."

Fortes's funeral will be among the largest in city history, attended by the mayor and city council, the chief of police, and the Park Board, and will include five minutes of silence which will be observed throughout the city. Over the next five years, funds will be raised to construct a fountain in his memory, which will be placed in Alexandra Park. In 1986, Fortes will be named Citizen of the Century by the Vancouver Historical Society.

"He was a real asset to the city and his death comes as a shock and a blow to the thousands who knew and loved his cheerful ways and hearty greetings," the paper concludes. "Three generations of Vancouver folk have known and loved Joe, and there will be genuine sorrow that his advice of 'Kick yo' feet, ma'am,' will no longer be heard."

Joe Fortes teaching a woman to swim at English Bay, 1905.
IMAGE COURTESY OF THE VANCOUVER ARCHIVES (CVA 677-421, PHOTOGRAPHER STUART THOMSON)

FEBRUARY 5, 1953

LOCALS REJOICE WITH THE NEWS THAT, after years of provincial control, the BC government has decided to scrap consumer price controls on milk products.

"A decrease of two to three cents a quart on milk was forecast here Wednesday night," beams a front-page article in the *Vancouver News-Herald*. "Leaders in the milk industry all agreed the move will result in a drop in the price of milk."

The move, intended to make British Columbia more competitive in the dairy market, ends a government-mandated premium of two cents on all carton-packaged milk (which is currently sold at between 21 and 24 cents, depending on the product). While Vancouverites are pleased with the news, it is also favourably received by provincial retailers, with Walter Kraft of Canada Safeway Ltd. announcing that it will allow Safeway stores "to sell packaged milk at the same price as milk in glass."

Although it is agreed that there will certainly be a drop in the price of milk, there is no consensus on the exact amount.

"Whether it will be one cent a quart or even three, nobody knows," a spokesman for the Lower Mainland producers' association says in an interview. "It might take six months before the whole business straightens itself out."

February 5 appears to be something of a historical crux point for headlines related to the dairy industry. On the same day in 1908, the *Vancouver Daily World* reported that "some five milkmen and restaurant-keepers are to be hauled to court to answer a charge of selling milk deficient in butter fat and in solids."

The case quickly stalled when it was discovered that "the list of other cases before the court was so lengthy that it was found impossible to proceed."

Milk Wagon, Dec. 7, 1934.
IMAGE COURTESY OF THE VANCOUVER ARCHIVES (CVA 99-4690, PHOTOGRAPHER STUART THOMSON)

FEBRUARY 6, 1922

Homeless man standing in front of train car, circa 1930.
Image courtesy of the Vancouver Archives (CVA 677-382)

"Three Thousand Addicts in City!" declares a front-page headline in the *Vancouver Daily World,* reporting on speeches given at three separate meetings held around town, meetings that served to once again stoke the flames of the city's growing drug panic.

"Before I became a member of an investigation committee I would not believe the terrible stories of drug trafficking as told by the press," explains Dr. A.P. Procter, official representative of the BC Medical Association, speaking to a crowd at the Colonial Theatre. "Since I have spoken to child addicts and heard their dreadful stories from their own lips I can only compare the sufferings they describe with the horrible tortures depicted by Gustave Dore in his famous pictures of the tortures of the damned, which I viewed in London."

Meetings of this nature have become common in Vancouver over the past year, spurred on by bigotry, hysterical coverage in the local and national media (the *World,* in particular, has been running overwrought, drug-related stories since early January), and a number of high-profile arrests in Chinatown.

Before 1908, narcotic substances such as cocaine, heroin, and morphine could be obtained through a doctor's prescription. Even after the passing of the nation's first anti-drug legislation, users were punished only with small fines, with a maximum sentence of one year for trafficking. However, with the 1920s has come a widespread sense of moral terror surrounding illicit drug use, resulting in a wave of increasingly harsh penalties and restrictive legislation (thanks in large part to the efforts of Vancouver South MP Harry H. Stevens).

"The cabarets and dance halls were the places where the majority of young people cultivated the dope habit," the paper explains. "The beginner usually started on cocaine which, although not getting such a grip on its user as morphine, causes insomnia, which in turn leads to the deadlier forms of drugs in vain efforts to obtain sleep."

Of the three meetings, two unanimously pass a resolution calling for prison terms of up to 10 years, "the inclusion of the lash in the sentence," and the deportation of all peddlers—though this deportation order would only apply to "aliens." While a number of causes for illicit juvenile drug use are cited, the blame for the opium trade itself is placed squarely on the shoulders of "Orientals" (though, the paper notes grudgingly, "There were quite a few white men engaged in the business").

"God is the only cure for the drug evil," Reverend B.H. West tells his congregation at South Hill Baptist Church. "People who take dope have rejected God and until they accept again the teaching of the Gospel a cure cannot be effected."

Despite the hysteria, later estimates will show that the total number of drug addicts in the entire province is only 2,000. By the end of their drug campaign, the *World*'s circulation will have increased by more than one-third.

FEBRUARY 7, 1925

A CELEBRATION FOR VISITING JAPANESE dignitaries suddenly turns deadly as a launch carrying crew from one of the ships docked for the occasion crashes into a CPR barge and capsizes in the First Narrows, resulting in 11 deaths.

"A liberty boat, carrying another 50 or 60 men back to the *Idzumo*, in tow of the launch, was cut adrift when the launch crashed into the barge," the *Vancouver Sun* will report several days later, "and these men were compelled to remain inactive aboard the liberty boat, while searchlights from the *Yakumo* and the *Nanoose* [the tug towing the barge] revealed the men from the launch struggling in the water and boats from the *Yakumo* working desperately to save as many as possible. The launch, which weighed about 10 tons and was covered in, is believed to have gone down like a plummet, giving its occupants no chance whatever."

The *Idzumo* is part of a three-ship convoy carrying visiting Japanese dignitaries to an official reception being held at the Hotel Vancouver, a reception hosted by Imperial Consul Isago Gomyo and his wife as part of a weekend of celebrations by the city's Japanese community. The drowned men (as well as two who are rescued but later succumb to hypothermia) are part of a crew of more than 2,000 midshipmen, officers, and sailors in town for the festivities. At the time of the accident, the launch and liberty boat were returning to the *Idzumo* from celebrations on shore, and the crash is believed to have been a result of darkness and pilot error.

"According to Captain Singleton of the *Nanoose*, he had passed the three warships and was heading for the First Narrows when the launch, having failed, evidently, to observe the transfer [in tow], cut across the bows of the barge," the *Sun* will continue.

The Idzumo in Burrard Inlet, Feb. 1925.
IMAGE COURTESY OF THE VANCOUVER ARCHIVES (Bo P97)

"Captain Singleton immediately stopped the tug and let go the tow line to reduce the speed of the barge but the latter crashed into the [boat] which sank immediately."

Rescue efforts will continue through the night, fishing survivors from the water with the aid of searchlights. In the days to follow, divers and boats will retrieve the launch, and the remaining bodies from the 172-foot-deep harbour, and the civic, provincial, and federal governments will send their condolences. Key CPR officials however, will work hard to distance themselves from the tragedy.

Despite the incident, the imperial consul's reception will proceed as planned.

FEBRUARY 8, 1914

MUSIC HALL SENSATION MARIE LLOYD lies low on the Sabbath, after a week's engagement, and a high-profile battle with Mayor Truman Baxter and city officials—one that resulted in her being banned from Vancouver stages following allegations of "objectionable features."

"Mayor Baxter had heard rumours that she intended to say some spicy things about the city's chief magistrate and some other Vancouver people on the last day of her engagement," the *Vancouver Province* will report in the next day's paper, "and his worship accordingly decided early in the day to call Miss Marie off the stage."

Lloyd, whose propensity for lewd insinuations and saucy double entendres has for years brought her into conflict with authorities, was preparing to finish the last of her Vancouver performances when she received the news of her mandated cancellation—minutes before she was to take the stage.

"I am at a loss to understand the reason which prompted the mayor on Saturday to take such a high-handed proceeding as to stop my performance just as I was going onstage," Lloyd complains. "I consider the treatment accorded me by the civic authorities as nothing less than a gross insult—an affront unjustified by any action of mine."

Marie Lloyd, circa 1900.

In the face of Lloyd's complaints, and amid the public outcry from members of Lloyd's audience—many of whom were unable to receive a refund—Mayor Baxter is unrepentant, citing "blue" material in her performance from the very beginning.

"After witnessing the performance on Monday night I talked it over with all the aldermen, the chief of police and others," explains Mayor Baxter, "and all of them were more or less of the opinion that Marie Lloyd's act was a disgrace. I then instructed License Inspector Jones to have the objectionable features removed and the performance on Tuesday night was all right."

Lloyd will continue to cause a scene throughout the remainder of her time in Vancouver, at one point storming the headquarters of the *Vancouver World* (which published an unfavourable article about her common-law husband) and creating such a fuss that the police will have to be called. Despite the negative publicity, Lloyd will continue to have a successful career as an entertainer until her death following a collapse onstage in 1922.

Among the "objectionable features" described as "a disgrace" by Mayor Baxter: a moment where Lloyd raised her skirt to show off her ankle.

FEBRUARY 9, 1891

Vancouverites are introduced to "the showplace of the Pacific Northwest" as the Vancouver Opera House—the city's first entertainment venue—opens its doors at 765 Granville with a performance of *Lohengrin*.

"The theatre was a place of plush and velvet, plaster cherubs and gargoyles," famous Vancouver promoter Ivan Ackery will note in his 1980 autobiography. "Patrons marvelled at its drop curtain, said to be one of the two finest in the world. It was an oil painting of the Three Sisters, Canmore's famous mountains, by a great artist. The work was unsigned, but some people thought it had been done by Lafayette. It took two flat cars to transport the curtain by rail from New York."

The 1,200-seat venue, financed by the CPR in exchange for land concessions, cost roughly $200,000 to construct, and will, during its 30 years of operation, play host to a number of famous acts, including Sarah Bernhardt, Mark Twain, and a live production of *Ben Hur* (which will include an actual chariot race onstage). A seat in the gallery is available for the princely sum of $1, orchestra seats cost $3, and a box for six can be as much as $20. (In the beginning, men and women will be forced to purchase tickets from separate box offices.) According to Ackery, the venue is as much a social as an entertainment centre, with "a special place on the left-hand side under the boxes" popular as a discreet place for high-ranking CPR men to entertain local prostitutes.

"The Vancouver Opera House was the principal entertainment center in the city," Ackery will note, "and streetcars used to line up to wait for the late theatre crowd, wreaking havoc with the traffic."

With the growing success of the vaudeville circuit, dozens of other venues will spring up on Granville Street, earning it the nickname "Theatre Row." Owing to failing business, the CPR will sell the venue in 1911, though it will remain operational on Granville Street (first as the Orpheum, later as the movie house Lyric Theatre) for another 49 years.

Audience at the Vancouver Opera House, Oct. 30, 1903.
Image courtesy of the Vancouver Archives (Bu P389)

Flashlight of Audience Attending
Henry W. Savage's Production
"King Dodo"
with
Richard Golden
Vancouver Opera House., Vancouver, B.C.
Oct 30., 1903.
Seating Capacity 1200 Attendance 1590   H.O. Lee

FEBRUARY 10, 1947

CRITICISM OF BC's ARCHAIC LIQUOR LAWS once again dominates discussion as the editorial page of the *Vancouver Sun* dedicates a significant portion of its content to demanding "Better Liquor Regulations."

"On the eve of the opening of the Legislature, the word from Victoria is that British Columbia's government is going to do very little to improve the drinking habits of the people of this province," the editorial gripes. "The evidence suggests that the government feels that so long as the people who do drink can get all the beer and 'hard stuff' they want in the beer parlors and liquor stores, they will be content with the existing uncivilized conditions."

Liquor consumption and the laws surrounding it have been a source of debate in British Columbia for close to 60 years. Before 1900, BC's saloons were permitted to remain open 24 hours a day, seven days a week (even flying in the face of Sunday closing laws). And before the onset of Prohibition, British Columbians consumed roughly twice the national liquor average. However, with the introduction of the Liquor Control Board in 1921, severe restrictions were placed on the sale of alcohol. For more than 20 years, only hotel "beer parlours" have been permitted to sell liquor, and only in the form of beer by the glass, at a government-mandated price of 10 cents. These establishments are forbidden from advertising, serving food, playing music, having windows, or serving more than one brand of beer. In addition—in a misguided attempt to combat venereal disease—women are forced to sit in a separate section. The restrictions have subsequently led to a roaring trade for illegal "bottle clubs," unregulated establishments where patrons bring their own liquor and are charged exorbitant fees for "set-ups" (a glass, mixers, and ice).

"There will be no beer and wine licenses for ordinary restaurants, because the Attorney-General is reported to believe that most of these are family eating places and people do not want liquor served in places where they eat with their children," the editorial continues. "But surely the Attorney-General knows better than that. In other places having up-to-date liquor laws, both types of restaurants—those having licenses and those preferring not to have them—flourish side by side. Similarly, according to these reports, beer parlors will continue to be dismal, cheerless places for the swilling of beer, No meals or music."

Public pressure to liberalize the province's liquor laws has been steadily increasing since the end of World War II, but despite a plebiscite and two government reports, little will change until the late 1970s, when diversified licences and legislation allowing the creation of neighbourhood pubs will finally break the hotel industry's near-monopoly on the sale of alcohol.

As of 2012, British Columbia liquor licences will remain the most expensive, time-consuming, and difficult to obtain in Canada.

FEBRUARY 11, 1912

Following continual complaints from homeowners, Alderman James White announces his intention to form a special committee to investigate the high cost of living in Vancouver.

"That there is being made by both wholesalers and retailers an unreasonable amount of profit, Alderman White is convinced," the *Vancouver Sun* will report the following day. "But just the extent of unreasonable profit has not been determined and it is for such determination the commission is suggested."

White, who has investigated the situation on his own for some time, calls for the formation of a city committee to inquire into costs city-wide, consult with homeowners, and, if necessary, convene a full inquiry, with a board able to question witnesses under oath, and with an eye to finding the "cause" of the problem.

"The cost of living in Vancouver has become a serious problem to many persons, particularly those who receive the lowest wages, who form as much the backbone of a community as wealthier persons," White explains at a press conference. "I have personally investigated to some extent enough to convince me that there is something radically wrong, which the council may remedy and thereby make Vancouver not only the most attractive investment city on the Coast, but a city where a man of average means and income may live and enjoy life and bank a small percentage of his wages if he is of a thrifty disposition."

In addition, White notes, while wages have risen throughout the previous few years, they have not necessarily risen with the cost of living. And, although the alderman initially intended to present his motion to council on the morning of February 12, he has decided on a brief delay, so that he may compare Vancouver

Alderman James White, circa 1910.
Image Courtesy of the Vancouver Archives (Port P240, Walter H. Calder, photographer)

with the economic conditions present in the east.

"The average man of family desires most of all a home which he may call his own," White concludes. "But how may he accomplish such ambition when the cost of living is so high it takes all he earns to feed, clothe and care for his family? . . . The constant hustle for enough money merely to exist is decidedly discouraging."

FEBRUARY 12, 1951

AFTER A MONTH OF DELAY, council passes a bylaw allowing Mayor "Friendly" Fred Hume to donate all but a dollar of his annual salary to charity.

"Vancouver now has a dollar-a-year mayor," reports the *Vancouver Sun*. "The remaining $7,499 will be allocated for miscellaneous grants, social assistance and the mayor's fund so that His Worship will be able to give the money to worthy causes as he requested last month."

The measure, which passes by a vote of five to three, allows the mayor—already a millionaire as the head of his own electrical contracting firm—to distribute the majority of his $7,500 annual salary to charities as grants or in the form of social assistance. Despite Hume's best intentions, the move is heavily criticized by other city officials, such as Aldermen Bert Showler, R.K. Gervin, and Archie Proctor. Proctor in particular chides the mayor in council, criticizing him for setting a "dangerous precedent . . . embarrassing to future mayors and aldermen."

"When I decided to give my services to the city and suggested that the money could help less fortunate people, I didn't expect to be the butt of sarcasm and dirty letters," Hume thunders. "I don't like it. It's up to the next mayor what he does with his salary. If he can afford to give it away, God bless him. If he can't, that's his business. That's the way I feel. This is my business—it's none of yours."

Hume will go on to become one of Vancouver's most popular mayors, serving for a further seven years, and for the remainder of his career, he will refuse to collect any more than a dollar a year.

Fred Hume, Jan. 1951.
PHOTOGRAPH BY THE PROVINCE NEWSPAPER (VPL 42585)

FEBRUARY 13, 1954

MILITARY INVESTIGATORS DESCEND on North Vancouver, and local papers report on the discovery that, one day earlier, a defective compass and a thick bank of fog caused a USAF pilot to crash his fully armed F-86 Sabre Jet into the side of Grouse Mountain—less than 200 feet from the chairlift.

"It was awful low when it came out of the clouds, and it was going very fast," explains six-year-old Robin McPherson, the only eyewitness to the crash, in an interview with the *Vancouver Province*. "Then it sort of zoomed up and went in the trees on the side of the mountain. I didn't hear any noise like a bang."

The plane, which crashed shortly after noon on February 12, had taken off from McChord Field in Tacoma on a routine training mission, piloted by Second Lieutenant Lamar Barlow. Sixty miles from Vancouver, Barlow began to experience instrument trouble, making a confused mayday call somewhere over Blaine. Hopelessly lost, the pilot was directed to Vancouver, though he had less than 15 minutes of fuel remaining.

Questions will later be raised about how Barlow ended up so far into Canadian airspace, in an aircraft so heavily armed (each of the 24 rockets on board had the explosive power of a 250-pound bomb), especially once local reporters are prevented from photographing the wreckage on the grounds that its weapons and radar systems are classified.

"Jagged metal and ripped fabric was spewed for hundreds of feet around," reports the *Sun*. "A parachute ripped open by the impact dangled from a tree. There was no sign of fire."

Miraculously, no one was injured other than Barlow, whose body is found still strapped into his harness. Large portions of the wreckage came to rest within 15 feet of the home of Ray Nunn, who awoke to find portions of fuselage strewn all across the area behind his cabin.

"All our boys are instructed to jump by parachute if they get into a tight spot," Major C.D. Sawtelle will tell the *Province* two days later. "However, if he knew he might kill many other people if he left his plane, he would decide to stick with it."

The F-86 is the second aircraft known to have collided with Grouse Mountain.

FEBRUARY 14, 1859

CONFUSION REIGNS AND TEMPERS FLARE as Governor James Douglas declares that a site has been chosen for the capital of the fledgling colony of British Columbia—Queensborough.

The site of the yet-to-be-built city, recommended by Lieutenant-Governor Richard Moody, is selected for its "great facilities for communication by water, as well as by future great trunk railways into the interior," and for its distance from the border and defensible position on the Fraser riverbank in case of American attack. The decision comes as a surprise to locals, many of whom assumed that the capital would be established in nearby Fort Langley, and serves to inflame the tempers of land speculators, who, combined, had spent more than $66,000 on property in anticipation of the decision.

"What a grand old Park this whole hill would make!" Moody will write to Douglas in early December (while bemoaning the thorny consistency of the underbrush and referring to the nearby forest as "vexacious").

Pressure to make the capital a world-class city is strong, but, as Moody will quickly discover, the process of surveying, clearing, and laying out a brand new city in such a remote location is equally troublesome. By the end of the year, most of the main streets will have yet to be constructed.

"The people [of Queensborough] seemed peculiar," MLA and Speaker of the Legislature J.S. Helmcken will later recall in his memoirs, and they "hated Victoria—sitting over hot stoves in stores or publics, eating crackers and drinking water or some apparently equally innocent beverage—indeed they seemed to live on these and politics—the latter being sufficiently exciting."

Nonetheless, Queensborough will remain the capital of British Columbia until 1868, when an unfortunate combination of near-sightedness, intoxication, and underhanded tactics by local politicians (Helmcken among them) during a key debate will result in it losing the title to Victoria.

The name "Queensborough", meanwhile, will never be favourably received in England, and in July 1859, Queen Victoria herself will change it to "New Westminster."

Columbia Street in New Westminster, 1890.
IMAGE COURTESY OF THE VANCOUVER ARCHIVES (CVA 677-282, PHOTOGRAPHER CORNISH)

FEBRUARY 15, 1965

AT EXACTLY NOON AT JERICHO AIR FORCE BASE, Canada's new flag is unfolded and raised, making it the first ceremonial raising of the Maple Leaf anywhere in the country.

"Four trumpeters, using yard long ceremonial trumpets gave a flourish for the new nylon flag as 300 army and air force personnel stood smartly to attention," reports the *Vancouver Province*. "Capt. Roy Forbes read the flag proclamation. [Two chaplains] blessed the two Red Ensigns as they came down and a neatly folded new Maple Leaf flag on a pillow."

The Red Ensign has been Canada's official flag since 1946, though it had been used in an informal capacity for close to 80 years and was promoted by such figures as Prime Minister John A. Macdonald. Before that, the official flag was simply the Union Jack.

"If our nation, by God's grace, endures a thousand years, this day, the 15th day of February, 1965, will always be remembered as a milestone in Canada's national progress," Prime Minister Lester Pearson will say during his public address in Ottawa. "It is impossible for me not to be deeply moved on such an occasion or to be insensible to the honour and privilege of taking part in it."

"God Bless our flag!" he will conclude, "and God Bless Canada!"

The only flags raised before the Jericho ceremony were in Victoria (at sunrise) and at UBC (where it was quietly hoisted at 7:15 a.m.); however, neither of these events was marked by any form of celebration.

"All vessels in the harbor switched to the Maple Leaf flag," reports the *Province*, "except those who had none. They were ordered to fly no flags."

Vancouver schools and other civic institutions have yet to raise the new flag because, unfortunately, very few are available in British Columbia.

"They are expected," the paper reports, "within weeks."

A flag-raising ceremony for the dedication of the foremast to the HMCS Vancouver, at Kitsilano Beach, 1937.
IMAGE COURTESY OF THE VANCOUVER ARCHIVES (BE P60)

FEBRUARY 16, 1966

LOCAL DAILIES REJOICE with the news that, after several days of furious debate, council has decided to accept an anonymous $1.5 million donation to furnish the city with its own planetarium.

"The decision came after a fight-filled 75 minutes of debate in which council also officially accepted the offer of the anonymous donor who wants to build the planetarium for the city," reports the *Vancouver Sun*, and "approved appointment of museum architect Gerald Hamilton for the planetarium job as well."

The dispute, which will continue to simmer in the days to come, revolves around the location of the proposed space centre. While Mayor Bill Rathie favours the development of a former RCAF base located near the foot of the Burrard Street Bridge, a similar $1 million donation was recently offered to the Park Board for the construction of a conservatory, woods museum, and planetarium at Little Mountain.

"A planetarium is a dome-shaped building in which the con-stellations are projected on the ceiling from a special machine," reports the February 14 edition of the *Vancouver Sun*. "The visitors, who are seated, can be given the impression of riding through space."

By the end of 1966, the location of the new planetarium will be settled, once it is combined with a $3.5 million cultural complex intended for the Kitsilano RCAF facility as part of a city centennial project.

Though the donor of the $1.5 grant will originally elect to remain anonymous, by September he will have been revealed as lumber millionaire H.R. MacMillan, whose conditions for giving a grant to the facility include the inclusion of at least 300 seats, a land donation from the city, and a provision that only the finest

Exterior of the H.R. MacMillan Planetarium, Feb. 17, 1972.
PHOTOGRAPH BY W.E.K. MIDDLETON (VPL 54587)

instruments be purchased (with, for reasons unexplained, preference given to equipment manufactured in Japan).

The H.R. MacMillan Planetarium will open in October 1968 and, within two months, will have proved so popular with the public, it will have surpassed all economic estimates.

FEBRUARY 17, 1903

THE PROVINCE REPORTS ON A "largely attended and most enthusiastic" conference, presided over by Vancouver MP R.G. MacPherson, aimed at "the total exclusion of Orientals" from work on the soon-to-be constructed Transcontinental Railway.

"An Easterner converted," the article reads gleefully. "An exceedingly interesting address dealing with the Transcanada railway project was made by Mr. O.E. Talbot, MP for Bellechasse, who stated that he had conversed with Mr. MacPherson on the Oriental question.

"To tell the truth," Talbot says to the crowd, "we men of Quebec are the most easy men to convince in the world. That is, we leave it to the people who come from the portion of the country affected and then act as they advise. Thus we consider that when a British Columbia member of parliament advises Oriental exclusion, he knows what he is talking about, and we therefore support him."

For decades, anti-Asian sentiment has been stronger in Vancouver than anywhere else in the country, supported by the public and championed by politicians at the local, provincial, and federal levels. In fact, scarcely four years later, the city will give birth to the Asiatic Exclusion League, a group whose motto is simply "to keep this Province and this Dominion for the White Man, by stopping any further Oriental Immigration."

"If you want to see British Columbia a white man's country for yourself and for your children, you must take prompt action," the text of a league recruiting pamphlet, published in Vancouver, will read. "It is rapidly becoming a brown and yellow country. At the present rate of birth increase, there will be within seven years, more Japanese births than white births in the Province of British Columbia. The Asiatic menace is not a theory; it is a fact."

Racial prejudice will continue to play a large part in the lives of Vancouverites and their representatives in the decades to come. In 1907, an early meeting of the Asiatic Exclusion League (held with the blessing of Mayor Bethune) will lead to the city's worst race riot, and in the early 1940s, pressure from prominent Vancouver politicians will persuade Prime Minister William Lyon Mackenzie King to call for the internment of the province's entire Japanese population.

"The Asiatic Exclusion League believes that the proper place for the Asiatic is in Asia," the pamphlet will conclude, "not in reducing the standard of living and making British Columbia a colony of Asia."

Annual membership in the league will cost 25 cents.

Unidentified Asian family, outside Wah Chon's Washing and Ironing, circa 1895.
IMAGE COURTESY OF THE VANCOUVER ARCHIVES (CVA 178-2.8)

FEBRUARY 18, 1982

"POLICE PUSH PUSHERS in 'Granville Maul'" reads the headline of a full-page story in the *Vancouver Sun* as the paper provides its readers with an in-depth look at the soft-drug capital of Vancouver—the 800-block of Granville Street.

"The summer crowds may be gone," the paper begins, "but under the flickering neon glow of Theatre Row, the drug dealers carry on, police or no police . . . The 800-block, the drug dealers' place of business, is the main battleground of the soft drug war in the city."

The Granville Street drug trade has grown steadily in recent years, ever since a number of blocks were closed to vehicular traffic in 1974 (in a misguided attempt to make the downtown core more people-friendly). Thanks to a lack of foot traffic, a non-existent residential population, and the opening of nearby Pacific Centre Mall, the area has become a ghost town for all but the dealers and the police department.

"I think it's like a war down here," a drug dealer known only as "John" tells the paper. "I told the cops that once and got a few pokes in the stomach for my troubles."

"The dealers sell 'soft drugs'—hashish, marijuana and acid, a chemical hallucinogen," the article continues. "Most are easily recognized by their clothes—dirty jeans and leather or wool lumber jackets are favored—and by their hair—1960s long. One dealer called his attire his 'calling card.' Standing alone or in pairs along the mall, the dealers offer their wares in barely audible mumbles."

Though police action will have some effect, Granville Street won't see any significant change until the early 1990s, when a city council decision to rezone the area to allow for residential use will

The 800 and 900 blocks of Granville Street, circa 1967.
IMAGE COURTESY OF THE VANCOUVER ARCHIVES (CVA 672-1, PHOTOGRAPHER B.C. JENNINGS)

result in a proliferation of upscale and middle-class developments, restaurants, and nightclubs. These developments will lead, in large part, to a reduction in single room occupancy hotels on Granville Street and the subsequent displacement of the low-income population housed within.

"We have regained some measure of control," Superintendent Hank Starek reassures the public in an interview with the *Sun*. "We are beginning to see increasing numbers of families and shoppers in the area."

A moment later, he adds: "It's still one hell of a focal point for soft drug sales."

FEBRUARY 19, 1938

AT PRECISELY 6:31 A.M., a mysterious explosion shakes Metro Vancouver. The shock lasts less than one minute, rattling windows, shaking buildings, and awakening residents across the city.

"Vancouver city and district was shaken by a mystery blast or quake shortly after 6 o'clock this morning, the roar and subsequent shake awakening householders, rattling dishes in cupboards and, in some instances, even moving furniture," reports the *Vancouver Sun*. "Records of the seismograph at the Gonzales Heights Observatory, Victoria, show absolutely no trace of an earth shock although officials there admitted the possibility of a purely localized tremor."

Theories abound in the wake of the incident, ranging from earthquakes to avalanches to bomb plots, and both City Hall and local dailies are swamped with phone calls by Vancouverites convinced that a ship has exploded in the harbour. The noise is heard and the tremors are felt as far east as the Second Narrows Bridge, and as far north as the Capilano Suspension Bridge; however, despite extensive searching, no cause can be found. No seismic activity is detected outside the city limits, and even UBC geology professor M.Y. Williams, contacted by the *Sun*, is unable to offer any explanation.

"Thorough check of all possible places where blasting operations might be conducted also failed to reveal any clue to the mysterious blast or tremor," the paper continues. "Suggestion has also been voiced that the blast and tremor could have been caused by a meteor crashing into the mountains on the North Shore. The theory is receiving little credence, however, particularly as there have been no reports of such a falling body having been seen."

The cause of the explosion will never be determined.

FEBRUARY 20, 1910

POLICE KEEP THEIR DISTANCE and casual racism abounds in the local dailies as a violent knife fight breaks out among a "dusky fraternity" of African-Canadians in a Pender Street barbershop.

"There was a dark time in a Pender east barber shop late Saturday night," the *Vancouver Daily World* will explain, glibly, the following day, "when a sextette of colored gentlemen held a veritable indoor championship meet . . . Today the dusky fraternity are anxiously waiting for the return to life of a well-known instructor, who is swathed in plaster of Paris and thread, as a stitch in time is all that holds life within his dusky form."

The fight, which begins in a nearby residence, quickly draws a crowd when it moves down Pender Street, even prompting the appointment of a de facto referee. Although a number of serious injuries are sustained by participants and their "seconds," including deep cuts to the hands and face, the *World* will maintain a decidedly tongue-in-cheek tone when referring to the brawl.

"So interested in the fun did they become that the shout of 'time' was not heard," the paper will report.

Several minutes later, all attempts at order are abandoned, with the first "knockout" being the referee himself. Despite the serious nature of the fight, police are not notified before or afterward, and public pressure to investigate is minimal (citizens, the paper notes, "are somewhat interested").

"Two of the 'sleepers' have been on the 'out' list ever since," the *World* will report, "although two doctors have been constantly in attendance with their needles and thread."

"Had a sewing machine been requisitioned," the paper will conclude, "the job would have been finished in a few hours."

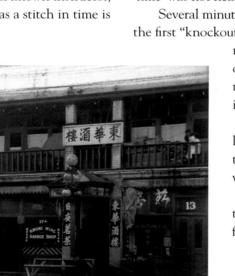

A barbershop on Pender Street, circa 1910.
IMAGE COURTESY OF THE VANCOUVER ARCHIVES (CVA 789-46)

FEBRUARY 21, 1970

Newspapers set on fire during a strike at the Vancouver Daily Province, 1946.
IMAGE COURTESY OF THE VANCOUVER ARCHIVES (CVA 1184-2560, PHOTOGRAPHER JACK LINDSAY)

AFTER A WEEK WITHOUT A SINGLE DAILY NEWSPAPER because of a strike by Pacific Press employees, the first issue is published of the city's newest news source: the *Vancouver Express*.

"This is both a birth and a death notice" reads an announcement on page 4. "We herewith announce the birth of the *Vancouver Express* and the certainty of its death at an uncertain future date."

The strike is the second for Pacific Press in less than three years, the result of foundering contract negotiations, and the company's apparent willingness to engage in strikebreaking tactics (such as installing a helipad to deliver scab workers behind picket lines). Conditions are already tense, and with the prospect of a lengthy job action ahead, the publication of an independent newspaper is proposed to union membership by Mike Tytherleigh, former editor of the now-defunct *Vancouver Times*.

"At a union meeting I suggested—why don't we start our own paper?" Tytherleigh will recall in a 2001 conversation with author Marc Edge. "Having worked with offset printing at the ill-fated *Times*, I knew how easy it was to produce a paper. Later in the week, I was called to a meeting of the union bosses, including the poobah from New York, to discuss the feasibility. I said there was no need for discussion because we were well under way with a planned, 12-page paper to be published on the Saturday."

The first edition is a complete sellout, running so many copies that the press at Broadway Printers breaks down. And, in the weeks to come, as advertisers clamour for space in the city's only news source, the *Express* will swell from 12 pages to more than 40. Despite having no wire service, no typewriters, no city directory, and only three telephones, the founding staff of 10 will manage to produce the paper three times a week (though all contributors will write without bylines to avoid potential Pacific Press repercussions).

After three months without the *Sun* or the *Province*, Pacific Press will agree to a proposal put forth by mediators, a proposal that rules overwhelmingly in favour of the unions, and the *Express* will fold.

The strike will not be the last for Pacific Press—it will experience a total of six over a period of 17 years. And, in 1978 when employees once again walk off the job, the *Vancouver Express* will return for a further eight months.

FEBRUARY 22, 1955

ON THE HEELS OF A SENSATIONAL *Maclean's* article declaring Vancouver the drug capital of Canada, the *Vancouver Sun* dedicates nearly its entire front page to reports on the city's "mounting narcotics problem."

"Get tough with drug traffickers!" reads one such article, written by well-known celebrity and nightlife columnist Jack Wasserman. "Send dope smugglers to jail for 25 years! Increase penalties for pushers!"

Wasserman, recounting an interview with George W. Cunningham (deputy commissioner of the US Treasury Department's Bureau of Narcotics), shares the latest wisdom from Washington on how to cut "illegal traffic in narcotics to the minimum."

"If your city starts free [treatment] clinics you'll get every addict who can make it there," Cunningham warns, "and they'll get there if they must run, fly, or even crawl on their hands and knees."

Among Cunningham's suggestions are lengthy prison terms for "pushing," compulsory "drug-cure" treatment for addicts, and 25-year minimum sentences for smuggling. Most helpfully, he recommends that police "eliminate the market."

In addition to piquing the interest of local papers, the *Maclean's* article has also prompted an official response from the Vancouver Police Department, with Police Chief Walter Mulligan announcing that, to augment the efforts of the four-man Drug Squad, "every man on the force from now on will check every known addict and pusher wherever found and without regard to other duties."

There are close to 1,500 addicts in the city, the *Sun's* editorial page reports, with "at least 500 more at present undetected." Substantial front-page real estate is dedicated to how to properly spot any such addicts. But, according to Cunningham, the city's worst criminal element is the quiet spectre of the "Addict-Pusher."

"You don't buy dope in Sunday Schools," he asserts, "nor in churches. You get it in honky-tonks, cheap night clubs, and other places where the addicts hang out."

However, in referring to a current campaign in the US that calls for the death penalty for trafficking to teenagers, the deputy commissioner is hesitant.

"If you make the penalties too harsh," Cunningham replies, "the juries won't convict."

FEBRUARY 23, 1969

"HOVERCRAFT SWOOSHES OVER TO NANAIMO IN 42 MINUTES," reports the *Vancouver Province* as North America's first scheduled hovercraft service begins operation, running twice daily between Nanaimo and Vancouver.

"It was just fantastic," gushes Byng Heeney, executive vice-president of Pacific Hovercraft, Ltd., in an interview with the paper. "Mind you, there were a few empty seats on the first trip to Nanaimo at 8 o'clock this morning but on the way back and on the other return trip we actually had to turn passengers away."

The 35-seat vessel departs from the north end of Granville Street at 8 a.m. and 3 p.m., takes less than an hour to reach its destination, travels at 50 miles an hour, and costs $7 each way. Its inaugural voyage is hampered by high winds and rough seas, but the reception, as reported by the *Vancouver Sun*, is generally positive.

"Bumpy, but not uncomfortable," says William Saunders, one of the hovercraft's first passengers. "Nobody seemed upset by the conditions."

"The hovercraft is not as comfortable as the BC ferry but it's sure faster and I guess that's what counts since it is mainly for the businessman," says Karen Henderson, another passenger.

Other opinions include: "A good trip. I'd have paid double," "It was good fun, but a bit noisy," and from Pacific Hovercraft president Barry Jones, "These conditions are the worst under which we will operate."

FEBRUARY 24, 1887

AN INAUSPICIOUS DAY DAWNS in Vancouver history as, at "around midnight," following a venomous public meeting, an angry mob marches on a Chinese camp near False Creek and engages in the city's first race riot.

"When the Chinamen saw all these men coming, they were terrified," city pioneer W.H. Gallagher will recall in a later interview with archivist J.S. Matthews. "The crowd came up to the camp singing 'John Brown's Body,' and such songs; the Chinamen poked their noses out from beneath their tents; the 'rioters' grabbed the tents by the bottom and upset them, the 'war cry,' 'John Brown's Body,' still continuing. The Chinamen did not stop to see; they just ran. Some went dressed, some not; some with shoes, some with bare feet; the snow was on the ground and it was cold. Perhaps, in the darkness, they did not know that the cliff, and a drop of twenty feet [was there]; perhaps some had forgotten; some may have lost direction. The tide was in; they had no choice; and you could hear them going plump, plump, plump, as they jumped into the salt water. Scores of them went over the cliff— McDougall was supposed to have two hundred of them up there."

"It was a weird scene to those standing on The Bluff," the *Daily News-Advertiser* will report the next day, "and looking down on the fire, inside which were burning the bundles of clothing and bedding, which were thrown down from the hill from time to time, whenever the fire grew dim and appeared to require replenishing."

This is not the first time Chinese workers have been expelled from Vancouver. In fact, several "committees" have previously been assembled with the intention of removing Chinese from the city, committees that have included, among others, Mayor Malcolm McLean. Tensions have been high between the city's Caucasian and immigrant communities throughout January and February 1887, and the discovery that contractor John "Chinese" McDougall intends to use Asian labour to clear land for the CPR has caused considerable upset among white workers.

The morning following the riot, virtually all of McDougall's workers will be herded to the dock and forced onto a steamer bound for Victoria. In response, the government in Victoria will suspend the city's charter and declare martial law, vowing to find and convict those responsible. However, because of a lack of co-operating witnesses, few charges will be laid, and no convictions will result.

"I have heard it said that four Chinamen were tied together by their pigtails and thrown in the creek at McDougall's camp," Gallagher will recall. "If so, I know nothing of it. I do know that some of them were tied together by their pigtails to prevent them escaping in Chinatown the following morning."

Chinatown businesses damaged in the race riot of 1907.
PHOTOGRAPH BY PHILIP T. TIMMS (VPL 939)

FEBRUARY 25, 1937

AN ERA OFFICIALLY BEGINS as Vancouver's citizens see their first mention in print of the "insanity-inducing herb" known as "Marihuana."

"This is the first case involving marihuana," explains an article in the *Vancouver Province* in reference to a suspicious death where the drug was found in the stomach of a corpse, "which has become a scourge in the United States, to come to the attention of Vancouver authorities . . . Marihuana is smoked in cigarette form by addicts. It is thought possible that the man chewed and swallowed one or more of the cigarettes, which are called 'Mary Warners' by those who use them."

Drug prohibition laws in Canada effectively began in Vancouver after a 1908 visit by Deputy Minister of Labour William Lyon Mackenzie King led to the creation of the *Opium Act*, the country's first anti-narcotic legislation. Push from moral reformers on the West Coast also led to stiffer penalties being enacted in the 1920s. In 1923, cannabis was added to Canada's restricted substances list. Before 1961, cannabis was involved in only 2 percent of drug arrests nationwide, and on only six occasions in Vancouver over the same 38-year period.

Though the official cause of death in this instance is never revealed, police suspect that the drug (also known as "Mexican hemp," the article points out) found in the victim's stomach "may have figured in."

As the years progress, Vancouver will come to play host to more drug users than anywhere else in the country. By the late 1950s, Columbia and Hastings will be named in a *Maclean's* magazine article as "Canada's most notorious underworld rendezvous." However, by the 1960s, a number of organizations will have become active in promoting the legalization of marijuana, though these groups will mostly be demonized in the media and written off as "hippies" and "beatniks." The war on marijuana will ultimately give birth to Operation: Dustpan in the 1970s, a controversial police offensive against soft drugs which will culminate in the infamous Gastown Riot, one of the most notorious examples of police brutality in the city's history.

By 2011, marijuana exports from British Columbia will total close to $6 billion (40 percent of Canada's total production). Authorities will estimate the number of grow operations in Greater Vancouver at more than 8,000.

FEBRUARY 26, 1942

Automobiles confiscated from Japanese "evacuees" at the PNE Grounds, March 10, 1942.
IMAGE COURTESY OF THE VANCOUVER ARCHIVES (CVA 1184-88, PHOTOGRAPHER JACK LINDSAY)

"TREND OF THE TIMES IN VANCOUVER!" declares a joyous headline on the front page of the *Vancouver Province* as, following the adoption of Order-in-Council P.C. 1486 two days earlier, an order is sent from Justice Minister Louis St. Laurent to remove and intern the more than 21,000 members of British Columbia's Japanese population.

"Without fuss or friction, a change that may have a significant bearing on British Columbia's future is taking place in Vancouver," reports the *Sun*. "The Japanese are moving out, and Canadians are moving in. There are new faces behind the counters in establishments formerly operated by Nipponese, and it is expected their number will increase as the exodus from the coast gathers momentum."

The order, approved by Prime Minister Mackenzie King, is based heavily upon the recommendations of Vancouver Centre MP Ian Mackenzie (a vocal supporter of anti-Asian organizations such as the White Canada Movement), and is issued despite assurances from the country's top police and military leaders that there is no danger of either Japanese sabotage or a Pacific Coast invasion.

"Every person of the Japanese race shall leave the protected area aforesaid forthwith," the order declares, in addition to establishing a dusk-to-dawn curfew and restrictions on Japanese possession of automobiles, cameras, and radio equipment.

"The presence of thousands of Japanese on the Pacific coast adds enormously to the dangers of hostile attacks which may be made very soon," states a resolution sent to Ottawa by the Vancouver Real Estate Exchange, urging internment as soon as possible. "It is generally recognized that it is the intention of many of the Japanese to support their countrymen in the event of an invasion."

Within weeks, Vancouver's Japanese citizens will have their property confiscated and they will be placed in internment camps elsewhere in BC. There, they will spend the next three and a half years living in stables, barnyards, and subhuman environments, while the "Custodian of Aliens" auctions off their clothes, homes, and personal property—often at below market value.

"It is the government's plan to get these people out of BC as fast as possible," Mackenzie will later explain. "It is my personal intention, as long as I remain in public life, to see they never come back here. Let our slogan be for British Columbia: 'No Japs from the Rockies to the seas.'"

At the end of the war, those interned will be offered two choices: deportation, or transfer to another province. When total financial losses to Japanese Canadian citizens are calculated in 1986, the number will exceed $400 million.

FEBRUARY 27, 1976

A VANCOUVER SUN EDITORIAL BEMOANS the plight of Vancouver's male population, following a city council decision to "crack down" on massage parlours.

"City council's bold decision to crack down on massage parlors undoubtedly comes as bad news to all those timid men who have finally worked up enough courage to at least contemplate their first visit to one of the notorious squeeze-and-pound emporiums," reports the *Vancouver Sun*'s Christopher Dafoe. "Some of us will now never know what it feels like to be tied into a granny knot by a bored beauty dressed in nothing more concealing than a glazed smile."

The bylaw, approved February 24, places local massage parlours and nude modelling studios under tough new regulations, including a $3,000 annual licence fee (well above average); officially enforced sizes for doors, rooms, and lighting; and the requirement that all masseuses wear non-transparent garments covering the body from the neck to the knees. Sleeves must also reach the elbow, and hours are sharply regulated.

"He simply can't stand seeing us have a good time," complains a local—referred to in Dafoe's column only as "Jock McSporran"—about Alderman Harry Rankin, who spearheaded the initiative. "Businessmen, tired or otherwise, make him see red, and when he thinks of us enjoying ourselves in pleasant surroundings he reaches for his revolver. The class war has moved to a new front."

McSporran also tosses out other allegations, among them the idea that council's concern over nude photography businesses and body-painting is "simply another example of council's notorious hatred of culture and the arts."

Massage tables at the Pacific Athletic Club, Aug. 25, 1936.
IMAGE COURTESY OF THE VANCOUVER ARCHIVES (CVA 99-4463, PHOTOGRAPHER STUART THOMSON)

Rankin, however, is vehement in his support of the new regulations, claiming that massage parlours exploit women "in the most obnoxious way."

Opinion is sharply divided. While some aldermen support banning massage parlours altogether, others support simple regulation, for fear of driving the business underground. The sole dissenter on council is Alderman Fritz Bowers, who claims that "the city should not be in the business of regulating morals."

"Inflation finished off late Roman civilization," Dafoe continues, "just as it is finishing off ours, and Romans who were taking a beating at the bank enjoyed a quick visit to the masseuse to help them forget their money worries."

Every one of council's regulations will remain on the books into the 21st century, with licence fees for "body-rub parlours" continuing to be among the five highest in the city.

FEBRUARY 28, 1958

"Tim Won't Return to His Beloved Park" reads a headline in the *Vancouver Province* reporting on the deteriorating health of Stanley Park's last official resident: Tim Cummings.

"William Timothy (Tim) Cummings has left his beloved Stanley Park—probably for good," reports the paper. "Nearly blind and suffering from a congestive heart trouble, Tim has been a patient in General Hospital since last December."

Cummings, who has spent the entirety of his 77 years living in the Brockton Point cottage where he was born, is the only resident officially permitted to remain following the forced eviction of Stanley Park's families in the late 1880s, when the site was declared a public greenspace. Ever since, Cummings has paid $5 a month to occupy his family's tiny green cabin as part of an "understanding" with the Park Board, outliving his younger brother and sister, and becoming a familiar sight at Brockton Point, where he could be seen each day raising and lowering the flag in his front yard.

"A powerfully built longshoreman in his youth, Tim spent most of his time fishing for flounders, cod and sea bass almost off his front stoop," the paper reports. "The last tenant in the park, Tim knew every inch of his 1,000 acre birthplace. He has hunted it for bear, deer, and blackberries."

Following a brief hospital stay, Cummings will die on March 11, 1958. In the days to follow, his ashes will be scattered in the waters near his cottage. And, despite protest from a number of prominent sources (including the *Vancouver Sun* and city archivist J.S. Matthews), and a campaign to have the building preserved as a historic site, Cummings's cabin will be declared unsalvageable and torn down in December 1963.

"We felt we owed it to Tim to let him live out his days in the parkland where he was born," Park Board superintendent Stuart Lefeaux will explain in the March 11 edition of the *Vancouver Sun*. "His house will be torn down next week, but its site will always be 'Tim's Place' to us."

The Cummings' Cottage in Stanley Park, 1937.
Image Courtesy of the Vancouver Archives
(CVA 260-678, James Crookall, photographer)

MARCH 1, 1926

CITY ALDERMEN ARE "DIVIDED," reports the *Vancouver Evening Sun*, as they reveal a proposal put forward to change the name of Grouse Mountain to "Mount Vancouver."

"There is a certain sentimentality which clings to old names which makes some of the aldermen hesitate to recommend the change," reports the paper (which has been actively campaigning for the name change itself), though it is quick to point out that "Alderman G.H. Worthington, a member of the Greater Vancouver Publicity Bureau, was outspoken in his advocacy of the change."

The change, the paper reports smugly, is also supported by Alderman H.E. Hammond, who calls it "a good idea. As a businessman he recognized the wisdom of having a name for the North Shore all-year playground which would immediately identify it with Vancouver."

Several other aldermen are in support of the change (all of them members of the Greater Vancouver Publicity Bureau); however, this opinion is by no means universal.

"Ald. E.W. Dean approved the suggestion that a substantial memorial to Captain Vancouver should be erected in the city," the paper reports, "but said he opposed changing the name of Grouse Mountain."

Aldermen John Bennett and Angus McInnis are also opposed, with Bennett claiming that he is "attached to the name of Grouse Mountain," and McInnis saying he "liked the old names best."

"Alderman Almond pointed out that it was not as if the mountain in question was named after any great hero," the paper concludes. "Only for some such reason as that would the proposed change of name be likely to arouse a storm of opposition."

Grouse Mountain, 1929.
IMAGE COURTESY OF THE VANCOUVER ARCHIVES (CVA 99-3713, PHOTOGRAPHER STUART THOMSON)

MARCH 2, 1945

"RUNNING THE DOMINION GOVERNMENT is as simple as building a house," exclaims roofer-turned-Democratic-Party "founder and organizer" William R. Smith, as the *Vancouver News-Herald* reports on the first public address given by "Canada's Next Prime Minister."

"A dozen pink carnations danced continuously on the head table in the Hotel Georgia ballroom as the 'founder and organizer' of the Democratic Party of Canada literally pounded out his program," the paper says of Smith's speech, which is accompanied by more or less constant table-thumping.

"Four-fifths of the people in this country want to vote for me," Smith claims, speaking to a crowd of 133 at the Hotel Georgia, in what he says is "the first speech I ever made." Smith's campaign promises include doubling Canada's population (to "cut our taxes in half," he explains), giving jobs to "everyone," and the somewhat ambiguous pledge to turn Canada into "a republic."

"I was nailing on shingles and every day dozens of men from Shaughnessy Hospital went by," says Smith, describing his transformation from manual labourer to political powerhouse. "I threw down the hammer and picked up the pen. I said: 'This isn't going to happen anymore. We will soon have everybody cripples.'"

Smith, a self-proclaimed populist who intends to run as a candidate for Vancouver–Burrard, claims to have spent time in every district of the city, doing his utmost to determine the desires of the people. Among his more outlandish claims are that he is the first democrat in North America and that "Mackenzie King has a monopoly on typewriters." Smith will continue to campaign throughout 1945, assembling four other candidates under the Democratic Party banner, including his brother George, a semi-professional baseball player.

In the July federal election, his party will secure approximately .05 percent of the popular vote.

MARCH 3, 1945

Vancouverites mourn as the local dailies report on the sudden death of celebrated artist and author Emily Carr in a Victoria rest home, at the age of 74. Carr, a painter of considerable renown since she began exhibiting her paintings in 1908, has gained a reputation for her paintings, much of which is inspired by the First Nations people of the Pacific Northwest.

"Emily Carr was a shining link with the past," Nellie McClung, Carr's friend and fellow author will say in an interview with the *Vancouver Province*. "She was essentially a trailbreaker, not afraid to make a new pattern with her pen or a paintbrush. She wrote as she pleased, and painted her world as she saw it. Let us hope that her mantle will fall on many of our younger writers, who will carry on with diligence and courage for the enrichment of Canada's cultural heritage."

Despite her reputation, and her early success, Carr suffered a number of financial setbacks which left her on the brink of poverty for close to 15 years. Forced to raise sheepdogs and sell pottery and rugs to survive, she returned to the world of painting with a 1938 solo show at the Vancouver Art Gallery and, following an acute angina attack, turned to the world of writing only a few short years before her death. Carr's first book, *Klee Wyck* (translated as "The Laughing One"), a collection of sketches originally written for radio, garnered instant acclaim upon its publication in 1941, winning the Governor General's Award and being praised by the Canadian Authors Association as the "truest picture of any aspect of British Columbia life to appear in print."

"She moved among the tribes for half a century, chronicling their lives in both painting and writing," the *Vancouver Province* reports in a brief eulogy. "She was an individualist, she said, and consequently drew away from the 'old school methods of teaching.' She could not adequately describe Canada by using the 'cramped style of London and Paris.'"

Carr's health has been slowly deteriorating over the final eight years of her life, and a number of medical complaints, among them a heart attack, more than one stroke, and repeated angina attacks, have confined her to nursing homes. Though she has been preparing for the end for some time (in 1942, she directed a friend to bury some of her personal belongings in Beacon Hill Park), her sudden death comes only a few days before she was to be awarded an honorary doctorate by the University of British Columbia.

Upon her death, Carr will leave more than 100 paintings to the Vancouver Art Gallery. She will be buried in Victoria's Ross Bay Cemetery.

MARCH 4, 1971

NARY A WORD IS SPOKEN in either of the city's major dailies as, at 6:30 p.m., Prime Minister Pierre Trudeau weds 22-year-old Margaret Sinclair at a top-secret wedding ceremony in North Vancouver.

"It was a quiet and simple wedding, because they wanted it that way," Sinclair's mother will tell the *Vancouver Sun* the following day.

The pair are married at St. Stephen's Roman Catholic Church, close to the Sinclair family's home on Highland Drive, in front of only a handful of close friends and immediate family (of the 18 scheduled to attend, only 13 are present, with the other five stranded in Montreal because of inclement weather). The wedding is such a closely guarded secret that it even comes as a surprise to some attendees.

"We sort of expected it for the past few months," Sinclair's sister Janet will explain. "It was obvious to anybody close to the family that it was going to happen pretty quickly."

"Photographer Fred Schiffer, who took the wedding pictures, wasn't informed of the true identity of the parties to be married until the night before the wedding," reports the *Sun*. "Earlier he had been told the wedding would be between one of the other four Sinclair daughters and a 'gentleman of France with no family.' When the photographer learned he would be shooting the prime minister's wedding, 'he didn't sleep all night', according to his son, Roger."

The charismatic Trudeau, who will go on to become the country's third-longest-serving prime minister, is already well known countrywide for his reputation with women, and has often been referred to in the media as Canada's most eligible bachelor—linked to everyone from politicians to famous actresses, including Barbra Streisand. And, despite the pair's 33-year age gap, Sinclair's mother is supportive of the newlyweds.

"He may be old but he's young at heart," she will gush to reporters. "They are very well suited to each other and it has been a happy courtship. She's a very intelligent girl and she's a great sport. She can do anything he can do."

Trudeau will serve 15 years as prime minister and go on to be simultaneously one of the most admired and one of the most reviled figures in Canadian politics. The marriage, however, will be tumultuous from the very beginning. Sinclair, suffering from undiagnosed bipolar disorder and resentful of Trudeau's solitary nature and obsessive devotion to his work, will begin acting out only a few years later, threatening suicide with a kitchen knife, openly smoking marijuana at 54 Sussex Drive, and allegedly engaging in affairs with both Ted Kennedy and Rolling Stones guitarist Ron Wood.

The couple will separate in 1977.

MARCH 5, 1949

A SAD DAY DAWNS FOR RESIDENTS of Shaughnessy, Dunbar, and Kerrisdale as the "mansion district" faces the end of door-to-door bread delivery.

"Bakers here say the trend is away from door-to-door deliveries in what they refer to as 'better income districts,'" reports the March 4 edition of the *Vancouver Province*. "The housewife with a large grocery allowance spends less for bread than her sisters whose man carries a lunch-bucket."

"We can't make money on one or two loaves per household and the salesman can't show a profit," complains an unnamed manager of "one of the larger bakeries."

"What is bakery profit on a loaf of bread?" asks another. "My barber guessed two cents a loaf. I'd be delighted to settle for half of that."

Bread delivery has been on the decline for several years in Vancouver, part of a larger trend in other coastal cities. Bread salesmen (many of whom, the paper notes, only recently switched from horse-and-carriage delivery), who earn a wage plus commission for a 48-hour week, are being edged out of the market. Managers blame that fact on shorter working hours, higher wages, the removal of a federal government subsidy on bakeries (causing the price of bread to skyrocket by two cents a loaf), and a decrease in calls from affluent districts (with many of them being, they note with frustration, time-consuming "back door" calls). Of the estimated 500,000 loaves sold each week in the city, only one-fifth are sold by delivery, and only two remaining bakeries city-wide even engage in retail sales. Profits for a bakery are, on average, one-third of a cent a loaf in a "good" month, the managers calculate, with delivery operations averaging even less.

Vancouver's baking industry (represented by the Vancouver Master Bakers' Association) has found itself under a considerable amount of scrutiny over the previous 15 years, accused of price-fixing and artificially inflating profits. In 1937, the industry even found itself the subject of a city investigative committee.

Despite these hardships, overall bread sales remain unchanged, owing to a boom in the wholesale market, though some managers predict that the weakness in bread delivery may prophesy large-scale economic misfortune in the years to come.

"Recessions, in my years of experience," remarks an unnamed manager, ominously, "have been forecast in our graph of falling bread sales before they became apparent in general business."

MARCH 6, 1945

AT A LITTLE PAST NOON, in Vancouver Harbour, the SS *Greenhill Park*—a 10,000-ton government supply vessel, suddenly explodes, killing eight longshoremen, injuring 19 other workers, and shattering windows in nearly every office building in the downtown area.

"Downtown Vancouver was rocked by a series of blasts as the SS *Greenhill Park*, loaded with chemicals, blew up at noon today," reports the *Vancouver Sun*. "Flames and smoke shot 100 feet into the air as the explosions of the chemicals set off some of the ship's ammunition and also sent ship flares soaring into the sky in an awesome display of grim fireworks."

The ship, being loaded with lumber and destined for Australia, is wracked by three separate explosions as its cargo—liquor, distress flares, and a highly volatile chemical known as sodium chlorate (stored together in direct contravention of safety procedures)—ignites. Despite being showered with shattered glass, thousands of spectators will swarm from their offices to the waterfront to witness the aftermath of the blast, creating massive delays for ambulance crews and firefighters.

"The fire started from behind some cases," stevedore Ralph Atkinson explains in an interview with the *Vancouver Province*. "I saw the smoke, grabbed some fire extinguishers, but they would do nothing to stop the smoke. We knew there was some inflammable liquid in cans, also some flares. So we beat it out of the hole and I was the last one out . . . Somebody must have been smoking."

The findings of an inquiry commission released two months later will conclude that smoking was indeed a factor in the explosion on board the *Greenhill Park*, positing that "whisky

Man surveying the wreckage of the Greenhill Park, March 6, 1945.
IMAGE COURTESY OF THE VANCOUVER ARCHIVES (CVA 586-3565, DON COLTMAN, STEFFENS COLMER)

or more of the barrels, spilled into the surrounding combustible cargo and was ignited by a lighted match carelessly dropped by a longshoreman in the vicinity."

Despite extensive rescue attempts, eight longshoremen will lose their lives in the blast. The commission's report will cast blame both on stevedores, who are proven to have been stealing whisky from barrels on board, and on their superiors, who stand accused of loading improperly and neglecting basic safety protocols.

The damage to the docks is estimated in the neighbourhood of $20,000, and it will take local glass and window companies close to two weeks to complete all the necessary repairs. The *Greenhill Park* will later be purchased by a Brazilian company, repaired, and remain in service until the late 1960s.

MARCH 7, 1913

AFTER A LENGTHY BATTLE with breast cancer, noted Canadian poet and orator Pauline Johnson dies in Bute Street Hospital, three days shy of her 52nd birthday.

"Her death was not unexpected," the *Vancouver Province* reports, "as for the last fortnight she had been slowly sinking. She had, however, rallied several times during the last year from similar acute attacks, and it was not until last Tuesday that it was recognized she could hardly live through the week. Her last moments were peaceful, and she was fully conscious. Her sister, Miss Eva Johnson, was her constant companion for the last few days, though she was resting when the end finally came."

Johnson, the daughter of a Mohawk Chief, has always been known for celebrating her First Nations heritage, in everything from the content of her work, to the buckskin costume she designed for herself during her many years of touring. Despite her national fame and numerous speaking engagements, Johnson's finances quickly became precarious after she retired from orating in 1909. With the onset of cancer, she elected to spend her remaining years in Vancouver's West End. There, she recorded the words related to her by her long-time friend Chief Joe Capilano, as both were nearing the end of their respective lives—Johnson from cancer, Capilano from tuberculosis.

The resultant book, *Legends of Vancouver*, based on her conversations with Capilano, was released in 1910 (after appearing first in the *Vancouver Province*) and became an instant success, requiring multiple printings.

Funeral procession for Pauline Johnson, near Granville and Georgia, March 10, 1913.
IMAGE COURTESY OF THE VANCOUVER ARCHIVES (PORT P1422)

As part of the largest funeral in the city's history (eclipsed only by that of Joe Fortes in 1922), Johnson's ashes will be buried near Siwash Rock, making her the only person ever to have been officially buried in Stanley Park.

Legends of Vancouver will continue to be widely read into the 21st century.

> *There's wine in the cup, Vancouver,*
> *and there's warmth in my heart for you.*
> *While I drink to your health,*
> *Your youth and your wealth,*
> *And the things that you yet will do.*

MARCH 8, 1901

"CARNEGIE WILL GIVE LIBRARY" reports the *Vancouver Daily World* as the city receives news that multi-millionaire Andrew Carnegie has pledged $50,000 to the city for the purpose of building a free public library.

"Mr. Andrew Carnegie, the great iron and steel manufacturer, has decided to include Vancouver in the long list of towns, both in the United States and Great Britain, to which he has donated handsome sums of money for the erection of buildings to contain free libraries," the *Vancouver Daily News-Advertiser* will report the following day. "Within the past few months Mr. Carnegie has bestowed similar benefactions on two other Coast towns—Seattle and Tacoma."

"It is the best news we have had for many a day," beams Mayor T.O. Townley, "and, while of course I do not pretend to speak for the council, I can see no other end than that of the immediate acceptance of Mr. Carnegie's generous offer. The question of a site is, of course, an important one."

The money, gifted to Vancouver following a request made of the former steel magnate by MP George Maxwell, will be immediately accepted by city council, along with Carnegie's usual conditions: that the city donate the land and dedicate $5,000 a year to its upkeep. The Scottish-American multimillionaire (whose company, Carnegie Steel, was sold to J.P. Morgan only days earlier as part of the largest personal financial transaction ever recorded in its time) has made a habit of contributing to philanthropic causes over the previous 20 years, in particular to world peace initiatives, the Carnegie Hero Fund (which honours exceptionally altruistic deeds with a cash prize), and the construction of free libraries throughout Canada, the United States, and Europe.

After a lively referendum, the site of the new library will be fixed at Main and Hastings, where it will remain for more than 100 years, eventually being turned into the Carnegie Community Centre. By the time of his death at the age of 84, Andrew Carnegie will have donated more than $350 million of his personal wealth, aiding in the creation of roughly 3,000 free libraries.

The construction of the Carnegie Library, 1902.
IMAGE COURTESY OF THE VANCOUVER ARCHIVES (CVA 1376-27)

MARCH 9, 1977

AT 8 A.M., FOLLOWING MONTHS OF CHRONIC PAIN in his right knee and a subsequent diagnosis with osteogenic sarcoma, SFU kinesiology student Terry Fox undergoes an operation to have his leg amputated at Royal Columbian Hospital.

The operation, performed by Vancouver Canucks osteosurgeon Dr. Michael Piper, is the only option for dealing with the rare disease, and even following the amputation, a patient's average survival rate is only 50 percent. That said, Fox, a gifted athlete, will be up and walking on a temporary prosthetic limb less than three weeks later, and three weeks after that, he will play 18 holes of golf. His recovery will be swift in the months to follow, and he will join a wheelchair basketball team coached by Paralympian Rick Hansen. However, it is a small gift—a magazine left by his hospital bed the night before the operation—that sows the seeds for what will eventually become Fox's Marathon of Hope.

"The night before my amputation, my former basketball coach brought me a magazine with an article on an amputee who ran in the New York marathon," Fox will later write in a letter to the Canadian Cancer Society. "It was then when I decided to meet this new challenge head on and not only overcome my disability, but conquer it in such a way that I could never look back and say it disabled me. But as I soon realized that would be only half of my quest, for as I went through the 16 months of the physically and emotionally draining ordeal of chemotherapy, I was rudely awakened by the feelings that surrounded and coursed through the cancer clinic. There were faces with the brave smiles, and the ones who had given up smiling. There were feelings of hopeful denial, and the feelings of despair. My quest would not be a selfish one. I could not leave knowing these faces and feelings would still exist, even though I would be set free from mine. Somewhere the hurting must stop . . . and I was determined to take myself to the limit for this cause."

Three years later, Fox will dip his artificial leg in the Atlantic Ocean and set off from St. John's, Newfoundland. Although the return of his cancer will prematurely end both the run and his life, the Marathon of Hope and the Terry Fox Foundation will go on to raise as of 2012 an estimated $600 million for cancer research.

MARCH 10, 1927

At 6:15 p.m., THROWN OFF-COURSE by a powerful undertow, the 6,000-ton freighter SS *Eurana* collides with the Second Narrows Bridge, plowing through half of the fixed span just north of its swing structure and causing more than $10,000 worth of damage.

"With a thunderous crash of steel on steel, she ploughed into the fixed span, cutting off her forward works, her derricks, her great steel mast, her pilot house and chartroom," reports the *Vancouver Province*. "She finally came to rest with the east side of the bridge nearly touching her smokestack. Girders on the east side of the span were twisted and crumpled; the footwalk on that side was demolished."

The *Eurana*, bound for New York and carrying a cargo of lumber, sustains roughly $25,000 in damage as a result of the collision, heard nearly a mile away—though, miraculously, there are no injuries. It will take work crews nearly two hours to free the *Eurana* from where it has become wedged under the span, as they consider everything from acetylene torches to dynamite. Mercifully, the ship will be dislodged before any such action is necessary, when, at roughly 8:30 p.m., workers flood the hold and allow the freighter to drift free.

"The ship was in good position, headed right for the bridge," Captain W. Wingate will insist in an interview with the *Evening Sun*. "About 400 feet off the bridge she started to sheer. The helm was put hard over and the engines full ahead, the only possible way of straightening her up when it was evident that she was not going to straighten up and would hit the bridge. Both anchors were let go. Both anchors responded and that lessened the impact."

The ship Losmar in collision with the Second Narrows Bridge, April 1930.
PHOTOGRAPH BY JACK CASH (VPL 86904)

Despite the *Province*'s colourful description, the structure is insured against damages. Within the hour, it will be reopened to vehicle and pedestrian traffic. Ships have collided with the Second Narrows Bridge with alarming regularity since it opened in 1925. Shallow water, unpredictable currents, and its own unfortunate, low-slung structure have led to such frequent traffic delays, it has been nicknamed "The Bridge of Sighs" by Vancouverites.

The *Eurana* accident won't be the last in the bridge's history. Two more freighters will collide with the structure in the ensuing three years, and a third—the *Pacific Gatherer*—will do such significant damage that the bridge will be closed for four years.

In 1960, it will be replaced by the Ironworkers Memorial Bridge.

MARCH 11, 1910

THE SQUAMISH NATION loses a dedicated champion as, after a lengthy struggle, Chief Joe Capilano succumbs to tuberculosis at the age of 60.

"Chief Joe Capilano is dead," reports the *Vancouver Daily World*. "This is a little statement of fact that will bring sadness to many, both in the circles of the aborigine and in the homes of the whites."

Joe, a respected carver and storyteller, was also a tireless advocate for the rights of his people, even going so far as to travel to England to personally present a petition on Native land claims to King Edward VII. Joe's stories, as told to poet Pauline Johnson, formed the basis for her final and most widely read book, *Legends of Vancouver*.

"Chief Joe was known to be not a man of marvellously strong physique and he frequently required the care of a physician," the paper recalls, "though his faith in medicinal men was, according to his own telling, somewhat shattered when a medical practitioner who had doctored the Indians for years allowed himself to die."

Capilano's death has been expected for quite some time. As the *World* notes, "Chief Joe himself always presented a smiling and confident face to friends or one utterly stoically expressionless to strangers." The Capilano family has been tied into the fabric of British Columbia's history for centuries: his wife, Mary Capilano (who will survive him by 30 years), is the granddaughter of George Mathias, who welcomed George Vancouver upon his landing at Point Grey in 1792. And the Capilano family will remain a dominant force in the Squamish nation for a further five decades, when Joe is succeeded as chief by his son Mathias Joe, who will grow up to become a celebrated carver in his own right.

Although Joe Capilano didn't live to see the changes to Native rights that he fought so hard to secure, Chief Mathias Joe will inherit his father's desire to agitate for the rights of his people. In 1949, he will be the first First Nations person to cast a ballot in British Columbia.

Chief Joe Capilano's mausoleum, 1920.
IMAGE COURTESY OF THE VANCOUVER ARCHIVES (IN P14, PHOTOGRAPHER W. J. MOORE)

MARCH 12, 1977

"Granville Island Plan Set," exclaims the *Vancouver Sun* reporting on the official opening of the $2.4 million Granville Island seawall and the subsequent unveiling of federal government plans to transform the land from a "somewhat dishevelled industrial area" into an artisans' paradise.

"A farmers' market, theatres and an art school are among projects being studied as early steps in the redevelopment of Granville Island," writes the *Vancouver Province*. "[Canada Mortgage and Housing Corporation Consultant Norm] Hotson outlined plans for gradual transformation of the island. It could include recreation areas, artists' shops and studios, museums and restaurants, while retaining some industries."

The redevelopment plan, a long-time pet project of Vancouver Centre MP and Justice Minister Ron Basford, has been in the works from the early 1970s as part of an overall scheme to remove heavy industry from the False Creek basin, replacing it with residential development. Granville Island (known as "Mud Island" until the late 1930s) has historically been considered an eyesore by Vancouverites since it was constructed in the early 1900s, dredged up from the mud flats of False Creek and leased to all manner of industrial and manufacturing companies. Discussion surrounding a facelift for the island has been ongoing since the 1960s; however, plans to transform the 41-acre site (which was an actual island until 1956 when additional dredging turned it into a peninsula) only began in earnest in 1973. While many buildings will be repurposed, several businesses, including Ocean Cement, will be permitted to stay.

"This is a recycling project," Hotson explains. "It will be a link with the past."

Entrance to Granville Island, circa 1976.
Image Courtesy of the Vancouver Archives (CVA 1135-37, William E. Graham, photographer)
Image Copyright: City of Vancouver

In the months to come, there will be no shortage of critics of the project, including the *Vancouver Sun*, the Downtown Business Association, and even the city director of planning, Ray Spaxman, with concerns raised over cost, pollution, and potential competition between the island and similar boutiques and public markets in Gastown.

Despite the opposition, the Granville Island Public Market will have its grand opening in March 1979. By the early 1980s, the island will have become not only a hub for artists, but also one of the city's most popular tourist attractions.

It will remain under the management and ownership of the federal government into the new millennium.

MARCH 13, 1922

"PROVINCE BROADCASTS NEWS AND MUSIC BY RADIO!" declares the front page of the *Vancouver Province* as, thanks to the paper's own broadcasting equipment, the city gains its first radio station.

"For the first time in the history of the Canadian West, radio 'waves' carried the news of the day to scores of districts," the *Province* reports proudly, "many of them so much beyond the reach of the mailed evening newspaper that news with them by ordinary channels is often three or four days old."

The half-hour broadcast begins at 8:30 p.m. and includes news coverage and musical selections. It is sent from a "radiophone" transmitter inside the Merchants' Exchange Building and comes after weeks of testing and experimentation. Other newspapers will quickly follow suit with their own broadcasts, including the *Vancouver Sun* and the *Vancouver Daily World*, both of which will begin broadcasting within two weeks.

"Bright and early this morning, from points up and down the Coast, messages were received describing the clearness and satisfactory nature of the service supplied last night," the paper continues smugly. "The greatest distance covered was recorded by the government station at High River, Alta., which is 600 miles away and across the Rockies."

According to the article, the broadcast was "rather better in clearness and quality than the best 'wire telephone' that has ever been used. And as for the music, you close your eyes and you imagine you are listening to a phonograph in the same room with you."

Future programs will include news coverage, music, and even live concerts.

The station will continue to broadcast until March 1940.

A giant radio in Victory Square, as part of a sales promotion, 1930.
IMAGE COURTESY OF THE VANCOUVER ARCHIVES (CVA 99-4144, PHOTOGRAPHER STUART THOMSON)

MARCH 14, 1972

THE BAYSHORE INN IN COAL HARBOUR receives an extreme and last-minute request when the top four floors are unexpectedly rented by an eccentric out-of-town guest: Howard Hughes.

"Nobody knew he was coming," bellman Stan Yip will explain in an interview conducted years later with the *Winnipeg Free Press*. "We were told he had called from his plane and wanted the top four floors. The manager told him we were full. Hughes said: 'If I don't get the rooms, I'm buying the hotel.'"

Unusually, the reclusive 66-year-old aviator, filmmaker, and billionaire chooses to walk into the hotel's side lobby himself, freshly barbered (Hughes rarely has his hair cut), wearing a bathrobe, pyjamas, and sandals, and remarking "Hey, this is pretty nice," before disappearing up the elevator and commandeering the top two floors of the building for himself and his aides.

Hughes's arrival will go unnoticed by the city's media for several days because of his requests for privacy and because he hasn't been seen in public in close to 15 years. In fact, by the time a spokesman confirms his arrival, the *Sun* and *Province* will already be speculating that he has departed again. Photographers will be unable to confirm his identity, and rumours will abound that he is sneaking out to watch Canucks games, or tour Stanley Park at night. In reality, Hughes—who suffers from severe obsessive-compulsive disorder and an addiction to prescription painkillers—will never leave the penthouse suite. Hughes, who takes up a new place of residence every six months to avoid paying taxes, will remain at the Bayshore until September, continuing a lengthy tradition of bizarre behaviour. (He reportedly has his hair and nails cut only once a year, refuses to bathe or wear clothes, and, because of his obsession with germs, will only accept items wrapped in Kleenex.) This tradition will go on unabated until his death in 1976.

"I remember how his staff had instructed our head chef to cut his food into small exact squares," Yip will explain in a 2004 interview with the *Vancouver Courier*. "All of the security were Hughes men. They operated completely separate from the hotel. I don't know of anybody in the hotel who ever saw him, but the publicity never died down the whole time he was here."

Photographers will camp outside the hotel for weeks, hoping for a snapshot of the reclusive billionaire, with one even attempting to fly past his penthouse in a hang-glider. However, as the *Province* notes, guests displaced by Hughes's sudden appearance are less taken with his arrival.

"You could say I am bugged," says Dunlop Tire sales manager Wayne Smith (in town for the Western Tire Dealers Conference). "We made a deal here for accommodation and I don't know why we should get turned out with 15 minutes' notice, Howard Hughes or not."

MARCH 15, 1969

"FOOL LET OFF—BUT WITH A WARNING" reads an article in the *Vancouver Province* reporting on the arrest of Joachim Foikis, the city's official Town Fool, on the charge of "creating a disturbance."

"Drum-beating Town Fool Joachim Foikis was cleared Friday of a charge of creating a disturbance but was told he should cool 'silly symphonies' in the downtown area in the future," reports the paper. "Foikis was arrested at Granville and Broadway last Saturday as he stood in the midst of a crowd of 200 people who spilled out of a meditation session with Zen Buddhist philosopher Alan Watts. Police picked Foikis out as the leader of the crowd as he waved his fool's baton in tune to the sounds of bass and snare drums, cymbals, flutes and tambourines."

Foikis, who conducted his own defence at the proceedings, called a number of witnesses, all of whom called the affair "a happy, spontaneous and innocent gathering." The Crown, however, was not so convinced, alleging, according to the paper, "although there was no viciousness attached to the gathering, it had not been a 'happy happening', but rather a 'silly happening.'"

Joachim Foikis is a familiar figure in Vancouver, having received in 1968 a Canada Council Grant to serve as the city's official Town Fool to "promote self-awareness of the entire community." His previous activities have included attending city council meetings in a jester's outfit (his customary attire), snarling up traffic by travelling down Main Street in a cart pulled by donkeys, and hosting spontaneous street parties—activities that will eventually get him profiled in the *New York Times*.

"There's a time and place for most things," Magistrate Morris Mulligan tells Foikis. "I don't think the corner of Granville and Broadway between 10 and 11 at night is the right time or the right place for this thing of yours. But on the whole of the evidence I must dismiss the charge and you are free to go."

Less than a month later, Foikis will use the last $500 of his grant to host a street party for Downtown Eastside residents.

MARCH 16, 1895

ABLE TO STAND THE OUTRAGE NO LONGER, the *Province* publishes a scathing editorial on the scandalous state of the CPR's *Empress* steamships.

"That the CPR has given Victoria the go-by as a port of call or at least sojourn for her *Empress* line of steamers may be a matter past praying for," the article seethes, "but the accommodation afforded to passengers in embarking and disembarking is an abuse still very much alive."

The *Empress* ships—so named because they include the *Empress of India*, *Empress of China*, and *Empress of Japan*—are operated by the railroad's Canadian Pacific Steamship Company as a means of transporting goods and passengers to and from "the Orient." The ships themselves are a relatively new acquisition, having been in service for only six years; however, opening up trade routes with the Far East (in addition to the handsome government subsidies the vessels currently enjoy) has brought untold profit to the CPR in transporting Chinese silks and other commodities to North America.

"The gangway is an ingenious contrivance," the paper continues with rancour. "It consists of a single plank of Douglas Fir, and like all great inventions is remarkable for its simplicity. It offers great advantage over common or garden gangways in that it is extremely dangerous to life and limb, and thereby introduces an element of pleasurable excitement—not to say hazard into the voyage—which is not generally included in the price of a first-class fare."

Despite the *Province*'s complaints, the *Empress* ships will remain a part of BC's transportation network for decades to come, eventually moving soldiers (in addition to thousands of Chinese labourers) to the Western Front during World War I.

The fleet will remain in operation until the 1960s when the advent of air travel will render it redundant.

Passengers on board a steamer leaving Vancouver, 1920.
IMAGE COURTESY OF THE VANCOUVER ARCHIVES (CVA 99-1255, PHOTOGRAPHER STUART THOMSON)

MARCH 17, 1939

"THE OLD PIER GOES" reads a headline in the *Vancouver Daily Province* as the demolition of the West End's beloved English Bay Pier enters its final stages.

"English Bay pier is nearly a thing of the past," the paper laments. "The thirty-year-old structure, rotten with age, becoming a menace to public safety, is on its way out . . . The big square timbers, the planking, has been wrecked and sold for firewood. The piling is being cut up as cordwood. The pillars and rails are stacked awaiting buyers and what a sentimental period they represent."

The pier, a local landmark since its construction in 1909, has faithfully served the citizens of the West End for decades, both as a promenade and as an accommodation for boats (though a number of collisions with those same boats over the years necessitated a series of costly repairs). Despite its sentimental value, and a high-profile campaign in the early 1930s to revitalize the pier (a plan that included a lower car deck, cafés, and a glass-domed *Palais de Danse*), the city has opted instead to demolish the structure, in keeping with its plan to convert the West End's waterfront back into unspoiled parkland. Back in February, the choice to demolish the promenade briefly led to talk of several new structures, including a new "breakwater masonry pier," as part of an unemployment relief scheme. Despite support from the city's tourist association, and the mayor himself, the plan never came to fruition.

"The pier came to have a sentimental value as a landmark dating back for 30 years," concludes W.H. Roberts of the English Bay Protective Association. "We were a little shocked to learn it was coming down, but, frankly, it rather spoiled the view and was, in itself, no great asset."

English Bay Pier, 1905.
IMAGE COURTESY OF THE VANCOUVER ARCHIVES (CVA 677-227)

MARCH 18, 1910

THE VANCOUVER WORLD REPORTS ON THE LATEST THREAT to menace the city's population, an issue that has long been "a bugbear" to local law enforcement: Chinese lottery games.

"It will be well for those who are in the habit of frequenting and playing the Chinese lottery games to know that they are playing at an unlawful game, and subject themselves, if caught, to a heavy fine or jail term," police court prosecutor J.K. Kennedy proclaims.

His declaration follows the prosecution of Wily Lo and Charley Sing, after a raid on their Hastings Street "gambling den" resulted in a three-month prison sentence for each man. Illegal gambling has long been a source of frustration to local law enforcement, a frustration made more pronounced given that most previous cases have been overturned on appeal. The issue of vice crime in Chinese neighbourhoods is a popular one with *World* publisher L.D. Taylor, an issue that will continue to occupy significant front-page real estate for the remainder of the decade. The campaign will climax in 1920, with a series of sensationalized, xenophobic stories on Chinese drug lords. In 1920, the *World* will pressure city officials (who will, in turn, pressure provincial and federal politicians) into a commitment to stamp out the Chinatown "dope trade."

"Many of those who have gone into these places have felt safe owing to the police being unable to get a decision from the courts declaring the lottery to be a gambling game," the paper concludes. "They did not think they were breaking the law, and consequently spent thousands of dollars on the lottery. For the benefit of those who are addicted to such practices, it would be well to bear in mind that any person looking on at an unlawful game is guilty of an offense, and liable to a heavy fine, as well as those who actually play the game . . . Now that the appeal has been quashed it is altogether likely that the police will clean out all Chinese lottery games wherever they exist, many of which are carried on behind tailor shops and Chinese places of business."

Each gambler found on the premises is fined $25. *World* publisher L.D. Taylor will go on to become Vancouver's most-elected mayor, notorious for his lax approach to vice crime.

MARCH 19, 1974

ON THE HEELS OF AN UNPRECEDENTED letter-writing campaign, a lengthy "Save the Orpheum" drive, and a city feasibility study, Vancouver city council votes 10 to 1 to purchase the historic Orpheum Theatre, thus rescuing it from being gutted by Famous Players and turned into a multiplex.

"Mayor Art Phillips told council the federal government has agreed to put up $1 million toward the $3.9-million purchase price and will put up a further $1 million for renovations," reports the *Vancouver Sun*. "The only dissenting vote came from Ald. Harry Rankin who said he was not disputing the desirability of the city having another theatre. He said his quarrel was with council's sense of priorities in spending the sum involved when there are many other needs that clamour for money."

The Orpheum (originally known as "The New Orpheum") has been a city institution since its construction in 1927. Originally a vaudeville house, it was later purchased by Famous Players and transformed into a movie theatre. However, the news that the corporation was planning to gut the building's interior and create multiple auditoriums caused a massive public outcry and gave birth to the "Save the Orpheum" campaign.

"When word of Famous Players' plans for the theatre reached the public, City Hall was inundated with 8,000 letters from citizens, with only ten of them in favour of the destruction," former Orpheum manager Ivan Ackery will later recall in his memoirs. "The others were shocked, angry, pleading. Two petitions bore 1,000 signatures. Never before had the city had such an overwhelming reaction to the impending loss of an old building. Even Christ Church Cathedral, which is a beloved and historic site, inspired only 300 letters to prevent its destruction."

The campaign (which will include a fundraiser by none other than Jack Benny) will result in a commitment of $2 million from the federal government, with the city contributing the remainder of the $7.1 million sale, and the intention being to transform the movie house into a new civic theatre. Despite receiving no provincial assistance, the renovations will proceed, and the Orpheum will reopen in 1977 as the permanent home of the Vancouver Symphony Orchestra.

It will be designated as a National Historic Site of Canada in 1979.

The "New Orpheum" under construction, 1927.
IMAGE COURTESY OF THE VANCOUVER ARCHIVES (CVA 447-397, PHOTOGRAPHER WALTER E. FROST)

MARCH 20, 1925

IN THE WAKE OF THE JANET SMITH SHOOTING—the city's most notorious unsolved murder case—a group of men in Ku Klux Klan regalia arrive at the Point Grey home of R.P. Baker and kidnap his 25-year-old houseboy, Wong Foon Sing.

"After blindfolding him and tying his arms, his captors took him to a car and forced him to lie down on the floor of the back seat," Edward Starkins will recount in his 1985 book, *Who Killed Janet Smith?* "They set out on a long drive, during which one man kept his foot pressed down on his back . . . Still blindfolded, he was taken into a building and up a flight of stairs, then told to remain still while a hard, heavy object was attached to each of his legs. The rope around his body was removed. Some time later, realizing that he was alone, Wong removed his blindfold to discover that he was in a dark room where the windows had been covered with heavy black paper. His feet were shackled to a chain bolted to the floor."

For the next six weeks, Sing will be held captive in a Shaughnessy attic, repeatedly beaten, threatened with death, and faced with near-strangulation by his mysterious captors, all in the hopes of eliciting a confession. The Janet Smith case has gripped Vancouver since it was first reported in the local dailies in July 1924, with Sing, who found the body, seen as the prime suspect. The Shaughnessy nursemaid, found dead at the bottom of a basement staircase with a single gunshot wound to the head, has been the topic of furious discussion ever since, including rumours that Baker is involved in the illicit drug trade and that Smith was murdered at a drug-fuelled high society party (in some versions, by a high-ranking political figure).

Six weeks later, local dailies will report that Sing has been found wandering deliriously along Marine Drive. Although no evidence links Sing to the crime, and Attorney General A.M. Manson apparently admits Sing isn't even a suspect, the houseboy will be immediately charged with murder and held under a "privacy ban," preventing him even from conversing with his attorney. Although the Klan—active in the Vancouver of the 1920s—is initially suspected, it will be revealed during the sensational criminal trial which follows, that the kidnapping was in fact organized and financed by the Point Grey Police Department, *Point Grey Gazette* publisher and Marpole mayor J.A. Paton, and with the blessing of Attorney General Manson himself. The resulting scandal will send several of the kidnappers to prison and finish Manson's political career.

Though indicted on charges related to the kidnapping, J.A. Paton and every member of the Point Grey police will receive a last-minute stay of prosecution from the deputy attorney general. Paton will go on to become a prominent MLA, speaking in favour of Japanese internment, and his paper, the *Point Grey Gazette*, will go on to become the *Vancouver Courier*. Sing, his hearing permanently damaged as a result of his torture, will return to China less than a year later.

Smith's murder will never be solved.

Man in Ku Klux Klan regalia, outside of the organization's headquarters at Glen Brae, Nov. 1925. The mansion will later go on to become Canuck Place.
IMAGE COURTESY OF THE VANCOUVER ARCHIVES (CVA 99-1499, PHOTOGRAPHER STUART THOMSON)

MARCH 21, 1985

IN FRONT OF A CROWD OF SUPPORTERS (including Rolland and Betty Fox), and with an inventory that includes one custom-built wheelchair, one spare frame, a motorhome, an escort van, 80 pairs of deerskin curling gloves, and 15 bottles of Shur-Grip, Paralympian Rick Hansen launches his international Man in Motion tour at Oakridge Centre.

"Although dark clouds briefly threatened to dampen things," the *Vancouver Province* reports, "the 27-year-old wheelchair athlete started his 18-month tour on time at 9 a.m. to the cheers of 300 spectators."

"This is very special to us and we hope it's special to you," Hansen tells the crowd. "Thank you all."

Hansen, who lost the use of his legs following a car accident when he was 15 years old, has spent much of the previous year training, organizing, and fundraising for the 24,900-mile marathon, which is intended to take him across more than 100 major cities in 34 countries, on five continents, with the goal of raising $10 million for spinal cord research. Though prominent sponsors include McDonald's, Nike, and Expo 86, the Man in Motion tour has been in a state of financial desperation for almost a year. Soliciting money from a donated office in the Guinness Tower and using office supplies pilfered from the Jim Pattison Group several floors below, Hansen's core group of volunteers are still woefully short of their targets, with only $90,000 of the $750,000 for operational expenses they'd hoped to raise.

"School kids sold oranges and washed cars to raise a few bucks for the fund," writes the *Sun*'s Jim Taylor in a column unfortunately titled "Jockwatch." "Prime Minister Brian Mulroney sent a congratulatory telegram—thus far in lieu of cheque. But the people were there. Hundreds of them, picking up the fund-raising appeal carried yesterday morning on virtually every radio station and re-routing to Oakridge to be briefly a part of something they sensed could be great."

Though the marathon gets off to a less-than-perfect start (the motorhome containing the five-person support crew will be in an accident before it's even left the Oakridge parking lot), and despite some early hardships (notably bad weather and a dead alternator), Hansen and his crew will successfully reach Bellingham on his first day. The Man in Motion tour will go on to become more successful than anyone had imagined, ultimately raising $26 million for spinal cord research.

The tour crew will also, by Hansen's estimation, be involved in an impressive 553 accidents.

MARCH 22, 1937

At approximately 2 a.m., a three-alarm fire begins in the Pender Street offices of the *Vancouver Sun*, raging out of control for more than two hours and doing roughly $200,000 in damage.

"On their arrival the firemen found both street and alley showered with broken glass from the explosion and flames pouring out of windows on the second floor, where the editorial rooms are located," reports the *Province*. "Business office, editorial rooms, mailing room, gymnasium and photographic studio, which were housed in the building, were destroyed, with all their equipment."

Less than 15 minutes after it begins, the fire has already engulfed all four floors, causing windows to explode, and flames to shoot from the roof, more than 50 feet into the air. Janitor Jack Johnson suffers minor burns and smoke inhalation as a result of attempting to combat the blaze.

"Heavy black smoke continued to pour from the building as the flames ate their way through the roof," the paper continues. "The rear of the structure was a wall of flame, and the dense smoke forced firemen to work in short shifts on their high ladders."

Though the cause of the fire cannot be determined, it is presumed that it began on the building's lower floors, quickly spreading up the elevator shaft before consuming the building and its contents. Miraculously, there are no serious injuries, and the paper's presses, housed next door, are largely undamaged. In the early hours of the morning, writers and editors are able to clear space in the bindery next door, and, despite the setbacks, they manage to bring the morning edition out on time.

Vancouver Fire Department in action, circa 1917.
Image Courtesy of the Vancouver Archives (CVA 99-725, Stuart Thomson, photographer)

"In newspaper circles there is sympathy and admiration for the management and staff of the *Vancouver Sun*," the *News-Herald* will report the following day. "The sympathy is because of the serious dislocation of the structure of organization, the loss by fire and water of so many accustomed tools of daily use, and filed away against need . . . The admiration is because the traditions of journalism were so competently maintained."

"It was 9:15 a.m.," the *Sun*'s Alan Morley will write triumphantly that morning. "The *Vancouver Sun* was doing 'business as usual.' The deadline was coming up for the noon edition. And here's your paper, mister!"

MARCH 23, 1936

WITH NEWSWORTHY EVENTS in woefully short supply, the *Vancouver Sun* combs its archives for happenings in years past as part of its popular "This Day in History" section.

"Ten Years Ago" important mentions include the victory of the New Westminster Adanacs over Duncan in a senior basketball tournament, and word that "Edward McDougall, well-known contractor believes that Vancouver is to have its greatest year in this line of business."

"Twenty Years Ago" there is word that the Vancouver Fire Department was able to save the $70,000 home of J.B. Johnston on Angus Drive. The fire, which began at roughly 6:20 a.m., still managed to do $1,000 of damage.

And "Forty Years Ago" two noteworthy items are the victory of E.B. Deane over J.H. Senkler in a local billiards tournament, and the news that "the mangy dog which has been such an eye sore around town for the last few weeks has at last been destroyed."

Charles E. Jones' dog "Smoky" (not set to be destroyed), circa 1935.
IMAGE COURTESY OF THE VANCOUVER ARCHIVES (CVA 371-1201)

MARCH 24, 1949

Workers operating a butter-wrapping machine, circa 1940.
IMAGE COURTESY OF THE VANCOUVER ARCHIVES (CVA 1184-1786, PHOTOGRAPHER JACK LINDSAY)

VANCOUVERITES REJOICE and manufacturers prepare as, for the first time since 1886, the BC legislature legalizes the sale and production of a highly contentious food product: margarine.

"The manufacture and sale of oleomargarine in British Columbia became legal today," reports the *Vancouver Sun*. "The Legislature gave its approval Wednesday to the margarine measure which specifies the amount of yellow colouring allowed in it, requires clear labelling that it is not butter and makes restaurants inform the public when they are serving it instead of butter. The 'Farm Bloc' in the Legislature softened most of their opposition as the bill was given approval because they had won their fight against completely unrestricted sale of oleo. Several uttered minor protests against allowing any yellow in oleo at all, but there was no attempt to call a recorded division on the question."

The legalization (following a 70-year ban) comes after a furious battle between margarine manufacturers and the BC dairy industry, which has, for decades, been fearful of the product's impact on its business. Margarine, which has been illegal in Canada since 1886, was still referred to as a banned substance in British Columbia until the passage of the legislation, on the advice of Attorney General G.S. Wismer (a figure seen as sympathetic to the butter lobby), even after the federal government ruled that its restriction of the low-cost alternative was unlawful. However, after legalization in other provinces, and a letter campaign to Wismer himself from more than 1,500 BC women (a campaign spearheaded by pro-margarine forces, among them shopping columnist "Penny Wise" and Point Grey MLA Tillie Rolston), the legislature at last passed *An Act Respecting Oleomargarine*.

A number of restrictions will remain, among them, that margarine not be used in any provincial institution and that the substance not be permitted to resemble butter in either shape or colour. Successive attempts in the early 1950s to remove restrictions on the colour of margarine will be defeated, thanks in large part to strenuous objections from the butter lobby. Despite initial enthusiasm, the papers caution that bulk production will not be available until early April.

"The Vancouver plan operators said that their product would not be on the market," the *Victoria Daily Colonist* will report, "until it is 100 per cent perfect."

That December, Vancouver will go on to produce the first commercial margarine in the country.

MARCH 25, 1937

Helena Gutteridge receives the oath of office, March 30, 1937.
IMAGE COURTESY OF THE VANCOUVER ARCHIVES (PORT P276.1, PHOTOGRAPHER GREGORY E. D'ARCHY-HODSOLL)

LOCAL PAPERS BUZZ with the news as, following a close race, suffragette, social reformer, and Cooperative Commonwealth Federation candidate Helena Gutteridge is elected as the city's first female city councillor.

"Helena Gutteridge created history in Vancouver Wednesday, when she gained a seat on the city council," the *Vancouver News-Herald* explains, "the first woman ever to become an alderman in the city."

The victory is Gutteridge's third attempt at obtaining a council seat, including a failed bid only two months earlier (because of a series of technicalities, the city has held three elections in four months). However, following the sudden death of Alderman L.D. McDonald, a by-election was called, allowing the CCF candidate to triumph over her closest opponent, Alderman H.L. Corey, by 358 votes. The paper is quick to point out that the turnout was only 17 percent of the electorate and the contest was initially far too close to call.

"While Ms. Gutteridge finally triumphed by a plurality of 358 the contest during the count appeared very much closer," the paper continues. "Ex-Ald. Corey took the lead at the outset and held it for some time. Then Miss Gutteridge began to pull up as polling stations favorable to the party were heard from."

The country's first female alderman—Calgary's Annie Gale—was elected more than 20 years earlier, and since then, a number of other cities have followed suit. City elections have seen female councillors before. In fact, this by-election marks the sixth time a woman has run for civic office in Vancouver. Gutteridge, who has gained a reputation during her 20 years in the city campaigning for women's suffrage, organized labour, and the rights of the unemployed (and who was instrumental in the CCF's decision to enter civic politics), will make an unusual addition to city council, proposing such radical notions as subsidized housing, extending the civic franchise to all residents (not just property owners), and even—in a move unusual for the time—opposing a motion restricting trade licences for Asian citizens. Nonetheless, Gutteridge will be the only one of the three CCF members on council to survive a December election. (The party's overtly socialist leanings will lead to its sound trouncing by the newly minted Non-Partisan Association.) Her final months in office will be spent campaigning for a comprehensive subsidized housing program.

At the end of her term, she will lose her seat to Alderman Corey. Although in later life she will feel defeated by her inability to bring about comprehensive change to the city's housing policy, she will live to see the opening of both Little Mountain and Orchard Park social housing projects in the early 1950s.

MARCH 26, 1915

"VANCOUVER MILLIONAIRES Win Hockey Championship of World," exclaims a headline in the *Vancouver Province* as, in the Denman Arena in front of 5,000 fans, Vancouver wins the Stanley Cup.

"The Vancouver team outplayed the Ottawas from every standpoint," the paper gloats, of the team's 12 to 8 victory over Ottawa, "but the superb checking back and untiring persistency of the coast forwards proved a tremendous factor in the ultimate result."

"They outplayed us in all departments," Ottawa manager Frank Shaughnessy admits after the game. "Your forwards came back so fast and outskated our men so that the defence did not get much chance."

This year marks the first time that the respective champions of the Pacific Coast Hockey Association and the National Hockey Association have officially competed for the Stanley Cup (a two-game series between Toronto and Victoria the previous year was deemed ineligible), and marks the farthest west the cup itself has travelled in its history. The Millionaires have already soundly defeated the Senators in the first three games of the best-of-five series, led strongly by the efforts of Fred "Cyclone" Taylor.

"The final game of the series was the least exciting," the paper complains. "The Ottawas appeared to realize that they were up against a better team and their methods lacked the dash and vim of the other games, though they tried hard for a while. Both teams played loosely and the hockey served up was notable chiefly for its lack of class. For a world's championship event it was indeed a rather poor exhibition."

The Millionaires (awarded $300 a player for the win) will make it to the playoffs five subsequent times (twice as the Vancouver Maroons) without success, and the team will eventually fold in 1926.

The game will mark the city's only Stanley Cup victory.

The event does not even make the front page.

Fred "Cyclone" Taylor, 1919.

IMAGE COURTESY OF THE VANCOUVER ARCHIVES (CVA 99-778)

MARCH 27, 1978

Nat Bailey receives an award for "Cleanest Kitchen" from the Junior Chamber of Commerce, April 20, 1956.
Photograph by Vic Spooner (VPL 83008)

Self-made millionaire, White Spot founder, and baseball enthusiast Nat Bailey dies in Vancouver General Hospital at the age of 76.

"Bailey's trademark was he always seemed to wear a bow tie," fellow entrepreneur Ben Wosk will recall in a March 28 interview with the *Vancouver Sun*. "That I would rather think would be a hangover from selling peanuts in the ball park. When he was worth $10 million, he always wore a little stubby bow tie."

Born in Michigan, Bailey moved to Vancouver with his family in the early 1900s, selling popcorn and newspapers at Granville and Davie at the age of 17. As his success grew, Bailey bought a truck and expanded his operation to include soft drinks, ice cream, and hot dogs, which he sold on city streets, in parks, and on beaches. He was also a lifelong sports enthusiast; in addition to working wrestling and boxing matches as an announcer, he sold hot dogs and other confectionary at baseball games in the city's Athletic Park, and thanks to his eccentric style of dress and distinctive voice, he became a well-known local personality.

"He had this great tenor voice and it sprang from a throat of pure leather," the *Sun*'s Jim Kearney will recall in a lengthy eulogy. "Meanwhile, it never heard of laryngitis. It couldn't afford the luxury, for there was no PA system in Brown's ballyard. Just Nat and his megaphone to announce the lineups, pitching changes and all other pertinent information. But that was only part of his job, merely temporary interruptions as he went about the business of lobbing hotdogs and peanuts to the top rows of the stands; flawlessly fielding the nickels and dimes that came flying back."

In 1928, Bailey—a three-pack-a-day smoker—opened White Spot (distinctive for being the city's first drive-in) on South Granville. While the franchise foundered during the Depression, it eventually became a local institution, enjoying such popularity that it was later purchased by the American-owned General Foods, whose holdings include Maxwell House Coffee, Kool-Aid, and Jell-O. Bailey continued his local philanthropic work, putting large amounts of money into the Vancouver Mounties Baseball Club and involving himself with a failed attempt to bring the city its first NHL franchise.

White Spot Limited, meanwhile, will be purchased by BC property developer Peter Toigo (in a Canada-wide sale that includes all 54 Kentucky Fried Chicken Outlets and other franchises). Toigo's company, Shato Holdings, will have by the year 2000 expanded the chain to include 60 restaurants and 40 Triple O White Spot fast-food locations in Canada and Hong Kong.

Less than a week after Bailey's death, Capilano Stadium will be renamed "Nat Bailey" in his honour.

MARCH 28, 1954

WITH POLIO SEASON QUICKLY APPROACHING, there are renewed calls for better sanitation by the residents of South Vancouver, many of whom (despite repeated appeals over the previous 40 years) still live without even a basic sewer system.

"Deadly polio germs lurk in open Vancouver ditches into which septic tank sewage seeps during poliomyelitis outbreaks," declares the *Vancouver News-Herald*. "Fifty of the 120 polio cases reported in Vancouver proper last year occurred in South Vancouver, by far the highest incidence for any one area of the city. Medical men say it would be wrong to assume this is a result of South Vancouver having the highest percentage of septic tanks . . . but they unhesitatingly point out that the presence in the city of large numbers of septic tanks which discharge unabsorbed sewage into open ditches is a decided health menace."

Fear of the degenerative disease—which destroys motor neurons and most often affects young children—has been steadily growing throughout the 1940s and 1950s, with outbreaks becoming more and more common in areas with poor sanitation (the disease being spread by fecal-oral contact), consigning thousands of children and adults to lives of weakness, paralysis, and withered limbs, and many thousands more to life inside the dreaded Iron Lung. While portions of the city of Vancouver have had a sewer system since the end of 1888 (laid out at the same time as many of its streets), South Vancouver—a separate municipality until 1929—is still serviced only by a network of septic tanks.

"Our taxes are high, but we don't mind as long as we get the services they're supposed to pay for," says Ray Oates of South Vancouver. "We want sewers before we want an auditorium."

Drainage ditch on Main Street, circa 1910.
IMAGE COURTESY OF THE VANCOUVER ARCHIVES (A-16-22)

Mercifully for the residents of South Vancouver, Dr. Jonas Salk will have developed the world's first polio vaccine by the following year. As a result of Salk's work (as well as a live vaccine developed in the 1960s by Dr. Albert Sabin), poliomyelitis will be eradicated from the Americas by 1994.

The residents of South Vancouver, on the other hand, will be waiting for a comprehensive sewer system until at least the mid-1960s.

MARCH 29, 1898

CLOSE TO 25 ARTICLES and advertisements appear in the 10 pages of the *Vancouver Daily News-Advertiser*, all of them aimed at Klondike-bound miners and prospectors, as the fledgling city scrambles to cash in on gold rush fever.

"The rush has begun!" declares an article published that same week. "There is plenty of gold at the other end. Every advice from there is more encouraging."

The Yukon gold rush, touched off only one year earlier by the *Seattle Post-Intelligencer*'s report of a "ton of gold" unearthed near Dawson City, has prompted tens of thousands of hopefuls to quit their jobs and leave their families, to journey north. And, with Vancouver essentially the last supply post before the Ashcroft and Stikine trails (heavily promoted for circumnavigating Alaska and thus keeping prospectors entirely on British soil), and with word that Mounted Police will turn away anyone with less than a ton of supplies, the city is now in the middle of a pronounced economic boom—one that will last into the 1900s and see its population double effectively overnight.

"This is undoubtedly the greatest mining camp the world has ever seen," exclaims another article referring to Dawson City, "and there will be more gold shipped from here in the next two or three years than has ever been shipped from one camp . . . If prospects hold out, there is room within a radius of one hundred miles from here for two hundred thousand miners to be employed successfully."

This is hardly the first time gold rush fever has struck the Lower Mainland. In 1859, news of gold strikes on the Fraser River brought 30,000 prospectors to the area, resulting in $10 million in gold being removed by prospectors. And, with this new boom in full swing, even products without a solid Klondike connection are being trumpeted as necessities by local merchants. ("No Man," declares an ad in the *News-Advertiser*, "should leave for the Klondike without a supply of Vaseline.")

Unbridled gold rush enthusiasm will continue to grow well past the end of 1898. A banner at the bottom of the December 31 edition of the *Vancouver Daily World* will declare: "VANCOUVER IS THE GATEWAY TO THE KLONDIKE. It Poossesses [sic] Unrivalled Outfitting Advantages."

A group en route to the Klondike, gathered outside of Johnston, Kerfoot and Co., Cordova Street, 1898.
IMAGE COURTESY OF THE VANCOUVER ARCHIVES (STR P336)

MARCH 30, 1967

AFTER MONTHS OF UNFAIR, alarmist reporting on the realities of the youth movement in the local papers, and cruising on a tide of libertarian, peace-and-love sentiment surging up the coast from San Francisco, a manifesto is drafted by a group of Vancouver artists, poets, writers, and free thinkers, with the aim of providing the city with "a truly free press."

"To all those interested in fighting lies/propaganda/terrorism," it reads, "the events of the last few months in Vancouver have made it clear that the time has come to establish a truly free press."

The document, attributed to Peter Auxier, Pierre Coupey, Dan McLeod, and Rick Kitaeff, and drawn heavily from Quebec's Refus Global, goes on to detail the aims of a free press in Vancouver, aims that include "to fight repressive legislation, the abuse of police power . . . to invite free exchange of opinion, radical or otherwise . . . to uphold civil liberties [and] to discuss issues, not to condemn people."

The Vancouver of the late 1960s is a ripe battleground for Canada's emerging counterculture movement. With a rabidly pro-development mayor (who will, at one point, refer to hippies as "scum"), a notoriously stodgy middle class, and an increasingly aggressive police force, youths inspired by the spirit growing out from Haight-Ashbury's hippie scene will begin to establish their own identity in Vancouver. They will experiment with sex, drugs, and alternative ways of thinking, and move into a series of rundown houses in the Kitsilano area later known as "Chemical Row." In the months to come, with dozens of flower children arriving in the city each day, council will appoint a three-man "Special Hippie Committee" dedicated to examining the "problem" of the city's growing counterculture, and a number of

Dan McLeod awarding a prize record to a contest winner outside Georgia Straight headquarters, circa 1968.
IMAGE COURTESY OF UBC RARE BOOKS AND SPECIAL COLLECTIONS, GEORGIA STRAIGHT COLLECTION

hippie-centric business will spring up along Fourth Avenue.

"Human Beings! Artists! Angels! Children of the New Sun!" the manifesto concludes. "If you wish to discuss the aims of a free press, its name, the means to set it up, its floating editorial board, its stance and scope, come to 883 Hamilton Street, April 2nd."

Though a call for cheques is issued in the name of Gastown Press, the counterculture newspaper will soon have a different name: the *Georgia Straight*.

MARCH 31, 1908

"CITIZEN FACES GRAVE CHARGE," reads a headline in the *Vancouver Daily World* as, following his "sensational" arrest the previous afternoon, wealthy engineer George A. Walkem appears in police court, on the charge of having counselled his lover to have an abortion.

Although Walkem, head of the prestigious G.A. Walkem and Co., is released on $6,000 bail, the story will continue to grow more sensational as the case develops. Walkem is initially accused of having advised lover Blanche Bond to visit a Seattle doctor for an abortion operation (in March of the previous year), but courtroom testimony will reveal an affair packed with lurid detail, including abandonment, death threats, coercion, and false promises of marriage.

"The story of Miss Bond was told under great difficulty," an article in the *Vancouver Province* will explain, when Bond takes the stand in early April, "it being necessary to give her temporary rests. She said that she met Walkem in July of 1906. He continued for a long time coming to her house almost every night. He had first furnished her with one kind of medicine, later supplying another. When he asked her to go to Nanaimo for an operation, she refused. He threatened to cut his throat, and alarmed over this threat the girl said that she consented to go to Seattle."

Bond is described by an April 18 *News-Advertiser* article as "a handsome woman" who "excited the compassion of every one that saw her." She tells of her affair with Walkem over two days in a weakened and hysterical state, fainting regularly and having to be carried into the courtroom on a chair. Following the operation, according to Bond's testimony, she and Walkem took a trip to Portland, whereupon he abandoned her and returned to Vancouver, advising in subsequent correspondence (read at great length in the courtroom), "Now Blanche, dear, take my advice and tell nothing to anybody." Bond will also claim that Walkem repeatedly expressed a promise to marry her (a statement that draws murmurs of disapproval from the courtroom and the local papers). In the context of early 1900s British Columbia, the charges against Walkem are serious indeed; taking steps to produce a miscarriage is an offence punishable by a maximum of life in prison.

The proceedings will continue well into May, and take an even more sensational turn as Bond's brother (who brought the charges forward in the first place) attacks Walkem outside the county court. Walkem, for his part, will cast doubt on Blanche Bond's sanity, at one point alleging that Bond threatened his life with a revolver. However, after several weeks of testimony, Walkem will be found guilty by the jury on both counts. Following the trial, Bond will depart for San Bernardino, California, and Walkem's lawyers will be said to have obtained a confession stating that her entire testimony in the original trial was untrue.

"The Walkem case is one that is in very bad odor with the public," an April 11 article in the *Vancouver Daily World* will complain, "and it makes bad copy."

The charges will be dropped on appeal. Abortion will only be fully legalized in 1989.

APRIL 1, 1968

COUNCIL CHAMBERS BECOME THE SITE of a merry celebration as Joachim Foikis, Vancouver's Town Fool, receives word he has been awarded a $3,500 grant from the Canada Council for the Arts.

"When I read about it this morning, I saw red," fumes Mayor Tom Campbell in an interview with the *Vancouver Sun*. "An old-age pensioner, who's worked all his life for his country, gets $1,200 a year. Here's a fellow who refuses to work and they give him a $3,500 young-age pension. Couldn't we use it for public housing for senior citizens, retarded children, pensioners, deserving students?"

The 35-year-old Foikis, a former social worker with two degrees, has been the city's self-declared "Official Fool" for more than a year. Well known around the downtown courthouse, and notorious for attending council meetings in full fool's motley, Foikis claims as his stated mission to "spread joy and confusion," while at the same time mocking "the 4 pillars of society: money, status, respectability, and conformity." Among his most notable acts: hosting numerous impromptu street dance parties, petitioning council for a "Fool Tax" (one cent per ordinary citizen and two cents per politician), bringing a troupe of mimes and a loaf of bread to the annual general meeting of the Architectural Institute of BC, and purchasing a donkey cart which he will ride through the streets at rush hour.

"Most people on city council are real estate moles who have their heads stuck in the ground and no vision," Foikis says in response to Campbell's reaction. "Tourism isn't my aim, but I am of more value to Vancouver than $4,000 worth of tourist billboards. The people of Vancouver need the sort of thing that I am doing so that they will awaken from their sleep and arise from the dead."

The Canada Council grant draws considerable ire from residents city-wide, including lawyer Peter J. de Vooght, who threatens a writ of prohibition in an attempt to keep the Fool from his money. However, the grant will be paid, and Foikis will remain the city's official fool for the remainder of 1968.

"Our needs are slight, so I can work for a year at a good salary, then take a year off to read," Foikis will explain in a later interview with the *Sun*'s weekend magazine. "It is foolishness that man should be the servant of money. Money should be the servant of man."

Ultimately, Foikis will become so popular that he will be invited to Ontario and booked for speaking engagements, he will be featured in an article by the *New York Times* Press Service, and even make it into the 1968 *Encyclopedia Britannica Yearbook*. Following his retirement from fooldom, Foikis will spend 14 years in self-imposed poverty on Lasqueti Island before finally settling in Victoria. And, in 2007, at the age of 72—in a sad but fitting end—Foikis will fall to his death while dancing to a band in Victoria's inner harbour.

"It was something to get outside myself," he explains of his chosen profession. "I was too introverted. But now I have met so many people. And I have helped quite a few in their folly, I think. The time will soon come when I will no longer be a fool. I would like to go back to my books. Maybe I would study at university again. Maybe there would be someone to take my place. There will always be a need for a fool."

Joachim Foikis, April 3rd, 1968.
IMAGE © VANCOUVER SUN. PHOTO CREDIT: KEN OAKES.

Mayor Campbell 'Sees Red'
Over Fool and His Money

APRIL 2, 1868

The legislature, circa 1890.
IMAGE COURTESY OF THE VANCOUVER ARCHIVES (CVA 677-505, SAVANNAH PHOTOGRAPHERS)

DISAPPOINTMENT REIGNS throughout the Lower Mainland as, following a disastrous speech by MLA William Franklyn, New Westminster loses its status as British Columbia's capital.

"There is a ridiculous side to most subjects," J.S. Helmcken, Speaker of the Legislature, will later recall. "The Capital question is not an exception. Of course everyone was earnest and serious, [Franklyn] among the number, altho opposed to the Resolution, he was genial, near-sighted, and liked a drop of the creatur occasionally."

Considerable debate has swirled around the placement of the province's capital over the past two years, leaving MLAs bitterly divided, with some favouring its current site at New Westminster, and others recommending it be moved back to its original location—Victoria. And, going into the debate (the continuation of one begun at the previous session in 1867), no clear victor is evident.

"We counted the noses of our friends—and found ourselves in a pretty tight space," Helmcken will explain. "The Governor, if he laid any pressure on the official members, could decide the matter either way he chose."

However, the proceedings take a turn for the farcical as Franklyn, a former magistrate with a reputation for drink, takes the floor. In an attempt to address worries that navigating the Fraser River could prove difficult, Franklyn compares it with navigating Calcutta's Hooghly River.

"Mr. President," he begins, "when I went up the Hooghly forty years ago, the navigation was very intricate, the river full of shoals and sandbanks, a very great deal worse than the Fraser River."

Unfortunately, Franklyn's love of "the creatur" will serve to be his undoing. Each time he completes the first page of his speech, William George Cox, an MLA sympathetic to the Victoria cause, places it back on the top of the pile, and Franklyn, sufficiently intoxicated, simply picks up the sheet, and begins again with "Mr. President. When I went up the Hooghly forty years ago . . ." Franklyn's speech will continue in this manner for several more minutes, until Cox delivers the *coup de grâce*: removing the lenses from Franklyn's spectacles so he, in Helmcken's words, is "unable to see the Hooghly or anything else."

"Well we must not laugh," Helmcken will explain, "the room was full of people—and we must burst, so I proposed a recess for half an hour— contrary to rule of course. We all adjourned to the annex—and burst! . . . The half hour expired—we all return to the chamber, as grave as Councilmen ought to be."

Within the hour, Victoria will be named the capital of British Columbia, and Helmcken, Cox, and their supporters will spend the evening in a New Westminster hotel fearing for their safety.

Franklyn will lose his post as MLA shortly thereafter.

APRIL 3, 1956

ONE "BANDIT" IS KILLED, another is wounded, and an RCMP officer is hospitalized with seven gunshot wounds as a Coquitlam Royal Bank becomes the scene of a "roaring" shootout between masked robbers and police, following a dramatic, failed midday bank heist.

"The armed holdup was staged by four masked men, who shot it out with four RCMP Officers from Maillardville and Burnaby," reports the *Vancouver Province*. "Within minutes a parking lot outside the bank was spattered with blood, and strewn with currency from a shopping bag used in the raid."

The thieves, who enter the building shortly after it opens, declare "This is a holdup! Get busy," and force tellers to fill a large

Police patrol cruiser, 1914.
IMAGE COURTESY OF THE VANCOUVER ARCHIVES (A-30-69, PHOTOGRAPHER A. J. SELSET)

shopping bag with bills. However, within minutes the building is surrounded by RCMP officers, alerted by the safe's silent alarm. The first to enter the building is 29-year-old "Bud" Johnstone.

"I ran into the bank and said to the manager, 'Anything happening?'" Johnstone will recall in a bedside interview with the *Vancouver Province* later that day. "He nodded his head and I soon found out why he didn't speak, as the man who had him covered behind the counter took a shot at me."

"He leaped up and opened fire in return," the paper explains. "Two of the bandits fell to the floor, picked themselves up and all three started running from the bank."

The two bandits struck by Johnstone's volley of bullets collapse in the parking lot, as Johnstone himself smashes through the bank's front door and pursues the remaining suspects through the parking lot. Panicked, one of the robbers (already holding the Bank Manager hostage) fires, hitting Johnstone and knocking him to the ground.

Despite being shot a total of seven times, Johnstone manages to kill one fleeing bandit, wound another, and bluff a third into surrendering (despite his gun having already run out of ammunition). The fourth bandit escapes in a getaway vehicle, but, following an intense police chase, the vehicle will be run off the road and will overturn in a ditch.

All of the money will be recovered, and, despite his extensive injuries, within hours of the shootout Johnstone will be in Royal Columbian Hospital, listed in Good condition.

"Every time I got shot," Johnstone will explain, "I thought to myself, 'This must be it.'"

APRIL 4, 1917

AFTER YEARS OF OPPOSITION, numerous defeated bills, and a provincial referendum, the women of British Columbia are finally granted the right to vote following a unanimous decision in the legislature.

"The bill did not require much discussion," reports the *Vancouver Province*, "as the proposal to make effective the women suffrage plan undoubtedly met with the approval of both sides of the House, as well as the people of the country."

BC is the fifth Canadian province to grant the franchise to women, though female property holders province-wide have been able to vote in municipal elections since 1873. However, as the article is quick to point out, "Conservatives in the House had voted against it when suffrage bills had been introduced . . . [Premier Brewster] himself had voted against it because he and other Conservatives had not then believed that the time was ripe. But their views had changed, particularly because of the noble part the women played in the war."

The only dissenting opinion is presented by one Captain Hayward, who has voted against the measure four previous times, and, while grudgingly giving suffrage his approval, who notes that he "did not think the majority of the women in the province really wanted the vote in the past or at the present time."

"I do not think women care tuppence about politics," he declares, before being silenced by the Speaker of the House, "and they will likely astonish both political parties when they mark their ballots."

The story is presented on page 14 of the *Province*, after boxing and tennis news, social announcements, and an article about an irrigation bill.

Vancouver's "Pioneer Ladies" drinking tea at the Diamond Jubilee, 1946.
IMAGE COURTESY OF THE VANCOUVER ARCHIVES (CVA 371-2016)

APRIL 5, 1958

SHIPPING COMPANIES AND NAVIGATORS breathe a sigh of relief as, at 9:31 a.m., 125 miles northwest of Vancouver, the notorious Ripple Rock is destroyed by 1,400 pounds of explosives.

"A split second before there was sudden agitation on the surface of the narrows, where the notorious 'ripple' signal was plainly visible in the ebbing tide," the *Vancouver Province* will report in its April 7 edition. "Then suddenly, the sea opened up in a breath-taking eruption. Observers in the bunkers about 6,000 feet away felt a brief tremor underfoot like a short earthquake shock. A great mushrooming cloud of water, rock and gas came, spreading, pluming, churning, in ever increasing intensity."

The blast, fired by Dr. Victor Dolmage, and part of a three-year, $3 million public works project, is deemed a "complete success" by Works Minister Howard Green, and brings an end to the infamous Seymour Narrows navigation hazard that has claimed 120 ships and the lives of 114 mariners since 1875.

The blast—billed by the *Province* as "man's biggest non-atomic explosion"—fires approximately 375,000 tons of rock more than 1,000 feet in the air, creating a small tidal wave in the process. Despite the magnitude of the blast (achieved by having the 10-person engineering team tunnel under the rock and place explosives at its base), no one is injured, and very few people in nearby Campbell River even notice the explosion. This is the third attempt to remove Ripple Rock in the past 15 years; two previous operations were performed in 1943 and 1945, but neither was successful. The 1,375 tons of Nitramex 2H, specifically developed for the project by the Du Pont Corporation, were, the paper notes helpfully, "enough to lift the Empire State Building one mile into the air."

The explosion of Ripple Rock, April 1958.
IMAGE COURTESY OF THE VANCOUVER PUBLIC LIBRARY (VPL 1808)

Following the blast, the Seymour Narrows inside passage will be ultimately made safe for coastal shipping interests, which represent a $100 million annual business in BC.

"Few fish were killed by the blast," the paper assures its readers, "mostly ling cod, young rock cod, and red snappers."

APRIL 6, 1886

"WHEREAS IT IS EXPEDIENT that the inhabitants of the tract of land known as the Town of Granville and vicinity should be incorporated: Therefore, Her Majesty, by and with the advice and consent of the Legislative Assembly of the Province of British Columbia, enacts as follows: from and after the passing of this Act the inhabitants of the tract of land hereinafter described in the second section hereof, and their successors shall be, and are hereby declared to be, a body politic and corporate in fact and in law, by the name of 'The City of Vancouver.'"

With these words (and numerous others), the City of Vancouver is officially incorporated, as the Lieutenant-Governor of British Columbia signs the *Vancouver Incorporation Act* into law. At the time of incorporation, the population of the growing community sits at roughly 5,000, and the bill itself was presented by a citizen's committee in mid-January (after urging from local politicians, CPR affiliates, and land speculators), with a 125-signature petition attached. To commemorate the occasion, a ceremony is held at the home of City Constable Jonathan Miller, on the corner of Carrall and Water Streets—a building that will, less than a month later, serve as the sole polling booth for Vancouver's first civic election.

The act sets the new city's boundaries as "commencing at the low-water mark on the south shore of Burrard Inlet" and extending to what will later be Nanaimo Street to the east, 16th Avenue to the south, and Alma Street to the west. The act further states that the mayor and aldermen must "reside within the city, or within two miles thereof," be "a male of the full age of twenty-one years," and be the owner of property over $1,000 within the city limits.

Vancouver's first council, outside of a makeshift City Hall, shortly after the Great Fire of 1886.
IMAGE COURTESY OF THE VANCOUVER ARCHIVES (LGN 1045, PHOTOGRAPHER HARRY T. DEVINE)

The new city council is also granted power to pass, alter, and repeal bylaws, among them those "for the prevention of sales . . . of any goods, chattels, or other personal property whatsoever, excepting the selling of milk, drugs, or medicine on Sundays," and "for preventing vice, drunkenness, profane swearing, obscene, blasphemous, or grossly insulting language, and other immorality or indecency on any of the streets."

Within five years, Vancouver's population will top 13,000.

APRIL 7, 1933

AFTER ONLY A WEEK OF DEBATE, *An Act Respecting Sexual Steril-ization* is passed in the BC legislature, ostensibly giving the super-intendents of provincial mental institutions and schools for the delinquent the power to sterilize patients deemed "mentally unfit."

"Where it appears to the Superintendent of any institution within the scope of this Act that any inmate of that institution, if discharged therefrom without being subjected to an operation for sexual sterilization, would be likely to beget or bear children who would have a tendency toward serious mental disease or mental de-ficiency," reads the text of the act, written by Dr. J.G. McKay and Riverview superintendent A.L. Crease, "the Superintendent may submit to the Board of Eugenics a recommendation that a surgical operation be performed upon that inmate for sexual sterilization."

The act passes "without formal division," according to session-al clippings, with the support of a number of prominent medical authorities, though there is some opposition from Liberal leader T.D. Patullo and local representatives of the Catholic Church. Discussion of the sterilization issue has been ongoing throughout the late 1920s and early 1930s, both in British Columbia and as part of a worldwide eugenics movement popular in Britain, Germany, and the United States (California, in particular, is a strong pro-ponent of the practice), as a result of fears about crowding and the overburdening of mental institutions.

According to the law, consent of the inmate is required; however, final say on whether an individual is capable of giving consent is left to medical professionals. On July 5, 1933, the act will come into effect, and soon afterward, a Board of Eugenics (including McKay) will be created.

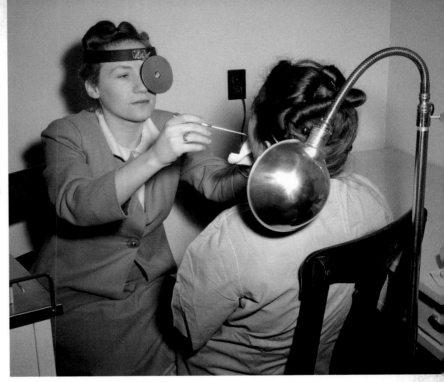

Doctor and patient, circa 1940.
IMAGE COURTESY OF THE VANCOUVER ARCHIVES (CVA 1184-1800, PHOTOGRAPHER JACK LINDSAY)

Ultimately, 64 individuals will be sterilized between 1935 and 1973. Only seven will be male, including a man with a "mentally defective" IQ of 54, one labelled "manic depressive," and another described as "promiscuous." The remaining 57 patients will be female, sterilized for reasons such as postpartum depression, epilepsy, and, most commonly (in 35 of the cases, according to a 1945 Essondale Report), for sexual promiscuity.

Among the case notes for these women will be phrases such as "sexual colouring to ideas," "sexual propensities," and "talked freely of sexual experience."

The act will be repealed in 1973.

APRIL 8, 1935

"20,000 People Cheer Woods in Death-Defying Dive Here," reports the *Vancouver News-Herald* as, in front of a formidable crowd (including Mayor Gerry McGeer, who endorsed the event), stuntman and daredevil Ray Woods leaps headfirst from the Burrard Street Bridge.

"Defying the elements, the diver took off from the windy side of the Burrard Bridge, to the choppy water 110 feet below," exclaims the paper. "And so nonchalant was he, that he took off backward, making a perfect back 'jack-knife' dive . . . The dive, in fact, was made possible only through special permission of the mayor, who over-ruled an old civic bylaw which for a time threatened to prevent the visiting diver from doing his amazing leap."

To Woods—the owner of a diving school in his hometown of St. Louis—the 110-foot drop is "relatively easy." In fact, the leap from the Burrard span is his 161st jump, in a career that has taken him all over Canada, the United States, and Mexico, and seen him drop from structures as high as 170 feet. Despite the drop and the powerful impact, Woods resurfaces almost immediately, to the cheers of the raucous crowd, a feat accomplished through the strategic use of padding, including a steel-ribbed corset and rubberized chest-plate. Although his feat is by far the most impressive, Woods isn't the only one to risk death that afternoon.

"The crowd on the bridge itself had lined the eastern rail, in expectation of seeing Mr. Woods go off that side to the smooth water below," the paper confides. "On his arrival, however, they started a mad dash across the span roadway, risking death or injury from the hundreds of automobiles speeding by."

Woods will continue to dive from municipal structures until 1937, when a miscalculation on San Francisco's Oakland Bay Bridge will leave him a quadriplegic. Despite five crushed vertebrae and a gloomy prognosis from doctors, Woods will miraculously regain mobility in his upper body. His diving career, unfortunately, will be finished.

"I dived because I loved to travel and that was the only way I knew to see the country and get paid for it," Woods will tell a Michigan newspaper in 1939. "I have no regrets. I've seen most of the United States, Canada and Mexico. I've crammed three ordinary lives of excitement and sight seeing into my 32 years. And before long I'll be walking again."

The opening of the Burrard Street Bridge, July 1, 1932.
Image courtesy of the Vancouver Archives (CVA 99-2656, photographer Stuart Thomson)

APRIL 9, 1975

"SOUND VISITATION WAS COSMIC TURKEY," complains *Province* music critic Jeani Read, reporting on the "extra-terrestrial Muzak" of the latest band to grace the stage at the Pacific Coliseum: Pink Floyd.

"There was, indeed, a time sometime when heavy, amorphous, out-tripping concerts—head music—were a significant force in rock," Read complains. "There was also a time sometime when [Pink Floyd was] an extraordinary band to listen to, live . . . But what Pink Floyd is doing now is painfully anachronistic besides being insufferably boring."

The band, playing to a crowd of nearly 17,000 and accompanied by a dazzling light show, multiple circular screens, and speakers placed strategically around the venue, began the show by treating the crowd to never-before-heard tracks from the upcoming album *Wish You Were Here*, including the opener "Shine on You Crazy Diamond," before finishing out the performance with hits from *The Dark Side of the Moon*. Read, however, remains unimpressed, going on to criticize nearly every aspect of the band's performance, including its "limited scope," "rough, borderline inept vocals," and "debilitating single-mindedness of approach."

"What was billed as some kind of sound and light show visitation turned out to be more cosmic turkey than cosmic circus," Read claims. "Pink Floyd could possibly still write some decent score for general entertainment sci-fi flicks. But, judging from their most recent material, which occupied the first half of their performance, they might even have trouble with that."

Five months later, *Wish You Were Here* will debut at number one in the United States and Britain, and, with the eventual release of *Animals* and *The Wall*, Pink Floyd will cement its place as one of the most successful and iconic rock bands of the decade.

Read herself will eventually move into lifestyle reporting, going on to author columns such as "Bachelor of the Week" and "Girl Talk."

Sound technicians setting up for a show at the Pacific Coliseum, circa 1970.
IMAGE COURTESY OF UBC RARE BOOKS AND SPECIAL COLLECTIONS, GEORGIA STRAIGHT COLLECTION

APRIL 10, 1985

CONTROVERSY ROCKS THE PNE'S AGRODOME as 20-year-old East Vancouver native Michael Olajide becomes Canada's new middleweight champion—by delivering a sucker punch to his opponent after his trainer has already thrown in the towel.

News of Olajide's win is greeted by a chorus of boos from the 4,100-person crowd after his controversial ninth-round victory over Winnipeg's Wayne Caplette, but despite the backlash, officials declare the victory perfectly legal.

"The corner is not allowed to throw in the towel," the referee explains to the seething crowd. "The referee is the only man who can stop the fight."

"Wayne Caplette is an experienced fighter," Olajide tells the *Vancouver Sun*. "He has been in the ring for a long time. He should know better than to drop his gloves when he's standing right in front of me."

The ticket, which also included the Canadian featherweight title bout, is Olajide's first time in the ring in close to a year. After having approached six other fighters, and being turned down by all of them, he has spent close to a year training and increasing his strength (to the point where two of his sparring partners quit).

"Michael Olajide Jr. showed no pity, no compassion, and, as it happens, not much class when he saved his most savage work of the evening for precisely the moment a game Wayne Caplette had clearly abandoned his hopes of taking the Canadian middleweight title," reports the *Sun*'s James Lawton. "Nobody said boxing was a place for pity and compassion, no more than it is for idle dreams."

Caplette will only enter the ring once more following the Agrodome bout, losing by KO to Virgil Hill in Williston, North Dakota. He will retire shortly thereafter. Olajide will become a fight consultant for motion pictures, as well as going on to choreograph and star in his own line of fitness videos.

A boxer working out on a punching bag, 1942.
IMAGE COURTESY OF THE VANCOUVER ARCHIVES (CVA 1184-1462, PHOTOGRAPHER JACK LINDSAY)

APRIL 11, 1903

"No More Japanese Will Come Here," reads a joyous headline on the front page of the *Vancouver Daily Province*. The article quotes a message sent from the consul-general of Japan:

"I cabled my Government two weeks ago, advising it to pursue its policy of restriction of emigration of Japanese to Canada. The reply I received was that the Government of Japan was not desirous of forcing its emigrants into British Columbia, against the wishes of the people of that province."

"It seems to me," the cable continues, "that the people of British Columbia should stop agitating themselves over the immigration of Japanese labour and begin to exercise themselves over the possibilities of trade with the Orient, of which Canadians have as yet failed to realize the importance."

An unidentified Japanese woman and boy, circa 1905.
Image Courtesy of the Vancouver Archives (CVA 287-10)

APRIL 12, 1910

Portrait in the Hollow Tree, Stanley Park, circa 1900.
IMAGE COURTESY OF THE VANCOUVER ARCHIVES (LGN 713, PHOTOGRAPHER NORMAN CAPLE)

THE LOCAL DAILIES BUZZ AS, following a recent Park Board decision to remove close to 70 trees from the city's premier tourist attraction, the "Stanley Forest Controversy" comes to a dramatic head.

"This meeting is of opinion that a great deal of unnecessary and regrettable damage has recently been caused by the wholesale slaughter of trees in Stanley forest," reads a letter drafted by the newly formed Lovers of Stanley Forest Committee. "The park commissioners are elected without requiring any previous experience or training on their part for the work of the commission, and without sufficient consideration of their suitability for the positions they are to occupy."

The 12-person committee, angered by the park commissioners' management of Stanley Park (construction of a recent fire break, a road-widening project, and the clearing of 68 trees from the property are among the chief complaints), issues a number of demands alongside its letter, among them halting all further deforestation, appointing an "expert forester" to assist with all future decisions, and changing the park's name to "Stanley Forest."

"They are barbarians who would add to the destruction today," committee member Walter Moberly asserted at the group's first meeting the day before, "and in my view they should be prosecuted to the full extent of the law. I would be glad to move a resolution to that effect."

However, unbeknown to the committee, the board's deforestation plan is part of an attempt to contain a recent outbreak of Hemlock Looper, which has led to the death and defoliation of a number of trees throughout the park. In fact, thanks to the infestation, the committee will have one of its wishes indirectly granted: shortly thereafter, Ottawa will dispatch noted entomologist James Swaine to study the situation. Unfortunately, Swaine's report will lead to an era of more active forest management in Stanley Park, recommending widespread use of toxic insecticides, as well as the removal of all of the park's hemlock trees (which Swaine considers a weaker species) and their subsequent replacement with Douglas fir and red cedar.

The Swaine Report will ultimately transform the Park Board's forestry strategy and the landscape of the park itself, changing it from a diverse and unruly patch of trees to a tamed and manicured tourist attraction, resulting in the replacement of innumerable hemlocks, the levelling of a large patch of trees near Second Beach, the excavation of Beaver Lake (not to mention the removal of its beavers), and the creation of Lost Lagoon.

Insect and fungal outbreaks will continue throughout the next decade, culminating in 1929, when the Park Board will approve the spraying of the entire park with lead arsenate. Insect spraying via airplane will be a common Park Board practice until at least 1961.

APRIL 13, 1903

AFTER ORGANIZING A SYMPATHY STRIKE of local longshoremen against the Canadian Pacific Railway, union activist Frank Rogers is shot on Abbott Street by a railway company strikebreaker.

"I did not have any trouble or row with anyone that night," Rogers will tell police after being rushed to the city hospital. "Neither did Larry O'Neill, nor the other man who was with me, that I know of. I do not know who shot me, but I think it must have been [a strikebreaker] or some of the special police. I had had no trouble with anyone for some time past. I did not see anyone else going down on to the wharf with us."

The 30-year-old Rogers, a stevedore and president of the BC Fishermen's Union, has been a consistent thorn in the side of local business owners (particularly cannery owners) since his arrival in Vancouver in the late 1890s, organizing strikes in the summers of 1900 and 1901, and working tirelessly since to advocate for workers' rights.

"Rogers was an organizer, one of the best the fishermen ever had," fisherman Mike Vidulich will recall years later in an interview with *BC Historical News*. "The canners could never buy him."

Tensions have been running high between rail workers and the CPR for months, with workers on strike since the end of February, and the railroad vowing to spend more than $1 million on special police and spies to end the labour action. Rogers, who had been keeping a relatively low profile (he was arrested numerous times throughout 1900 and 1901 in connection with picket-related activities), nonetheless organized the sympathy strike of longshoremen when he caught word that CPR employees were to walk off the job in late February. On the evening of April 13, on his way home from a Gastown restuarant, Rogers is shot in the stomach while investigating a commotion on some nearby railway tracks.

Despite being moved to the city hospital, Rogers will die the following morning from an inoperable wound. Two weeks later, Rogers' alleged killer, CPR strikebreaker James MacGregor, will be brought to trial in a Vancouver courtroom. Unfortunately, a high-paid lawyer provided by the railroad, and the inexplicable change in testimony by a key witness (also a CPR employee), will allow MacGregor to go free. He will vanish from Vancouver a short while later.

Rogers' funeral, three days later, will be attended by more than 800 mourners. The anchor-shaped wreath laid on his headstone will read "Martyr."

APRIL 14, 1964

MUSIC LOVERS REJOICE as singer, pianist, and TV personality Nat "King" Cole plays to a full house at the Queen Elizabeth Theatre.

"Trim, elegant, and super professional, Cole gives every appearance of being one of the most completely at-ease figures in show business," gushes the *Sun's* William Littler. "His easy vocal delivery, his ready smile and lively eyes, his casual, at-home manner on the stage are all attributes of the born performer."

The Alabama-born Cole, who rose to prominence as a jazz pianist, and whose record revenues are said to have single-handedly built Capitol Records, delights audiences with renditions of "Straighten Up and Fly Right," "Unforgettable," and "The Christmas Song" (the fourth and final version of which, recorded in 1961, will go on to become an enduring seasonal classic).

Cole (a 3-pack-a-day smoker, who credits cigarettes for his distinctive sound) sings, plays the clavietta, and occasionally the piano alongside a 12-person chorus, and an orchestra which features a number of Vancouver musicians, performing with a voice "that was pure Cole—warm, slightly husky, now soft and easy sounding, now strong and rhythmic."

Cole has been to Vancouver at least once before (in May of 1958), and the performance comes after what will turn out to have been his final television appearance, on The Jack Benny Program in January.

This will also turn out to be the singer's final Vancouver appearance; later in 1964, he will be diagnosed with lung cancer, and despite surgery to remove his left lung, Cole will die in February of 1965 in Santa Monica, California.

"It was a show that certainly had style," the paper concludes. "Rarely has the Queen Elizabeth Theatre played host to such a relaxed, friendly, and thoroughly professional two and one-half hours of entertainment."

APRIL 15, 1970

DRINKING ESTABLISHMENTS CITY-WIDE brace themselves, and 19-year-olds rejoice, as at the stroke of midnight BC becomes the first province in Canada to drop its age of majority from 21 to 19.

"It was the magic night when all 19- and 20-year-olds became adults with all the privileges of adulthood and they indulged their new freedom by jamming in bars and pubs," explains the *Vancouver Express*. "The nightclubs were caught only by the edges of the storm as the determined new adults caught second shows after the bars closed."

The new *Age of Majority Act*, first introduced on March 4 by Attorney General Leslie Peterson and supported by all parties, is aimed at bringing "the governing of our young people out of the Middle Ages."

"By reducing the age to 19," Peterson insisted, "a precedent has been set for Canada—which I hope might be followed in other provinces."

Before the new legislation, adulthood was classified according to the provincial *Infants Act*, a bill that designated any person under the age of 21 as an "infant." A proposal to amend the *Infants Act* was introduced on two separate occasions by Member of Parliament Garde Gardom, the second as recently as January. With the drafting of the *Age of Majority Act*, 19-year-olds and 20-year-olds are entitled not only to enter bars and nightclubs, but also to enter into marriage contracts and to vote. Naturally, the measure is not without its detractors.

"A guy can't even get a drink for all those teeny-boppers," a disgruntled patron of The Ritz bar complains to the *Express*.

A Vancouver bar, circa 1972.
IMAGE COURTESY OF THE VANCOUVER PUBLIC LIBRARY

Even some students are opposed to the reforms, with one complaining to the *Victoria Colonist* that it "takes the thrill out of becoming 21. And I don't think the kids are aware of all the extra responsibilities this brings."

An additional side effect of the new legislation is a sudden insistence by bar owners on valid picture ID.

"It was bad enough trying to determine who was 21," one exasperated club owner tells the *Express*, "but it will be murder separating the teenagers."

Other Canadian provinces will quickly follow suit, with Saskatchewan introducing a similar bill the same week, and Alberta reducing its age of majority to 18 in 1971.

APRIL 16, 1990

CONSIDERABLE MEDIA ATTENTION and public debate begin to swirl after the discovery of more than 20 squatters who have taken up residence in four empty houses on Frances Street. With city-wide vacancy rates below 1 percent, and BC being the only province in Canada without rent-control legislation (abolished in 1984), the Frances Street squats immediately become emblematic of the overall housing crisis affecting many Vancouverites.

Despite eviction threats from owner Ning Yee, and rumours of "Assault by Trespass" arrests by the VPD, the squatters quickly gain widespread community support, including an endorsement from the Grandview–Woodland Area Council and a front-page article in the *Globe and Mail*.

"Part of the reason the coverage was so positive was, I think, because we were presented as 'helpless homeless,' driven to desperate acts by the housing crisis," Keith Chu, a Frances Street squatter, will write in the summer 1990 issue of *Artest Magazine*. "We were very much 'victims,' and therefore acceptable . . . The media definitely changed everything. Since then we haven't heard from Ning Yee and we are moving happily into our fifth month."

Over the next seven months, the squatters will host community events and barbecues, and consistently avoid any attempt at eviction, ultimately becoming one of the most successful public squats in North America.

"I remember reading in the newspapers about Jack Poole and the Vancouver Land Corporation," Chu will recall, "about how they were going to build several hundred units of housing for moderate income earners, about their operating capital of $25 million, funded by union pensions and the city of Vancouver. Poole was quoted as saying that they were going to try extra hard so that some of the one bedroom apartments might be as low as $600. It turns out that this year they'll be building less than 50 units of housing. Meanwhile, on Frances Street, 25 people have provided housing for themselves, with no operating capital, no bureaucracy and no rent. Imagine if $25 million was given to people to squat the several hundred buildings and apartment units left empty for months by real estate speculators and to do their own repairs. More housing would be 'created' than Jack Poole could ever dream of . . . Instead, in other cities, developers and city councillors have responded to squatters by vandalising empty houses. Electrical wiring is ripped out, toilets are plugged with cement, windows are smashed . . . It's amazing what lengths some will go to keep others homeless."

In late November 1990, the city will deploy more than 100 officers armed with sniper rifles, riot shields, assault rifles, and dogs to evict the Frances Street squatters. Shortly thereafter, the houses will be declared a public nuisance and demolished.

Police descend on the Francis Street Squats, November 1990.
IMAGE COURTESY OF THE UBYSSEY.

APRIL 17, 1934

"WHO IS BC's BEST WHEELBARROW PUSHER?" asks a front-page headline in the *Vancouver Sun* as the paper announces the date of its sixth annual Walking Marathon.

"How good are you at pushing a wheelbarrow for eleven miles?" the article asks. "If you think you have ability at this form of pastime you can pick off a nice prize in connection with the sixth annual Vancouver Sun Walking Marathon."

The paper offers prizes ("if enough entrants are received to make the race worth while"), an entry form, multiple "classes" (with or without the aforementioned wheelbarrow), and the assurance that any devoted walker can enter, regardless of skill level.

"Every class of walker is provided for in the various classes in the Marathon," the paper explains. "This is shown by the entry this morning of F. Bell, a man of 75, who is willing to test his speed against other veterans in 'F' class for men of 65 and upwards."

The paper outlines a number of entrants already registered, including the entire Patterson family of 2234 Alberta Street.

The walking marathon will take place as planned, with more than 250 entrants, with victory in the "main event" (the 'B' category for men between the ages of 17 and 40) secured by 1933 champion Norman Walton. However, the most surprising victory of the day will go to 80-year-old Fred Fowler, who will defeat every one of the other nine challengers in the "much-discussed" wheelbarrow category.

In 1985, the *Sun* will begin to sponsor an athletic event of a different kind, with the creation of the Vancouver Sun Run.

A man in a wheelbarrow, 1892.
IMAGE COURTESY OF THE VANCOUVER ARCHIVES (STR P82, PHOTOGRAPHER BAILEY BROS.)

APRIL 18, 1976

"VIOLENCE IN HOCKEY?" begins an editorial in the *Vancouver Sun* as the newspaper takes sharp aim at allegations of brutality in the city's most beloved sport.

"If there is any trend towards violence in hockey," the editorial argues, "the leagues are perfectly capable of controlling it themselves, they've been telling us. And telling us and telling us—while the ribs get speared, the eyes jabbed, the legs gashed, the jaws broken, and the skulls fractured. In the last 3½ months, at least 21 persons—mostly players, but some coaches and spectators as well—have been hauled before courts in seven provinces and charged with assault, or something similar, as a result of incidents at hockey games. Two have been fined, one was jailed and the rest are awaiting trial. That wouldn't suggest violence, would it?"

League officials are less sympathetic toward the editorial's point of view, with NHL president Clarence Campbell quoted as saying: "It's just the product of the imagination of a lot of kooks who know nothing about it."

The editorial then goes on to detail a series of aggressive "free-for-alls" which have taken place in Quebec, North Vancouver, and Toronto over the past few days, and echoes Attorney General Garde Gardom's call for corrective action by league officials rather than government.

Violence in hockey has a history as long and storied as the sport itself; however, in the early days of the 20th century, it was dealt with in a very different fashion. Before the institution of a penalty system in 1912 by the Pacific Coast Hockey League (a precursor to the NHL), players themselves were fined by the league for infractions. In the very first Stanley Cup playoff (a three-game series between the Toronto Blue Shirts and the Victoria Aristocrats), a fight between two players actually brought one game to an end, with warnings from the police inspector on the scene that "any more pugilistic exhibitions would be treated just as if they had occurred on the street and arrests would be made."

"A few life suspensions here and there, a few $10,000 fines on individuals would clean things up in short order," the article concludes. "Public tolerance will stand only so much of this nonsense before the demands that governments step in and take control of the game become too shrill for Mr. Gardom and other politicians to ignore."

"The hockey people should be given one more chance," it concludes. "One, and no more."

APRIL 19, 1884

WEST COAST FIRST NATIONS PEOPLE are forced to take their most important spiritual and social ceremony underground when an amendment to the federal *Indian Act* is signed in Ottawa for the express purpose of banning the potlatch.

"Every Indian or other person who engages in or assists in celebrating the Indian festival known as the 'Potlatch' or the Indian dance known as the 'Tamanawas' is guilty of a misdemeanor," states the text of the act, signed by Prime Minister John A. Macdonald, "and shall be liable to imprisonment for a term not more than six nor less than two months in a jail or other place of confinement."

"The *Indian Act*, which is the Dominion Law governing all Indian affairs, makes it a criminal offence for any person or Indian to take part in one of these gatherings," Indian Affairs agent William Halliday will later write in his memoirs, "and many people who do not know any better, are governed by sentiment in the matter, and not having fully gone into the merits or demerits of the Act, feel that a wrong has been done the Indians in passing this statute."

In typical colonial fashion, the potlatch ban aims at "civilizing" the indigenous people of the Pacific Coast by westernizing their behaviour, suppressing a ritual that the Department of Indian Affairs classifies as a "wasteful and destructive custom." The potlatch—a ritual gift-giving ceremony for occasions from births to marriages, to the dedication of a new house—is viewed by westerners with suspicion and alarm, amid allegations of cannibalism and sexual promiscuity. (The marriages performed at the potlatch are not binding, Halliday will note with horror, allowing the woman to leave a union at any time, "if she felt so disposed.")

A potlatch in Alert Bay, 1926.
PHOTOGRAPH BY ALBERT PAULL (VPL 1709)

For more than a decade, the legislation will go unenforced. Even with the first prosecution in 1898, Judge Matthew Baillie Begbie will be unwilling to convict because of ambiguity surrounding the term *potlatch* itself. All this will change in 1919, when Halliday and Superintendent Duncan Campbell Scott will begin the most aggressive campaign to date against the practice. Halliday, also a Justice of the Peace, will successfully petition to have the crime transformed from an indictable offence (requiring a trial by jury) to a summary offence (requiring a conviction by judge alone). By the end of 1921, dozens of people will be faced with a grim decision: give up their traditional customs forever, or be sentenced to hard labour in Oakalla Prison.

"They seem to utterly lack that fine feeling which we commonly call sentiment," Halliday will conclude of the First Nations people of BC, "and their ideas are very gross."

The ban will not be repealed until 1951.

APRIL 20, 1995

4/20 Celebrations at the Vancouver Art Gallery, April 20, 2013.
IMAGE CREDIT: MIRANDA NELSON

STARTING AT NOON, more than 200 people begin to gather in Victory Square for the city's first 4/20 celebration, an event that, according to BC Marijuana Party Leader and "Prince of Pot" Marc Emery, is the first of its kind anywhere in the world.

"My store manager Danna Rozek and an employee named Cindy Lassu came up to me in early April 1995, and said, 'Marc, can we have a 4/20 celebration on April 20th next door in Victory Park?'" Emery will recall in an April 2010 interview with *Cannabis Culture* magazine (which Emery publishes). "I responded, 'Like, on 4:20 in the afternoon on April 20?' and they said, 'No, like all day on April 20.'"

Though Emery initially dismissed the idea as decadent, the employees of his HempBC Store (located across the street from the Victory Square Cenotaph on Hastings Street) decide to go ahead and organize the event, which features speeches and performances by local bands, and which will continue free from police interference until 7 in the evening.

"On April 20, 1995, it was a beautiful sunny day, and 6 cables ran from various electrical outlets at Hemp BC 75 feet to Victory Square to supply power for the PA system, the microphones, amplifiers," Emery will continue in a 2012 editorial for the *Huffington Post*. "The party began around noon but because it was a very new idea, never done on April 20 any time before, there were about only 150 people by 2 p.m., peaking at 250 people at 4:20 p.m. Nonetheless, open pot smoking went on for about 6 hours without any police interference, much to my surprise, only 25 feet from a major intersection of Hastings and Cambie. Everyone who came seemed to have a wonderful time."

The term "4/20" has been in semi-regular usage in North America since the early 1970s, when it was coined by a group of teenagers in San Rafael, California, who would regularly meet in the woods outside their high school and smoke pot near a bust of Louis Pasteur. These same students (known as the "Waldos") later passed on the phrase (shortened from "4/20 Louis") to the Grateful Dead, with whom they regularly associated after the band fled Haight-Ashbury to set up shop in Marin County. The phrase continued to spread among Deadheads countrywide throughout the 1970s and 1980s. In the early 1990s, it began to appear regularly in issues of the subculture's staple publication, *High Times*.

In cities around the world, 4/20 celebrations will begin to crop up, and in 1996, the Vancouver event will draw more than 500 people. By 1997, the event will attract more than 1,000 supporters, necessitating a move to a new location outside the Vancouver Art Gallery. The celebrations will continue to interfere with city-wide productivity into the new millennium; the 2012 event (reported to cost more than $20,000) will attract close to 20,000 people.

In 2005, Emery will be extradited to the US and sentenced to five years in federal prison for selling marijuana seeds through the mail.

APRIL 21, 1939

Respectable citizens breathe a sigh of relief as, following years of discussion and a string of highly publicized murders, city officials discuss the possibility of bulldozing one of Vancouver's most misunderstood neighbourhoods: Hogan's Alley.

"To the average citizen, Hogan's Alley stands for three things—squalor, immorality and crime," states the *Vancouver Province*. "But is Hogan's Alley the blemish on the face of this city it is claimed to be?"

Located between Union and Prior, the alley has long been considered a hub of vice and crime, home to bootleggers, prostitutes, and a number of colourful characters, including saloon owner "Queen Kathleen" Newman, and "Mayor" Carl Malchi. It was named, according to a May 1964 *Province* article, for a "mysterious, open-handed Irishman who never made the city directory." It has also become emblematic of Strathcona's larger black community. Spurred on by a number of recent murder investigations and by the city's rabid slum clearance mandate, officials—including members of the building department and the chief sanitation inspector—have been sent to determine whether wholesale demolition is warranted.

"Hogan's Alley has the name which conjures up images of bootleggers, canned-heaters, prostitutes and all types of criminals," the paper continues. "Police records bear this out. But detectives are inclined to laugh at the thought of the city's centre of crime being one small lane . . . Other lanes in the district are crowded with just such dwellings. In them dwells humanity at a low ebb, because of poverty, the evils of drink and dope, and other factors which create such slums."

Hogan's Alley, 1958.
Image courtesy of the Vancouver Archives (Bu P508.53, photographer A.L. Yates)

"The whole district is one in which police have a great deal of trouble," explains Chief Constable W.W. Foster. "There are many people in the alley who are just poor—not criminals. Others, of course, we are called in to deal with."

After the inspection, the demolition of several Hogan's Alley huts will be mandated, as well as the repair of several others, in keeping with the slum clearance mindset popular with city officials of the 1950s.

Following a slow exodus of many of its most prominent citizens, Hogan's Alley will eventually be bulldozed in 1964 to make way for the Georgia Viaduct.

APRIL 22, 1954

THE *VANCOUVER NEWS-HERALD* announces that, after a three-year battle for funding by "prominent Vancouver citizens," $100,000 in grants from the provincial government will furnish Vancouver with a brand new aquarium.

"All types of BC fish will be on display," notes the article, "as well as fish from all points down the Pacific, and tropical varieties."

Carl Lietze, president and co-founder of the Vancouver Public Aquarium Association, tells reporters "Vancouver's aquarium will have a setup second to none on this coast," adding that "the San Francisco aquarium, regarded as one of the finest in the US, have [*sic*] no tanks as large as some of those planned for Vancouver."

"We have the whole-hearted backing of the whole fish industry in the province," Lietze says, "as well as UBC officials."

The original city's original "aquarium" was opened at English Bay Pier in 1938; however, it was little more than a single, small room containing several fish tanks (not to mention its star attraction, Oscar the Octopus).

Two years later (with financial assistance from timber baron H.R. MacMillan, as well as $100,000 from each of the federal and civic governments), Canada's first "official" public aquarium will open its doors. In 1964, it will become the first facility in the world to house an orca and will remain one of the five largest aquariums in North America.

Early Vancouver "Aquarium" exhibits, Sept 27, 1922.
PHOTOGRAPH BY DOMINION PHOTO CO (VPL 21348)

APRIL 23, 1975

CONFLICT ENSUES between politicians and police in the suburb of Port Coquitlam, reports the *Vancouver Sun*, over a city council decision to impose a curfew on all children under the age of 15.

"Each night at 11 o'clock the fire department will sound a siren to warn juveniles to get off the city streets," explains the paper. "Council instructed its staff to finish drafting a bylaw that would carry a $5 maximum fine for parents or guardians who permit their children or wards to habitually contravene the bylaw."

Mayor Jack Campbell is in wholehearted support of the bylaw, explaining that it will "draw to the attention of the proper authorities parents who are delinquent in their responsibility to their children."

"He said the bylaw would show youngsters who now are left to roam at will that someone cares about them and wants them home," reports the paper. "[Alderman] Phil Ranger, in supporting the bylaw, said it was a safety measure for young teen-agers who have not as yet become hardcore delinquents and would teach them they must learn to respect the law."

Local law enforcement, however, is less enthusiastic about the move, with the RCMP's Marvin Young claiming that the bylaw would do little besides "result in the RCMP becoming a taxi service to return young people to their homes." Alderman George Laking is a particularly vocal opponent of the measure, noting the need for congenial relations between police and the city's juveniles, and the inherent difficulty in applying the term "habitual" to simple curfew violations.

"[Laking] said that since the RCMP say they meet with little success in having charges laid against juveniles," the *Sun* concludes, "the curfew would be just more unenforceable legislation."

APRIL 24, 1955

"STEEL RAILS CARRY FINAL LOAD," reads a headline in the *Vancouver Sun* as the paper reports on the retirement of the last of the city's streetcars after more than 60 years of operation.

"Sunday was a day of pleasant nostalgia, optimistic future gazing and talk of the last, the first, and the best for thousands of Vancouver citizens who joined with BC Electric in celebrating 'rails to rubber' day," the paper writes. "'The last streetcar ride is the best' was the unanimous opinion of old and young alike as they grabbed the nearest of a steady stream of streetcars without any waiting, got on without paying and rode without a grouch or a frown from fellow passengers."

The streetcars, which are being replaced by "trolley coaches" in a city-wide conversion, have operated since 1890, and to honour the history of the system, several vehicles are made available specifically for "the oldsters—only those who were pioneer residents of Vancouver before 1900."

"Today, work crews are already busy ripping up sections of the track and tearing down the single electric wires that were the streetcars' source of power," the article continues. "Sunday night the last of the streetcars were pulled across the Kitsilano trestle over False Creek to their resting place at the Kitsilano barns."

The conversion of electric rail-based public transport to bus lines has been an ongoing theme throughout North America since the mid-1930s, with automakers and tire manufacturers such as General Motors involved in (and later convicted for their involvement in) elaborate operations to purchase and dismantle streetcar systems across the United States. While GM's involvement was by no means the only factor in these conversions, and no evidence exists that they had any direct influence over Vancouver's "rails to rubber" movement, it nonetheless fuelled a broader push toward car dependence and celebration of personal auto ownership. Speeches canonizing the past and celebrating the future were given throughout Sunday's "day of celebration," including ones by BC Electric head Dal Grauer, Mayor Fred Hume, and Donald Hyde of the American Transit Association.

"And then," the paper explains, "the people and the streetcars, the never-to-be-seen-again streetcars, went home. They went with a fond farewell. Now, on with the completion of 109 miles of repaving to make way for the new trolley coaches."

Electric streetcar on Davie Street, 1944.
IMAGE COURTESY OF THE VANCOUVER ARCHIVES
(CVA 586-1872, DON COLTMAN AND STEFFANS COLMER, PHOTOGRAPHERS)

APRIL 25, 1899

Police occupying Deadman's Island, circa 1913.
IMAGE COURTESY OF THE VANCOUVER ARCHIVES (ST PK P330, PHOTOGRAPHER BROADBRIDGE BULLEN)

"LUDGATE'S MEN ARRESTED; Vancouver's Mayor Makes Good on His Threat," reads a headline in Toronto's *Daily Mail and Empire*, reporting on a high-profile clash between city council and big business, a clash that resulted in the first-ever reading of Vancouver's riot act—the battle over ownership of Deadman's Island.

"Theodore Ludgate, the lessee of Deadman's Island from the Federal Government, this morning landed thirty men on the island, and at 6:30 was met by Mayor Garden, City Solicitor Hamersley, and Capt. Tatlon, chairman of the Park Commissioners, and thirty special police officers," the paper reports. "Mr. Ludgate commenced the cutting of a tree, followed in turn by his men, all of whom were at once arrested."

Ludgate, a lumber baron from the US who leased Deadman's Island (a former Squamish Nation burial ground and a disposal site for bodies infected during an 1888 smallpox epidemic) from the federal government with the intent of building a sawmill, has been embroiled in a battle with the city for months. Despite the federal government's support of Ludgate's mill project, Mayor James Garden has thus far refused to recognize the project, threatening to dispatch a contingent of 25 police to the island if Ludgate begins to build. Ludgate, however, emboldened by federal support, was unfazed, stating in the April 24 issue of the *Mail and Empire* that, rather than cave to the pressure, he would send 50 of his own men to begin work immediately.

"If the policemen arrest them, it will be a sorry day for Vancouver," Ludgate explained in an April 24 interview, "as I am instructed by Attorney-General Martin of British Columbia that the island is mine by lease, and if the policemen try to stop me they are trespassers, not I, and a huge mass meeting will be at once called of citizens who will request Mayor Garden and the Council to resign as misrepresenting the city's interest."

"I was terribly frightened," Ludgate's widow will explain in an interview with archivist J.S. Matthews. "A great big policeman, Mr. Murphy, came to the house, and tried to persuade Theodore not to cut the trees on Deadman's Island, but Theodore replied, 'I've got five hundred axes all ready.' I feared they might kill him."

Following the arrest of Ludgate's men (and Garden's reading of the riot act), the case will be postponed in police court, pending a discussion in city council. Police guards will be posted on the island for years, and the case will ultimately be taken to the Privy Council. Ludgate's lease will eventually be ruled valid; however, by the time the legal mess is sorted out, it will be 1911.

Ludgate will clear a number of trees from the island, but the mill will never be constructed.

APRIL 26, 2000

LOCAL PAPERS RECOIL at the revelation in the *Anglican Journal* of a soon-to-be released report that reveals First Nations children in BC residential schools in the late 1940s and early 1950s were used for "health experiments."

The experiments, conducted over a period of five years and overseen by the Department of Indian Affairs chief dental officer H.K. Brown, involved tinkering with diet and deliberately denying basic dental care to First Nations students (without their knowledge or consent) in an effort to study the effects of fluoride and vitamin C treatment.

"No specialized, over-all type of dental service should be provided, such as the use of sodium fluoride, dental prophylaxis or even urea compounds," reads a 1949 memorandum by Dr. Brown, concerning an experiment on students at a Port Alberni residential school. "In this study dental caries [tooth decay] and gingivitis are both important factors in assessing nutritional status. The caries index could be upset by such specialized dental measures as those referred to above; and dental prophylaxis could alter the gingival picture sufficiently to make it of questionable value as a possible index of Vitamin C deficiency."

For close to a century, BC's residential schools were responsible for forcibly removing tens of thousands of First Nations children from their parents. In the course of their "education" and assimilation, they were exposed to disease and malnutrition, and often subjected to physical and sexual abuse. In fact, according to a damning 1907 report prepared by the Department of Indian Affairs chief medical officer Dr. Peter Bryce, an average mortality rate of 30 percent was documented in BC residential schools, with basic hygiene and ventilation being completely ignored, deliberately exposing otherwise healthy pupils to tuberculosis. Bryce, a physician behind the passage of the first *Public Health Act* in the country (in Ontario), was appalled at the conditions he observed throughout Canada's residential schools; however, after he submitted his findings, Dr. Bryce was promptly removed from his post, and the recommendations of his report were largely ignored by the department superintendent, Duncan Campbell Scott. Complaints regarding the state of residential schools in Western Canada didn't begin with Bryce; they can be found as early as 1897 in a memorandum composed by the clerk of the Schools Branch of Indian Affairs, Martin Benson.

"It is scarcely any wonder that our Indian pupils who have an hereditary tendency to phthisis [tuberculosis], should develop alarming symptoms of this disease after a short residence in some of our schools," the memo reads, "brought on by exposure to draughts in school rooms and sleeping in overcrowded, over-heated and unventilated dormitories."

In spite of government's attempts to quiet him, Bryce would go on to publish *The Story of a National Crime*, an 18-page pamphlet detailing the deplorable state of native residential schools and the determined inaction of federal employees (and Scott in particular). The pamphlet was largely ignored, and it won't be until 2009 that the Canadian government will officially apologize for its involvement in the residential school system, rolling out a $1.9 billion compensation plan for survivors.

Classroom at Nanaimo Indian School, 1942.
IMAGE COURTESY OF THE VANCOUVER ARCHIVES (CVA 586-835, PHOTOGRAPHER WARNER WILLIAMS)

APRIL 27, 1969

JOACHIM FOIKIS, Vancouver's self-appointed Town Fool, spends the last $500 of his Canada Council Grant money on a street party for Downtown Eastside residents.

"A fool's music broke the drab routine of Vancouver's skidroad Sunday," reports the *Vancouver Sun*. "About 200 derelicts danced, sang, wore daffodils, and even laughed as they took part in a 'happening' at Pioneer Park. Their faces brightened as Town Fool Joachim Foikis handed out bongo drums, flutes, tambourines, daffodils, and even food."

"[The homeless] have not had so much fun in the last 20 years," says a grinning police constable, stationed nearby.

Foikis, who received the grant in 1968 (fittingly enough, on April Fool's Day) for promoting "self-awareness of the entire community," is a common sight in the downtown area, strolling

the streets in his "fool's motley," showing up to dance at nuclear demonstrations, and giving strangers a ride down city streets in his donkey-drawn carriage. In fact, his willingness to poke fun at city officials and raise awareness of important issues is so successful, he will eventually be profiled by the *New York Times*.

While more conservative taxpayers observing the "skidroad party" scoff at Foikis's use of public funds, UBC fine arts teacher Herbert Gilbert claims that the Fool has earned his grant money.

"Foikis has sparked a vitality here where everything else has failed," he says. "I have traveled around the world but nowhere have I found this kind of an atmosphere. It's like something you would expect in Tangier or Istanbul, but it's right here in Vancouver. Foikis has done a good job. He has planted the seeds of a relaxed humanism. He has peeled off the masks of fear. He's done something to get people mixing together as human beings."

Joachim Foikis, circa 1968.

APRIL 28, 1947

"TCA THREE TO VANCOUVER TOWER. By the range at 7,000 on instruments. Westbound at 11:13."

With these words, Trans-Canada Airways Flight 3 vanishes into thin air in the skies near Vancouver Airport, less than 20 minutes before it is due to land.

"The message to the control tower indicated the plane was inbound, would be landing within a matter of minutes," reports the *Vancouver Sun*. "Clearance—permission to land—would have been asked when the plane was over Point Grey, three to four miles from the field. The call for clearance never came."

The plane, a Lockheed Lodestar, is inbound from Lethbridge and reported to have been carrying seven Vancouverites among its 12 passengers and three crew. Though the first search planes will take off less than two hours later, and the hunt will involve helicopters, boats, and divers, and cover close to 12,000 miles, no sign of the aircraft will be found. Dozens of reports will be investigated, placing the crash site in Belcarra, Nanaimo, or the Gulf Islands, or at the bottom of the Strait of Georgia. The search, supervised by the Royal Canadian Air Force, will be abandoned after two weeks.

"What happened to the plane and its passengers after Capt. W.G. Pike made his routine check to the range tower 2.5 miles east of the airport on Lulu Island may never be known," the article continues. "Pike spoke normally and clearly. The ceiling was 5,000, and he was flying on instruments. It was raining heavily, but landing conditions were not considered difficult."

It won't be until 1994, on North Vancouver's Mount Elsay, that the wreckage will at last be discovered.

The nose of an airplane, circa 1930.
IMAGE COURTESY OF THE VANCOUVER ARCHIVES (TRANS P82)

APRIL 29, 1959

In the inside pages of the *Vancouver Province*, journalist Jean Howarth publishes an article on the execution of Leo Anthony Mantha, the last prisoner to be hanged at Burnaby's Oakalla Prison.

"He came into the bleak little concrete room looking frozen and expressionless and he didn't say anything," Howarth writes. "The murmur of the priest's prayers came with him. After half a minute the priest stopped praying, because there wasn't anything to pray over any more."

The 31-year-old Mantha, executed at 12:07 a.m. the previous day, was sentenced to death for the murder of his lover, fellow seaman Aaron Jenkins, whom he killed after hearing the news that Jenkins intended to leave him and marry his girlfriend. Mantha's final hours were spent quietly: a T-bone steak for dinner, a cigarette, time spent praying with the prison chaplain, and a mild sedative (less than usual for a condemned man, the guards noted). The execution took place in an elevator shaft modified for precisely the purpose, under the watch of a federal hangman.

"There was silence for a minute," Howarth writes. "And then we heard the shuffle of feet and Leo Mantha came in behind him. The priest's voice murmuring prayers. The hangman put his strap around his legs and pulled a black cloth over his head and the noose. And stepped back and reached down to a little lever on the floor. Only I put my hands over my face then because I was sick."

Oakalla, opened in 1912, has been the site of every prison execution in British Columbia since 1919. Although capital punishment is legal countrywide, a recent change in public opinion (not to mention the vocal opposition to the practice voiced by

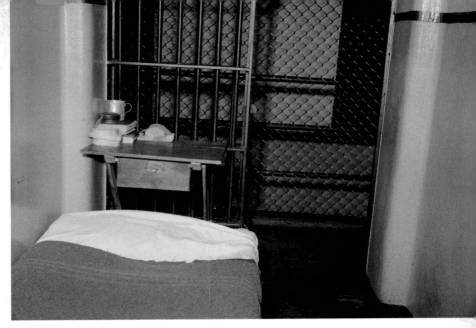

Interior of a cell at Oakalla Prison, circa 1940.
Image courtesy of the Vancouver Archives (CVA 1184-2266, photographer Jack Lindsay)

Oakalla's own warden, Hugh Christie) has resulted in a growing number of Death Row prisoners instead having their sentences commuted (including a prisoner scheduled to be hanged the same day as Mantha).

"I went to see Leo Mantha hanged because I do not believe in capital punishment," Howarth concludes. "It was my idea to go. A man had been assigned to the job and the managing editor did not want to let a woman go. None of my superiors did. It made them uncomfortable."

Though other prisoners will be sentenced to Death Row in British Columbia in the 15 years to follow, all of them will have their sentences commuted before they reach the gallows. Capital punishment will be removed from the *Criminal Code* in 1976.

Oakalla will be decommissioned in 1991, and in 1993, it will be bulldozed to make way for a condominium project.

APRIL 30, 1937

IN A LETTER TO THE *VANCOUVER SUN*, Dora Kitto (Honorary Secretary of the Canadian Anti-Vivisection Society) speaks out against the evils of the newest craze to hit the Lower Mainland: vitamins.

"The word 'vitamin' (which means nothing at all) has become a research slogan," Kitto declares. "Even modern fiction has adopted it. A correspondent in the '*Times*' asked 'Are There Vitamins?' To this we reply that vitamins are hypothetical and illusory substances."

Kitto goes on to denounce the "menace" of vitamins and vitamin research, citing a number of newspaper and magazine editorials on the subject, including one in the January issue of the *Medical Times* which declares them to be "an obsession and a danger." In particular, Kitto urges authorities to put an immediate end to vitamin testing on animals, a practice she equates to "animal torture," despite the United Kingdom's Medical Research Council being fully in favour of the idea. Kitto's arguments are part of a debate on the effectiveness of vitamins that goes back years and has filled the pages of newspapers such as the *London Times* and the *Daily Telegraph*.

"Our foodstuffs should not be tampered with and made artificial," Kitto concludes, going on to quote a physician known as Dr. J. Oliver. "So why should an army of research workers be wasting their time and our money on endless experiments on animals to prove or disprove something which cannot be of the slightest importance to the diet of the ordinary individual in civilized countries?"

Men taking part in a healthy lifestyle at Brockton Point, circa 1897.
IMAGE COURTESY OF THE VANCOUVER ARCHIVES
(SGN 981, WILLIAM M. STARK, PHOTOGRAPHER)

MAY 1, 1972

AFTER A YEAR OF SERIOUS MONEY WOES, and following a vote of 282 to 100, the congregation of Christ Church Cathedral votes to demolish the historic structure and replace it with an office complex known as Cathedral Place.

"Despite last-minute pleas for reprieve, Christ Church Cathedral Monday night was served notice of demolition," reports the *Vancouver Province*. "Nearly 400 members of its congregation voted 72.1 per cent in favor of replacing the 83-year-old building with a $7.6 million complex of office buildings and a new, underground cathedral."

The decision to destroy the historic church, first built in the early 1890s, comes as a result of a significant cash crunch being felt by Anglican dioceses countrywide. Each diocese, Christ Church included, will be receiving $400,000 less in annual operating funds, a development that has left the church scrambling for other revenue options. The office complex—designed by famed architect Arthur Erickson—would include a partially underground church, a chapel, offices, and meeting rooms, and bring the church itself a minimum of $75,000 in annual operating funds (with a potential maximum of $112,000 once the tower is full). Spearheading the initiative thus far has been Reverend Herbert O'Driscoll, the dean of the facility, who has also recently aroused the ire of the church's older parishioners by sponsoring monthly rock masses. The controversial proposal has met with serious resistance province-wide, drawing the ire of opponents such as prominent MLAs, UBC planning professor Brahm Weisman, and *Vancouver Sun* journalist Allan Fotheringham.

Christ Church Cathedral, at the corner of Georgia and Burrard, 1894.
IMAGE COURTESY OF THE VANCOUVER ARCHIVES (CH P73)

"My generation will inherit a city that has no soul," a 16-year-old boy will protest at a public meeting. "If you destroy this and replace it with a monument to materialism, you'll be left with an empty meeting place."

Despite the scheme being approved by the archdiocese in New Westminster, the issue will remain a contentious one for a further three years, before, in the face of public pressure, city council will deny Cathedral Place a development permit. Christ Church Cathedral will remain in serious financial trouble until it manages to broker a sponsorship deal with a multinational development company, which agrees to sponsor the cathedral, to the tune of approximately $300,000 a year for 105 years, in exchange for relaxed building-height restrictions in its development nearby.

The cathedral will be designated a Class A Heritage Site in 1976.

MAY 2, 1986

"THE PARTY'S ON!" exclaims a banner on the front page of the *Vancouver Sun* as, under a light drizzle at 8:30 a.m., Expo 86 opens its gates to the world.

Within two hours, 5,000 visitors will be on site, including Prime Minister Brian Mulroney, Premier Bill Bennett, and Prince Charles and Princess Diana (whose activities the *Sun* details in two separate columns). The fair includes pavilions from 54 countries and nine corporate sponsors. The day's entertainments include a Musqueam welcome dance, the Harbour Symphony (100 boats blowing their whistles and horns in unison), and the comic stylings of mascots Goose and Beaver, "representing Canada's best-known creatures."

"I feel like a proud father," beams Premier Bill Bennett in an interview with the paper. "People have lined up . . . even in this unusual weather. You bet I am excited. You could feel it on the site all last week as everyone was getting ready for today and I know it will last all summer."

One person who doesn't share Bennett's enthusiasm is Vancouver mayor Mike Harcourt. Harcourt—suddenly dropped just two days previous from the welcoming party for Charles and Diana at their official arrival ceremony—calls the development "an insult to the mayor's office." The mayor has also been dropped from four other functions set to be attended by the royal couple, even though all indications from the province were that he was slated to attend.

"I think there are more civilized ways of doing things," Harcourt says.

More than 22 million people will ultimately attend the exposition, making it one of the largest cultural events in

Expo, 1986.
IMAGE COURTESY OF THE VANCOUVER ARCHIVES (2010-006.392)
IMAGE COPYRIGHT: CITY OF VANCOUVER

BC's history and leading its organizers to declare the fair an unparalleled success.

"Expo 86 was truly everything that the people of British Columbia dreamed it would be," the fair's final report will gush. "As Canadians, we wanted to show the world that we could honour a great heritage—Montreal's Expo 67—and live up to our reputation as an international host."

Of the $802 million in expenditures, roughly $491 million will be recouped.

MAY 3, 1886

499 ABLE-BODIED MEN (women have not yet been granted the vote) make their way to the city's only polling station, as mayoral candidates Richard Alexander and Malcolm MacLean square off in Vancouver's first civic election.

"The first election was a hot election, the hottest I have known in Vancouver," pioneer V.W. Haywood will recall in an interview with archivist J.S. Matthews. "We wanted to put MacLean in, and we did it. I had a vote because I rented a piece of ground on what is now Cordova Street from Arthur Sullivan, built a cabin on it, and voted on that cabin as a tenant. There was a lot of people who voted who did not have a vote. Lots of people coming in here, stopping in hotels; they had no qualification, but, as I said, we wanted to put in MacLean, and we did."

The proceedings are rife with fraud, intimidation, and other underhanded tactics, as both sides take advantage of the utter disorganization of the proceedings. MacLean, a local real estate agent, is the clear underdog in the race, having only a few dollars in his pocket. However, MacLean also has the good fortune of having been hand-picked as a candidate and bankrolled by disgruntled loggers frustrated by their treatment at the hands of Alexander, manager of the largest employer in town, the Hastings Mill.

"I asked him if he would run for mayor," city pioneer J.T. Abray will recall in a conversation with J.S. Matthews. "MacLean said, 'Why, I have no dollars for an election.' I replied, 'We have a few dollars; if you'll make up your mind to come out.'"

Voting will remain close throughout the day, with Alexander bringing over a boatful of supporters from Victoria (accompanied by a brass band playing "Hail to the Chief"), and MacLean's supporters quickly capitalizing on the fact that there is no voters list.

"Everybody who had a lease had a vote," Abray will recall. "I had a restaurant on Columbia Street, where the old City Hotel was. Upstairs I had thirteen boarders—remember, thirteen roomers upstairs. Then I had a shack on Hastings Street, next to the present Woods Hotel—right between it and the present City Hall; it was only one room, but I made it into four leases; so with the four leases in the shack and thirteen roomers at the restaurant I had seventeen leases, and a lease entitled you to a vote. It did not matter who you were; you could not let a day like that pass without voting."

By the end of the day, 499 citizens have cast their ballots, and MacLean, the underdog, stands victorious by only 17 votes. Alexander's supporters scream their outrage, and MacLean's camp jubilantly parades him around town in a rented vehicle, before both parties retire to the balcony of the Sunnyside Hotel to make their respective speeches.

"MacLean spoke first," pioneer George Schetky will recall, "and made some nice remarks, thanked them, and spoke the usual post-election pleasantries. He was well received, and stood back. Then Alexander appeared, and said bluffly and bluntly, 'Well, I am defeated; it was a case of might against right.' Then you should have heard the boos."

Sunnyside Hotel, June 1888.
IMAGE COURTESY OF THE VANCOUVER ARCHIVES (BU P371, PHOTOGRAPHER R.H. GARDINER)

SUNNY SIDE HOTEL.

WATER ST.

The Great Eastern Photographic and Advertising Company.

MAY 4, 1964

THE LANDSCAPE OF STRATHCONA is set to be forever altered as, after years of decline and the exodus of many of its notable citizens, the city decides to bulldoze one of Vancouver's most colourful neighbourhoods: Hogan's Alley.

"Shed a tear for Hogan's Alley," reports the *Vancouver Province*, "because its thieves, cut-throats and characters have gone where the good thieves go, and even old buildings are about to make way for progress."

Hogan's Alley, considered a breeding ground for vice and crime up until the mid-1950s, was also at one time among the city's best-known black neighbourhoods. Gaining a nefarious reputation thanks to a number of highly publicized murders in the first half of the 20th century, the alley has always had its own unique flavour (the addresses are all followed by a ½), and was called home by a number of bizarre characters, among them gin-joint owner "Queen Kathleen" Newman, "Mayor" Carl Malchi, and even the mysterious Hogan himself. Though his first name has been lost to history, the alley's alleged patriarch is remembered by Queen Kathleen as "a real swinging sort," a gregarious Irishman known for his social prowess and roaring parties.

The demolition of Hogan's Alley is in preparation for a city freeway plan under Mayor (and former property developer) Tom Campbell, a plan that includes the construction of the new Georgia and Dunsmuir Viaducts, and the bulldozing of large portions of Strathcona and Chinatown. Although the wholesale destruction of the Hogan's Alley has been called for by community groups for decades, the area has, in recent years, retreated to the fringes of public awareness.

Portraits of Hogan's Alley resident Fielding William Sprotts, May 28, 1935.
IMAGE COURTESY OF THE VANCOUVER ARCHIVES (PORT N3.2)

"For 40 years Hogan's Alley was the despair of successive city councils and clean-up groups, and then—about 10 years ago—the old spirit died in a sudden wave of respectability," the *Province* continues. "Today it is unmarked and unmourned, and the rows of cabins are utilized by respectable, silent Chinese. Even the name Hogan's Alley disappeared from sign posts and the postal guide a year ago, although the postman still trudges the ancient gravel lane. Even this peaceful scene will soon be gone, for the whole area where Hogan was a happy host is scheduled to disappear under Phase Three of the city's redevelopment program."

Following the construction of the viaducts, and the demolition of Hogan's Alley, the city's freeway project will languish. By the early 1970s, in the face of uncertain finances and strong local opposition, it will be abandoned altogether.

MAY 5, 1967

Amid a storm of anti-hippie sentiment, the first issue of the *Georgia Straight* appears on Vancouver's streets, with a cover price of 10 cents.

"It was fuelled by large amounts of idealism," Pierre Coupey, one of the *Straight*'s founding editors, will explain. "The idea was to give voice to an anger against establishment values, and their assumption of power. People were crying for a voice. It was fundamentally, in the beginning, opposed to private ownership, and was designed primarily as a collective to fight for social justice. Vancouver had, at that time, a very repressive Mayor, Tom Campbell, and there was a very repressive ethos within the police force. It was the beginnings of drug culture. We were finding a sense of ourselves as writers and activists, and we had a desire to work for social justice. There was a sense among us that the World Order needed to change, and we felt that we were in a position to effect that change. It was this convergence of energies, where one refuses to knuckle under, and behave oneself."

The *Straight* is one of dozens of underground, activist publications that have sprung up all over North America, making up the Underground Press Syndicate, whose other member publications include such papers as the *East Village Other*, the *Los Angeles Free Press*, and the *Inquisition*. The paper is tied directly to the city's growing hippie community, and several of its creators and early contributors—including Rick Kitaeff, Dan McLeod, and "Zip" Almasy—are already well-known counterculture figures, known to both the public and the police.

"At one time I had an escort of 2 or 3 police cars following me on a regular basis," Coupey will recall. "We were always getting

The Georgia Straight, Vol 1, Issue 1, May 5, 1967.
Image Courtesy of Pierre Coupey

tickets and getting pulled over for minor infractions. Rick Kitaeff fought most of that in court; he got more tickets than all of us."

The paper will create such a controversy that not a single printer in town will dare to touch the second issue.

However, by the end of 1967, its circulation will be well over 60,000.

MAY 6, 1959

EMPLOYEES ARE OVERWHELMED, several children are lost, and a group of pranksters push the emergency stop on the escalators as 10,000 customers flock to 41st and Cambie to view the grand opening of what the *Vancouver Sun* hails as "Canada's Most Beautiful Shopping Centre": Oakridge.

"Flags flew crisp in the breeze, commissionaires' medals glinted proudly in the sunshine, and everyone, it seemed, felt in a bit of a fiesta mood," the article gushes. "Within an hour of the opening, the 2,500-car parking lot was jammed."

"Woodward's is symbolic of Vancouver," declares Mayor Tom Alsbury in his speech to the assembled crowd. "As the city grows, so grows Woodward's!"

The $10 million, 32-acre shopping centre (which the previous day was featured on 16 pages and in 46 separate articles in the *Sun*) is said to be the largest in Western Canada, boasting 39 specialty shops, a bank, a drugstore, a truck tunnel for deliveries, and a restaurant known as the Oakridge Room. To the tune of bagpipes, Mayor Alsbury (sharing the platform with retail giant Charles Woodward, who owns the development and whose new location takes up three entire storeys) opens the doors to the facility, first turning a large gold key in an imaginary lock.

"Eagerly clutching their money, the spectators surged forward to the swirl of bagpipes," the article continues. "Cashiers were soon playing a merry tune with their cash registers. Harassed Department Managers answered questions, gave directions, and, in the middle of it all, tried to get acquainted with new staff members."

In the years to follow, Oakridge will become surprisingly successful, owing in large part to its location near the geographic

Oakridge Shopping Centre, Sept 1970.
IMAGE COURTESY OF THE VANCOUVER ARCHIVES (CVA 800-1989, PHOTOGRAPHER AL INGRAM)

centre of Vancouver, and a national trend toward the building and frequenting of shopping centres. Oakridge will welcome its 10-millionth shopper in 1963 and, shortly thereafter, apply for a rezoning permit to expand the centre (a plan quashed after city council—in a precedent-setting move that will quickly become commonplace—demands community amenity contributions in exchange).

"The huge centre, situated at 41st and Cambie," the *Sun* concludes, "is already hailed as Canada's most lovely centre. Every customer comfort and convenience went into the planning and construction."

MAY 7, 1907

SHORTLY AFTER NOON, a number of Vancouverites are—in the words of the *Province*—"suddenly stricken with kinetoscopitis" as renowned filmmaker William Harbeck records a six-minute black-and-white film that will become famous as the earliest surviving footage of the city.

"The attacks became epidemic shortly after noon," the paper explains, "but the results so far have not proved serious. Kinetoscopitis is not nearly as serious in its effects as spinal meningitis."

Harbeck, a flamboyant and successful Seattle filmmaker who has made his name recording vistas throughout the US, Canada, and Mexico, is working under contract to the CPR's "Department of Colonization," providing the company with short films intended to "put Western Canada on the motion picture screen in a scenic, industrial and comic form."

Harbeck shoots 2,000 feet of film from the deck of a moving streetcar, hand-cranking the camera, the paper notes, at a rate of 16 frames per second, travelling through the streets of Vancouver, beginning at Robson and Granville. As the paper explains, with many Vancouverites having never seen a film crew in action, the results are often amusing.

"Well-known businessmen would be walking along the street evidently engrossed in deeply considering some real estate deal," the *Province* explains, "but as soon as they caught sight of the big camera they would straighten up, throw out their chest and try to look as if they owned the whole street. Even out in the residential sections fond mothers brought out their babies and posed by the gates as the picture-taking car went past."

Granville and Robson, circa 1907.
IMAGE COURTESY OF THE VANCOUVER ARCHIVES (CVA 677-586, PHILLIP TIMMS, PHOTOGRAPHER)

Harbeck will go on to produce 13 such films for the CPR, including a similar streetcar picture of Victoria, and *The Ship's Husband*, a comic feature about a marital mix-up on board a CPR ferry. In fact, the railroad will be so impressed with his work, that they will renew his contract and eventually send him to Europe, where he will screen a number of his films and study with French filmmaker Léon Gaumont.

By 1912, with his international popularity at its zenith, Harbeck will take a contract which will prove to be his last, recording the maiden voyage of White Star Line's newest and most modern vessel: the *Titanic*.

MAY 8, 1970

WINDOWS ARE SMASHED, property is damaged, and arrests are made as a "Sip-In," staged in The Bay's cafeteria by members of the Youth International Party, degenerates into a riot.

"The Vancouver Youth International Party demands an immediate end to all discrimination against hip people in the Hudson's Bay cafeteria," states a press release made by the group. "In support of this demand, Yippies will stage a peaceful sip-in (sit-in) in the Bay cafeteria this Friday, May 8, from 7 to 9 p.m. We will remain sipping our coffees in the cafeteria until the Bay management promises—in writing—to end all harassment against hip people."

The Sip-In, which begins peacefully enough, draws close to 200 people (including several plainclothes police officers). But, despite the Yippies' call for a peaceful protest, the crowd quickly becomes so boisterous that employees close the cafeteria.

"The demonstration was loud," a *Georgia Straight* correspondent using the pseudonym "Tony Tugwell" will explain. "People chanted, banged spoons on the tables and snake-danced around the room."

Within an hour, word circulates that a large contingent of police have blocked all the exits, and panic begins to spread among the demonstrators. Moments later, amid fears of police brutality, the Yippies leave the building; however, once on the street, the protest suddenly erupts into violence. The crowd quickly doubles in size, and protesters—many angered by the May 4 Kent State shootings—proceed down Georgia Street, smash windows in the American Consulate, and burn an American flag in the street.

Yippies invade Blaine, May 9, 1970.
IMAGE COURTESY OF UBC SPECIAL COLLECTIONS GEORGIA STRAIGHT COLLECTION

"A dance in the intersection of Granville and Georgia liberated that zone," an anonymous Yippie will write in the pages of the *Straight*. "The pigs again set up around us and again we floated through their lines. Marching arm in arm up Granville shouting and laughing a head-strong undercover pig blew his cover and tried to bust a brother on the sidewalk. This being quickly discovered— us being psychically in tune with each other—he was immediately grabbed and overcome."

Protesters will continue to Granville Street, smashing the windows of a CIBC bank, pulling down trolley lines, and finally marching on police headquarters to demand the release of five people arrested in connection with the demonstration. Three people are hurriedly released on bail, and the crowd is then broken up by police.

The following day, between 400 and 500 Yippies will "invade" the US border town of Blaine, Washington, and cause more than $50,000 in damage.

MAY 9, 1967

AFTER THREE YEARS OF WORK and several attempts to get a bill through the House of Commons, the Bank of British Columbia is officially launched. The bank, originally conceived of by Premier W.A.C. Bennett as a response to Central Canada's domination of the banking industry, has already raised close to $2 million in funds, mostly from prominent local investors.

"The Bank of British Columbia will be a great national institution. With head office in Vancouver, we hope it will have a strong orientation toward BC and toward the Pacific trading rim, which will in fact make us an international bank," says chairman Einar Gunderson, at a press conference held at the Hotel Vancouver. "As quickly as we can hire and train management and personnel and set up physical locations and administrative controls, we are going to open branches in the principal areas of BC on an expanding scale."

As originally proposed by the Social Credit Party, the bank would have been able to operate with the provincial government as a primary shareholder. However, the incorporation bill was soundly defeated in the Senate amid concerns that it would become a "political bank." After a clause was inserted to prohibit the government from participating in ownership or operation of the bank, a new bill was passed in the House of Commons to incorporate the institution.

"It is fair at this point to note that the Premier and members of the cabinet had on numerous occasions stressed that the government's only interest in obtaining shares was to strengthen and support the bank," Gunderson states. "While the government or crown agencies cannot now participate in ownership or operation

A Bank of British Columbia branch on Pender Street, May 1974.
IMAGE COURTESY OF THE VANCOUVER ARCHIVES (CVA 778-308)

of the bank, your board of provisional directors is assured that the interest and backing of Premier Bennett and the government is as strong as ever."

The Bank of British Columbia will officially open its doors on July 18, 1968, alongside a heavy marketing push; newspaper ads will boast of female tellers in miniskirts. ("But don't let them fool you into thinking they're without brains," one advertisement will claim. "They're smart in the head, too.")

The bank will reach the height of its power in 1984, with close to 1,400 employees, $2.7 billion in assets, and branches in Alberta, Saskatchewan, and Manitoba. However, in 1986, after recurring financial difficulties, it will be acquired by the Hong Kong Bank of Canada, and less than 10 years later, it will be dissolved altogether.

MAY 10, 1886

One week after the fledgling city's first civic election—one that saw underdog real estate agent Malcolm MacLean defeat Richard Alexander by a margin of only 17 votes—Vancouver city council meets for the first time.

"There were insufficient chairs," Vancouver pioneer William H. Gallagher will later recall in an interview with the *Vancouver Historical Journal*. "Charlie Johnson found some in the prisoners' cells and passed them out into the court room; there was some agitation, some shuffling about; Mayor MacLean was standing at the head of the table. Then he sat down, and was the only man sitting down when he called the meeting to order. His Worship was very business-like and prompt."

The meeting takes place in the sitting room of the city courthouse on Water Street, a building that also serves as the jail, the polling station, and the home of Vancouver's first constable, Jonathan Miller. The room—with jail cells along one wall and lit by a single coal lamp—is packed to the gills, with more than 20 aldermen and other observers crowded around one another, eager to witness the historic event. However, as Gallagher will recall, the proceedings quickly stall when it is realized that neither the mayor nor any of the aldermen have any experience in politics.

"Charlie Johnson, who up to that time had been master of ceremonies all day, whispered to me, 'What do we do next?'" Gallagher will recount. "I was a young man, it is true, but I had once been through a similar experience in Wolseley, Manitoba, and had a general idea of the procedure. I replied, 'If you'll wait a moment, I'll show you,' and I went out into the street and around to Tilley's Stationery Store, bought a pen, a bottle of ink, a pad of paper, and, returning, wrote down on the head of the first sheet, 'City of Vancouver.' Then I said to Charlie Johnson, 'Better elect a city clerk.' Then I wrote something brief about 'Meeting of City Council, sworn in by Chas. Gardner Johnson,' and pushed the pad in front of Tom McGuigan."

"The second appointment," Gallagher will explain, "was G. F. Baldwin as City Treasurer, but they had not, as yet, twenty-five cents of civic funds for him to take care of."

A photograph of John Innes's The Builders, depicting the first meeting of city council, circa 1886. Photograph circa 1943.
Image courtesy of the Vancouver Archives (City N22.6, photographer of painting, W.J. Moore)

MAY 11, 1951

Vancouver mayor "Friendly" Fred Hume runs into considerable opposition from both city council and local contractors as he suggests scrapping plans to construct the Cambie and Granville Street Bridges, and filling False Creek with concrete.

"I'm amazed that the Mayor would come up with such a suggestion in view of previous engineering reports that the cost of filling in False Creek would be prohibitive," says Alderman Alex Fisher in an interview with the *Vancouver Sun*. "The city had a hard enough time getting the crown land necessary for the footings of the proposed Granville Street Bridge, and if the contracts for the bridge have been signed and sealed, that's the end of the matter."

Hume's initial idea (which has been in the newspapers for several days) calls for filling in portions at the site of Granville and Cambie Streets, and building low-level spans in those areas, noting that "eventually, the entire False Creek area could be filled in for secondary industry." Hume, who opposed the construction of both bridges in his election campaign, continues to press for engineering reports and feasibility studies, despite contracts having already been signed and construction beginning within the month.

Land reclamation projects are not uncommon in a city with land value as high as Vancouver's. Indeed, Granville Island, a mile and a half of land in the Main Street area (where Pacific Central Station will later be built), and the land under the Georgia Viaduct are all reclaimed land, dredged up from the bottom of the inlet amid similar debate during the early part of the century.

The Granville Street Bridge under construction, looking north down Granville Street, May 13, 1953.
Image courtesy of the Vancouver Archives (LGN 1048)

"Filling in of False Creek is the natural answer to the problem of traffic and industrial congestion in that area," explains Alderman R.K. Gervin in an interview with the *Sun*. "Industry would move either to Burrard Inlet or the Fraser River. I predict this will eventually happen, but it won't be overnight."

The plan will never receive any serious attention in council.

MAY 12, 1886

IN THE COURTHOUSE ON WATER STREET, the second meeting of Vancouver's first city council takes place. Its main order of business: drafting a petition to the Governor General requesting control of the Dominion Military Reserve, a request that will result in the creation of Stanley Park.

"Whereas it is advisable that permission should be given to the Mayor and Council of said City of Vancouver to have control of said Reserve," reads the text of the petition, "in order that it may be used by the inhabitants of the City of Vancouver as a Park. Your petitioners therefore pray that said Reserve should be handed over to the said Corporation to be used by them subject to such restrictions as to Your Excellency may seem right, to be and to be held by them as a Public Park."

Urban greenspaces have recently become a fashionable concept across North America (as part of a move away from the heavy industrialization in the British Isles), but, in reality, the driving forces behind the petition to lease the 1,000-acre peninsula as a park are land values and the Canadian Pacific Railway. In early January 1885, then CPR vice-president W.C. Van Horne wrote the federal government to request transfer of much of the Stanley Park lands for the railway to sell. Unfortunately, the Dominion of Canada at the time still considered the area necessary for national defence purposes, and his request was refused. The CPR has been heavily involved in the sale of real estate (acquired at no cost in the form of land grants) in Vancouver in recent years. Rebuffed in its attempts to secure the land, and fearful that the release of such large portions of property would ultimately drive land values down, the company began using its influence to ensure that the property would remain off of the market.

Entrance to Stanley Park, circa 1890.
IMAGE COURTESY OF THE VANCOUVER ARCHIVES (LGN 1048, PHOTOGRAPHER HARRY T. DEVINE)

The motion to draft the Stanley Park petition is made by Alderman Lachlan Alexander Hamilton, who is by no coincidence also CPR Land Commissioner. It is supported by Mayor MacLean, who also happens to be the brother-in-law of Member of Parliament Arthur Wellington Ross, a realtor and CPR instrument who made an identical request of council six weeks earlier and was rejected. After a year of behind-the-scenes manoeuvring and petitioning of government, Stanley Park will be granted to the city in June 1887.

"The Minister reports that he sees no objection to this proposal," an Order-in-Council dated June 8, 1887, will read, "provided the Corporation keep the park in proper order, and the Dominion Government retain the right to resume the property when required at any time."

Stanley Park will have its official opening in September 1888. No mention will be made of the dozens of families who made their home in the park for generations, all of whom were unceremoniously evicted.

MAY 13, 1907

A PETITION IS PRESENTED TO CITY COUNCIL requesting that the residents of District Lot 301, otherwise known as "No Man's Land," be allowed to become a part of the City of Vancouver.

"This district is a sort of buffer between Vancouver and South Vancouver," claims the *Vancouver Daily World*, referring to the land that will one day be the area between Main Street and Clark Drive. "It is 35 chains by 72 chains and contains 114 blocks, and runs from Clark drive to Westminster avenue. Mr. William Ash, one of the oldest residents in that section, is very enthusiastic about having the section annexed to the city."

Ash isn't the only resident of the 142-hectare area eager to be part of the city. A poll conducted by the *Province* indicates that 90 percent of residents are in favour of the idea, with property owners even willing to assume their share of current civic debt. At this point in history, the City of Vancouver is comparatively small, bordered by the Municipality of Point Grey to the west and the City of South Vancouver to the southeast, with each municipality having its own police force and government. Lot 301, originally purchased in 1870 by real estate agent Henry Valentine Edmonds (who subdivided the lots himself and named all the streets after friends and family), is still relatively wild, with no sewers, no sidewalks, and no connection to the municipal water supply. Residents live among countless wild animals, including cougars and bears. Crossing over is common between No Man's Land and Vancouver proper, with the potential for residents of each district to work in the other, and even among Vancouverites, the boundaries of the areas are not always clear.

Ken and Theresa Quinley with their pet bear cub, 1910.
IMAGE COURTESY OF THE VANCOUVER ARCHIVES (CVA 7-29, PHOTOGRAPHER JAMES L. QUINEY)

"A good many of the residents in lot 301 work in the city and might as well be citizens," the paper continues, descending into editorial. "There are many improved streets in the district now and many improvements are being made . . . Ash met people walking through 301 on Sunday and in conversation learned that they did not know that they were outside the city limits."

However, despite the hopes of No Man's Land petitioners, council will vote against annexing the district after hearing from a delegation of Lot 301's residents who are opposed to the move. Further, it will be alleged that petitioners boosted their numbers by collecting signatures from people not even allowed to vote in the district.

"Mr. G.W. Thomas held that this proposal had, in a sense, been sprung on the people of 301," the *World* will report several days later. "As soon as an inkling of it was heard it was found that there was going to be a strong opposition. The majority, he was assured, did not wish to be affiliated with the city at present."

District Lot 301 will be incorporated into the City of Vancouver four years later.

MAY 14, 1906

FOLLOWING A BOTCHED HEIST, notorious bandit Bill Miner (who holds the distinction of being Canada's first train robber) is captured by Mounted Police in his camp outside Kamloops.

"The three bandits who held up the CPR westbound express near here last Tuesday night, and who have given the provincial police so hard a week's work, were run to the ground in a secluded thicket near Douglas Lake late yesterday afternoon," reports the *Vancouver Province*. "The entire gang was captured, and their leader nurses a wounded leg as a result of a short but sharp skirmish with Provincial Constable Fernie and a small detachment of Northwest Mounted Police."

The heist itself, which took place on April 29, was an utter failure, netting the bandits a total of $15.50 (and some catarrh pills). And, although Miner—known as "The Gentleman Bandit" because of his impeccable manners while committing robberies—has become infamous over the course of his long career throughout the US and Canada, his capture is a relatively unimpressive affair.

"The camp was quietly surrounded, and we commenced to close in on them," explains North West Mounted Police Constable William Fernie in an interview with the *Province*. "A fusillade of shots from the brush showed that they had spotted us and intended to put up a fight. This intention was altered after some score of shots had been exchanged and one of the men, supposed to be the leader, had gone down with a bullet in his thigh. They surrendered without further resistance and we took them into custody."

Miner and gang members Louis Colquhoun and William "Shorty" Dun (who chastises officers after his capture by jeering, "It's a damned pity you didn't put the bullet through my head") are

Bill Miner in custody, circa 1906.
IMAGE COURTESY OF THE VANCOUVER ARCHIVES (PORT P572)

immediately taken into custody and transported to Kamloops. Despite Miner's notoriety, it takes a day for police to even identify him. Having gone to ground after his last robbery, he has lived quietly in the interior under the name "George Edwards." (The *Province* initially writes that the gang's leader is a man who has "been around Aspen Grove for some months, and has some mining interests there. Little is known of him.") However, Miner will be identified early on May 15 and sentenced to life imprisonment in New Westminster's British Columbia Penitentiary.

He will stage a daring escape just over a year later and will never be recaptured in Canada.

MAY 15, 1976

"OPENING CLOSES BRIDGE," writes the *Vancouver Sun* as, with little fanfare, the Arthur Laing Bridge is officially opened—even though it's been in use since the previous August.

"The official opening of the $23 million Arthur Laing Bridge will disrupt traffic between Vancouver and the airport on Saturday morning," the paper reports, bitterly, as traffic is rerouted to the nearby Oak Street Bridge.

The bridge itself has been at the centre of several controversies since it was first discussed in the late 1960s. Originally planned as a toll structure, it met with heavy opposition from locals who forced the federal government to pay for the span out of general revenues. In addition, because of disagreements at the federal, municipal, and provincial levels, the bridge offers no increased access to the city for residents of Richmond and Sea Island, with two proposed ramps abandoned in favour of a circuitous route designed to discourage commuter use.

A bridge has existed in the Marpole area since 1889. The original Marpole Bridge—a road-level span constructed out of timber and steel that was in place for only three years—was later replaced by a notoriously inconvenient swing bridge, which stood between 1901 and the late 1950s. (Records show that it was opened 7,015 times in 1954 alone.) The current structure (originally known as the Hudson Street Bridge) was named in honour of Senator and former Liberal Party Leader Arthur Laing, a long-time resident of Sea Island and a tireless advocate of British Columbia.

The battle over commuter use of the Arthur Laing will remain ferocious for close to 10 years, with Richmond and Sea Island residents supporting the construction of local access ways, and the City of Vancouver and GVRD bitterly opposing it.

"If you make more facilities for automobile commuters you get a lot more auto commuters," Mayor Art Phillips will say in a 1976 interview with the *Vancouver Province*, adding that opening the bridge for commuter use would create "the type of city development that we don't want to see happen."

The bridge will be opened to bus and truck traffic in 1977. After years of pressure from Tory MP Tom Siddon, on-ramps to facilitate Richmond traffic will be constructed in 1985.

The original Marpole Bridge, predecessor to the Arthur Laing, 1900.
IMAGE COURTESY OF THE VANCOUVER ARCHIVES (SGN 1119)

MAY 16, 1908

"SPECIAL ATTRACTION AT THE PANTAGES" reads a small advertisement in the *Vancouver Daily News-Advertiser*. "Manager George Calvert, of the Pantages Theatre, takes great pleasure in announcing that there will be an extra act on the bill this afternoon and this evening, namely 'Jeff,' the Boxing Kangaroo. This animal is claimed to be an adept in the boxing line, in fact almost as good if not better than an ordinary boxer and he has proved a great attraction wherever he has appeared. This is an act that will greatly please the ladies and children and there should be a large turnout of them at all the performances to-day."

Other notable advertisements run in the same week include "A Neat and Attractive Home in Grandview" for $3,600, "Teleconi, The Great Vibratory Treatment" (claiming to cure paralysis, rheumatism, and other ailments), and a product known simply as "Coke."

"Just the thing at this season of the year," the ad reads. "Coke meets the ease exactly. A little kindling and a shovel or two of coke will take the chill off and make the house comfortable. Try a ton or half a ton, and judge for yourself."

Mayor L.D. Taylor shakes Babe Ruth's hand on the stage at the Pantages, Nov. 29 1926.
IMAGE COURTESY OF THE VANCOUVER ARCHIVES (CVA 1477-106, PHOTOGRAPHER DOMINION PHOTO)

MAY 17, 2010

A mock trial being performed at Vancouver Heights Presbyterian Church, Jan. 1922.
IMAGE COURTESY OF THE VANCOUVER ARCHIVES (CVA 99 – 3204, PHOTOGRAPHER STUART THOMSON)

SIX YEARS AFTER A POLICE RAID on the BC legislature, the fraud and breach-of-trust trial of Dave Basi and Bob Virk seems poised to begin in BC Supreme Court. Unfortunately, given what the *Vancouver Sun* calls "last-minute snags" (which can't be reported because of a publication ban), the proceedings are postponed by one more day.

After years of similar delays, Basi and Virk (ministerial aides to Finance Minister Gary Collins and Transportation Minister Judith Reid) stand accused of leaking confidential government documents related to the privatization of BC Rail to lobbyists in exchange for money and favours. The case is alleged to stretch much further into the Liberal government than simply Basi or Virk, and the witness list provided by the Crown includes many of the key players in the first Gordon Campbell administration. However, by October, after the testimony of only two witnesses, both Basi and Virk will suddenly plead guilty, receive two-year house arrest sentences, and have their $6 million in legal fees passed on to BC taxpayers. Much of the evidence in the proceedings (pointing to far deeper involvement in corruption, bribery, nepotism, and media manipulation by the provincial Liberal Party) will never see the light of day.

"David Basi and Bob Virk are guilty alright—guilty of being unwitting pawns in a much bigger chess game where all the other players came out winners," reporter and trial observer Bill Tieleman will later write in an article for BC online magazine *The Tyee*.

Tieleman will add that "Basi and Virk do not deserve to spend a single day under house arrest, let alone the two years less a day they were sentenced to last week under a guilty plea bargain

agreement," going on to liken them to "the ill-fated Rosencrantz and Guildenstern—a pair of minor actors working for the corrupt King Claudius who are sent off unsuspectingly to their deaths by the scheming Danish prince Hamlet—Basi and Virk were simply hung out to dry after police raided the BC legislature."

After the abrupt end to the trial, and with mounting evidence of direct intervention in the judicial process by government, deliberate mishandling of the case by the RCMP, the involvement of Bruce Clark (brother of Christy Clark), and the appointment of a Special Prosecutor who had ties to the Liberal government, Tieleman and others (including Dave Basi himself) will continue to call for a public inquiry. These calls will go unheeded, and none of the other corporate or political players involved in the process will be charged or penalized.

"I want my kids to know that their dad had integrity, that their dad does sleep with a clear conscience at night," Basi will say to the *Vancouver Sun* at the conclusion of the trial. "I know some people who don't, I'll tell you that much, and they're very relieved today."

MAY 18, 1960

PARENTS AROUND THE VANCOUVER AREA prepare to lock up their children as the *Vancouver Sun* reports on a police raid at Spanish Banks during a "high school liquor-and-sex party."

"It was a real drunken sex orgy—and they seemed to be really enjoying it," an unnamed officer is quoted as saying. "I don't know what to think of our younger generation any more."

"Royal Canadian Mounted Police said they found girl's under-clothing and torn dresses scattered about the beach when they raided the party attended by about 200 students," the paper reports, with horror. "They said the students were from Sir Winston Churchill, Lord Byng, and Magee schools."

However, officers on the scene find no evidence of weapons, no liquor, no one complaining of any injuries, and very few high school students. After investigation by the RCMP, the party is proven to be part of a charity clothing drive. Events turned briefly violent after the party was crashed by "greasers" with chains, pipes, beer bottles, and guns.

"There was no sex," student representative Bob McConnell will explain. "It was too cold and wet and there were too many people around."

"What was described in a front-page story in the *Vancouver Sun* Wednesday as a shot-punctuated high school liquor-and-sex beach party," the *Province* will declare cheerily the following day, "just was not so."

BC Tel employees at a beach bonfire, circa 1940.
IMAGE COURTESY OF THE VANCOUVER ARCHIVES
(CVA 1184-2805, PHOTOGRAPHER JACK LINDSAY)

MAY 19, 1967

SHORTLY BEFORE 11 A.M., teller Sharon Biagoni is forced to hand over nearly $3,000 in cash as the Canadian Imperial Bank of Commerce becomes the latest victim of the city's most notorious holdup man: Rubberface.

"Rubberface, Vancouver's most persistent bank bandit, struck again today," the *Vancouver Sun* reports. "He got away with $2,925 from the Canadian Imperial Bank of Commerce, Pender and Burrard, in at least his seventh holdup in more than three years."

Rubberface, described by Biagoni as "middle-aged, about five-foot-five," with one side of his face "distorted with vertical lines in his cheek, like a man who had suffered a stroke," is believed by police to be a daring makeup artist who has, in various disguises over the course of his three-year crime spree, made off with roughly $14,000 in stolen cash. Throughout this time, the criminal's MO remains remarkably consistent: his face is always marred by some obvious disfigurement (for a December 1966 robbery, he treated his skin to give it an unusually ruddy appearance), he usually strikes in the late morning, and although he claims to carry a gun, one is never produced.

"Police said he told the girl he had a gun under his coat, but she did not see a gun," a May 20 article in the *Sun* will recount. "Bank Manager D.A. Mars said Miss Biagoni gave Rubberface the money, and another teller standing beside her sounded the alarm. He said the raider walked out of the bank, and no attempt was made to chase him."

No arrests will be made. As of 2008, Vancouver will be known officially as the bank robbery capital of North America.

Bank vault, circa 1934.
IMAGE COURTESY OF THE VANCOUVER ARCHIVES (CVA 586-1006, PHOTOGRAPHER WILLIAMS WARNER)

MAY 20, 1929

Discussion continues in a city subcommittee, following a proposal by Mayor W.H. Malkin, advocating the elimination of horse-drawn traffic from the Granville Street Bridge.

"Mayor W.H. Malkin suggested banning slow-moving traffic from the bridge altogether," the *Vancouver Star* reports, "stating that it is absolutely essential that drastic measures be taken to speed up traffic on that thoroughfare."

Based on traffic codes used in various US cities, the bill was translated into "legal phraseology" only one day earlier by subcommittee members J.B. Williams and Oscar Orr, solicitor and assistant prosecutor, respectively. The proposal, which has yet to be voted on by council, also calls for the installation of automated traffic lights (linked by underground wiring), despite the exorbitant extra cost of $8,500.

Automobile ownership is still a relatively new phenomenon in British Columbia. Between 1920 and 1929, the number of cars in the Lower Mainland has steadily risen from 6,500 to 36,500. Because of this growth, traffic safety has become a strong local concern in recent months, prompting the passage of new bylaws restricting jaywalking and mandating regular brake checks, the creation of a local Safe-Driving Club, and multiple articles in local dailies dedicated to traffic safety tips (including, helpfully, "Don't drive at all with defective brakes").

"If the measure is adopted by the council, as passed Friday, traffic, both vehicular and pedestrian, will be subject to the provisions of the bylaw," the *Star* continues. "Pedestrians will be required to observe the traffic regulations in regard to crossings of streets and observance of signals at all intersections where signals are in operation. While pedestrians are not prohibited from crossing streets where they desire, nevertheless the requirements of the new bylaw are that they must give way to vehicular traffic at signal-regulated crossings or trespass at their own risk."

The proposed bylaw also happens to coincide with Traffic Safety Week, a cause taken up in earnest by former BC Attorney General A.M. Manson.

"The motor vehicle is a new contraption," Manson warns in an article in the *Vancouver Province* published the same day, "a vehicle of pleasure and business, and a weapon of death."

Horse-drawn traffic on Abbott Street, circa 1891.
Image Courtesy of the Vancouver Archives (Trans P24)

MAY 21, 1941

WITH THE BOMBING OF LONDON still fresh in the minds of Vancouverites, the dailies tell locals of an impending "trial blackout" at 10 p.m. the following evening.

"At 9:50 . . . warning signals, by police and fire department sirens and factory whistles, will inform the populace of Greater Vancouver that the heralded blackout will take place in 10 minutes," reports the *Vancouver News-Herald*. "Within that time in every building in the greater city and beyond lights should be switched off, outside lights and Neon illumination darkened, so that by 10 p.m. not a light of any description will be visible from the sky or any point of the city."

Over the space of two days, the *Sun, Province*, and *News-Herald* meticulously detail the rules for the trial blackout, which is scheduled to last exactly 15 minutes: all lights in homes and businesses must remain off, all automobiles and vehicles (including bicycles) must be parked, and all skylights must be covered. Phones are not to be used unless absolutely necessary, and residents are required to remain in their homes. The only lights where these rules won't apply are navigation lights in the harbour and running lights on seafaring vessels. At the same time, a "nerve centre" will be put into operation at City Hall, where a telephone switchboard will dispatch services to the sites of "the supposed bombing of a house here, the dropping of a fire bomb there, the killing and wounding of people in several parts of the city as homes are demolished about their ears."

The blackout will be reported by military observers to have been "95 to 98 per cent successful," with one of the few visible lights coming, unusually, from the City Hall "nerve centre," where a door will have been left ajar.

"Five minutes before 10 o'clock the city was a blaze of color with bright lights outlining the main streets in clear pattern," the *Vancouver Province* will write following the blackout. "Two minutes after 10 the city was a black mass spread beneath our plane. It was impossible to pick out any of the landmarks which had been so clearly visible before."

"The blackout is something unique in Vancouver," explains Major S.C. McLennan, in charge of the experiment, in an interview with the paper, "and something which I sincerely hope will never become a necessity."

MAY 22, 1970

THERE IS NO WORD OF CELEBRATION in either of the city's major papers as, after years of waiting, the Vancouver Canucks officially join the NHL.

"Having been skivvied to the tune of $6 million for an NHL franchise that was considered grossly over-priced at $2 million just two years ago, the owners are now being dunned for a $1.2 million payment by the Western Hockey League," complains the *Province*'s Eric Whitehead. "The Canucks are countering with an offer of $500,000 plus placement of their current WHL franchise elsewhere—Calgary preferred—and a continuation of regular payments from this franchise to the WHL office."

The Canucks' eminent departure from the WHL has caused all manner of legal woes, with the league demanding $1.2 million in compensation for the team's departure. (Ordinarily they collect 5 percent of a team's annual gross.)

"Vancouver has now been awarded a final franchise, not conditional on anything," general manager Bud Poile tells reporters, defiantly, at a press conference. "We had to guarantee to indemnify the NHL against any damages arising from our leaving the WHL and to convince them we've made a legitimate effort to settle our differences."

Vancouver's fight for an NHL franchise has been a lengthy one, with the city having already been passed over in 1965 in favour of six American cities. However, following the efforts of a number of locals—among them Nat Bailey and former mayor Fred Hume—and

the payment of the aforementioned $6 million, the Canucks were granted the 14th NHL franchise in early 1970. The team's final WHL season was a triumphant one, going 8–0–3 in the playoffs and winning the coveted Lester Patrick Cup.

The fledgling team's first NHL game will be played October 9, bringing dignitaries from around the province, including Premier W.A.C. Bennett, Mayor Tom Campbell, and Chief Dan George.

It will be a 3 to 1 loss against the LA Kings.

The Vancouver Canucks, 1946.
IMAGE COURTESY OF THE VANCOUVER ARCHIVES
(CVA 586-4280, PHOTOGRAPHER DON COLTMAN, STEFFENS COLMER)

MAY 23, 1914

AFTER SEVEN WEEKS AT SEA, the 376 passengers aboard the steamship *Komagata Maru* (all of them British subjects of South Asian descent) arrive in Burrard Inlet. They are summarily denied entry into Canada on the basis of their race, touching off what will become one of the most notorious incidents of prejudice in Vancouver's history.

Anti-Asian sentiment already runs deep in Canada, with a number of federal and provincial laws designed specifically to discourage immigration from India, including requirements that each new arrival must be in possession of $200 (when the average immigrant makes only $2.25 a month) and must have arrived via a "continuous journey"). These laws are supported by prominent federal and provincial politicians, and even by Vancouver's mayor, Truman Baxter.

"I have no ill-feeling against people coming from Asia personally, but I reaffirm that the national life of Canada will not permit any large degree of immigration from Asia," federal politician Henry Herbert Stevens tells the crowd at an anti-Asian rally organized by Mayor Baxter. "I intend to stand up absolutely on all occasions on this one great principle—of a white country and a white British Columbia."

His speech, the papers report, is followed by "thunderous applause."

The passengers, who refuse to return to India, will remain in Burrard Inlet for close to two months, resisting multiple attempts to drive them from the area, and actively clashing with police and civilians.

"Howling masses of Hindus showered policemen with lumps of coal and bricks," the *Vancouver Sun* will report of one such incident. "It was like standing underneath a coal chute."

Attempts to starve the passengers out will also be foiled, this time by members of the city's Asian community, who will secretly smuggle food aboard. It will only be after the appearance of a Royal Canadian Navy gunship that the boat is finally driven from Burrard Inlet and forced to return to India.

In 2008, the BC legislature will officially apologize for its part in the incident, followed three months later by an apology from Prime Minister Stephen Harper himself. In 2011, a monument to the incident will be donated to the Vancouver Park Board. It will be installed on July 23, 2012—98 years later—in Harbour Green Park.

Passengers on board the Komagata Maru, July 1914.
IMAGE COURTESY OF THE VANCOUVER ARCHIVES (CVA 7-123, PHOTOGRAPHER JAMES L. QUINEY)

MAY 24, 1908

A BIZARRE PIECE OF HISTORY is made in the streets of Vancouver as Deputy Minister of Labour William Lyon Mackenzie King arrives from Ottawa, on a brief visit which will accidentally give birth to Canada's first anti-drug legislation.

King, in town to investigate damage claims made by local businesses during the infamous race riots of the previous September, has noticed a number of unusual items on the list of damages declared by merchants, among them claims for loss of revenue by several Chinatown opium manufacturers.

"I desire respectfully to bring to the attention of Your Excellency in Council a matter of serious significance and importance which was disclosed during the course of the inquiry under the present commission," King will write upon his return to the capital. "In the investigation of the different losses, a claim was made for $800 by each of two opium manufacturers on account of loss of business for six days, their places of manufacture having been closed for that length of time in consequence of the riots. I was somewhat surprised at the presentation of claims for losses in such a business. There does not appear, however, to be any existing legislation prohibiting the importation of crude opium, or its manufacture in Canada, and the only restraint upon the manufacture of that article in the city of Vancouver is the municipal regulation requiring the taking out of a license and the payment therefore of a fee of $500 before the manufacture can be carried on within the city limits."

As it turns out, the Vancouver factories are not the only two manufacturing opium in the Lower Mainland. There are "three or four" in Victoria and another in New Westminster, and as King will note with particular horror, "they sold to white people as well as Chinese." Until this time, narcotics such as cocaine, heroin, and morphine could be purchased at the local pharmacy (in the early days, opium manufacture was subject only to a $500 fee). It is only toward the end of the first decade of the 1900s that drug use begins to be seen as immoral, with widespread denunciation of even the mildest of mood-altering substances.

"This industry, I believe, has taken root and has developed in an insidious manner without the knowledge of the people of this country," King will conclude. "Its baneful influences are too well known to require comment. The present would seem an opportune time for the government of Canada and the governments of the provinces to co-operate with the governments of Great Britain and China in a united effort to free the people from an evil so injurious to their progress and wellbeing. Any legislation which may be directed to this end, will have the hearty endorsement of a large proportion of the Chinese residents of this country, who, as members of an Anti-Opium League, are doing all in their power to enlighten their fellow citizens on the terrible consequences of the opium habit, and to suppress, as effectually as possible, the trade which, for so many years, has been carried on with impunity."

The *Anti-Opium Act* will be passed in Parliament before the end of the year. By the early 2000s, an estimated $2.3 billion will be spent annually countrywide on drug enforcement.

MAY 25, 1930

Local fishermen rub their hands in anticipation as local papers report on the progress of a plan to drain Stanley Park's famous Lost Lagoon and fill it with fresh water.

"Vancouver is to have its own 'fisherman's paradise,' almost in the centre of the city," the *Vancouver Province* reports. "Lost Lagoon, at the entrance of Stanley Park, is being rapidly converted into a fishing preserve, and by the end of two weeks will once more ripple its shores against the willows and cedars that grace its shady banks."

The 41-acre, artificial lagoon, which until recently received its water supply from pipes in Coal Harbour, has been drained and is being gradually refilled via a pipe system from Second Beach. This is not the first major change for the picturesque lagoon, so named at the turn of the century by poet Pauline Johnson. Before the completion of the Stanley Park Causeway in 1916, it was simply a brackish tidal shallow, a part of Coal Harbour that stood between the downtown peninsula, and the park itself. (Until the installation of a bridge in 1888, visitors had no choice but to cross using a precariously placed log.) Virtually dry at low tide, Lost Lagoon nonetheless remained a popular canoeing spot for decades, especially after the creation of the causeway (a task accomplished simply by dumping ash and street sweepings into the lagoon) stabilized its water levels and permanently turned it into a de facto duck preserve. At the time of the causeway construction, numerous other proposals were put forward, including draining the lake altogether to turn it into an athletic field.

This change will not be the last for Lost Lagoon. In 1937, an attempt to add water lilies will end in failure, and the installation of a $32,000 fountain in the midst of the Depression will cause a local uproar. Briefly, a plan will circulate to transform the area into a bathing beach (after excessive pollution in English Bay forces its closure); however, no such action will ever be taken.

The trout-fishing program will prove a financial success, though it will eventually be discontinued, along with the use of any water craft in Lost Lagoon's waters.

"Speedboats" on Lost Lagoon, 1929.
Image courtesy of the Vancouver Archives (CVA 99-1957, photographer Stuart Thomson)

MAY 26, 1995

About 1,200 Vancouverites, along with politicians and dignitaries from the civic, provincial, and federal levels (as well as an additional 1,000 unfortunate observers forced to wait outside because of fire regulations), are on hand as the city opens the brand new, $30 million downtown library at the corner of Homer and Georgia.

"Kids screamed. Adults quizzed the librarians on CD-ROMs, how to use the computerized card catalogue, and whether they were really settled in yet," writes the *Vancouver Sun*'s Frances Bula. "Sound bounced everywhere in the library's open design, which has several areas where people can look up or down at all seven floors from balconies or walkways."

The library building, which took 26 months to construct, is only a part of the $114 million Library Square facility, which also includes an office tower (leased to the federal government), a "green roof," and a restaurant bar. On the day of its opening, the library itself is home to one million books; 150,000 audiotapes, videotapes, and CDs; and roughly 6,600 periodicals. The building was also, supporters note with pride, designed with an eye for energy efficiency, using programmable thermostats and high-efficiency ventilation fans for an estimated annual energy savings of $190,000.

Before the move to Library Square, the city's books were housed at a $2.5 million facility on the corner of Robson and Burrard, a site that had served as a downtown library since 1957. At its opening, this library had housed 817,000 books and also featured a "Bookmobile," which was intended to promote literacy in out-of-the-way areas.

Despite the excitement surrounding the new library, a less-than-expected return on the sale of the Robson and Burrard property quickly put the project into a serious budget crunch. The plans for a $500,000 rooftop garden had to be abandoned, and a number of other aesthetic flourishes were shelved because of financial constraints.

By opening day, the facility is still left with a budget shortfall of $5 million.

Construction of the new Main Branch of the Vancouver Public Library, May 25, 1995.
Image Courtesy of the Vancouver Public Library (Oi-Lun Kwan, photographer)

MAY 27, 1959

AT EMPIRE STADIUM, in front of more than 19,000 people—a record crowd for a high-school sporting event—18-year-old sprinter Harry Jerome breaks the local speed record for the 220-yard dash.

"If anything, that record-breaking crowd will best remember a fleet-footed athlete from North Vancouver high school," reports the *Province*. "His name: Harry Jerome. This North Vancouver flier's name was on everyone's lips. No wonder. Jerome amazed all who watched with his phenomenal speed and grace. But the thing they will remember most will be his performance in the 220 and 100 yards. In that order."

Jerome's official time is recorded as 21.9 seconds, which is notable for beating—by 0.1 of a second—the record set 31 years earlier by fellow Vancouverite Percy Williams, a sprinter who went on to win two gold medals at the Amsterdam Olympics, and who remains the city's most celebrated Olympic athlete. Jerome also manages to come close to Williams's record for the 100-yard dash, with officials agreeing that, had the track been in better condition, he would have at least equalled Williams's time.

According to the paper, Jerome's only wishes are to "get through Grade 12 and make the BC team which will go back to the Pan American Games trials in Toronto."

For his promise on the track, Jerome will be wooed by several prominent American univer-

sities, eventually receiving a scholarship to the University of Oregon and going on to win a gold medal at the Commonwealth Games. Thereafter, there will be heavy local pressure for Jerome to equal his predecessor's achievements. By the time he arrives in Rome for the 1960 Olympics, local media will already be predicting a gold medal. Unfortunately, a pulled muscle will force Jerome to withdraw in the semifinals. The backlash at home will be severe, with some publications even labelling him a "quitter."

Despite the media's continually harsh treatment of the sprinter (a second injury, suffered during the 1962 British Empire Games, will result in similarly heartless commentary—even going so far as to label poor performance "pulling a Jerome"), Jerome will go on to win a bronze medal at the 1964 Tokyo Olympics, bringing home Canada's first track medal in 28 years.

"It was funny," Jerome will tell the *Toronto Star*, "but I quit running as a juvenile because I couldn't beat anyone. I was too small to play football and couldn't hit well enough in baseball, so running seemed like the only sport. But as a juvenile, I was a flop—couldn't even place in a high school meet."

Harry Jerome will die unexpectedly following a seizure at the age of 42.

Harry Jerome breaks Percy Williams' record, May 27, 1959.
IMAGE COURTESY OF THE NORTH VANCOUVER ARCHIVES (5349)

MAY 28, 1886

In George Schetky's clothing store, a meeting is held to organize a volunteer fire brigade for Vancouver—less than a month before the city burns to the ground.

"In April 1886, the city of Vancouver was incorporated and except for the small fire company manned by the men at the Hasting's [sic] Mill, the townsite's fire protection consisted of citizens with buckets, picks, and shovels," fire department historian Alex Matches will later explain in his book *Vancouver's Bravest*. "To correct this situation, a meeting was held on May 28 at George Schletsky's [sic] clothing store to organize Volunteer Hose Company No. 1. Shortly after, a hook and ladder company was formed and by June 2 the fire brigade was properly organized with Sam Pedgriff elected chief."

However, at this point, the brigade has little in its inventory besides buckets, shovels, and enthusiasm. A lack of civic funds means that the fledgling hose company can't afford to purchase a fire engine. Before the creation of Volunteer Hose Company No. 1, the only thing even remotely resembling a fire department in Vancouver was the "Darktown Fire Brigade," a group of 23 men dressed in blackface, who hauled a decrepit hose reel around during Dominion Day Parades, and sported the motto "We Git Dar." Following the meeting, Pedgriff will petition city council for support, and in lieu of funding, fire brigade members will subsequently be exempted from military or jury duty.

The department's lack of a fire engine will prove disastrous in June, when the city will be entirely destroyed by fire in the space of less than an hour. However, following the Great Fire, the townsite of Granville will commit to the purchase of its first piece of firefighting equipment: a Ronald fire engine, complete with four reels, and 2,500 feet of hose. Membership dues will be fixed at "two bits" per month, and the brigade will have its first chance to use the engine less than two months later.

By the end of the 20th century, the Vancouver Fire Department will employ more than 800 people, serving the city from 20 fire halls.

Mercifully, none of them will be dressed in blackface.

The Dark Town Fire Brigade, 1888.
Image courtesy of the Vancouver Archives (FD P1, photographer Bailey & Neelands)

MAY 29, 1875

FOLLOWING A SERIES OF MISFORTUNES, and an illness that has spanned close to nine years, saloonkeeper, riverboat pilot, and Vancouver pioneer John "Gassy Jack" Deighton dies at home at age 44.

Deighton has long been plagued by chronic health problems (thought variously to have been tuberculosis, congestive heart problems, or an excess of red blood cells) which involve difficulty breathing, a purplish complexion, and swelling of the extremities so severe that, in some cases, he required crutches. Despite visits by three different doctors, his condition continues to worsen, and by the evening of May 29, he is dead. His last words are directed at his pet mastiff, howling outside the window, and will be variously reported as "You son of a bitch! There's something going to happen!" and "Damn that dog. I wish he'd shut up."

Less than 10 years after his arrival, Deighton has made himself a name and a fortune as a saloonkeeper in the fledgling city of Granville (a British Admiralty Chart of the day clearly labelled the area "Gastown"), serving drinks to loggers and millworkers, and regaling them with the long-winded stories that gave him his nickname. He is widely regarded to have been among the first white settlers on Burrard Inlet, and his Globe Saloon was the area's first bar.

"Captain Deighton was original in his way, and his name became almost a household word with most of our citizens," his obituary in the *Mainland Guardian* will recall. "Although uncouth occasionally in his language, he possessed a good heart, and was never niggardly with his gifts when he found an object for his generosity. An Englishman by birth, he had a good deal of that humour so common with his countrymen, and which rendered him famous in this district; had fortune favoured him in his early years with a blessing of a good education, he would have been, we doubt not, a valuable and useful citizen. As it was, though restricted in his means of action, he filled his position with credit."

Deighton's wife—a 17-year-old Squamish nation woman named Madeline—will be unable to deal with the duties required in the wake of her husband's death. Consequently, his body will remain in its bed for six days before Jonathan Miller (the city's first constable) will arrange a coffin and burial. Despite the discovery of a secret will, Deighton's brother and sister-in-law will ravage what is left of Gassy Jack's estate, leaving his only beneficiary— a handicapped teenage son—without a cent.

MAY 30, 1985

MORE THAN 5,000 PEOPLE GATHER to watch and cheer, and the front page of both local papers is plastered with the news that, one day earlier, Vernon resident Steve Fonyo completed his 8,000-kilometre "Journey for Lives," becoming the first disabled Canadian athlete to run across the country, and raising more than $13 million for cancer research.

"Not even the weather could rain on Steve Fonyo's parade," reports the *Vancouver Sun*. "Trudging through a downpour most of Wednesday, the 19-year-old cross-Canada runner, escorted by two Mounties in scarlet, made a soggy but triumphant arrival at the end of the Trans-Canada Highway."

Fonyo, whose 425-day, 7,924-kilometre trek began in early March 1984, was at first heavily criticized by the media for emulating Canadian icon Terry Fox (Fonyo appropriated many of the customs of Fox's "Marathon of Hope," including dipping his prosthetic leg in the sea, and carrying a jar of Atlantic Ocean water with him across the country). In recent months, though, public opinion has turned decidedly in his favour.

"All I want to say is that I couldn't have done it without you," Fonyo tells supporters. "I've been on the road for over a year—14 months. Missed a lot of home, missed a lot of things I like to do and I just want to say that I couldn't have done it without you. I couldn't have done it without the RCMP and my sponsors helping me. I just want to say: thank you Canada."

Fonyo's victory ceremony will include speeches of praise from Premier Bill Bennett, Lieutenant-Governor Robert Rogers, and federal Health Minister Jake Epp, along with congratulations from Brian Mulroney and the Canadian Cancer Society (with whom it is alleged Fonyo has a "tumultuous relationship"). The runner will be awarded the Order of Canada in 1987.

Unfortunately, in the years to follow, Fonyo will repeatedly run afoul of the law, pleading guilty in 1996 to 16 charges in an Edmonton courtroom, including aggravated assault, assault with a weapon, fraud (upward of $10,000), and possession of a stolen vehicle. An alcoholic and a cocaine addict, he will also be convicted five times of driving under the influence.

His Order of Canada will be revoked in 2009.

MAY 31, 1976

AFTER MONTHS OF PREPARATION, and considerable media discussion, Habitat—the United Nations Conference on Human Settlements—officially opens in Vancouver, with an address by Prime Minister Pierre Trudeau.

"We have entered, willingly or otherwise, the era of a community of interest, vital to the survival of the species," Trudeau tells the assembled delegates. "No nation can afford to isolate itself in self-contemplation, clasping to its breast its possessions in denial to others."

The conference, billed as "one of the most important conferences of the UN" by Secretary-General Kurt Waldheim, has a number of broad goals, chief among them "solving settlement problems."

"The world community is fully aware that living conditions and patterns of human settlement are not satisfactory at all in most parts of the world," Waldheim tells the delegation. "If something is not done and done quickly, the situation will deteriorate dramatically."

"In most countries, there is enough to fulfill basic needs," adds Habitat Secretary-General Enrique Penlosa. "But in most countries a minority is overusing resources and there is not enough left to meet the minimal needs of the majority . . . The new style will provide for the minimum needs of everyone."

A number of committees are assembled, meeting in conference rooms across the city, representing the first time the international community has convened to discuss the challenges of an increasingly urbanized world. Years of work have been put into defining and refining the issues to be discussed, and the conference draws all manner of interested parties to Vancouver, even giving birth to an unofficial "Habitat Forum," whose organizing committee, the Vancouver Symposium, includes noted anthropologist Margaret Mead.

Unfortunately, despite its lofty goals and broad aims, the Habitat conference will ultimately be a dismal failure, hijacked by political interests and transformed instead into a forum for the Israel-Palestine question and for a voting bloc of Third World countries known as the Group of 77. Despite being largely progressive, the final statement of principles, known as the *Vancouver Declaration*, will be viewed as a disaster by the international media. Because of the statement's implicit support for an equally disastrous anti-Semitic UN resolution passed one year earlier (also thanks to the Group of 77), not a single First World country at the conference will vote in the document's favour.

The organization UN–Habitat, which is born from the conference, will do very little in the ensuing decades, finally receiving an overhaul in the 1990s.

JUNE 1, 1967

"HAIRY HIPPIES OFFERED TRIM," reads a headline in the *Vancouver Sun,* reporting that a local barber now offers free haircuts to city hippies, claiming he "owes them a favour."

"It's the least I can do after the way the hippies have boosted the hair-cutting trade," claims Bill Partridge, the Vancouver barber who offers the service. "Look at it this way: until this hippy phase started there were a lot of respectable people who grew their hair long. Now, they have it cut short because they don't want to be branded as hippies."

Partridge proposes the creation of a barbers' committee, with the aim of providing the service on a large scale to the city's hippie community. However, with one exception, the idea is soundly dismissed by both hippies and barbers alike, and fewer than 10 haircuts will ever be given.

"A lot of these hippies are intelligent people with a lot to offer society," Partridge insists, "but what employer is going to give them a job when they've got long hair? It's a tragedy that they're wasting their talents. If I could get a few of them in the chair and give them free haircuts, they could start playing a useful part in society."

A hippie couple on Granville Street, 1968.
IMAGE COURTESY OF THE MUSEUM OF VANCOUVER (FONCIE PULICE, PHOTOGRAPHER).

JUNE 2, 1937

VANCOUVER MOURNS THE LOSS of businessman and "Merchant Prince" Charles Woodward, founder of Woodward's Department Stores.

"Charles Woodward, who would have been 85 in July, died at 4 o'clock this morning in the General Hospital after an illness of six weeks," the *Vancouver Province* reports. "His death was not unexpected, as he had been sinking for some days."

Woodward, whose beginnings in business coincided with the early development of the city, arrived in 1891 from Hamilton, Ontario, and opened his first store at the corner of Westminster and Harris Streets (later known as Main and Georgia). Despite several setbacks and early financial difficulties, Woodward opened his second store (constructed over a frog pond) at Hastings and Abbott, and by 1912, he was not only a millionaire, but one of the most successful businessmen in the country.

"He was the only man in business in Vancouver who could boast that he had been continuously in the same business for forty-five years," the paper continues. "His rise to fame and fortune epitomized the story of the poor boy gaining success on the basis of honesty and sound business principles."

Despite aspirations of retiring, Woodward continued to oversee every aspect of his empire, with multiple locations throughout Vancouver, and he even expanded the enterprise westward into Alberta. Following the patriarch's demise, Woodward's will continue to be a notable part of Vancouver's retail landscape for decades (its "$1.49 Day" sales will be a city staple) under the capable direction of his sons William and Percival and, later, grandson Charles "Chunky" Woodward. It will also become the owner and primary financier behind Oakridge Mall in the 1960s. However, the recession of the 1980s will all but devastate the Woodward's empire. Following years of financial difficulty, Woodward's will file for bankruptcy in 1992, and its assets will be sold to the Hudson's Bay Company.

"Mr. Woodward was one of the builders of our commercial world," laments Mayor G.C. Miller. "He was one of those whose pioneering efforts assisted immeasurably in the growth of this city during its earlier years. In his death Vancouver has suffered a distinct loss."

Beacon on the top of Woodward's Department Store, 1938.
IMAGE COURTESY OF THE VANCOUVER ARCHIVES (VAN SC P114)

JUNE 3, 1972

AS THE ROLLING STONES PLAY to thousands of appreciative fans, police clash with more than 2,500 rioters outside Pacific Coliseum, in a battle that involves fists, rocks, knives, Molotov cocktails, and a homemade bazooka, and puts close to a dozen people in hospital.

"About 30 policemen suffered injuries ranging from cuts and bruises to concussions and broken bones," the *Province* reports. "Most seriously injured were Sgt. Stan Ziola, who received a concussion and a broken bone in his chest, Const. Koos Dykstra, who sustained a broken wrist, and Const. Peter Barnes, who received a severe concussion."

Molotov cocktails are hurled at passing police cars, a railroad spike is fired from the homemade bazooka, and one youth is arrested for wielding a heavy length of chain with a hook at one end. The skirmish, which lasts for roughly three hours, is believed by police to have been orchestrated by the notorious Clark Park Gang, a group of youths from East Vancouver that has already been the target of a five-month undercover investigation.

"The PNE looks upon the [riot] group as being not in any way rock fans but trouble makers who were there for the sole purpose of making trouble," says a PNE spokesman.

Thirteen arrests are made in connection with the riot, with a further nine in the days to come, and the level-headed police response provides some redemption for the VPD after years of allegations of brutality.

However, shortly thereafter, following the ambush of a uniformed constable by several "Clark Parkers," a secret police "Heavy Squad" will be deployed, armed with baseball bats, for the express purpose of disbanding the Clark Park Gang. Rumours will abound of members being brutally assaulted, tossed into Burrard Inlet, and fired at with live rounds.

Within two months of the Heavy Squad's deployment, the Clark Park Gang will cease to exist.

The Rolling Stones play the Pacific Coliseum, June 3 1972. (VPL 86279)

JUNE 4, 1946

Pallbearers carrying L.D. Taylor's coffin, June 1946.
IMAGE COURTESY OF THE VANCOUVER ARCHIVES (CVA 1477-972)

AN ERA ENDS AS FORMER PUBLISHER, prospector, fugitive, and Vancouver mayor Louis Denison Taylor dies at St. Paul's Hospital, only weeks before his 89th birthday.

"A wonderful old man died in Vancouver yesterday" reports the *Province*, "one who had known the city from the days of its youth and had served it long and faithfully, often at great loss to himself. This was Louis D. Taylor, who passed away within six weeks of his eighty-ninth birthday. Had he lived and had his strength permitted, he would, no doubt, have had his place in the Jubilee celebrations. But death intervened."

Taylor, a striking figure in his trademark red tie, served as Vancouver's mayor for a total of 11 years and will remain the city's most-elected politician, having won the mayoralty on eight occasions. Throughout his lifetime, he wore many different hats: newspaper subscription agent, banker, publisher of the *Vancouver Daily World*, city licence commissioner, and, briefly, prospector. However, as personal correspondence will later reveal, L.D. was also a fugitive: upon his arrival in Vancouver at age 39, he was fleeing embezzlement charges stemming from his involvement in a Chicago bank, a secret he kept all his life. Virtually penniless, Taylor began making a name for himself in local politics, finally winning the mayoralty in 1910 after several hard-fought campaigns.

Taylor courted controversy with his "Open Town" policies—designed to focus police resources on violent crime and away from vice crime, and his career was marked by unsteady finances, allegations of corruption, and even insinuations by the *Province* (with whom he enjoyed a longstanding feud) that he was a socialist. During Taylor's career, and thanks to his influence, a number of major changes took place in Vancouver: the amalgamation of the city with Point Grey, the construction of the international airport, the institution of eight-hour days for civic employees, and the establishment of a city planning commission, among others. Unfortunately, Taylor's perceived leniency toward crime would end up destroying his political career. In April 1928, a public inquiry was held into widespread corruption in the police force, alleging that the Vancouver Police Department accepted bribes from bars and brothels all over town in exchange for protection. The inquiry was a disaster for Taylor; he never again won the mayoralty, and in what would prove to be his final campaign, he received only 1 percent of the vote.

"L.D. was perhaps never a great mayor," the *Province* continues. "But he was a competent and enterprising mayor and he had the city's best interests always at heart and the years gave him vast experience. No one who saw him preside at a meeting of the City Council in his best days could doubt his ability."

When Taylor is buried, his trademark red tie will be buried with him.

JUNE 5, 1959

"ENGLISH BAY MAY GET SECOND SAND COVER," reads a headline in the *Vancouver Province* as the Park Board discusses the latest phase of its English Bay beautification plan: expanding the beach area by more than four times.

"They spend millions on Waikiki Beach," explains an unnamed Park Board spokesman in an interview with the paper, "and we are getting the job done for about $7,000."

Thus far, 70,000 cubic yards of sand have been dredged from the bay as part of a sweeping plan (begun in 1929) to beautify the coastline between English Bay and the Burrard Street Bridge. Other projects have included the demolition of some West End waterfront properties and industry, the razing of the old English Bay Pier, and the widening of the grass "laying out" area. Over the next three years, the work will include a number of other demolitions and "greening" along the waterfront. In addition, the sand will be levelled and specifically cultivated into a 30-degree slope to allow for optimum swimming conditions.

"The job's been done carefully," beach supervisor George Burrows will reassure, "There's a 30-degree slope with no holes or steep drop-offs anywhere."

The sand for the beach is dredged from the bottom of the inlet by public works and will total approximately 100,000 cubic yards when the project is completed on June 12.

"The perfect sand we want doesn't exist around here," complains the Park Board spokesman. "River sand is easy to get at about $2 a cubic yard but there is a lot of black material in it and it is very fine. It will certainly be an improvement. We may have to try other sand for the upper beach and laying out area next year."

English Bay, 1905.
IMAGE COURTESY OF THE VANCOUVER ARCHIVES (BE P12.05, PHOTOGRAPHER PHILIP T. TIMMS)

JUNE 6, 1933

"SNAKES ALIVE!" declares a headline in the *Vancouver Sun*, reporting on numerous sightings of an eight-foot-long serpent said to have made its home in the gardens and back alleys of the Grandview area.

"It was first seen a week ago by a woman who was going back out into her back garden," the paper reports. "She dashed back to the telephone and notified the police. The police came 'snake hunting' but the elusive reptile had wiggled off. Monday night, another housewife saw it in her garden, but again it got away before police arrived on the scene, and it was last observed heading for the bush in the 1900 block East Second Avenue."

A number of rumours emerge about the origins of the snake, among them that it "escaped from a carnival show on the Exhibition grounds last year," but no concrete proof will ever be uncovered.

"Whatever, or whoever the Grandview Snake is," the *Sun* concludes, "it has instituted a reign of terror in that district."

A "serpent" in the garden of a home in the 1500 block of Marine Drive, circa 1920. IMAGE COURTESY OF THE VANCOUVER ARCHIVES (CVA 371-358)

JUNE 7, 1989

The Vancouver Canucks and general manager Pat Quinn court controversy during the sixth round of the NHL entry draft when they select an 18-year-old, 185-pound rookie from the Soviet Union—Pavel Bure.

Considerable fuss is made over Bure's selection because the record-setting rookie was being courted by a number of other teams (including the Detroit Red Wings and the Edmonton Oilers), all

of whom were told that he was ineligible for the draft for at least another year, having not played the requisite 11 international games. Several complaints will be filed, a number of irate Detroit representatives will storm the stage where the draft is taking place, and in May 1990 Bure will be deemed ineligible by the NHL. However, after serious investigation, chief scout Mike Penny will discover that Bure has in fact played 12 international games, and on the evening of the 1990 NHL draft, the league will reverse its decision.

The battle to employ Bure as a Vancouver Canuck will continue for a further 12 months because of contract negotiations and the need for the right winger and his family to defect from the Soviet Union. The team will be forced to pay a $250,000 transfer fee and to buy out his existing $800,000 contract with the Russian Ice Hockey Federation.

Pavel Bure will debut at the Pacific Coliseum in November 1991 in front of a crowd of 16,123. His four-year deal, worth $3 million, makes him the highest-paid player on the team. He will go on to score 34 goals in his first season (in spite of playing in only 65 games), will be the first Canuck to win the Calder Memorial Trophy, and will join the Canucks for the Stanley Cup Final in 1994 against the New York Rangers.

No mention is made of Bure's drafting in any of Vancouver's major newspapers.

A Vancouver Canucks game, 1946.
Image courtesy of the Vancouver Archives (CVA 1184-2505, photographer Jack Lindsay)

JUNE 8, 1933

LOCAL SWIMMERS BLUSH with modesty as, after 41 years, the city issues a bylaw amendment allowing men to go topless on Vancouver beaches.

"Trunks will be a correct attire for men on Vancouver's beaches this summer," an article in the *Vancouver Sun* explains. "This city lined itself up with many of the outstanding resorts of Great Britain when the Park Board at its regular meeting Thursday, approved of amendments to the present bylaw regarding bathing suits."

Etiquette surrounding beachwear, part of the Victorian social code for decades, was made official with the 1892 passage of Bylaw 135, which forbade any Vancouverite from bathing or swimming in English Bay or Burrard Inlet without "a bathing dress covering the body from the neck to the knees" (though, in a peculiar bit of specificity, this restriction only applied between 8 a.m. and 6 p.m.), under threat of a $100 fine or a two-month prison term (with or without hard labour). However, in the years following, attitudes have softened, in keeping with changing social mores worldwide, allowing male Vancouverites to expose themselves as never before.

"No person shall wear any bathing suit to any extent transparent," the text of the bylaw, drafted by the police commissioner, chief of police, and city prosecutor, warns, "or any bathing suit not entirely modest in make and style . . . Men's trunks of sufficient height to cover the stomach with a three-inch of leg square cut, shall be deemed to be entirely modest within the meaning of this section."

"It shall be unlawful," the bylaw adds, "for any person wearing a bathing suit to lower or roll down such suit while on a public bathing beach."

English Bay, circa 1920.
IMAGE COURTESY OF THE VANCOUVER ARCHIVES (CVA 677-96, PHILLIP TIMMS, PHOTOGRAPHER)

BATHING BEACH ENGLISH BAY, VANCOUVER B.C.

JUNE 9, 1920

WITH PROHIBITION IN FULL SWING, the *Vancouver Sun* reports on the latest developments in the case of two men caught in New Westminster with a car full of bootleg liquor.

"The evidence showed that the liquor was hidden in various portions of the car," the paper reports. "[Driver Ray] Smith was employed in Vancouver by another man, who does not appear, owing to the fact that he and a woman in the car when it was searched, managed to make their escape."

Smith, the two unidentified suspects, and accomplice Robert Waite (using the alias Arthur E. Murphy and in possession of a phony US Customs badge) broke down on Sixth Avenue the previous Friday, where the "queer behaviour" of its occupants aroused the suspicions of the local police chief, who immediately searched the vehicle. Although 31 bottles of whisky were discovered inside, Smith and Waite have since been released on $100 bail.

Prohibition, which has been in effect since 1917, has been an utter failure in British Columbia; a roaring bootleg trade, high policing costs, and a loophole that allows the purchase of "medicinal" liquor (in 1919, 181,000 liquor prescriptions were written by BC doctors) has kept the legislation from having any lasting effect. By 1919, the provincial government will in fact have sold $1.5 million in "medicinal" liquor, and Walter Findlay, the prohibition commissioner, will himself have been sentenced to two years in jail for bootlegging seized provincial alcohol. After only three years of Prohibition, British Columbians will vote in October 1920 to repeal the measure in favour of government-regulated sale.

Smith is fined $75 for illegal possession of liquor. Waite, who fails to appear in the courtroom, simply forfeits his bail. Under the new provisions of the *Prohibition Act*, the car—believed to be worth close to $3,500—is impounded by the police.

An Attorney General's report, published four days earlier, reveals that, in the previous fiscal year, the BC government made an estimated $733,000 on the sale of medicinal liquor.

RCMP liquor seizure, Dec. 6, 1932.
IMAGE COURTESY OF THE VANCOUVER ARCHIVES
(CVA 99-4273, PHOTOGRAPHER STUART THOMSON)

JUNE 10, 1947

Youth gangs again dominate local headlines as the *Vancouver Province* reports on the police breakup of a "fracas" between two rival groups of "hoodlums" on the Vancouver College campus.

"I don't like to classify these young men as ordinary hoodlums or hooligans," says Magistrate Mackenzie Matheson, who fines each of the youths involved $10 in police court, "but they are almost certainly getting into that class."

Fred Herzog North Vancouver, 1958
© Fred Herzog, 2013 Courtesy of Equinox Gallery, Vancouver

The fight, involving a gang from Kerrisdale and another from East Vancouver, is allegedly instigated by the East End Boys, in retaliation for a similar rumble at the PNE's Happyland earlier that same week.

"We were even numbers then," recalls Wilbur Clarke of the Kerrisdale Boys, "six of us to seven of them, so we said to come up to the school grounds. They said they wanted to fight. We said all right."

The rumble is broken up by police before any serious harm can be caused; however, though the number of participants is small, the spectacle draws close to 300 observers. Youth gangs have called Vancouver home throughout the 1940s, many associated with particular geographical areas and sporting colourful names such as the Alma Dukes and the Homer Street Gang. Rumbles and drag races have been common features of the seemingly endless turf disputes between the factions, a trend that will continue throughout the 1950s and climax with the park gangs of the 1960s. The most notorious of these, the Clark Park Gang, will be responsible for a 1972 riot outside a Rolling Stones concert at the Pacific Coliseum which will put more than a dozen people in hospital.

"I think the police are to be congratulated on the work they did in preventing more trouble," Magistrate Matheson beams. "Of course, you can't put old heads on young shoulders. You young men have a lot to learn. One thing they have to learn is they can't settle civic differences by fists."

JUNE 11, 1976

AFTER 12 DAYS OF INFIGHTING, political agendas, and frustration on all sides, the United Nations Habitat Conference winds down with the adoption of the *Vancouver Declaration*—a disastrous document voted against by virtually every First World country at the conference.

"The United Nations' conference on human settlements was smashed apart in its final hours Friday night by the political power of the third world," writes the *Sun*. "A recommendation closely linked to the previous UN resolution equating Zionism with racism, which sent shockwaves around the world last year, was approved by the majority of the delegates. Canada and 14 other nations were therefore unable to vote in favor of the *Vancouver Declaration of Human Settlements* which was intended to be the crowning achievement of Habitat."

Despite the fact that the conference was hailed as the dawn of a new era in global discussion, it was quickly hijacked by political interests and dominated by issues such as the Israel–Palestine feud, and the sheer voting power of the Group of 77 (a voting bloc of 113 developing nations), leading conference president Barney Danson to plead: "For the sake of God and the sake of our children I beg you—and I do not beg easily—to stay with what this was all about."

"Continuation of this sort of tactic doesn't bode well for my country's support and participation in future UN conferences concerned with substantial global problems demanding global attention," states US delegate Christian Herter Jr. "[The *Vancouver Declaration*] deplores racism while at the same time expounding its own particular brand of racism."

Thanks to the sheer numbers of the Group of 77, the *Vancouver Declaration* was redrafted to include more radical, economic, or politically motivated clauses, such as the ability to safeguard homelands from "foreign aggression," and includes a paragraph urging all people and governments "to join the struggle against any form of colonialism, foreign aggression and occupation, domination, apartheid and all forms of racism and racial discrimination, referred to in the resolution as adopted by the General Assembly of the UN."

And, owing to the fact that the document now contains reference to an earlier UN resolution (also forced through by the Group of 77) equating Zionism with racism, no First World nation at the conference votes in its favour, with Australia, Belgium, Canada, Denmark, France, Ireland, Israel, Italy, Luxembourg, the Netherlands, New Zealand, Norway, the US, and West Germany voting against.

The *Vancouver Declaration* will ultimately be implemented, but UN–Habitat, the organization born from the conference, will go on to achieve very little.

JUNE 12, 1933

AFTER DECADES OF SERVING in an unofficial capacity, Major James Skitt Matthews is appointed by Order-in-Council as Vancouver's first archivist at a monthly pay rate of $25.

"I know he went to work as a voluntary public officer and virtually without pay to establish the archives," former park commissioner R. Rowe Holland will explain at a 1953 celebration where Matthews will be granted the key to the city. "He has contributed not only his inspired and indefatigable time and effort to the creation of the archives, but has literally sacrificed every material thing he had in the world to the achievement of this great objective."

The fiery Matthews has served as the city's self-appointed record keeper for the past 33 years, first housing his collection in every nook and cranny of his Kitsilano home, and then in 1931 (through special arrangement with the library board) in a decrepit attic room in the Carnegie Library at Main and Hastings.

"There was neither heat, electric light, water, janitor service, telephone, typewriter, supplies or salary," Matthews will explain of his accommodations. "With no funds save his own, he furnished it with a discarded desk, a chair held together with wire; a waste paper basket without a bottom, and a cardboard merchandise carton for a fyling [sic] cabinet. Bookshelves were created with boards separated between blocks of wood . . . On the glass pane of the upper half of a plain door, he affixed by the gum of its flap a business envelope on which he had written 'City Archives'; the title he chose."

Disagreements with the library board began almost immediately. Upon learning of the board's plans to co-opt his materials

Major James Skitt Matthews at his desk, 1941.
IMAGE COURTESY OF THE VANCOUVER ARCHIVES (PORT P567, PHOTOGRAPHER BENJAMIN W. LEESON)

and designate an archivist of its own, Matthews secretly removed every piece of archival material to his home. In the early months of 1932, he began writing City Hall to request facilities and a salary. For close to 40 years, Matthews will remain custodian of the city's records, clashing with generations of mayors and aldermen (at least three mayors will attempt to retire him), and often ignoring or terrifying archives visitors (in one instance physically tossing out an unfortunate Swiss post-graduate student who accidentally dropped a file on the floor).

"For the more than 30 years I have known him, he has been mad as a hatter," a friend will recall. "Literally so. If he had not had the backing of the Vancouver Historical Society and its numerous influential members, he would have ended his irate days in Essondale. And yet—and this is why I admired him—in all that time he was the only character in town who could bully the bejeesus out of every mayor and council this town ever had."

Matthews will remain city archivist until his death in 1970 (at age 92). Some two years later, his vast collection of records, interviews, and photographs will be moved to its new home in the Major Matthews Building in Vanier Park.

JUNE 13, 1886

The day after the Great Fire, June 14, 1886.
IMAGE COURTESY OF THE VANCOUVER ARCHIVES (CVA 1477-416)

DESPITE VALIANT ATTEMPTS to keep it contained, a small brush fire near False Creek suddenly rages out of control, and in less than 45 minutes, the entire city of Vancouver has burned to the ground. Started in the early hours of the morning by CPR clearing crews near the Yaletown engine roundhouse, the blaze is whipped into a frenzy by a strong gust of wind, and the resultant fire destroys more than 1,000 buildings and claims (by the estimate of eyewitnesses) more than 20 lives.

"The city did not burn; it was consumed by flame," eyewitness W.F. Findlay will recall years later in a conversation with Vancouver's first archivist, J.S. Matthews. "The buildings simply melted before the fiery blast. As an illustration of the heat, there was a man (driving horse and wagon) caught on Carrall Street between Water Street and Cordova Street; man and horse perished in the centre of the street. The fire went down the sidewalk on old Hastings Road, past our office, so rapidly that people flying before it had to leave the burning sidewalk and take to the road; the fire traveled down that wooden sidewalk faster than a man could run."

Within minutes, the city is an inferno, and locals are forced to abandon their homes and personal property, taking refuge in wells, inside buildings, or leaping into the waters of False Creek to escape being burned alive. The heat is so intense, it will later be revealed that the bell at St. James Church has been melted into slag. By nightfall, the survivors have assembled at the base of Mount Pleasant, just outside the city limits, in what Findlay will call "the sorriest looking procession Vancouver had, and I hope ever will see." Only a handful of buildings remain in the wake of the blaze, and survivors (including Mayor Malcolm MacLean, who lost both of his properties—neither insured) will have little besides the clothes on their backs, lacking even basic necessities such as food. Luckily, word of the devastation has made its way to New Westminster, and by midnight, food and supplies have begun to arrive.

"It was never known, and never will be, how many lost their lives," Findlay will recall. "Of all the remains found, three only, those found at the corner of Hastings and Columbia streets, were recognisable by their features; then, too, we made an effort to keep the number as low as possible. Three bodies were taken out of a well down near St. James Church on Cordova Street East; at the time, there were some shacks down there. They were evidently husband, wife and little daughter . . . [who] saw the fire coming, rushed away, and seeing a well, jumped into it. There was three or four feet of water in the well, and their clothing was unharmed by fire, but their faces were livid; the fire had, apparently, swirled over the well, and they had been suffocated, not burned. They were well dressed; the lady had gloves on her hands."

In the wake of the destruction, rebuilding will begin in earnest. Some 12 hours later, spaces will be cleared, and new construction will have begun. Within five weeks, the city will have been largely rebuilt.

JUNE 14, 1994

VIOLENCE ERUPTS ON ROBSON STREET as a 3-2 loss by the Vancouver Canucks to the New York Rangers in Game 7 of the Stanley Cup Finals sparks one of the largest riots the city has ever seen, one that leaves more than 200 people injured and causes more than $1 million in property damage.

"The party degenerated into a melee," the *Vancouver Sun* will report the following day. "With the streets clogged with people, fights broke out, windows were smashed, and objects were thrown at police."

As the riot progresses into the early morning, police cars are overturned, buildings are looted, more than 50 windows in the Eaton's storefront are smashed, and a Molotov cocktail is thrown through the window of Duthie Books before a riot squad is able to disperse the crowd with the help of tear gas. Ryan Berntt, earmarked by VPD officers as one of the incident's main agitators, is shot in the head with a rubber bullet and will spend the next four weeks in a coma, awakening with permanent brain damage. In fact, the riot control efforts are so widespread that VPD officers (540 in total) run out of tear gas and are forced to call for additional supplies.

"I climbed up [to the roof of] Joe Fortes to see what was happening," eyewitness Liz Parker will explain in an interview with the *Sun*. "Police helmets were flying and I saw the riot shields come out. I'm really ashamed. I didn't think Vancouver would be like this."

The riot goes unreported in early editions of the *Sun*. Despite the presence of alcohol and a crowd of roughly 60,000 clogging the streets, the violence in fact caught the Vancouver Police Department completely by surprise.

"Police prepared, but little street trouble expected," read the headline to the previous day's edition of the *Sun*.

"We don't anticipate any need for them Tuesday night," spokesperson Anne Drennan was quoted as saying, "but, should it happen, we will be prepared."

The Stanley Cup Riot, June 14, 1994.
IMAGE © VANCOUVER SUN (STEVE BOSCH, PHOTOGRAPHER)

JUNE 15, 1956

The opening of the Vancouver Aquarium, June 15, 1956
(VPL 40142)

AT 2:45 P.M., with the turn of a beribboned key and after five years of steady work, the Vancouver Aquarium opens—making history as the first public aquarium in the country.

"Official opening of Canada's first public aquarium in Stanley Park Friday was the proudest moment of a lifetime for Carl L.A. Lietze," reports the *Vancouver Sun*. "Officials at the ceremony praised Mr. Lietze as the man who made the aquarium dream come true. The aquarium was born in Mr. Lietze's basement five years ago when his son began keeping fish in glass tanks."

"The man named most responsible for the spanking new educational and research centre in Stanley Park became interested in aquariums when his teen-age son built one in the basement of his home," adds the *Province*. "When the house was crammed with 25 fish tanks, he decided Vancouver should have a public aquarium."

Lietze, who founded the Vancouver Public Aquarium Society five years earlier, has been tireless in his efforts to obtain funding for the facility, pestering politicians, forging alliances with business interests (including timber baron H.R. MacMillan), and managing to secure $100,000 in funding from each level of government. Construction began in spring 1955; however, with all available funds tied up in construction, curator Murray Newman (still a student at UBC, with no formal experience in the area) was left without a cent to spend on the facility's fish. Through a fundraising partnership with the downtown Hudson's Bay, and with assistance from provincial and federal fisheries workers as well as a number of UBC students, the aquarium was stocked and staffed—for less than half of the estimated $30,000 needed to complete the task.

Following a luncheon, guests and dignitaries are invited to tour the facility, where more than 200 species of fish are on display.

"Even people who never go near the water can become experts on kinds of fish found in interior and coastal waters overnight," the *Province* declares. "The aquarium is divided into tropical fresh water, cold fresh water, and cold salt water fish. Specimens range from 'Black Mollies,' to the man-eating fish from the Amazon in the fresh water section . . . The fish have been begged, borrowed and bought. Many curator Murray Newman and his staff have fished out of the sea themselves."

Attendance during that first weekend will be close to 10,000. The Vancouver Aquarium will eventually grow to become the largest in Canada, covering more than 9,000 square metres, employing roughly 400 people, and containing 9.5 million litres of water and 70,000 animals.

As of 2013, it will be considered one of the top five aquariums in the world.

JUNE 16, 1928

STREET VENDOR, SPORTS ANNOUNCER, and high school dropout Nathaniel Ryal Bailey opens Vancouver's first drive-in restaurant at the corner of 67th and Granville—the White Spot Barbecue.

"It was far out in the bush when it opened but it was the city's first drive-in," the *Vancouver Province* will later report, "and had the best fried chicken in the Lower Mainland."

Since 1918 the business—evolved from Bailey's boyhood days selling snacks at ballparks and city beaches— has served ice cream, hot dogs, and cold drinks to sightseers at Marpole's Lookout Point, from a travelling lunch counter built into Bailey's Model-T Ford. The business takes a decisive step forward with the opening of the barbecue, which features a 25-car parking lot, a rustic log cabin, and, in front of the building, a cut of beef roasting on a roaring fire. The location is staffed by two—a cook and a manager, who also doubles as a "carhop"—and features meals presented on long, white planks, which can be slid through a car's window to serve as an impromptu food tray.

Originally set to be named The Granville Barbecue (and changed at the last minute after a friend of Bailey's suggested he name it after a White Spot restaurant in Los Angeles), the Marpole lot originally cost $11 to clear—a transaction that left Bailey overdrawn by $7. Peers will initially be skeptical of the business; Marpole is still considered remote by 1920s standards (it won't even be considered part of the city limits for another six months); however, the growing popularity of the automobile will cause White Spot's sales to soar. The barbecue will become so successful, a second White Spot will be opened in 1930. Unfortunately, the demolition of the nearby Marpole Bridge (reducing automobile

The original White Spot on 67th and Granville, April 14, 1936.
IMAGE COURTESY OF THE VANCOUVER ARCHIVES (CVA 99-4929, PHOTOGRAPHER STUART THOMSON)

traffic substantially) and the Great Depression will force Bailey to close his second location almost immediately, and by the early 1930s, White Spot will be verging on bankruptcy.

"The onset of the Depression sent the restaurant's revenue plummetting [*sic*]," the *Sun* will report, "and for a number of years the profits from his ball-park concessions and his ice cream truck were all that kept the White Spot from economic oblivion."

As the decade continues, Bailey's fortunes will turn around, allowing him to expand the original barbecue, buy up adjacent lots, and reopen in 1937 as the White Spot Restaurant and Drive-In. This building—with a dining room added in 1938 and extensive renovations in the 1970s—will remain in use for a further 39 years, even outliving its founder. (Bailey will die in 1978, after having sold his company to General Foods for $6 million.)

The building will be destroyed by fire in 1986.

JUNE 17, 1958

NINETEEN MEN ARE KILLED and dozens more are injured as, at 3:40 p.m., two sections of the partially completed Second Narrows Bridge collapse during construction in what will become known as the deadliest industrial accident in BC history.

"At first, it looked like our bridge was falling," Ben Hallman, a motorist on the nearby old Second Narrows Bridge, will recall in an interview with the *Province*. "Then we saw the two sections crash into the inlet. The air was filled with shouts and cries for help. Fifty men must have gone down with the bridge. They didn't have a chance. It all happened within a moment—a moment of horror."

The collapse of the $16 million structure, which will later be attributed to a faulty calculation on the part of a junior engineer (who himself perishes in the collapse), comes only a year into the construction of the much-debated span. A number of workers will be swept out to sea by the strong current, while others will be trapped below the surface, pinned by falling debris, dragged down by heavy tool belts, or clipped onto the girders by safety harnesses.

"Several workmen escaped by running to the solid section of the bridge as they heard first rumblings of the quake-like roar which accompanied the collapse," the paper continues. "As they reached safety they could hear the cries of dying and injured men, clinging or pinned to wreckage or struggling helplessly in the rushing water. But they were unable to help them."

"It was hell," survey crewman Art Pielon, aboard a boat north of the span, will explain in an interview with the *Vancouver Sun*. "Men flashing around in the water and screaming for help. I grabbed everyone I could see swimming. I only bothered with the live ones. I left the dead."

The collapse of the Second Narrows Bridge, June 17, 1958.
IMAGE COURTESY OF THE VANCOUVER PUBLIC LIBRARY

A large-scale rescue operation is undertaken almost immediately by police, pleasure-boat operators, and a team of divers. Because of their efforts, a number of injured workers are pulled from the inlet, and taken to hospital. A Royal Commission will later rule that the collapse was the result of engineer error, with Dominion Bridge (the contracting company, which should have caught the flaw in the design stage) accused of cutting corners in a race to get the project completed.

The span will later be rebuilt, and upon its opening in 1960, plaques will be placed on either end to commemorate the workers who died during its construction.

In 1994, it will be renamed the Ironworkers Memorial Bridge.

JUNE 18, 1973

PLANNERS BEAM AND RESIDENTS GROAN as new turning restrictions and traffic barriers are erected in the West End—the first part of a city plan to reclaim the area's residential character.

"New traffic patterns in Vancouver's West End will work like a charm—if Monday's first day results are anything to go by," reports the *Province*. "Traffic barriers and turning restrictions went into operation as part of a city planning program to return West End residential streets to local use."

The barriers are placed on Gilford, Chilco, and Pendrell, along with a number of additional turning restrictions on Georgia, as part of a joint initiative (unusual for the time) between the city's planning and engineering departments. Following a 1971 report, planners concluded that the West End (by the 1960s among the highest-density neighbourhoods in North America) should be reimagined for the 20th century, shying away from the frenzied high-rise developments and automobile congestion of previous decades.

"Most drivers paused to gaze at the bright yellow and blue barriers stretching diagonally across lanes in the middle of the block with trees in garbage cans at either end, before taking an unexpected detour home," continues the *Province*. "Rush hour 4 to 6 p.m. traffic along Georgia, heading for Lions Gate Bridge was unusually light and steady. The only unexpected delay was a momentary wait while a mother goose and her goslings waddled across the road west of Chilco."

The barriers (the first of their kind in North America) are only the beginning; two years later, the city will implement the 1975 West End Plan, an initiative (based on extensive citizen

The West End, circa 1970. Image Courtesy of the Vancouver Archives.
IMAGE COPYRIGHT: CITY OF VANCOUVER (CVA 1435-132)

input) calling for reduced building heights, neighbourhood parks, and a new community centre. Ultimately, the West End Plan will not only transform the neighbourhood, but mark a total shift in perspective in terms of city planning. The new approach will favour neighbourhoods over automobiles, halt the construction of residential high-rises until the 1980s, and ultimately evolve into a concept that will become well known and widely used among planners worldwide: Vancouverism.

Naturally, not everyone is enamoured of the changes.

"It's the most idiotic thing this city has ever devised," sputters one resident. "It's a good idea to reroute traffic, yes, but all they had to do was put no access blockades at the end of the roads at Georgia. These things are ugly—we don't need them. They'll just foul up traffic here. Now I have to travel three blocks out of my way to get out."

JUNE 19, 1912

"FEMALE POLICE SWORN," reads a headline in the *Vancouver Daily News-Advertiser* as, following a ceremony the previous morning, Vancouver becomes the first city in Canada to employ female constables.

"Back in 1912 it became apparent that some women with authority had to be there so that the frailer sex would be properly taken care of and an air of propriety given to the station," an article in the July 1926 edition of the *Greater Vancouver Police Gazette* will recall. "The arrests of women was very much on the increase, and it was felt that if a permanent woman was added to the force and given authority, it would do away with the necessity of sending out for some other of that sex so that a female prisoner could be searched."

The two constables (who receive $960 a year and are referred to as "Matrons" in all police annual reports up until 1919) are 47-year-old Lurancy Harris and 34-year-old Minnie Millar, both of whom will go on to distinguished careers with the VPD, and whose duties include (according to the *News-Advertiser*) "the work of reclamation and administration in connection with the female morality question."

Less than six months into her career, "Ma" Harris will receive international attention for escorting murderer Lorna Matthews on a 2,000-mile train journey to face trial in Oklahoma. The trip will see her name in newspapers across the US, and she will receive a hero's welcome when the pair arrives. She will subsequently become an inspector in the Women's Division, responsible for patrolling nightspots, remaining vigilant for signs of female immorality.

Minnie Millar will go on to make the first arrest by a female officer in the Vancouver Police Department; in 1926, she will arrest William Borden for indecent conduct toward women at a public beach.

Female police officers in Vancouver will only be granted a uniform beginning in 1947, and it will be 1973 before they are allowed to carry firearms.

As of 2012, 24 percent of the city's police force will be female.

Lurancy Harris, circa 1914.
IMAGE COURTESY OF THE VANCOUVER ARCHIVES (A-30-83, PHOTOGRAPHER A.J. SELSET)

JUNE 20, 1938

"VIOLENCE AND GAS BOMBS IN SUNDAY AFFRAY," reads the front page of the *Vancouver Province*, reporting on a large-scale riot that occurred the previous morning, in which hundreds of downtown store windows were smashed and more than $35,000 in property damage was caused in a fracas that will become known as Bloody Sunday.

"What we in Vancouver have said for weeks would happen, has happened," argues a *Province* editorial. "The unemployed 'sitdowners' have been evicted from the Post Office and the Art Gallery, and the sequel has been $30,000 damage to Vancouver citizens' property."

The root of the trouble was a month-long, "sit-down" protest at the Vancouver Art Gallery, and the Main Post Office at Granville and Hastings, attended by more than 1,000 jobless protesters.

The protesters, hit hard by nine years of economic depression, and angered by the apparent insensitivity of government to the plight of the unemployed, had been occupying both premises since May 20. The violence began in the small hours of Sunday morning when VPD officers assembled out-side the art gallery and the post office, and, in what would quickly become a notorious example of police brutality, used tear gas and truncheons to evacuate both buildings. Forty protesters (none of them armed) were sent to hospital, including protest organizer Steve Brodie, who was brutally beaten, and Arthur Redseth, whose eye was knocked from its socket by a police baton.

In retaliation for the police eviction, hundreds of protesters (along with a number of spectators along for the ride) streamed along Cordova Street, smashing windows and destroying whatever property they could find along the way.

"They heaved stones, planks, bottles," the *Province* reports, "anything they had. Some used their feet."

By afternoon, close to 15,000 people had gathered at Oppenheimer Park to protest the brutality of police. However, despite the destruction and widespread public support for the protesters, neither the federal nor provincial governments will agree to offer any further aid to the unemployed, and the Depression will continue largely unabated until the onset of World War II.

"The real blame for this regrettable situation that has been allowed to develop in Vancouver must be placed squarely on the shoulders of the institution of the government of Canada," the *Province* editorial continues. "First of all these men must eat. Next, they must be given opportunity to become self-supporting. These unemployed men want work and they want pay—surely they have a right to both."

Police disperse a crowd during a riot on Powell Street, 1935.
IMAGE COURTESY OF THE VANCOUVER ARCHIVES (CVA 371-1127)

JUNE 21, 1963

"LIQUOR LAW UNCIVILIZED," reports the *Vancouver Sun* as City Magistrate Bernard Isman takes sharp aim at the province's liquor laws.

"It's unfortunate the laws in this province aren't a little more civilized," Isman states in an interview with the paper. "There shouldn't be any more restrictions on the sale or partaking of liquor than there are on eating or smoking."

Isman's remarks come after imposing a $50 fine on Jocelyn Gamanche and three others for possessing liquor in an unlicensed nightspot known as Johann Strauss Kaffeehaus. Prosecutions for unlicensed liquor have been on the rise throughout the summer of 1963, in keeping with the province's draconian liquor laws. Those laws restrict the serving of alcohol to hotel beer parlours, where, since 1925, only beer by the glass has been available. This situation has led to the proliferation of dozens of underground "bottle clubs," which allow unlicensed booze and provide expensive mixers instead. The city even has a "Drunk Court," which levies fines and can even sentence repeat offenders to prison time at Oakalla.

"He said he can't see anything wrong with permitting a person to take a bottle into a restaurant or cabaret, buy ice and mixer there, and have a few drinks," the paper reports of Isman's position. "He said he imagined hundreds of people get away with drinking in unlicensed places every night and only a few get caught."

Several weeks later, Johann Strauss Kaffeehaus itself will be charged with allowing unlicensed liquor, along with the owners of three other nightspots including the Smilin' Buddha Cabaret, The Livin' Room, and Hofbrau Haus Cabaret.

The charges against Strauss will be dismissed in early October.

Youth and liquor at an unidentified outdoor event, circa early 1970s.
IMAGE COURTESY OF UBC RARE BOOKS AND SPECIAL COLLECTIONS, GEORGIA STRAIGHT COLLECTION

JUNE 22, 1964

MAYOR BILL RATHIE and Vancouver aldermen receive a sobering result from city voters when, in a survey conducted by Ben Crow and Associates, 8 out of 10 taxpayers rate council's conduct as "fair-to-poor."

"Most voters of Vancouver consider their city council foolish and incompetent," declares the *Vancouver Sun*. "They also regard the council as a bickering, arguing, indecisive, immature, petty, and myopic group."

The survey was commissioned by the mayor after a public plebiscite (necessary for the city to borrow additional money from the federal or provincial government) defeated council's proposed $48.5 million capital works program. It was intended to examine the reasons for the public's animosity toward the plan, however, as gleefully reported by the *Sun*, the survey instead reveals a widespread dissatisfaction with city officials themselves.

The paper reports that half of city ratepayers "stated they were dissatisfied with council" and that civic officials have been guilty of "spending money poorly."

Rathie and his associates are hardly the first to be targeted by the *Sun*. A 1938 editorial rated Mayor George Clark Miller and his council as "the most inept, the most inefficient and the most lackadaisical bunch of time servers we have yet had to suffer in civic affairs."

Aldermen receiving the oath of office, Jan 3, 1940.
IMAGE COURTESY OF THE VANCOUVER ARCHIVES (CITY P41)

JUNE 23, 1971

VANCOUVER MAYOR "TOM TERRIFIC" CAMPBELL CHOOSES, in his own words, to poke "the hornet's nest" when he arrives at the site of the youth-occupied All Seasons Park late in the evening to gloat in the face of community protesters.

The occupation, which has been taking place since the end of May, is in protest against the city's proposal to allow a Four Seasons Hotel to be constructed at the entrance to Stanley Park. The issue is already a contentious one around Vancouver, with a civic plebiscite on the issue showing Vancouver property owners to be split almost precisely 50–50, with half wanting the project to proceed,

and the other half wanting the land turned into a public park.

"You've lost," Campbell sneers, telling the youths that city property owners have fallen short of the 60 percent majority required to overturn the development.

"We've won, and we're just beginning to fight," shouts a youth.

"Go see a barber," Campbell retorts.

The confrontation continues in this vein for a further 20 minutes before Campbell is forced to retreat amid a roar of obscenities, narrowly avoiding a hail of crowd expectorate. However, despite Campbell's arrogance and undisguised support for the project, the vote will quickly polarize public opinion and force city council to re-examine the development.

"If this isn't a vote of nonconfidence in council, I don't know what is," says independent alderman Harry Rankin of the plebiscite. "They have been remarkably irresponsible and unresponsive to the wishes of the people."

All Seasons Park will remain occupied for the remainder of the year, and the hotel development will eventually be scrapped altogether. At the end of his term in 1972, Tom Campbell will choose to retire from civic politics.

The All Seasons site will later be transformed into a public park.

Tom Campbell confronts the All Seasons protesters, June 23, 1971.
IMAGE © VANCOUVER SUN

JUNE 24, 1955

THE CITY REELS AS ALLEGATIONS of widespread corruption in the Vancouver Police Department gain a sudden legitimacy after the attempted suicide of Detective Sergeant Leonard Cuthbert at police headquarters.

"He fired the shot that tore into the left side of his chest at 8:15 a.m.," reports the *Vancouver Sun*. "Vancouver General Hospital authorities said the bullet came within an eighth of an inch of his heart."

The allegations, published in the June 15 issue of Toronto-based scandal sheet *FLASH Weekly*, and the result of four years of work by sensationalist reporter Ray Munro, revealed that Cuthbert, Police Chief Walter Mulligan, and a number of lower-level police officers have been taking bribes for years from underworld figures in order to keep the police off their backs. Local papers initially condemned the story as fiction, including the *Province*, for whom Munro worked until quitting in frustration over its unwillingness to go after Mulligan. The mayor and city council sided with the VPD, and Mulligan himself immediately sued for libel. However, Cuthbert's suicide attempt lends legitimacy to the story, suddenly turning the Mulligan affair into the biggest news story in Canada.

"I'm sorry I missed my heart," Cuthbert tells the two detectives who discover him.

Cuthbert had been despondent in the days since the *Flash* report, having spoken freely of suicide and noting to friends that he had paid off his boat and his property taxes. In the minutes before pulling the trigger, he had confessed his involvement to Police Superintendent Harry Whelan, and as a result of Munro's work and Cuthbert's attempted suicide, a high-profile police inquiry will

Len Cuthbert testifying before the Tupper Inquiry, 1955.
IMAGE COURTESY OF THE VANCOUVER PUBLIC LIBRARY

immediately be launched, revealing the involvement of a number of figures on both sides of the law. It will ultimately become the largest police scandal in city history, exposing corruption at all levels of the VPD and giving a sizable black eye to Mayor Gerry McGeer, who had appointed Mulligan in an attempt to clean up the police department. Further, it will be revealed that the city's police commission had known about Mulligan and Cuthbert's activities since at least 1949 and chose to take no action—even after Cuthbert himself confessed to City Prosecutor Gordon Scott.

The Tupper Inquiry will result in Mulligan's dismissal, thanks to the testimony of several key witnesses, including Cuthbert himself (who will survive) and Superintendent Whelan (who, while blameless and having provided compelling evidence, will choose to shoot himself rather than have several embarrassing family secrets revealed at his cross-examination). Despite the publicity, no police officer involved in the operation will spend any time in prison.

Mulligan will flee the country before the end of the Tupper Inquiry, spending the rest of his career as a limousine driver at Los Angeles Airport.

JUNE 25, 1958

LOCAL DAILIES BUZZ WITH THE NEWS THAT, following years of plebiscites, lobbying, and prosecutions, a bylaw legalizing Sunday sports has been approved by council.

"Council Tuesday passed a bylaw authorizing the playing of, and charging admission for, the following: baseball, softball, ice hockey, ice and roller skating, rugby, soccer, Canadian football, golf, tennis, lacrosse, bowling (indoor and outdoor), cycling, badminton and swimming," the *Vancouver Sun* explains. "Other sports can be added at the discretion of council on application of interested parties. Among those omitted are American football, played by the University of BC and Vancouver College, and grass hockey."

The bylaw comes following a three to two BC Court of Appeal decision, which ruled in favour of allowing the practice. Vancouverites have been agitating for Sunday sports since 1949, when the first city-wide plebiscite on the issue was held. A number of other referendums have taken place throughout the early 1950s, amid heavy lobbying of the provincial government by city council, and a high-profile clash between the Lord's Day Alliance (a local group opposed to any Sunday activity) and the Vancouver Mounties, the city's professional baseball team (for whom Sunday games are a source of considerable revenue).

"Sunday sport supporters thought their battle won early this year when the legislature, acting on the passage of Vancouver's second plebiscite, amended the city's charter to permit commercial sport between 1 and 6 p.m. Sundays," a June 12 article in the *Vancouver Sun* explains. "Officials of the Lord's Day Alliance claimed the province did not have the power to pass the amendment."

The *Lord's Day Act*, a federal statute that prohibits a number of different activities on Sundays—among them the hiring of horses, the carrying of milk or cheese, and "all operations concerned with the making of maple sugar and maple syrup"—has been in place since 1907. However, the BC Court of Appeal ruling upheld the legislature's decision to at last allow Sunday sport. A mere two weeks later, the change has been written into a brand new city bylaw.

"I'm most happy the court of appeal brought down a favorable decision," gushed Alderman Ernie Broome at news of the June 12 decision. "It's very gratifying to know that finally the expressed desires of the people of Vancouver will be realized."

Although the case will be challenged all the way to the Supreme Court of Canada, Sunday sports will remain legal between 1 p.m. and 6 p.m. All other types of Sunday business and entertainment will remain illegal into the 1970s.

"This just the beginning," Alderman J.W. Cornett gripes. "Next it will be Sunday movies."

Baseball, 1918.
IMAGE COURTESY OF THE VANCOUVER ARCHIVES (CVA 99-602, PHOTOGRAPHER STUART THOMSON)

JUNE 26, 1890

Construction of the street railway on Granville, 1912.
IMAGE COURTESY OF THE VANCOUVER ARCHIVES (STR N244.2, PHOTOGRAPHER DAVID H. BUCHAN)

AMAZED CITIZENS GATHER and local papers rejoice as, after a year of planning and construction, the city's first electric streetcar makes its inaugural trip.

"Each car was filled by well to do citizens while a large number of small boys ran after it and at times had to exert themselves to their utmost to keep within any kind of speaking distance of it," the *Vancouver World* will report the following day. "A group of 30–40 mongols seemed especially astonished and could not suppress [*sic*] their ejaculations of curiosity."

While regular passenger service isn't scheduled to begin for several days, a test run of the entire 9.6 kilometre route (at a maximum allowable speed of 10 kilometres per hour) is deemed a complete success and followed by a day of free rides for the public. And, as Car Number 14 makes its rounds (though the company possesses only five cars, they have numbered them 10 to 15 to make the fleet seem more impressive) under the careful direction of conductor Dugald Carmichael, the event is hailed by locals as a historic event in the evolution of the city.

"The long distances one is obliged to travel in going to or from the various sections of the city rendered rapid locomotion necessary," the *World* will explain, "and this could only be obtained by means of electric power, which is now fast taking the lead all the world over. Not only to the business man who, in the heart of the city, finds it necessary to go at full speed in order to keep up with his work, but more especially to the residents in the suburbs, this electric tramway will indeed be a blessing."

The decision to switch from horse-drawn carriages to electric power caused a considerable amount of stir when it was first discussed.

While horse-drawn streetcars have existed since the 1860s, electric trams are still relatively new, with the first commercial streetcar in North America having only begun operation in Cleveland six years earlier. However, the Vancouver Electric Light and Railway Company (with future mayor David Oppenheimer serving as director) was convinced to sell its horses and stables, invest in wires and track, and ultimately take its place as only the third electric tramway in the country. (Victoria's began operation one year earlier.) Sensing the historic nature of the occasion, conductor Carmichael keeps the very first nickel fare, paid to him by passenger Lillian Parkes and later hanging it from his pocketwatch chain (though, as he will later note, he replaced it with a nickel of his own).

While initial revenues will be disastrous (the company will go into liquidation only two years later), the line will expand as Vancouver's population surges into the first decade of the 20th century. By 1910, the fleet will boast 232 cars, travelling as far as Kitsilano Beach and Oak Street.

The last of BC Electric's streetcars will be replaced by road buses in 1955.

JUNE 27, 1956

TEENAGERS REJOICE AND PARENTS RECOIL in horror as Bill Haley and the Comets introduce nearly 5,000 screaming fans at the Kerrisdale Arena to "the latest fad in modern music"—rock 'n' roll.

Vancouver Sun music critic Stanley Bligh, however, is disgusted by the scene, describing the concert as "the ultimate in musical depravity."

"It has nothing of social value," Bligh continues. "With measured beat it dulls the perception of the listeners; then gradually works them into a frenzy which could easily produce a form of hypnosis . . . The result is a cacophonous noise that might cause permanent harm to not fully developed adolescent minds."

Despite Bligh's negative reaction, the 31-year-old Haley and his eight-piece band (already worldwide sensations for bringing rock 'n' roll to mainstream white audiences) so engage the thousands present that the teenagers openly defy the arena's ban on dancing and take to the floor for the entirety of the band's three-hour set.

"The law surrendered the floor to twitching, gyrating youngsters," reports the *Sun*. "The hall became a seething mass of flailing arms and legs, twisting torsos."

"The energy was unbelievable," radio disc jockey (and MC of the concert) Red Robinson will recall years later. "I bring on [the opening act], and then I bring on Bill Haley and the Comets, and all hell broke loose. They're screaming, they're yelling—you can't hear yourself. It was incredible. And that's why a guy like Stanley Bligh couldn't believe the atmosphere in the place. It was electric. Totally electric."

However, as Robinson will explain, Haley is well aware of the limitations of his age and the depth of his new-found fame.

"I interviewed Bill backstage, and he told me something," Robinson will note. "I said 'Bill, this has got to be incredible. You're at the top of the charts, you're big worldwide.' And he said 'No Red, this'll probably be our last run for this year. There's this young guy out of Memphis they call the Hillbilly Cat. He's young, he's good-looking, and he does rock 'n' roll. And he's going to put us on the back shelf."

Only a few months later, the "Hillbilly Cat," Elvis Presley, will emerge on the world stage, cementing rock 'n' roll as a legitimate genre and, in the process, becoming the single most famous entertainer of his generation.

Bill Haley and Red Robinson, June 27, 1956.
IMAGE COURTESY OF THE RED ROBINSON COLLECTION.

JUNE 28, 1973

FOLLOWING AN UNREMARKABLE 13-episode first season, the *Vancouver Province* dedicates a full page to a made-in-BC television show renewed on an "act of faith," a show that is now head-to-head with *Hockey Night in Canada* as the country's most-watched program: *The Beachcombers*.

"*The Beachcombers* is a strange program to become such a success, because it lies in no particular category of television entertainment," the paper reports. "In the convoluted jargon of the broadcasting corporation, it is typed as a 'kid-ults' series; meaning, of course, its appeal lies with both children and their elders. Normally, trying to cater for such widely varying tastes would mean disaster, but somehow Gerussi and his small cast of Canadian actors have pulled it off."

The series, which stars veteran Canadian actor Bruno Gerussi, first aired in October 1972 and has, after considerable wrangling by CBC executives, been renewed for a 26-episode second season. The series—created by Marc and L.S. Strange as a replacement for the network's outdoor adventure hit *Rainbow Country* and tailored by executives to fit similar locations and characters—features a core cast of five, is filmed in the small Sunshine Coast town of Gibson's Landing, and costs approximately $50,000 an episode, which is inexpensive by Canadian TV standards. Early in 1973, the show has begun to enjoy a sharp rise in ratings as CBC broadcasts reruns throughout the summer hiatus in an effort to generate viewer interest.

"The other day I went over to Long Beach and I couldn't get out of the beer parlor for signing autographs," star Gerussi remarks.

However, despite its new-found success, the series is already plagued by problems and personality conflicts; creators Marc and L.S. Strange left the show before the beginning of the first season over disagreements with the CBC. In the months to follow, Bruno Gerussi's continued involvement will suddenly become very much in doubt as he engages in a high-profile war with story editor Suzanne Finlay over the poor quality of the series' scripts. By Season 5, Gerussi (notorious for his battles with the network and described affectionately as "a gigantic pain in the ass" by show co-creator Marc Strange) will be weary of *The Beachcombers* and on the verge of quitting, a decision only reconsidered after the return of Marc and L.S. Strange, who will take over the story department.

In the years to follow, *The Beachcombers* will become the most well-known series on Canadian television, employing hundreds of local actors, among them Jackson Davies, Pat John, and Moira Walley-Beckett (later a writer/producer on AMC's *Breaking Bad*).

The show will run for 19 seasons and be aired in more than 50 countries.

"Beachcombers" at Second Beach, circa 1890.
IMAGE COURTESY OF THE VANCOUVER ARCHIVES (SGN 5, PHOTOGRAPHER RICHARD H. TRUEMAN)

16. SECOND BEACH. VANCOUVER. B.C.

TRUEMAN. PHOTO.
VANCOUVER. B.C.

JUNE 29, 1956

AUDIENCES FILL TWO ROOMS at the Vancouver Art Gallery, spilling out into the hallway and taking up every available seat and space as the Vancouver area Flying Saucer Club plays host to Daniel W. Fry, "the man who touched a flying saucer."

"A room was reserved for 150," the *Vancouver Sun* reports, "but half an hour before his lecture began the crowd overflowed into a second room and into the halls. People shared chairs, sat on the floor, jammed into every inch of standing space."

Fry, a former explosives supervisor at New Mexico's infamous White Sands Proving Ground, claims to have been contacted on multiple occasions by an extraterrestrial creature named Alan (pronounced *A-Lawn*), who shared with him information about physics, the history of civilization, and the secrets of the lost lands of Atlantis and Lemuria.

"It was the evening of July 4, 1950, when a flying saucer whisked him from the desert to New York," the *Sun* reports. "He had just missed the bus that was to take him to Las Cruces with the rest of the camp to see a fireworks display. The trip to New York and back took 30 minutes. He was in bed before the other men returned to White Sands."

Vancouver Museum and Art Gallery, 1932.
IMAGE COURTESY OF THE VANCOUVER ARCHIVES (CVA 677-711.6, PHOTOGRAPHER PHILIP T. TIMMS)

Fry's talk, eagerly supported by the Flying Saucer Club, also includes a showing of a number of 16-millimetre films of his UFO encounters. Fry, who has since published a book about the experiences entitled *The White Sands Incident*, has become a minor celebrity among "West Coast saucerpeople" in recent years, both as the founder of Understanding, Inc., an organization dedicated to "preparing [humans] for their inevitable meetings with other races from space," and as one of the originators of the burgeoning "contactee" movement.

However, Fry has also failed a lie detector test about the incident (an experience he has dismissed as "far from unprejudiced"), and subsequent analysis of his amateur films will prove them to be faked. He will eventually retire to Alamogordo, New Mexico, and be awarded an honorary Doctorate of "Cosmism" from a mail-order outfit in London.

"The stocky associate of men of outer space told this tale with a straight face Thursday night," the *Sun* reports. "Not one person in the crowd that jammed two rooms in the Art Gallery laughed. They didn't even smirk."

JUNE 30, 1923

AFTER YEARS OF AGITATION by Vancouverites and British Columbians, *An Act Respecting Chinese Immigration* receives royal assent, effectively banning all immigration from China.

"The entry to or landing in Canada of persons of Chinese origin or descent irrespective of allegiance or citizenship, is confined to the following classes," reads the text of the bill, which goes on to name students, diplomats, and children born in Canada to Chinese parents. "No person of Chinese origin or descent other than the classes mentioned . . . shall be permitted to enter or land in Canada elsewhere than at the ports of Vancouver and Victoria."

Although many BC citizens and politicians have been pushing for total Oriental exclusion since at least the 1860s, the act itself is greeted with little celebration. Its supporters, who favour a total ban, still view it as conditional given its allowance of certain classes. Chinese labourers were originally brought to Canada in droves to assist with the construction of the Canadian Pacific Railroad, and Vancouver's West End was cleared largely as a result of Chinese labour. But anti-Asian sentiment in British Columbia—the province with the highest number of Asian citizens in the country, higher even than provinces with substantially larger populations—has remained at a consistent pitch for the better part of 60 years.

Neither is the act the first of its kind; in fact, it is preceded by a number of earlier measures designed to restrict Chinese immigration, including one enacted in 1885, another in 1900, and still another in 1903 (the latter imposing a substantial head tax on any new arrivals), enforced by fines of up to $3,000, deportation, or prison terms of up to 12 months. All decisions are made by the controller at the point of entry, and no appeals are possible.

For the next 44 years, only 24 Chinese immigrants will enter Canada.

Race won't be removed as a barrier to immigration until 1967.

JULY 1, 1936

CITIZENS DANCE IN THE STREETS, the local papers swoon, and a procession of gaily decorated automobiles parades through the streets as, on Dominion Day, Mayor L.D. Taylor cuts the silk ribbon on the newly completed Georgia Viaduct.

"The city now possesses a new artery of traffic that will be the means of saving much time to residents, merchants and others, as well as preventing much congestion on the down town thorough-fares," the *Vancouver Daily World* will report the following day. "The automobile parade, held in connection with the ceremony, came up to all expectations, some of the motor-driven vehicles being most handsomely decorated."

The $494,000 "incombustible" structure, which provides Vancouverites with an easy crossing over the waters of False Creek (land reclamation below is still several years away), is the result of three years of planning and construction, and is designed by Minneapolis contractor C.A.P. Turner (lauded as the inventor of the much-anticipated mushroom concrete column). First approved in 1912 after a design contest that saw entries from all over Canada and the US, the structure will be given all manner of official names, from the Georgia Harris Bridge to the King George V Bridge and even the William Hart-McHarg Viaduct (suggested by Mayor Taylor, after a local lawyer killed in action at Ypres), none of which will stick.

Though much fuss is made over its fireproof nature and innovative design, the viaduct contains a number of serious flaws in its construction—something that will become evident when, within 10 years, it begins shedding large chunks of concrete onto people and vehicles below. The concrete itself is riddled with weak spots, the supports are mismatched, and by the 1960s, portions of the span will have to be reinforced with wooden support beams to keep it from sagging.

Though it will remain in use into the 1970s, the viaduct will grow steadily more unstable, with a 25 mile per hour speed limit and 4-ton load ceiling established to preserve it until the construction of a replacement.

When the viaduct is finally demolished in 1971, portions of the concrete handrails will have become so brittle that workers will be able to remove them by hand.

Boats under the Georgia Viaduct, 1939.
IMAGE COURTESY OF THE VANCOUVER ARCHIVES (CVA 260-1038, PHOTOGRAPHER JAMES CROOKALL)

JULY 2, 1936

A LARGE NUMBER OF CITIZENS and roughly 200 invited guests assemble at 2 p.m. in Strathcona Park as former prime minister R.B. Bennett and Mayor Gerry McGeer lay the cornerstone for Vancouver's new $1 million City Hall.

"Although the addresses were in a serious vein, the gathering was in gay spirits," explains the *Vancouver Province*. "The official stand was brightly decorated with red, white and blue bunting and flags were plentiful. A huge Canadian ensign hung above the main archway, to the east of which the cornerstone was laid."

"This City Hall will be the guardian watchtower of your city," Bennett declares before the crowd. "It is worthy of your pride and should reflect your wisdom. It should be the symbol of your collective power—the sentinel overlooking your city."

Vancouver City Hall has changed locations a number of times over the years: council's first meetings were held in the city courthouse (which also served as the jail and the home of Vancouver's first constable, Jonathan Miller), subsequently moving to Powell Street, then Westminster (later Main) Street, and now—as construction takes place—into a temporary headquarters in the Holden Building on Hastings Street. Once completed, the building, which will contain extravagant fluted marble pillars and gold-leafed ceilings, will be an illustration of the stark division between the city's more affluent citizens and the thousands of unemployed protesters who have recently arrived from relief camps to take up residence in the downtown core—some of whom are going without even basic needs. Mayor McGeer is already deeply unpopular with the city's poor for his suppression of a number of workers' rights rallies. One bloody clash became known as the Battle of Ballantyne Pier, and at another McGeer personally read the riot act to striking workers in Victory Square. Furthering this reputation, the mayor has also been a strong proponent of extravagant celebrations to mark Vancouver's golden jubilee (including the City Hall project and a $35,000 fountain for Lost Lagoon), opting to fund them through special issue "Baby Bonds" of his own devising.

Construction of the facility will take five more months, reaching completion in early December, after 330 days, and funded by only 600 sponsors. Despite having spearheaded the initiative, McGeer will not be the first mayor to inhabit the new City Hall; he will be defeated at the polls by George Clark Miller and won't return to civic office for 10 years.

"This structure we are erecting will be the temple of civic government for many centuries to come," McGeer beams as architect Fred L. Townley presents him with a silver trowel.

Moments after McGeer turns the first symbolic shovelful of sod, a stray dog wanders into the area and urinates upon it.

City Hall, shortly after construction, 1937.
IMAGE COURTESY OF THE VANCOUVER ARCHIVES (CITY P21, PHOTOGRAPHER LEONARD FRANK)

JULY 3, 1906

Chief Joe Capilano (centre), prior to leaving for England, 1906.
IMAGE COURTESY OF THE VANCOUVER ARCHIVES (IN P41.1)

HUNDREDS OF SUPPORTERS MARCH in a procession to the CPR depot on Granville Street to bid farewell to Squamish Nation chief Joe Capilano as he departs for England to lay a petition for First Nations rights at the foot of the king.

"I go to see the King of England," Capilano says, addressing his supporters. "I will speak to him of what his Indian subjects want; I will tell you when I come back what he says. I will shake his hand in loyalty for you. He is king of the Indians and the whites. Under him, all are one big family. When I see the king I will tell him that his subjects are all faithful in British Columbia."

Capilano and a delegation of approximately 40 (dressed in traditional regalia) are seen off at the station by hundreds of supporters, as well as by the city comptroller (Mayor Buscombe sends his regrets at being unable to attend), before travelling on to Kamloops and finally departing for London, where Capilano will present the petition to King Edward VII. The document pleads for a number of basic rights for the country's First Nations inhabitants, among them expanded land reserves, the removal of policing by Indian Affairs agents (their traditional potlatch ceremonies having been declared illegal decades earlier), the ability to vote, and remuneration for land appropriated by white settlers (as promised, it notes, by Governor James Douglas).

"Perhaps we are among the most remote of your majesty's subjects, yet we give place to none in our loyalty and devotion to your majesty's person, and to the British crown," the petition reads. "We bring greetings from thousands of true and loyal hearts, which beat in unison beneath the red skins of our tribesmen, and it is because of our love to your majesty, coupled with the desire to live in harmony with the white people who are filling up our country, that we appeal to your majesty in person . . . We have no vote, if we had it might be different; but as it is we are at the mercy of those who have the vote, and alas! They have no mercy."

The First Nations people of the Pacific Northwest have been agitating for fairer treatment for decades; in particular, the Nisga'a have repeatedly petitioned local government and politicians in Victoria for the same rights. However, Capilano's voyage marks the first time a delegation has made an appeal directly to the British Crown.

"We are but poor ignorant Indians, and know nothing of the white man's law, but we are persuaded that your Majesty will not suffer us to be trodden upon, or taken advantage of," the petition concludes. "We leave ourselves in your Majesty's hands, and trust that we may be able to return to our people with good news."

Though the delegation will be well received in London, no changes to British Columbia's laws will take place, and it will be more than 40 years before First Nations citizens are granted the vote. While Joe Capilano won't live to see his people granted the rights he campaigned so tirelessly for, his son Mathias Joe will go on in 1949 to be the first First Nations citizen in British Columbia to cast a ballot.

JULY 4, 1886

VANCOUVERITES FLOCK IN DROVES to the Port Moody train station to see Canadian history being made, with the arrival of the country's first transcontinental passenger train.

"Arrival of the First Train!" beams the *New Westminster British Columbian*. "The locomotive and train were gayly decorated for the occasion, and the arrival was greeted with immense enthusiasm by those who had assembled to witness it. It is estimated that there were 1,500 people on the ground."

"There was quite a crowd at Port Moody to see the train come in," pioneer A.G. McCandless will later recall in a conversation with city archivist J.S. Matthews. "They climbed up an embankment above the track to watch the arrival . . . [The steamship *Yosemite*] was free to all of Vancouver who wanted to go up to Port Moody to meet the first train; consequently everyone who could get away got aboard, and too many people went for the food supply. The *Yosemite* was not prepared to dine so many; there was no place at the railway wharf, Port Moody, where anything to eat could be got; many had not had their breakfast; so many went hungry."

The train's arrival will be greeted with great excitement by locals (though, according to witnesses, nowhere near the 1,500 the *British Columbian* estimates), with Mayor MacLean reading a letter of welcome to arriving CPR officials and an official bouquet presented to a "Mrs. O'Neill," the first female passenger. While other trains have arrived in the area carrying freight and laying track, the CPR locomotive is the first to make the coast-to-coast trip carrying passengers. Less than one year later, a passenger train will arrive at the terminus in Vancouver itself. Locals swell with pride, and the event is considered so historic that there is a rush by

The arrival of the first train in Port Moody, July 4, 1886.
IMAGE COURTESY OF THE VANCOUVER ARCHIVES (CAN P1)

those present to collect souvenirs of the inaugural trip. (Lumps of coal from the locomotive will prove popular items.)

"The amazing success with which this work has been effected has already, by the admissions of all nations, become one of the most notable events to be embodied in the history of the 19th century," Mayor MacLean declares before the crowd. "We earnestly hope and trust that in its traffic operations it will be an equally great success; and in that view we cordially congratulate not only the Canadian Pacific Syndicate, but the Dominion of Canada at large, and indeed the whole British Empire."

"The first train," the paper notes, "was only 15 minutes late."

JULY 5, 1905

Vancouverites recoil in horror as, at approximately 8 p.m., while wading near the mouth of False Creek, eight-year-old Harry Menzies is nearly devoured by a shark.

"Ed Dusenberry, who lives nearby and has several small boats for excursion purposes on shore, was standing idly looking at [Menzies] playing," the *Vancouver Daily World* will report the following day. "His attention was suddenly attracted to a wave approaching the small boy, as though some other boy were swimming under water to grab the wader by the leg."

However, as the wave draws closer, Dusenberry spies a dorsal fin emerging from the shallow water and realizes with alarm that the wave is, in fact, an 1,100-pound shark, "of the genuine man-eating Hawaiian variety." Thinking quickly, Dusenberry arms himself with a long pike and dashes toward the water's edge, bellowing at Menzies to come ashore.

"The boy ran; the shark followed," the *World* will continue, "and in three seconds was hard and fast aground. Mr. Dusenberry lost no time. He grabbed the shark in the flank with the hook of the pike pole and tried to pull it ashore. Enraged by the pain the shark opened its mouth and showed the most ferocious set of teeth he had ever seen, something like a man would expect in a horrible nightmare."

As Menzies clambers safely ashore, Dusenberry impales the flailing shark, ramming the pike nearly eight feet down its throat. Despite the severity of its injuries, the creature will take two more hours to die, require 20 men to haul it out of the water, and, by the paper's estimation, bleed "nearly a barrel of gore."

The False Creek shark, as photographed by the Vancouver Daily World, July 7, 1905.

Only hours after pulling it ashore, the enterprising Dusenberry will erect a tent around the creature and begin charging 10 cents admission. Menzies, son of Hastings Mill foreman Ed Menzies, will escape unharmed.

The shark's species will never be definitively identified, and the reason for its presence in the waters of False Creek will never be determined.

JULY 6, 1967

TERROR GRIPS A QUIET POINT GREY NEIGHBOURHOOD AS, without warning, two people are seriously wounded, two others are murdered in their own backyard, and multiple houses are riddled with gunfire by a man who will become known as the Point Grey Sniper.

"I heard what sounded like a shot," John Walsh (who is standing outside with his friend Patti Barrass at the time of shooting) will recall in an interview with the *Vancouver Province*. "I thought it was a rifle. I suggested to Patti that we stop and turn back, but she said there didn't seem to be anything dangerous, so we went on. The next thing I knew there was another shot, and Patti fell."

Although the sniper only wounds Barrass, some of his other victims aren't so lucky. Mr. and Mrs. David Webster are both shot through the chest in their own backyard, before the gunman turns his sights on the home of Mrs. Hilda Baxter and fires several shots through her living room window. Baxter, hit in the arm, manages to call the police, but not before the sniper shoots into a gathering crowd outside.

"A young couple were talking on the boulevard," witness John McFarlane will recall in an interview with the *Province*, "and a man appeared in an upstairs window of the house across the street and shot the woman. She screamed for several minutes after she fell to the ground. Her companion tried to get to her but the man in the attic started to shoot at him."

For approximately 10 minutes, residents cower behind automobiles, and on the floors of their homes, before Vancouver police arrive and arrest without incident a 35-year-old former RCAF airman named Arthur John Towell.

Towell is talked into surrendering by his parents (with whom he lives and from whose home he launched his attack). When taken away by police, he is found to possess seven rifles, five handguns, one shotgun, and 2,366 rounds of ammunition. He is promptly charged with two counts of capital murder and two counts of attempted murder. He refuses to divulge any information to police or authorities, and the reason for his rampage is never uncovered. Following his trial in 1972, Towell will be placed in Riverview Mental Institution.

"I just don't understand it," one neighbour is quoted as saying. "His parents seemed like such nice people."

A backyard in Point Grey, 1960.
IMAGE COURTESY OF THE VANCOUVER PUBLIC LIBRARY (VPL 42285)

JULY 7, 1962

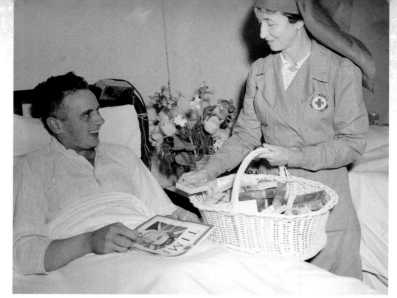

Red Cross Nurse handing out cigarettes at Shaughnessy Hospital, circa 1944.
IMAGE COURTESY OF THE VANCOUVER ARCHIVES
(CVA 586-2685, DON COLTMAN AND STEFFANS COLMER, PHOTOGRAPHERS)

WITH THE SASKATCHEWAN DOCTORS' STRIKE only a few days old, and in the midst of a countrywide debate that has been ongoing since 1961, politicians and doctors sound off in the editorial pages of the *Vancouver Province*, denouncing the "tragically controversial" principle of universal health care.

"The doctors would," one such editorial states, "oppose any national or provincial plan like the controversial one in Saskatchewan, on the grounds that it places medical direction in too great a degree under political control . . . Why, they ask, should BC have a compulsory, government-sponsored medicare plan when only 11 per cent of the people can honestly claim to need it? And this does not mean that the doctors want to ignore this unfortunate 11 per cent. They believe the provincial government could pay the medical insurance premiums for this group at far less cost than the price to taxpayers of so-called 'free' medical service for everyone."

Debate over public health care and insurance has been ongoing in Canada since it was first examined at a federal level back in 1919. Throughout its history, British Columbia has remained a leading proponent of subsidized health care, providing one of Canada's first provincial hospital insurance schemes in 1949. As far back as 1919, a BC government report called for a provincial health insurance system, and Premier Patullo's government drafted in 1935 one of Canada's first provincial health insurance acts, which advocated a flat-rate annual premium and provided for medical care (and even remuneration for income lost because of illness). However, since they were first discussed, these same measures have been strenuously opposed by the British Columbia Medical Association and its federal counterpart, the CMA; in fact, despite overwhelming public support, BCMA lobbying was entirely responsible for Patullo's decision to indefinitely postpone the 1935 *Health Insurance Act*.

In the decades to follow, public demand for and awareness of universal health insurance has continued to grow at an unprecedented rate. By the early 1940s, the first concrete discussions of a national health care plan began to take place, and while the CMA agreed with a federal care system (in principle), the association continued to oppose it in practice, demanding the right to oversee the system and levy fees. As a result of a 1964 Royal Commission's report, and in spite of continued opposition from Canada's medical professionals, universal health care will be introduced—beginning with British Columbia and Saskatchewan—in 1968.

"What the Commission recommends is that . . . as a nation we now take the necessary legislative, organizational and financial decisions to make all the fruits of the health sciences available to all our residents without hindrance of any kind," the commission's report will state. "There can be no greater challenge to a free society of free men."

JULY 8, 1934

Between 10,000 and 12,000 Vancouverites are on hand in Stanley Park, as the Vancouver Symphony Orchestra celebrates the official opening of the Marion Malkin Memorial Bowl with a two-hour program of classical music.

"For the playing of the musicians in their new surroundings in the great outdoors, it is a pleasure to say that it was invested with real expressive spontaneity and earned tremendous enthusiasm," reports the *Vancouver Province*. "As regards the acoustics of the Bowl, this writer found these eminently satisfying despite the views of

others who no doubt overlooked the fact that many of the listeners were roaming all over the lot and giving little or no heed to the music. Perhaps the freer use of amplifyers [sic] at future concerts will help along the good work. These, of course, should not be necessary if folks would only listen attentively."

The bowl is dedicated by Mayor L.D. Taylor, followed by a speech from W.H. Malkin, who provided funds for the structure and dedicated it to his late wife. The crowd remains undeterred by rain (which begins halfway through the performance), but because of a lack of chairs and insufficient amplification the audience misses many of the performance's subtler moments.

"No amplification whatever was used in the first half of the concert and in consequence it was difficult to enjoy the piano or pianissimo passages," gripes the *Vancouver Daily World*, "and this, with Dvorak's Symphony From the New World as the piece de resistance, was a marked drawback . . . After the intermission, with the amplifiers on, Strauss' 'Tales of the Vienna Woods' came louder and clearer but still not in sufficient volume to drown out the noise of shuffling, restless people who talked and clattered around looking for better places."

The Bowl's existence is the result of repeated lobbying by Vancouver Symphony Orchestra conductor Allard de Ridder, who convinced Malkin to finance the facility for use exclusively as a performance space for a summer concert series, sponsored by the BC Electric Railway. Starting in 1940, the venue will also be used to house Theatre Under the Stars.

"On the other hand," writes the *Province*, "do not forget it is not an easy matter to stand during the progress of a two-hour programme, which again prompts us to suggest that some thoughtful soul will provide much desired seating arrangements at the Bowl in the not-far-distant future."

Owing to rain, the orchestra will be forced to cut the performance short.

Malkin Bowl, circa 1940.
Image courtesy of the Vancouver Archives (CVA 1184-1963, photographer Jack Lindsay)

JULY 9, 1936

"ROTTING CARCASSES AT POUND Claimed to Be Health Menace," declares a headline in the *Vancouver News-Advertiser* as the heat of summer gives rise to a "dreadful stench" at the city's animal shelter.

"Vancouver's assistant poundkeeper charged Sunday that unnecessary delay in disposing of the bodies of dead animals during hot weather periods 'constitutes a menace to health,'" the paper continues. "The situation is aggravated," three-year pound employee Art Cornett, 43, added, "by the fact there is no proper sewer outlet for disposal of washing from the cages."

Generally, the animals—dead from natural causes or by euthanasia in the facility's gas chamber—are stored briefly on site before being transferred to the incinerator or the city dump. However, according to Cornett (who lives with his family in a home next door), it is often days before the corpses are disposed of. On site over the weekend, and fuelling Cornett's displeasure, were the carcasses of eight dogs and more than 20 cats.

"He said the dead animals were tossed into a 'chamber of horrors,'" the paper continues, "a small concrete box and allowed to remain there 'from Friday night to Sunday' in some cases. This weekend's hot weather resulted in 'what can only be described as a dreadful stench' in the area of the pound."

"I don't care if I lose my job over this," Cornett fumes. "But there's something wrong when these dead animals are allowed to remain on the premises in this kind of weather."

In the years to follow, euthanasia at Vancouver animal shelters will decline substantially. By 2010, of the 1,189 dogs brought to the city pound, only 25 will be put down.

A dog being released from the city pound, Aug 1942
(JACK LINDSAY, PHOTOGRAPHER, CVA 1184-947)

JULY 10, 1903

As Vancouver's population explodes, rapidly outpacing the growth of city infrastructure, local papers examine the latest addition to the waterfront's flora and fauna: human waste.

"Sanitary conditions that would be a disgrace to any city prevail along a portion of the waterfront and present a serious menace to the health of the residents of the locality in question, as well as to the city at large," reports the *Vancouver Province*. "At the foot of Burrard Street the sewer pipe has been broken off, and at low tide the mouth of the pipe is above the water. The quantity of sewage in evidence at low tide gives good grounds for alarm."

The reports come after numerous complaints regarding the city's current method of waste disposal (dumped raw into the waters of False Creek), with particular attention being paid to broken sewer outlets at the foot of Abbott and Columbia that have not been repaired, despite repeated appeals to council. In addition, due to tides, shallow pools of sewage are beginning to collect under some waterfront houses, with fears that they could serve as a breeding ground for polio and other diseases. The city itself will continue to lack a comprehensive sewer system well into the 1950s, with some sewage being deposited raw into local waters (from close to 60 known locations) and other areas relying on septic tanks (which will turn sections of the city into "a slime-covered, sewage-infected bog").

"There is no denying the fact that the need of some improvement in the disposal of the city's sewage is a pressing one, and should not be ignored if the public health is to be considered," the article continues. "As matters exist now, virtually all the sewage of the city that is discharged within an area bounded by Burrard Street and Columbia Avenue is allowed to float around on the waterfront, through the sewer outlets not being carried out far enough to prevent the discharge from being deposited on the shore in the vicinity."

Disposal of raw sewage into the waters of False Creek will continue unchecked for another 50 years. By the early 1950s, contamination of bathing beaches will have become so pronounced that the Park Board will be forced to close English Bay for swimming.

JULY 11, 1961

OUTRAGE ERUPTS IN CITY COUNCIL AS, after 60 years, Alderman Jack Moffitt suggests updating Vancouver's civic motto.

"Vancouver aldermen decided Tuesday it was time to bring the city motto up to the air age," the *Vancouver Sun* will report the following day. "When the debate came down for a safe emergency landing council voted 5 to 3 for the modernizing of the motto but only on the $15 badges the city is buying for aldermen to wear at ceremonial occasions."

Since 1901 the city crest has borne the words "By Sea and Land We Prosper," below the image of a logger and a fisherman. However, at Moffitt's suggestion, and after a furious session of debate, council votes to expand the motto to "By Sea, Land and Air We Prosper," though the high cost of replacing city stationery, paraphernalia, and badges worn by local police and firemen keeps the change from extending much past the ceremonial. And although the idea wins a majority in council, those opposed to the change are vocal in their displeasure; Aldermen Earle Adams and Bill Rathie are reported to have "tackled" Moffitt in the corridor after the session, and Alderman William Street dismisses the idea as "ridiculous."

"Cities don't go around changing their mottos," Street sputters at a press conference. "Next it will be 'By Sea, Land, Air and Space We Prosper.'"

This is not the first time council has attempted to add the word *air* to the city motto; an amendment in 1937 made an identical change but was abandoned two weeks later, again owing to cost.

"We applaud council's progressive thinking on such a vital issue," the *Vancouver Sun* will quip in its July 17 edition. "We only suggest aldermen take a close look at the crest itself, which depicts a logger and a fisherman . . . In future years, as amendments to the motto flourish, there will be room for a parking meter attendant, a dog catcher and a tax collector."

Debate will continue to rage throughout the week, and on July 19 Alderman Moffitt, thoroughly chastened, will withdraw the motion.

JULY 12, 1912

"ALEXANDER STREET TO GO BEFORE NEW YEAR," declares the *Vancouver Sun*, reporting on a meeting between Reverend A.M. Sanford (of the city's "Moral Reform Association"), Acting Mayor Sanford Crowe, and prominent city officials. Its stated intention: to "wipe out" the Alexander Street "restricted area" and the buildings being constructed there for "immoral purposes."

"Acting Mayor Crowe refused today to discuss the conference," the *Sun* explains, "but it has been stated on good authority that the police commissioners are now preparing to wipe out the restricted section."

Moral outrage over the city's red light district (which began on Dupont Street and, after moving several times, has finally settled in the area of Alexander Street) has been brewing for several years. The Moral Reform Association's recent publication of a pamphlet entitled *Social Vice in Vancouver*, which recommended the total eradication of the area, has done little to cool the fires.

"With the cessation of the vigorous criticisms from the Ministerial Association and Moral Reform Association," the *Sun* continues, "it is understood that the police commissioners are now ready to take action which would mean the breaking-up of the district referred to and the deportation of a great number of the inmates."

Brothels have been a familiar fixture in Vancouver since madam Birdie Stewart opened the first one in 1873 (the same year as the city's first school), and by the early 1890s, the city was home to close to 20. By the turn of the century, following a high-profile court battle between local madams and city council (who attempted to have brothels removed), local politicians and police chose to turn a blind eye to prostitution, provided it remained within a "restricted

Tiles in entranceway of Marie Gomez's former brothel on Alexander Street, April 1972.
IMAGE COURTESY OF THE VANCOUVER PUBLIC LIBRARY (VPL 85872X, CURT LANG, PHOTOGRAPHER)

area." Having first been pushed into Canton and Shanghai Alleys in Gastown, and then to an area just off Main Street, the city's brothels by 1912 have settled in the "Restricted Area," and thanks to a sustained economic boom, local brothel owners have been able to finance the construction of dozens of elegant buildings (conveniently located near the British Seaman's Mission). They operate with such impunity that, in many cases, madams (some of whom own their own establishments) have even spelled their names out in tiles on their front stoop.

However, within a year, owing to changes in the *Criminal Code* and agitation from moral reformers, arrests on Alexander Street will be stepped up considerably. By 1914, police will declare the area officially closed. Sex-trade workers will disperse to other parts of the city, and with the outbreak of World War I and a depression looming, prostitution will again return to the fringes of public awareness.

JULY 13, 1896

WITH A CITY-WIDE BICYCLE CRAZE reaching its height, and complaints rolling in from incensed pedestrians, council passes Bylaw No. 258, regulating the speed and freedoms of Vancouver's cyclists.

"The streets were largely macadam or wooden plank," city archivist J.S. Matthews will recall years later. "In winter, the macadam was muddy; the planks, frequently loose, had a nasty habit of squirting dirty water up the cracks between when a weight passed over, frequently soiling the trouser legs. This led to riding on the wooden sidewalks, especially in the dark or dusk. Pedestrians on these walks noised their objections with the result that a by-law regulating bicycle traffic and bicyclists was passed by the City Council. The fine for the first offence of riding on a sidewalk was five dollars. It was unlawful to ride a bicycle at night without a light. A license to ride was necessary, and the police were kept busy enforcing the law; a daily crop of charges were heard at the police court."

The bylaw requires that all riders equip their bicycles with a warning bell "that, when sounded, can be distinctly heard at a distance of at least 40 yards from such bicycle," forbids riding on sidewalks, and limits cycling speed to 8 miles per hour (with a 6 mile-per-hour maximum at intersections). However, as Matthews will note, while bicycle-related charges will be heard daily, the increase in enforcement (a $25 fine in most cases) will do little to curb the enthusiasm of Vancouver cyclists. In fact, bicycles will become so popular that the trend will lead to the construction of the city's first dedicated bike lanes.

"All kinds of gadgets were invented as accessories," Matthews will explain, "including 'fancy toned' bells (rung with the thumb to warn pedestrians to get out of the way), lamps of fancy design (which burned kerosene), extra hand brakes, handles and handlebars of high, low and medium twist, mud guards large and small, rims of wood and rims of polished metal; and they all had their advocates, some violent . . . The 'machines' were so numerous that the City Council ordered special bicycle paths constructed on those streets which were most frequently used. These paths were invariably cinder surfaced, and rolled flat, and ran along the edge of the street between the gutter and wooden sidewalk. They were about six feet wide, and constantly kept in order, level and smooth, by city workmen."

Local enthusiasm will continue to grow in the years to follow, with bicycling remaining popular among men, women, and even (as Matthews will note with chagrin) the elderly, and will lead to the creation of a number of cycling associations, including the Vancouver Cycling Association and the Terminal City Bicycle Club. However, in the years following the turn of the century, thanks to the introduction of the electric streetcar and the advent of the automobile, the bicycle craze will eventually die out.

"The bicycle paths fell into disrepair," Matthews will note, "and finally mysteriously disappeared."

The Vancouver Bicycle Club at Prospect Point, 1895.
IMAGE COURTESY OF THE VANCOUVER ARCHIVES (ST PK P174)

JULY 14, 1971

Maple Tree Square, Aug. 12, 1972.
IMAGE COURTESY OF THE VANCOUVER ARCHIVES (CVA 780-585)

"COBBLESTONES APPROVED," reads a headline in the *Vancouver Province* as, following three years of preparation, the construction of Maple Tree Square—the first phase of a Gastown beautification project intended to transform the decaying inner city area into a tourist hub—is approved by council.

"City crews will place red cobblestone brick, in a swirling pattern, from storefront to storefront on Maple Tree Square at the junction of Carrall, Water, Alexander, and Powell," the paper explains. "The $246,000 first phase, to be completed in October, will include underground wiring, antique street lamp standards, trees, benches, and ornamental furniture."

Revitalization of Gastown has been a local discussion topic for years, ever since fears of the area's demolition for a freeway in the late 1960s gave rise to a movement (backed by the community arts council) to save the historic area. The first phase of the $1.2 million plan (the remainder will be funded by grants from the federal and provincial governments) comes on the heels of Gastown's official designation as a provincial historic area earlier in the year, and it aims to transform the character of the area through the addition of cobblestone streets and sidewalk cafés, and a narrowing of its roadways to reduce vehicle traffic. Both BC Hydro and BC Tel have committed to burying their wires in the area in an effort to clear up the skyline, and a plan is also under way to convert the Stanley and New Fountain hotels into low-income housing to assist those displaced by the area's revitalization.

"Gastown can only be made natural again with the public areas getting some life into them," explains Larry Killam, a 32-year-old developer, one of Gastown's largest property owners and a strong proponent of the revitalization. "Gastown was built before bylaws were created."

Maple Tree Square was one of the city's earliest landmarks. Located outside Gassy Jack Deighton's Globe Saloon, it served as an unofficial meeting place and bulletin board, planted on the same block as Vancouver's first City Hall, which also served as its first courthouse and first jail. The revitalization project—which will include cobblestone streets, trees, and antique light fixtures along Water Street, as well as the Gastown Steam Clock—will take a further three years to complete. Prominent local property owners (Killam included) will commission a statue of Gassy Jack Deighton and, paying for it out of their own pocket, install it in Maple Tree Square without city permission.

The area will win an award from Heritage Canada in 1974 and be profiled in *Time* magazine.

JULY 15, 1959

MORE THAN 250,000 VANCOUVERITES CHEER and local dignitaries swoon as Queen Elizabeth and Prince Philip make a whirlwind 10-hour stop in Vancouver.

"The Queen and her husband cast a spell of friendship over the lower mainland Wednesday," reports the *Vancouver Province*. "The magic of her smile enraptured thousands who jostled good-naturedly on the street to get a glimpse of her charm."

The royal visit, which began in New Westminster at roughly 10 a.m., is described as her "busiest day" and "gruelling" by tour aides, and includes a total of 11 official functions in under 12 hours. Local papers dedicate considerable page space to every aspect of the Queen's stay in Vancouver, from her itinerary to her composure ("radiant") to her wardrobe (a "white satin evening dress with bodice and hem of appliquéd rose lace embroidered with pink crystals," confides the *Province*).

The Queen's official functions include the opening of the Deas Island Tunnel, a civic luncheon at the Hotel Vancouver (the dessert, featuring BC strawberries, is said to have been a particular favourite), a stop at Empire Stadium, a tour of Shaughnessy Hospital, dinner at the UBC Faculty Club, a brief sampling of Theatre Under The Stars, and finally an evening performance at Vancouver's unnamed civic auditorium—which, in a stunning display of originality, has been officially designated as the "Queen Elizabeth Theatre."

"Everyone cheered," writes the *Province*'s John Kirkwood. "The orchestra crashed out its mighty tribute and the massed chorus sang its heart out for a Queen . . . It was fitting that she should christen the theatre in her own name and by her own presence."

And, at 10:43 p.m., Queen Elizabeth and Prince Philip depart from the harbour aboard the HMCS *Assiniboine*, en route to Vancouver Island, a tour that will include Nanaimo, Chemainus, Duncan, and Victoria.

"The Queen seemed quite relaxed," Mayor Tom Alsbury tells the *Province*. "I suggested that she must find the tour a bit strenuous at times and she agreed but she was quick to say that her normal life at home was considerably less strenuous."

Only a few days later, claiming exhaustion, the Queen will be forced to postpone the northern leg of her Canadian tour. Upon returning to London, she will reveal that she is several months' pregnant.

JULY 16, 1952

LOCAL PAPERS PAY LITTLE ATTENTION AS, at an official ceremony in Stanley Park, the second Lumbermen's Arch is dedicated.

"Stanley Park's new Lumbermen's Arch was officially dedicated Tuesday by the head of the organization that made the new span possible," reads a brief article in the *Vancouver Province,* describing the ceremony (one which took place the previous day, presided over by city officials and representatives of the BC Lumber Manufacturer's Association).

A structure bearing the name Lumbermen's Arch has stood in Stanley Park for the better part of 40 years; the original structure, known officially as the Bowie Arch, was constructed in 1912 to honour the visiting Duke of Connaught, and was a much more elaborate, ornate structure, said to be held together without the use of screws, nails, or fasteners of any kind. Relocated to Stanley Park in 1913, the arch remained a popular destination for locals and tourists (hundreds of people carved their initials into its eight log supports) until, in advanced stages of decay, it was declared a hazard and demolished in 1947.

The new arch, completed in early May, is built from portions of a 65-foot red cedar felled in Stanley Park. It stands on a site that was once the location of one of the largest and oldest settlements on Burrard Inlet—the Squamish village of Khwaykhway. The interior of each log has been filled with concrete.

Controversy surrounding the correct spelling of the arch (Park Board literature and signage will refer to it as both Lumbermen's and Lumberman's Arch) will continue into the 1960s. In the 1980s, a proposal to replace the decaying memorial with a series of logging-themed totem poles will meet with much civic disapproval.

Lumbermen's Arch (originally known as the Bowie Arch), 1930.
IMAGE COURTESY OF THE VANCOUVER ARCHIVES (ARCH P41, PHOTOGRAPHER STUART THOMSON)

JULY 17, 1964

CITIZENS GASP AND ANIMAL RIGHTS GROUPS CRY "SADISM" AS, following a botched hunt in the Strait of Georgia, the Vancouver Aquarium accidentally becomes the first public aquarium in Canada to capture and display an orca.

"A harpooned, bullet-wounded killer whale was led into Vancouver harbor on a leash today, all in the interest of science," reports the *Vancouver Sun*. "Like a well-trained puppy, the whale followed the boat on the end of a 400-foot nylon rope attached to the harpoon."

The whale, which is towed (by the harpoon still buried in its flesh) under the Lions Gate Bridge to an improvised pen at Burrard Drydocks, was originally the target of an aquarium whaling vessel, under orders from director Murray Newman to kill the animal and to use its measurements to cast a life-sized, foam rubber replica. At this point, very little is known about killer whales: viewed only sporadically in the wild, they are still considered fearsome predators (newspaper stories discussing the aquarium's whale hunt refer to the whales as "sea monsters," with a "perfectly dreadful" disposition). In fact, so feared are the marine mammals that the Department of Fisheries has installed a 50-calibre Browning machine gun at Seymour Narrows.

However, the 5-ton whale (first nicknamed "Hound Dog" and later "Moby Doll") will defy all scientific expectation, proving to be a gentle, friendly, and highly intelligent guest during his stay in the drydock and later in a custom pen at Jericho Beach. In the weeks to follow (after the removal of the harpoon by nervous doctors), Moby will become a local celebrity, being viewed by more than 20,000 people and profiled by the international media, in the process transforming the scientific community's understanding of killer whales. Though Moby's pen could be easily destroyed at any time, he will never choose to do so, giving his handlers the chance to experience orca "language" first-hand and allowing UBC professor Pat McGeer to take the world's first orca electrocardiogram.

Sadly, Moby Doll will die after 87 days in captivity, from a fungal infection in his lungs. His passing will be mourned city-wide and even be noted in the *Times of London*. The Vancouver Aquarium's association with orcas will continue until 2001 when its last remaining captive whale, Bjossa, will be shipped to SeaWorld.

A moratorium will be placed on the capture of Pacific Northwest wild killer whales in 1976.

Dr. Murray Newman feeding Moby Doll.
IMAGE COPYRIGHT, THE VANCOUVER AQUARIUM.

JULY 18, 1921

THE STUDY OF THE ENGLISH LANGUAGE is transformed forever as the *Vancouver Sun* comes out with its very own "highly complimented" dictionary.

"While readers are eager for the book on account of its being authoritative and complete," reads an article in (unsurprisingly) the *Vancouver Sun*, "its absolute newness appeals to thousands . . . *The New Universities Dictionary* is new in all the word implies—new in contents, new in type, new in arrangement of helps to word study."

With breathless hyperbole, the *Sun* describes the towering achievements of its publication; compiled by university professors and said to be of particular importance to young people unable to attend school, the book is lauded as the only dictionary on the market that has managed to keep pace with the rapid evolution of the English language.

"Unaided, a young man or woman employed may learn the correct use of the English of modern business and society if they but follow the directions of the great university teachers," the article enthuses, "whose articles 'Standard English,' 'Practical Syntax' (which means: how to make good sentences), 'Punctuation' and 'Etymology' appear, plainly written in simple English."

The Sun Tower (originally The World Building) under construction, 1911.
IMAGE COURTESY OF THE VANCOUVER ARCHIVES (CVA 371-1274)

JULY 19, 1937

LOCAL BAKERIES PREPARE FOR SWEEPING CHANGES and ordinary citizens quiver with anticipation as after nearly a decade of waiting, sliced bread arrives in Vancouver.

"After every experiment has been made, and popularity assured, sliced bread comes to Vancouver," reads an article in the *Vancouver Sun*. "For a long time methods and recipes and machinery have been in process of improvement to slice bread automatically and to wrap it so that freshness can be assured to the last slice. Today, bread wagons of the makers of Purity Bread are carrying this new and better product."

Sliced bread, first produced in 1928 in the town of Chillicothe, Missouri (inventor Otto Rohwedder is said to have spent 13 years perfecting his bread-slicing machine before it was finally put on the market), was initially scorned by bakers, who charged that the thin, even pieces were likely to go stale more quickly than whole loaves. However, since the early 1930s, with the advent of Wonder Bread (which turned sliced bread into a national concern using its own version of Rohwedder's technology), the popularity of pre-sliced loaves has skyrocketed, causing a spike in North American bread consumption.

"People have found it is nicer to serve and quicker to prepare for the table," proclaims the *Vancouver Province*. "It does away with crumbs, cutting, and bread boards."

"Uniform slices!" exclaims an advertisement for Purity Redi-Cut Bread (the first to be sold in the city). "More slices per loaf! Toasts beautifully! Better flavor! 95% of all bread used in USA is sliced."

"I predict," says S.C. Boyd, manager of Robertson's Bakery, in an interview with the *Sun*, "that it will not be very long before every bakery in the city will find its customers calling for sliced bread to replace their usual whole loaves."

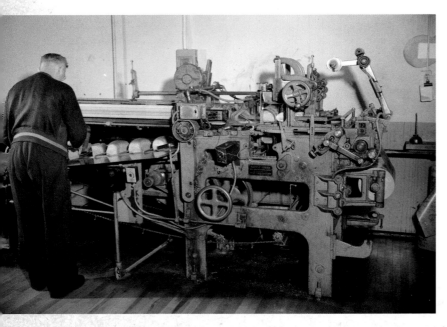

Man operating a bread-wrapping machine, 1945.
IMAGE COURTESY OF THE VANCOUVER ARCHIVES (CVA 1184-1815, PHOTOGRAPHER JACK LINDSAY)

JULY 20, 1885

WITH THE BLESSING OF THE PROVINCIAL GOVERNMENT, and the majority of Canadian citizens, the cosmopolitan landscape of the township of Granville is abruptly changed as *An Act Respecting Chinese Immigration* receives royal assent, imposing a substantial head tax on all Chinese immigrants.

"Every person of Chinese origin shall pay into the Consolidated Revenue Fund of Canada, on entering Canada, at the port, or other place of entry, a duty of fifty dollars," the act declares. "Every Chinese person who willfully evades or attempts to evade any of the provisions of this Act as respects the payment of duty, by personating any other individual, or who willfully makes use of any forged or fraudulent certificate to evade the provisions of this Act, and every person who willfully aids or abets any such Chinese person in any such evasion or attempt at evasion of any of the provisions of this Act, is guilty of a misdemeanour, and liable to imprisonment for a term not exceeding 12 months, or to a fine not exceeding five hundred dollars, or to both."

With the Canadian Pacific Railway nearing completion, and the need for inexpensive Chinese labour waning, the act is designed to staunch the flow of Asian immigration; in addition to the head tax, it also imposes severe penalties on any citizen who would attempt to transport Asian immigrants into the country, including severe fines, jail time, and the seizure of property. The act's passage is motivated as much by xenophobia as it is by fears of white labour being replaced by inexpensive Asian workers, and it becomes law in spite of federal government reports proving the value of Chinese labour in the construction of the railroad.

"This being the true state of the case, no rational being not unduly prejudiced against the Chinese could have been prepared for this measure of practical exclusion," reads an editorial (highly unusual for its time) in the *New Westminster British Columbian*, "which the timidity of the government, with one eye on British Columbia and the other on the labor vote, has hatched. To tell a Chinese labourer that, on his arrival in Canada he must pay a tax of $100 [*sic*], is to sentence him to poverty at home."

In the following decades, the head tax will be raised on several occasions, reaching its all-time high of $500 (the equivalent of two years' wages) in 1903, before the *Chinese Immigration Act* of 1923 will effectively ban Chinese immigration altogether.

By the time Chinese immigration is halted, the federal government will have collected upward of $23 million in head tax.

Men reading notices on Pender Street, circa 1936.
IMAGE COURTESY OF THE VANCOUVER ARCHIVES (BU N157.1)

JULY 21, 1969

WHILE THE REST OF THE WORLD is busy celebrating man's first steps on the moon, the *Vancouver Province* runs a full-page spread on another of history's milestones: the third annual Nanaimo–Vancouver Bathtub Race. The race, which occurred one day earlier, is described as "a stylish one, due to the large number of sunken baths," however, of the 300 tubs that left the starting line, 126 never made it out of Nanaimo Harbour.

"Slightly more than 70 seagoing plumbers received the coveted royal order of the golden plug, for finishing the 36-mile course at Kitsilano beach," the *Province* reports. "Glenn Filipponi, 14, of Coquitlam, was the race winner, with a time of two hours, nine minutes, 21 seconds . . . Each tub was accompanied by a more conventional escort boat, but in at least one case the escort boat broke down and had to be towed by the tub."

The race, the brainchild of Nanaimo mayor Frank Ney (who regularly participates in the event and tours neighbouring cities dressed in full pirate attire) as a way to put his city on the map, stretches from Nanaimo Harbour to the finish line at Kitsilano Beach. Since its inception, the event has been a regular part of Vancouver's annual Sea Festival.

Unfortunately, as the paper reports, the race was not without incident.

"One racer lodged a formal complaint against three tubs, including winner Filipponi's, charging they had jumped the starting gun," the *Province* explains. "Race officials solemnly questioned witnesses before declaring the official results."

At the finish line, Mayor Ney praised the racers for their "raw courage, and true bathtub seamanship," declaring proudly to the assembled crowd of 5,000, "we have again proven conclusively and incontrovertibly that BC leads the world in bathtub technology."

JULY 22, 1900

"Excitement at White Heat," reads a headline in the *Vancouver Province*. "Fishermen's Strike Rapidly Approaching Acute Stage."

"The striking fishermen on the Fraser River held an open air meeting at Steveston yesterday," the paper explains, "and, voting by secret ballot, decided almost unanimously to insist upon getting '25 cents or No Fish.'"

The fishermen's strike has already been in effect for close to three weeks, with total work stoppages all up and down the Fraser River, and patrol boats cruising the shoreline on the lookout for strikebreakers. Organizers and participants, which include First Nations, Japanese, and Caucasian fishermen, are campaigning for union recognition and for uniform prices for fish to match those south of the border. The division between fishermen and cannery owners is a bitter one, with canners threatening to evict fishermen from their bunkhouses and withhold food.

"Mr. Bremner, the dominion labour conciliator, was there to see what he could do to settle the unfortunate difficulty," the *Province* reports, "and when invited to address the meeting, said: That he had listened to Mr. Rogers and members of the Fishermen's union with pleasure, and was glad to hear the men's side of the story, but in view of the fact that they were to cast a ballot which might bind them to a certain price to be had for the fish, he would ask them to seriously consider the effect of their actions. Could the canners pay the price asked or not? He had been informed by a cannery owner, whom he knew personally, and in whom he had every confidence, that they could not."

Unfortunately the fishermen's strike has already begun to fray around the edges, and within days, Japanese fishermen will return

Salmon fishermen, 1943.
Image courtesy of the Vancouver Archives
(CVA 586-970, photographer Don Coltman, Steffens Colmer)

to work. The result will be internal conflict within the union, with Japanese fishermen assaulted, their property damaged, and their nets cut. Union vice-president Frank Rogers, the strike's de facto organizer, will be jailed overnight, and the Canadian militia will have to be called in to protect Japanese fishermen.

Within the week, all local fishermen will return to work, settling on 19 cents a fish and failing to win union recognition. For his demonstrated leadership during the dispute, Rogers will be elected president of the Fishermen's Union. He will continue to advocate for the rights of workers until, three years later, in the midst of a labour action, he will be murdered on Abbott Street by a CPR strikebreaker.

JULY 23, 1933

LOCALS MOURN AS, with its funding discontinued by the federal government, the Nine O'Clock Gun is fired for what appears to be the final time.

"The old muzzle-loader, which sends echoes reverberating back and forth between mountains and modern skyscrapers every night on the split second of 9 o'clock, was cast in 1816," the July 24 edition of the *Province* will report. "For nearly forty years it has given the correct time to ship and shore in Vancouver and before the days of wireless signals was important in correction of ships' chronometers."

And, while Ottawa has elected to phase out the gun (which costs $550 a year to fire) in the interest of economics, locals immediately begin a scheme to privately fund its operation. In fact, a number of $5 donations have already been collected by the Fire the Gun Committee and its chairman, W.R. Stokes, in hopes of keeping the 39-year-old tradition alive.

Though it has long since outlived its practical purpose, the gun is still fired 367 times a year (twice on Remembrance Day and twice on New Year's Eve), its three-pound charge released manually by Brockton Point lighthouse keeper J.H. Walsh.

And, as it turns out, mourning for the storied local tradition will have been premature; the next day, following a noon telegram from the director of the Department of Marine, J.H. Walsh will declare that Ottawa has agreed to continue funding the gun indefinitely. A small ceremony will take place at Brockton Point at 6 p.m., with W.R. Stokes proudly packing the barrel himself.

"On the suggestion of Colonel Spencer," the July 25 edition of the *Sun* will note, "a double charge of powder was rammed home to celebrate the occasion."

Though the gun will be silenced briefly between 1942 and 1943 as a war measure, and despite some electrical mishaps and its brief kidnapping in the late 1960s, the Nine O'Clock Gun will continue to be fired into the new millennium.

The Nine O'Clock Gun, 1943.
IMAGE COURTESY OF THE VANCOUVER ARCHIVES
(STEFFANS COLMER AND DON COLTMAN, PHOTOGRAPHERS, CVA 586-1646)

JULY 24, 1909

A LETTER IS MAILED TO THE MAYOR'S OFFICE warning of the latest danger to threaten denizens of Stanley Park: the public drinking cup.

"Dear Sir," reads the note sent from a Mrs. Benson of 1424 West Fourth Avenue. "Their [sic] is a great danger, let their [sic] be no mistake about this fact, that while it is the fashion to alarm the public about absolutely everything it eats, drinks or wears and while there is no doubt that certain faddists are carrying their messages to [sic] far there can be no two sides to the danger of the drinking cup."

Communal drinking cups are a familiar fixture throughout the North America of the early 1900s, before the proliferation of the modern drinking fountain (not to mention modern germ theory). They can be found everywhere from schools and parks to theatres and even apartment houses. Turn-of-the-century fountains, which like an ordinary faucet dispense water in a downward direction (upward-facing drinking fountains have not yet been invented), also feature a single metal cup or ladle chained to the fixture itself, from which to drink. Unfortunately, as medical professionals and the public are quickly coming to realize, the vessel also provides an ideal breeding ground for communicable disease.

"The mouth is one of the most effective of all our organs," the letter continues. "For the communication of disease and the rinsing of the cup does not remove from it the danger of contagion. Spending [sic] a short time in the Park and watch the people who drink out of one or two cups. We must bear in our minds whatever other precautions we may disregard we cannot lightly consider the public drinking cup used by all."

Mrs. Benson is not alone in her condemnation of the public drinking cup. Within two years, thanks to changing attitudes and the widespread proliferation of modern germ theory, a number of American states and Canadian provinces will have banned the offending vessel altogether. And, with the 1909 formation of the Haws Sanitary Drinking Faucet Company, the widespread popularity of the Kohler "Bubbler" (the world's first upward-facing drinking fountain), and the creation of the disposable Dixie Cup, Vancouver's public drinking cups will have, within a few short years, quietly vanished from existence.

As of 2007, the city will operate a total of 168 public drinking fountains.

JULY 25, 1970

"Subway Net to Serve City?" asks a headline in the *Vancouver Province* as a GVRD and provincial government study lays the groundwork for what will eventually become the SkyTrain system.

"A multi-million dollar subway in downtown Vancouver is being considered as one of the principal stages of a metropolitan rapid-transit network," the paper explains. "The underground system would be the nucleus for suburban transportation development over the next two decades."

The study, recommending a 20-year "master-plan," calls for electric rail as the most efficient type of transit, with a network of rail lines radiating from the downtown core. And, while a number of transportation options are discussed, the two most popular in the media are a monorail (similar to the type used in Tokyo) and a "French hovertrain that will speed passengers from Paris to Orleans on an inverted T rail at 188 miles per hour."

Transit will remain a priority for local government throughout the 1970s, and as part of a long-range regional plan for the 1980s, light rail will be adopted as the ideal commuter solution. While a number of possibilities will be discussed, the GVRD's underground rail system will be dismissed as financially unfeasible, with road-level trains considered the most affordable option. However, with the merging of Metro Vancouver's resources with BC Transit, the

Construction of the Dunsmuir Rail Tunnel, circa 1930s.
Image Courtesy of the Vancouver Archives (CVA 152-6.06, Leonard Frank, photographer)

timely purchase of the CPR's Dunsmuir Rail tunnel (said to take $50 million off the construction price tag) under downtown Vancouver, and the development impetus provided by the upcoming worldwide profile of Expo 86, a regional rapid transit system will suddenly become a reality.

Construction will begin in 1982, and the SkyTrain system will welcome its first paying customers on January 3, 1986.

JULY 26, 1888

AT ROUGHLY ONE O'CLOCK IN THE MORNING, after more than 50 years of faithful service, the SS *Beaver*–the most important steamship in the history of the Pacific Northwest—runs aground at Prospect Point.

"We were going to Nanaimo for bunker coal before going north to some island, Harwood or Thurlow Island," assistant engineer William H. Evans will later recall, "and from the time we left the dock until we were on the rocks was not very long. I think I was having a sleep and don't actually know who was on board except the crew, or if there were any except the crew. Anyway, I think the tide was pretty near high water, but still running in, because the captain hugged the shore pretty tight to get past the eddy off Observation Point, and the first thing I knew she hit, and that settled it."

Built in 1835 as the first steamship commissioned by the Hudson's Bay Company, the 101-foot paddlewheeler has, in its time, carried the HBC's James Douglas to Fort Langley (where he was sworn in as BC's first governor and in turn swore in Judge Matthew Baillie Begbie), played host to the province's first murder trials (which were held on its deck), and charted over 1,000 miles of coastline as an official survey vessel.

However, strong currents and pilot error will ground the ship permanently off Prospect Point, where it will remain, slowly decaying, eventually becoming a destination for sightseers and picnickers.

"We all got off," Evans will explain. "We were in too much of a hurry to pack up, and believe me, it would not have taken any of us three minutes to pack up, because in those days we travelled light. We all got off into the water and waded ashore; walked through the

The SS Beaver at Prospect Point, circa 1890.
IMAGE COURTESY OF THE VANCOUVER ARCHIVES (S-3-18)

park to the Sunnyside Hotel, and we were at rest, and peace. There was a peaceful calm settled down on us. The barkeeper, when he saw us, thought we had gone nutty because we had not long before left the bartender with goodbyes, and promised we would see him again, by and by, but he did not expect to see us that quick."

The *Beaver* will remain grounded near Prospect Point for the next several years, proving a popular photo opportunity for locals and tourists. There it will remain, until, dislodged by strong waves, it will sink in 1892.

JULY 27, 1938

CPR Pier D, on fire, July 27, 1938.
IMAGE COURTESY OF THE VANCOUVER ARCHIVES (CVA 152-12.5)

AT APPROXIMATELY 1:45 IN THE AFTERNOON, a small blaze starts on CPR Pier D at the foot of Granville Street and, within 15 minutes, has grown into the largest and most infamous waterfront fire in city history.

"I turned around to write a few words. Then back again," writes William Short of the *Vancouver Sun*. "The whole picture of the fire had changed. More than half of the pier was then in flames and white smoke started to come from a point where the Granville Street entrance should be."

Unfortunately, the city is woefully underprepared for marine firefighting emergencies, and as a result the fire (the most serious since 1930) rages unchecked for close to half an hour, with employees and volunteers doing their best to rescue railroad property before Vancouver's only fireboat (the ancient *J.H. Carlisle* anchored in False Creek) manages to make its way to the waterfront. Attempts to combat the blaze from the shore are largely unsuccessful, with the blistering heat keeping firefighters at a distance; flames grow to more than 100 feet high, reach the foot of Cordova Street, and threaten to engulf Piers B and C nearby.

"Everything was being consumed as the angry flames in their fury thrust forward and upward," the *Sun* reports. "A thrilling sight which filled one with awe at the realization of the helplessness of man before such fierce elements."

Burning oil and incendiaries (a ton of firecrackers among them) keep the flames burning for close to three hours. As fire department personnel note, with gratitude, a virtually windless day keeps the fire from spreading into the West End. More than an hour after the blaze began, a second firefighting vessel arrives from West Vancouver.

By the time the fire is finally extinguished at 4:52 p.m., CPR Pier D (as well as a VFD hose wagon crushed by debris) has been entirely destroyed. The CPR will estimate damages to the pier at more than $1 million. Following the blaze, a special fire defence committee will be convened to assess the city's marine fire preparedness, but, after a year of investigation, most of its recommendations will be shelved. The pier will never be rebuilt.

"Cause of the blaze," the paper reports, "was not immediately known."

JULY 28, 1922

AT 7:45 IN THE MORNING, after having been denied a last-minute appeal for clemency, 37-year-old Alex Paulson and 20-year-old Alan Robinson go to the gallows at Oakalla Prison, becoming the first white prisoners to be executed on the grounds.

"They kept their nerve to the end and gave no sign of breaking down from the moment when summoned from their cells to the adjustment of ropes around their necks on the scaffold by Arthur Ellis, the executioner," reports the *Vancouver Province*. "Both had nerved themselves to face the ordeal and both, according to prison officials, went through with it unflinchingly."

The execution comes after hours of intense communication via telegram and desperate attempts by defence lawyers for a last-minute postponement. The pair, convicted of the murder of well-respected businessman W.F. Salsbury in 1921, have remained on death row for the better part of a year. Their trial was a spectacular proceeding, with each man naming the other as the murderer and with Paulson ultimately turning king's evidence on his accomplice in exchange for a federal pardon. However, when the time to consider clemency arrived, neither federal nor provincial prosecutors were willing to uphold their promise of immunity, and Paulson too was sentenced to hang.

"Tell the boys to go straight," Robinson says as the noose is lowered over his head. "This game doesn't pay."

Paulson's last words are more succinct, saying only "Good-bye" before the men are dropped through the trap in the Oakalla exercise yard.

In the years to follow, there will be 44 official executions at Oakalla Prison before capital punishment is made illegal in 1976. Oakalla Prison will be decommissioned in 1991, and it will be bulldozed in 1993 to make way for a condominium project.

Isolation Unit at Oakalla Prison, circa 1950.
IMAGE COURTESY OF THE CITY OF BURNABY ARCHIVES (370-734)

JULY 29, 2009

Vancouverites head for the shade and turn up their air conditioners as a blistering heat wave subjects the city to the single hottest day ever recorded in its 123-year history. The 33.8 degree high—the result of an offshore high-pressure system that blocks cooler air from the Pacific—beats out the previous record of 33.3 degrees set back in 1960. When combined with heavy smoke from province-wide forest fires, the heat makes the summer truly something to complain about.

"Metro Vancouver's air advisory for the Lower Mainland asked residents to reduce emissions, and to ease up on strenuous activities if they are elderly or have cardio-respiratory conditions," reports the *Vancouver Sun*. "[Mayor] Robertson urged overheated Vancouverites to drink plenty of water and seek refuge at air-conditioned libraries, community centres, parks, pools and even the Sunset Ice-Skating rink."

On the bright side, seasonal water temperatures at Kitsilano Beach and English Bay are a full five degrees warmer than usual, bringing more than 14,000 people to Kitsilano alone and forcing the city to double the number of lifeguards on duty.

Summer heat at English Bay, circa 1929.
Image Courtesy of the Vancouver Archives (CVA 99-2046, Stuart Thomson, photographer)

"We born-and-bred Metro Vancouverites are simply not meant for the heat," complains Shelley Fralic in the next day's *Sun*. "We whine. And moan. If we wanted to be roasted alive, we say to anyone who'll listen, we'd move to the centre of the universe. Or Toronto."

JULY 30, 1910

A NEW ERA IN THE HISTORY of the city begins as, at the corner of Hastings and Cambie, the main branch of the Bank of Vancouver opens its doors.

"The new institution starts with a capital of two million dollars, and it is the confident hope of all good Vancouverites that it is starting on a long and honorable career," reports the *Vancouver Daily World*, "an early incident of which will be an important increase in the capital to its credit."

The company, whose Flack Block building also serves as its head office, voices its intention to remain fiercely loyal to the city

and province—even buying its furniture from local manufacturers. The institution also issues its own bank notes, which depict "scenes of the industries which bring prosperity to the province." The $5 bill features a shipping scene, the $10 depicts the lumber industry, the $20 shows salmon fishing, the $50 mining, and the $100 agriculture, all superimposed over a vista of the parliament buildings in Victoria.

"Yesterday was all bustle at the premises at the corner of Hastings and Cambie streets so that they might be in shape for the opening this morning," reports the *Vancouver Daily News-Advertiser*, "and while the interior has not been completed, still in a few days the bank will have quarters becoming an institution of this kind."

Two other branches of the institution are already open—one in East Collingwood and one at the Westminster Junction. Directors of the company include such BC notables as W.H. Malkin and Lieutenant-Governor T.W. Paterson.

"The gentlemen associated with the undertaking are of such standing in the West as to induce public confidence in any concern with which they may identify themselves," the *World* concludes, "and no doubt the Bank of Vancouver will speedily be recognized as being among those institutions which contribute to the high prestige which Canadian banking enjoys in the finance world."

Within five years, the bank will go into liquidation, having failed to acquire a significant depositor base.

Corner of Hastings and Cambie, 1913.
IMAGE COURTESY OF THE VANCOUVER ARCHIVES (CVA 371-2711, PHOTOGRAPHER RICHARD BROADBRIDGE)

JULY 31, 1944

CITIZENS CRINGE AND THE LOCAL DAILIES BUZZ as eight days of tension between counterculture youths and merchant sailors bubble over into the city's first Zoot-Suit Riot.

"Hand-to-hand fights between bands of noisy zoot-suiters and merchant seaman and sailors flared across downtown Vancouver over the week-end and left in their wake an injured policeman and at least one badly-mauled civilian youth and others with minor injuries," reports the *Vancouver Sun*. "Zoot suiters and merchant seamen have feuded since a week ago Saturday when a seaman was reportedly slugged unconscious outside a Granville Street café, but no violence had been reported until this week-end."

Squaring off in the dispute are groups of merchant seamen, and members of the Home Apple Pie Gang, an East End zoot suit crew that makes its headquarters at a café on Hastings and Princess. At the root of the trouble is a report (later found to have been false) by an inebriated sailor who claims that he was assaulted by a zoot suit gang on Granville Street. As a result, a number of fights break out city-wide between the rival factions, including a fight at Granville and Smithe (which leaves a zoot-suiter unconscious), one at Hastings and Princess (which sees a VPD officer struck in the face with a rock while trying to intervene), and one in the 900 block of Granville Street, which is viewed by more than 1,000 spectators.

The zoot-suiters, many from lower-income neighbourhoods in the East End, are unpopular with more affluent Vancouverites, their flamboyant style of dress (a *Sun* article notes with disdain that "the zoot suit reaches almost to the knee") flying in the face of wartime garment restrictions, which strictly regulate everything from jacket length to pant length to lapel size.

"Where local zooters get their illegal clothing is a mystery to the Prices Board officers here," an article in the August 1 edition of the *Sun* will claim. "They suspect some enterprising US Mail order house or black market tailors."

The next evening, a fight will break out on Princess and Hastings, and a procession of more than 100 will comb the streets of Vancouver. Sporadic violence will continue into the following weekend.

By the end of Sunday night, 11 people will have been arrested and six charges will have been laid.

AUGUST 1, 1928

LOCALS SWELL WITH PRIDE in all corners of the city as Vancouver sprinter Percy Williams, "the world's fastest human," wins his second gold medal at the Amsterdam Olympics.

"Percy Williams, the Vancouver sprinter who has so decisively 'cleaned up' at the Amsterdam Olympiad, will probably need an extra trunk to bring back the two laurel wreaths with which he is to be crowned," beams the *Vancouver Sun*, "and the host of congratulatory messages that have been sent him from the ends of the earth."

Upon his return home, Williams—gold medallist in both the 100-metre and the 200-metre dash—will receive congratulations from Mayor L.D. Taylor, Premier S.F. Tolmie, and even a telegram from Prime Minister Mackenzie King himself. In addition, he will be courted by a number of prestigious American universities and receive all manner of prizes, including a car, a set of golf clubs, and even a 12-gauge shotgun. Over the next two years, Williams will go on to win a gold medal at the inaugural British Empire Games, set a world record for speed in 1930, and win 19 of the 21 track meets he attends. In 1975, he will be declared Canada's all-time greatest Olympic athlete by the Associated Press.

In contrast to the euphoria of the crowd and the newspapers, the painfully shy Williams will never be comfortable with the spotlight. (An entry in his diary, made after winning the gold medal for the 100-metre dash, reads: "Well, well, well. So I'm supposed to be the world's 100 m champion . . . No more fun in running now.") In the years to come, he will vanish from the public eye altogether. Following an injury in 1930 that will end his sprinting career, he will retreat into a lifetime of quiet mundanity, selling insurance, and living with his mother.

Williams will continue to keep a low profile, being the only athlete to decline an invitation to a 1976 ceremony for all living gold medallists. In 1982, after years of living in obscurity, alcoholism, and arthritic pain, the world's fastest human will commit suicide, shooting himself with his Olympic congratulatory shotgun in the bathtub of his Vancouver home.

Percy Williams (third from right) at the Amsterdam Olympics, Aug. 1, 1928.
IMAGE COURTESY OF THE VANCOUVER ARCHIVES (CVA 99-3633, PHOTOGRAPHER STUART THOMSON)

AUGUST 2, 1918

THE CITY IS TAKEN COMPLETELY OFF GUARD when, in protest over the murder of labour activist Arthur "Ginger" Goodwin, the Vancouver Trades and Labour Council organizes a 24-hour general strike—the first in Canadian history.

"Though the possibility of a 'general strike' was talked of yesterday," reports the *Vancouver Province*, "few people imagined that it would actually occur. Today at noon, when the street cars faded off the street and the facts began to be realized the city was literally thunderstruck. Many people waiting on the downtown corners refused to believe that the proposed strike had been carried out."

Goodwin, a coal miner, union organizer, and socialist, has been involved in numerous unsuccessful strikes across the country, agitating for basic workers' rights (such as an eight-hour day) since at least 1912. Blacklisted in many provinces as a communist, and suffering from an unknown respiratory ailment (said to be tuberculosis), Goodwin fled into the BC forest when, after being repeatedly deemed unfit for duty, he was mysteriously (and some say suspiciously) called for service by the Canadian Army. Goodwin was tracked by a posse into the woods near Cumberland,

"Ginger" Goodwin

BC, and, for reasons unknown, shot in the back by Dan Campbell, a disgraced former constable for the Dominion Police.

The general strike will be received with considerable animosity by the public, with 300 men storming the Trades and Labour Council's headquarters on Dunsmuir Street, where the crowd will assault several individuals, force two labour agitators to kiss the Union Jack, and twice attempt to toss council secretary Victor Midgely out the window. By the following morning, the strike will be all but crushed, with local newspapers glossing over mob involvement and praising its actions against the city's "undesirables."

"This kind of thing will ruin the province," gripes Minister of Parliament S.J. Crowe. "If a few Red Socialists with pro-German ideas are going to run the whole country, it is about time we gave up, and believe me, I for one am not prepared to accept that proposition just yet."

Despite differing versions of the story (the police will claim manslaughter, while Campbell will allege self-defence), Campbell will never be tried for his part in Goodwin's death.

Ginger Goodwin in Cumberland BC, circa 1916.
IMAGE COURTESY OF THE CUMBERLAND MUSEUM AND ARCHIVES (C110-002)

AUGUST 3, 1910

THE VANCOUVER PARK BOARD receives a request from the Electric Railway Construction Company Limited proposing to surround Stanley Park with a railway line.

"Under instructions of clients who are now acquiring a Charter under name of Electric Railway Construction Company Limited, we beg leave to apply for a lease of a sufficient right of way on the foreshore around certain portions of Stanley Park between high and low water mark," the letter asks, "as may be necessary for a proposed electric railway."

The proposal, which calls for double-track electric streetcars (and overhead trolley lines) to run around the entirety of the park's waterfront, also suggests a number of "artistically illuminated" stations, a tunnel through Siwash Rock, and an elevator embedded at Prospect Point.

"It would form an added feature for Tourists, who could hardly fail to carry away with them much more favourable impressions of the park than it is possible for them to do at present," the letter continues. "It would enable those riding upon it, while enjoying the fresh ocean breezes, to contemplate the magnificent scenery of rock and forest on the one side and the wide expanse of waters upon the other."

Although a scenic railway encircling Stanley Park has been suggested once before (in 1906), the Park Board will remain opposed to the idea, citing damage to the park's scenic appeal. Undeterred, the Electric Railway Construction Company will continue to revise and resubmit its proposal into 1911, with the full support of the Vancouver Trades and Labour Council. Its final, desperate submission (in June 1911) will suggest a straight railway line, carving its way through the forest to connect with a potential ferry terminal at Siwash Rock.

The plan would, the company notes hopefully, allow increased accessibility to "900 acres of the most beautiful portion of the park which, at present, is absolutely inaccessible to any except good pedestrians, or the class wealthy enough to either maintain or hire suitable vehicles."

Map of Stanley Park, 1911.
IMAGE COURTESY OF THE VANCOUVER ARCHIVES (MAP 368A-R)

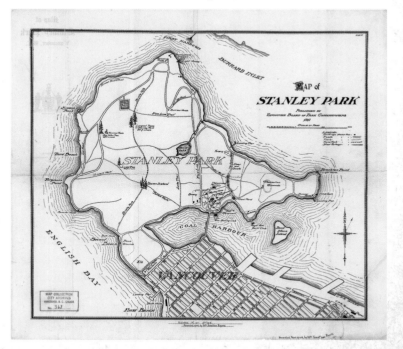

AUGUST 4, 1990

BC PLACE ECHOES WITH THE SOUND OF FANS, athletes, hot air balloons, a laser show, and a 200-member festival chorus as the stadium hosts the opening ceremonies of the third annual Gay Games, the first time the event has been held outside the United States.

"The Gay Games to me is a family event of another kind because of its sense of participation, of inclusion rather than exclusion," explains Max Reimer, producer and choreographer of the opening and closing ceremonies, in an interview with the *Vancouver Sun*. "There are many more than gays participating. This is not exclusively a gay event. It is a gay-awareness event."

The Games, said to have cost $2 million (and originally known as the Gay Olympics before an injunction was filed by the United States Olympic Committee), brings together 7,100 athletes (an estimated 300 of them heterosexual) and more than 2,000 volunteers, with close to 8,000 tickets sold. The opening ceremonies also feature more than 20 gay and lesbian bands, as well as a tribute to event founder Tom Waddell, a US Decathalon athlete who died following the 1986 Gay Games in San Francisco. The festivities will continue through the weekend as part of a major LGBT film, literary, and cultural festival known as Celebration '90, coinciding with the city's annual Pride Parade two days later (a parade that will attract close to 8,000, breaking all previous attendance records).

"It is so hyper, it's wonderful," beams volunteer services director Heather Williams in conversation with the *Sun*. "Everyone suddenly seemed to decide: 'This is neat, I want to be a part of it.' That's just fine with us."

Predictably, the event is not without its detractors; in recent weeks, a Fraser Valley congregation has bought advertising space in the local papers warning against an "impending sodomite invasion," and BC premier Bill Vander Zalm has refused to provide the Games with provincial funding.

"Perhaps I am missing the point, but I am somewhat confused by the declaration that the Gay Games are a celebration," writes Richmond resident Norma Plato in a letter to the *Vancouver Sun*. "The young athlete who first organized the games has since died of AIDS. AIDS, death and homosexuality are tragically connected. What has celebration to do with it?"

In addition, two young men are arrested following the discovery of homophobic graffiti outside BC Place, and by early evening, 40-year-old "preacher" Frank Soto (together with a 27-year-old male accomplice) has set up loudspeakers outside the stadium, making declarations such as "There will be no games in hell. Repent!"

Within minutes, Soto and his accomplice are surrounded by the Sisters of Perpetual Indulgence, a San Francisco–based group of activists who regularly dress in makeup and nun's habits. Shortly afterward, Soto's equipment will be dismantled by police.

The event will generate an estimated $18 million in tourist revenue.

AUGUST 5, 1965

AFTER ONLY 11 MONTHS, the final challenge to the city's Pacific Press newspaper monopoly disintegrates as the *Vancouver Times* publishes its last edition. "We're Taking a Pause," the headline will read the following morning, signalling the short-lived independent newspaper's abrupt—but entirely unsurprising—demise.

Started as an alternative to what it calls the "one-company control" of the Pacific Press papers (both the *Sun* and the *Province* became part of the same "holding company" in 1956), the *Times* has long struggled with low advertising revenues, a shaky editorial vision, and fiscal mismanagement (for example, staff once went through $200 of ballpoint pens in a single month), and despite its circulation, the fledgling publication can no longer afford to support itself.

"It is significant that until the end, the *Times* maintained a circulation of 40,000 copies a day," Jack Webster will report in an article for the *Vancouver Sun*. "These were people who liked the paper and wanted to see direct competition for the *Sun* and the *Province*. Other Vancouver people obviously resented the apparent monopoly of Pacific Press . . . The Times' promoters were banking, too, on advertiser resentment against Pacific Press. It failed to materialize."

Advertiser relations were never strong throughout the paper's run, largely, it is speculated, due to pressure from the Pacific Press papers, and the aggressive management style of owner "Val" Warren resulted in dozens of resignations, including, eventually, his own.

"Even before it published its first edition, the seeds of the *Times'* demise had been sown," writer and Vancouver newspaper historian Marc Edge will recount in his analysis of the paper. "Of the $1.8 million received from share sales by then, almost $1 million had gone to initial 'organization, development and finance costs.' By the time the first papers hit the streets, the *Times* was so cash-strapped that it had less than $200,000 on hand to meet working costs and a payroll of more than 300."

By the time the paper ceases publication, the newsroom consists of an editor, a managing editor, and two journalists. The *Sun*, by contrast, has a circulation of 240,000 and growing.

"It will be many years, I fear," Webster will lament, "before another effort is made to build a third daily newspaper from the ground up."

Province newspaper delivery boys, circa 1940.
IMAGE COURTESY OF THE VANCOUVER ARCHIVES (CVA 1184-863, PHOTOGRAPHER JACK LINDSAY)

AUGUST 6, 1884

NEWSPAPERS SPECULATE, decorations are furnished, and the populace hums with anticipation as Premier William Smithe, CPR vice-president W.C. Van Horne, and realtor Arthur Wellington Ross arrive to view the site of the railway's western terminus, in a town about to be transformed into "one of the great cities of the Pacific"—Port Moody.

"[Port Moody] has no rival," exclaims the *Port Moody Gazette*. "There is no place upon the whole coast of British Columbia that can enter into competition with it . . . These declarations are sweeping but incontrovertible."

From the time the CPR was formed in 1881, Port Moody has been the presumed location of the CPR's rail terminus, and, in anticipation of the delegation's arrival, the Elgin House hotel is "handsomely decorated with flags and evergreens" and festooned with two large banners, one that reads "CPRWT (Canadian Pacific Railway, Western Terminus)" and another that reads "Welcome Van Horne."

"He is evidently a man of large information and mature judgement," the paper exclaims of Van Horne, "quick to observe the natural advantage of different sections of the country, and a firm believer in the great future of British Columbia. It is his opinion that a city of 100,000 inhabitants will exist at the western terminus of the CPR in a few years, and though he made no direct reference as to the exact location of that future city, yet it was not hard to infer that Port Moody was in his mind's eye at the moment."

Unfortunately the *Gazette*'s announcement is premature; Van Horne, wholly unimpressed with Port Moody, has already turned his "mind's eye" toward a tiny, unincorporated logging village closer to Burrard Inlet. On the afternoon of the same day, the *New Westminster British Columbian* (whose editor, John Robson, is a provincial MLA with CPR connections) publishes word of Van Horne's intention to dispatch a surveyor to Coal Harbour to determine its feasibility as a rail terminus.

"There appeared in last Saturday's *Columbian* as choice an assortment of cast iron lies as it has been our lot to meet in a journalistic experience of some years," the *Gazette* will fume when it gets word of the story. "According to the paper referred to, Mr. Van Horne made some of the most extraordinary statements that ever fell from the lips of a man in his position. Now we have it on the best possible authority—from gentlemen who attended the meeting, and from Mr. Van Horne himself—that no such statements were made, nor was anything said that could be construed into such a meaning . . . At Port Moody we have every essential and the ROAD IS ALREADY HERE. That it will remain here for all time there is not the slightest reason to doubt—the contradictory and prevaricating *Columbian* to the contrary notwithstanding."

Shortly thereafter, Van Horne will dispatch surveyor Lachlan Alexander Hamilton to the tiny logging village of Granville, and by May 1886 (thanks in large part to a public address given by MLA and *Columbian* editor John Robson), the Burrard Inlet township will have been incorporated as the City of Vancouver. Shortly thereafter, Robson, Ross, and a select group of Victoria businessmen (all of whom quietly purchased land in the area following a tip from Van Horne) will become instant millionaires.

Map prepared by Port Moody real estate firms, 1884.
IMAGE COURTESY OF THE VANCOUVER ARCHIVES (MAP 316, PUBLISHER A. MORTIMER)

AUGUST 7, 1971

MORE THAN 2,000 PEOPLE GATHER in Gastown for the Grasstown Smoke-In, a street jamboree in favour of marijuana legalization that quickly turns into the most notorious example of police brutality in Vancouver's history.

The event, quickly dubbed "The Gastown Riot" or "The Battle of Maple Tree Square" by the media, begins peacefully enough, with organizers handing out Creamsicles, and students from Langara Community College parading about with a 10-foot joint made out of straw. However, claiming reports of rocks and bottles being thrown, four policemen on horseback suddenly charge into the crowd, followed by dozens of others, who indiscriminately attack those assembled with riot sticks.

"What did happen Saturday night in Maple Tree Square," *Vancouver Sun* columnist Allan Fotheringham will write several days later, "by the accounts of dozens of sober and sensible adults who were witness, was a disaster for future police public relations in this town. What happened was a police riot."

Both participants and onlookers are mercilessly beaten, with reports of police running down youth on horseback, attacking reporters, in one instance beating a girl in a wheelchair, and dragging a woman by her hair across half a block of broken glass.

"I wept openly," Gastown business owner Peter Fox will tell a public gathering of witnesses the following evening. "I have a law and order background. I have always believed that the police were right . . . I've always prided myself in thinking Vancouver was free of this sort of thing . . . but the senseless brutality that I witnessed created a great cultural shock in my life."

The Gastown Riot.
IMAGE © VANCOUVER SUN (AUGUST 9, 1971 EDITION) PHOTO CREDIT: GLENN BAGIO

In the end, 12 people are hospitalized, 79 taken into custody, and 38 charges are laid. By August 10, more than 100 sworn affidavits alleging police brutality will have been presented to city council, and the local media will be united in their condemnation of police. After several weeks of public pressure, a public inquiry will be held; however, 10 days and 48 witnesses later, the Dohm Commission will place blame for the riot squarely on the shoulders of the Smoke-In's organizers. No charges will be laid against any officer involved.

"The solution to a traffic tie-up was to break open heads," Fotheringham will write. "The mayor kept predicting a riot, it never came, so the police supplied him with one. If someone isn't sacked over this one, we live in a rather unpleasant town. Pigs is a dirty word, and no one likes to use it, but there were some pigs loose in Gastown on Saturday night."

AUGUST 8, 1887

AFTER MONTHS OF CONSTRUCTION, and opposition from certain stubborn aldermen, lamplighter Tim Clough is officially rendered obsolete as, for the first time, electric streetlights are turned on in Vancouver.

"People were tired of coal oil lamps," H.P. McCraney will recall years later in conversation with city archivist J.S. Matthews. "And in September 1886, three men—they were electricians—came up from Portland, Oregon . . . They had electrical equipment for sale, and approached local people to form a company, and so give the undertaking local 'colour.' The system did not spread far, just around Hastings, Cordova, Cambie, Carrall, Oppenheimer, Powell, Alexander, Cambie and Abbott streets."

The 32-candlepower carbon globes (more modern arc lights won't be installed until 1892) are powered by a low-output steam plant on the corner of Pender and Abbott, and, despite the novelty, require constant maintenance. In addition, the current generated by the plant itself is so weak that it only benefits the areas closest to the building; the streetlights on Granville Street receive such a weak current that they are barely able to illuminate.

"The joke at the time was," Matthews will later note, "that one needed a candle to find the electric light."

Images of electric light fixtures, 1913.
IMAGE COURTESY OF THE VANCOUVER ARCHIVES
(LGN 964, BC ELECTRIC RAILWAY COMPANY PHOTO)

AUGUST 9, 1907

Despite an extensive search by more than 30 officers, prison guards, and a bloodhound, police officially lose the trail of Bill Miner, one of North America's most infamous train robbers, who, a day previously, escaped with three accomplices from the New Westminster Penitentiary.

"It is the hunt for Bill Miner," reports the *Vancouver Province*, "the notorious desperado and convicted train-robber who, after having acknowledged that he had resigned himself to life in prison with its attendant good treatment for good conduct, cheated his confidants by planning and carrying out successfully one of the boldest coups ever attempted in the West."

The 65-year-old Miner, known as the "Gentleman Bandit" for his exceptional politeness while committing robberies (and who also happens to be Canada's first train robber), had been incarcerated for less than a year after a failed heist near Kamloops. By the time of his arrest (accepted with his customary good manners), he had achieved such fame that, when he arrived at the New Westminster prison, the tracks were lined with throngs of supporters.

"They excavated a hole under the wall near the brick smoke-stack," the *Province* recounts, "and escaped into another field of the prison grounds. Although this yard is surrounded by high fencing, the fugitives managed to scale this by means of a ladder, and got clear away into the surrounding brush."

Several promising leads begin to trickle in, and police believe the criminal to be "weak and probably footsore," but Miner's trail will remain cold. And, despite the boasts of Deputy Warden Bourke, the Gentleman Bandit will never be recaptured in Canada; after one more robbery, and two more daring escapes, Bill Miner will die of natural causes in a Georgia prison in 1913.

AUGUST 10, 1949

THESPIANS AND THEATREGOERS REJOICE as a proposal is put before council to relocate Theatre Under The Stars to a new home: a $600,000 artificial island in the middle of Lost Lagoon.

"Set in cement, the artificial island would have dressing rooms, scenery storage and electrical control rooms all below the surface of Lost Lagoon," reports the *Vancouver Sun*. "All that would be visible above the water would be a natural island of grass, trees and rock that would hold three or four sets during the Theatre Under The Stars season . . . Actors would reach the stage by a movable ramp or an underground causeway."

A model of the half-acre island has already been constructed, the first of five proposals aimed at expanding Theatre Under The Stars, proposals that include an amphitheatre at Little Mountain, an extension of Malkin Bowl, and two separate locations in the centre of Stanley Park. Rounding out the island model is a heavy growth of trees around the lagoon itself (intended to keep out non-paying customers), 7,000 seats installed at the site of the Lagoon Drive tennis courts, and a floating bandstand for the orchestra.

And, while the idea has excited the imagination, Park Board chairman Bert Emery cautions that it is by no means a reality.

"This Lost Lagoon model is not a recommendation," Emery explains to the *Sun*. "It is only a dream of what Vancouver must have if we are to give our citizens the best in open-air entertainment."

Lost Lagoon, circa 1946.
IMAGE COURTESY OF THE VANCOUVER ARCHIVES
(ST PK P197, OTTO FERNAND LANDAUER, PHOTOGRAPHER).

AUGUST 11, 1949

FOLLOWING A DARING STING OPERATION, *Vancouver Province* reporters Don McClean and Ray Munro capture the Lovers' Lane Marauder—a serial rapist who has been terrorizing couples in Stanley Park.

"Munro and I heard about the reports and rumours of robberies and of women being attacked in lonely spots in Stanley Park by two men posing as police morality officers, and decided we would try to get them," McClean will write in the following day's edition of the *Province*. "Only way to trap them, we figured, was to be decoys. I had felt that my training in the RCAF, though forsaken long ago for a typewriter, would come in handy. It did. And Munro, a handy man with his fists himself, took along his automatic."

Munro and McClean—who borrowed a red-haired wig from a friend and sported a sweater with "big boobies inside"—spent hours in Stanley Park, parking at the English Bay tennis courts, Pipeline Road, Third Beach, and Lumbermen's Arch.

"Taking no chances, Munro put his automatic and his flashlight on the seat beside us," McClean continues. "I attached to my wrist a billy I had borrowed from Traffic Officer Ed Comiskey. Then we did our decoy stunt—pretended to 'spoon.'"

The stakeout comes after months of rapes and assaults targeting couples in Stanley Park, assaults that follow a disturbingly similar pattern: two men, posing as the police Morality Squad, interrupt "spooning" couples, gang-raping the women, and savagely beating their male companions. According to Munro's autobiography (a self-serving, hyperbolic document that will also claim he is "one of the most honoured Canadians in history"), there have been 133 assaults in the previous 20 months, occurrences that have been kept out of the newspapers by the Vancouver Police Department.

Don McClean captures the Lovers' Lane Marauder.
IMAGE © VANCOUVER PROVINCE
(AUG 12, 1949 EDITION)
PHOTO CREDIT: RAY MUNRO

After several hours of waiting, Munro and McClean stop their car in a secluded parking lot near Brockton Oval. Within a moment, the driver's side door is hauled open, and a voice declares, "This is the Morality Squad!" McClean takes a swing into the darkness, connecting with his unseen assailant, and, after a ferocious brawl—Munro using his fists and McClean using the billy club—the two manage to wrestle their opponent into the back seat of the car (Munro's autobiography will claim he subdued the man solo).

In the days to follow, their assailant—a 32-year-old Coquitlam labourer named John K. Clark—will be held without bail on charges of impersonating a police officer. And, during his trial, thanks to the testimony of a 25-year-old victim from Courtenay, he will be definitively identified as the Lovers' Lane Marauder and sentenced to 15 years in prison and 10 lashes (five upon entry into jail, and five at the conclusion of his sentence), one of the heaviest sentences ever passed for rape in the country.

For their daring, McClean and Munro will be profiled in *Time* magazine. Munro will later be responsible for exposing Police Chief Walter Mulligan, leading to the largest police corruption scandal in city history.

Clark's accomplice will never be located.

AUGUST 12, 1907

At a meeting some 400 strong, the Asiatic Exclusion League is born in Vancouver, with the blessing of a number of city churches, prominent politicians, and the Trades and Labour Council. Its stated aim is "to keep Oriental immigrants out of British Columbia."

"After the most thorough examination that the Little Brown Man and his yellow cousins have yet received since the agitation against them, they were unanimously rejected as 'undesirables' at Labour Hall last night," reports the *Vancouver Province* gleefully, "their friendly opponents forming an Asiatic Exclusion League, the first in Canada. From every point of view 'the Jap' particularly was considered, and from every point of view found wanting in the qualities required in a white man's country, just because he is 'a Jap,' and the yellow can never assimilate with the white. Upon this all were agreed."

The league, which will quickly draft a petition to the federal government, has a number of high-profile supporters, among them Vancouver Member of Parliament R.G. MacPherson and Attorney General William Bowser.

"It is unnecessary for me to tell you that I am in full accord with your ideas of a league," Bowser writes in a letter expressing his regret at being unable to attend, "and only hope your efforts will be successful."

"Let me urge every one of you to become a missionary to preach this gospel of British Columbia as a white man's country," MP MacPherson tells the assembled crowd. "I have been called an agitator. Well, if to strive for that which is in the best interest of one's country is to be an agitator, then put me down as an agitator."

"There was," the *Province* notes, "an enthusiastic wave of applause."

Dupont Street (later Pender) in Chinatown, 1906.
Image courtesy of the Vancouver Archives (CVA 677-530, photographer Philip T. Timms)

AUGUST 13, 1958

"BEACHES CLOSED BY PARK BOARD," reads a headline in the *Vancouver Sun* as, following reports of excessive pollution, the Park Board bans swimming at all city beaches.

"[Lifeguards] have been told to keep children out and 'dissuade' adults," explains the *Sun*. "They have been told not to approach people until they are seen preparing to go in the water, and not to interfere with other beach activities."

The closures, posted on more than 500 signs and enforced by a team of 48 lifeguards, prohibit all paddling, bathing, or swimming in local waters, and come in the midst of a *Sun* series on the state of city beaches. The series reveals that, since the turn of the century, thousands of gallons of raw sewage have been dumped daily into English Bay, Burrard Inlet, and the Fraser River.

"Oceanographic studies show that water from both the Fraser River and Burrard Inlet circulates into English Bay to various degrees according to tide and season," an August 12 article explains. "This water carries with it considerable crude sewage adding to the large amounts already discharged into the beach areas."

Human waste in local waters has been a heavily discussed issue since the turn of the century. As early as 1903, locals complained of the excessive buildup of sewage taking place on the shores of Burrard Inlet. And a report, conducted in 1903 (while recommending utterly unhelpful measures such as dilution and diffusion), warned that local waters would become excessively polluted if a unified waste disposal strategy wasn't considered. (Even into the 1950s, BC lacks a basic provincial standard for bacterial testing.) This recommendation was later echoed by A.M. Rawn and

Swimming race at English Bay, 1905.
IMAGE COURTESY OF THE VANCOUVER ARCHIVES (BE P1 2.04, PHOTOGRAPHER PHILIP T. TIMMS)

Dr. Charles Gilman Hyde's 1953 report that urged construction of disposal plants at Iona Beach and on the North Shore.

"It is probable that," the report concluded, "unless corrective measures are taken to ensure the proper disposal of sewage, the degree of pollution will increase . . . until large areas of the beaches will no longer be safe for use."

Although the 1953 report has lain idle for five years, both the Iona Island and the Lions Gate Wastewater Treatment Facilities will be constructed by the early 1960s, followed by an additional three others, allowing for primary and secondary treatment of Metro Vancouver's sewage and drastically reducing pollution in primary contact areas. When pressed on whether swimmers at city beaches could be prosecuted for entering the water, an unnamed Park Board official is doubtful.

"At this stage, no," he says. "We want to see how it goes. We don't think [charges] will be necessary. We are not in the business of arresting people. We're supposed to be a 'fun' department."

AUGUST 14, 1907

"Cordova Street Lot Brings Big Figure," reads a headline in the *Vancouver World*. "Property Bought Two Years Ago for $8,600 Sells for $25,000—Building to Be Erected."

The 31-foot lot, purchased by C.S. Douglas (with two associates), contains little more than a decrepit building in need of replacement, with the new owners "considering the erection of a modern three storey building."

"The vendor was Mr. Angilo Calori, proprietor of the Hotel Europe," the paper continues, "who bought the property two years ago for $8,600. Eighteen years ago the same property changed hands at $8,000, which is an interesting item showing how slow property values rose during a period of years."

Property values will continue to increase substantially throughout the next five years, spurred on by investment by working-class people. (A 1912 survey conducted by the Ministerial Union of British Columbia will reveal that, during a single week in October, more than 40 percent of the land-purchase applications received were from the working class.) By 1912, Vancouver's property market will have become an orgy of borrowing, spending, and inflation, a place where, according to novelist Bertrand Sinclair, the common man would "go without lunch to make payments on plots of land in distant suburbs."

In the late 1870s, before the arrival of the CPR, land in what is now downtown Vancouver sold for approximately $1 an acre. Before that, the West End itself was granted to Englishmen Samuel Brighouse, John Morton, and William Hailstone for a total of 116 pounds—a sum thought to be so exorbitant that it earned them the nickname "The Three Greenhorns." However, by 1886, with the announcement that Vancouver would be the home of the CPR's coveted western terminus, property values began to skyrocket, and suddenly a lot near Granville and Dunsmuir was selling for $400. By 1893, a lot in the same area sold for $1,100, and by 1900, an adjoining lot was reportedly sold for $4,250.

By contrast, the average wage in the city is less than 50 cents an hour.

The Three Greenhorns, photo circa 1886.
Image Courtesy of the Vancouver Archives (Port P97)

AUGUST 15, 1895

To the delight of Vancouver audiences, and literati in general, the legendary Mark Twain appears for a rare speaking engagement at the Imperial Opera House on Pender Street. Twain, who has reportedly made more money from his works than any American author in history, has recently fallen on hard times and embarked

"Knowing for a fact that Samuel L. Clemens got up out of a sick bed (Mark was ill—not the bed)," reports the *Vancouver Daily World*, "and knowing that he was suffering severe physical pain, one can only imagine what a marvellous treat the audience would have enjoyed if the great humorist had been in proper fettle. As it was, those present were treated to 90 minutes of almost uninterrupted laughter. Almost is used advisedly because here and there there was a touch of real pathos."

Twain's stories, ranging from tales of his boyhood in Missouri and lectures on morality to an illustration of gender usage in the German language (accomplished by reading an English essay using German genders), cause the audience to roar with such laughter that at times he is inaudible. However, not everyone is as amused by the famous author's readings.

"Whether [the crowd's] anticipations were realized I cannot say," "Motley," a *Vancouver Province* critic, will write after Twain's Victoria engagement. "Mine were not and I wish Mr. Twain had read us a few more extracts from his sketches and other works . . . Nevertheless he impresses one as a reader of the first rank but only a second-rate speaker."

on a worldwide lecture tour to pay his creditors after a failed publishing venture. Despite being hoarse with a bad cold, the author and orator nonetheless manages to entertain a boisterous, standing-room-only crowd.

Mark Twain recuperates at the Hotel Vancouver, 1895.
Image courtesy of the Vancouver Archives (Port P329, photographer George T. Wadds)

AUGUST 16, 1910

FOLLOWING A SPEECH by Prime Minister Wilfrid Laurier, the Vancouver Exhibition has its formal opening at Hastings Park.

"Over 4,000 people passed through the turnstiles and as they inspected the splendid displays upon show in the industrial hall and its several auxiliary buildings," reports the *Vancouver Province*, "and wended their way through the grounds of Hastings Park their expressions of surprise and congratulations were heard upon every hand."

The brainchild of local industrial and business interests, the five-day fair aims to promote "practical and scientific husbandry," "encouragement of the cultivation of the beautiful," and a "healthy rivalry for supremacy and excellence in the minds of the rising generation."

"In the opinion of this meeting the time has arrived for the establishment of an Exhibition Association for Vancouver to embrace the Fat Stock, horses, dogs, poultry, also Horticultural, Agricultural and industrial interests," read the minutes from the Vancouver Exhibition Association's first meeting, "and also for the object of maintaining the City of Vancouver in that leading position she by rights should occupy."

Local fairs are relatively commonplace in the Lower Mainland of the early 1900s, with the New Westminster Agricultural Fair having been in existence (and having snapped up most of the lucrative provincial grants) since the late 1800s. The Vancouver association, eager for its own exhibition, fundraised for close to two years before its "preparation/opening" on August 15, a day that, the papers quickly note, included no competitions (except for the floriculture class).

Crowds on hand for the opening of the Vancouver Exhibition, 1925.
IMAGE COURTESY OF THE VANCOUVER ARCHIVES (CVA 99-3564, PHOTOGRAPHER STUART THOMSON)

"From the modest bowl of blushing wood flowers to the proud production of the Vancouver floral garden, wreathed and bound in all fantastic shapes, all classes are represented, and ably too, for the exhibit as judged upon yesterday was declared by one of the judges to be as good as he had ever had the pleasure of looking at."

Events begin at 11 a.m., including races, free vaudeville, and livestock, horses, poultry, and dog competitions. Most spectacular of all is a "high dive into a tank of flame." The event will become immediately popular with locals, with a total of 75,000 attendees in the first week and immediate talk of expansion (additions in later years will include a mineral exhibit and an international egg-laying contest).

The Vancouver Exhibition will change its name twice in the years to come, first to the Canada Pacific Exhibition and then, in 1947, to the Pacific National Exhibition.

AUGUST 17, 1938

Sai Woo Chop Suey House on Pender Street, 1936.
IMAGE COURTESY OF THE VANCOUVER ARCHIVES (CVA 260-452, PHOTOGRAPHER JAMES CROOKALL)

LOCALS MURMUR THEIR DISAPPROVAL as restaurant owner Charlie Ting reopens his business, in defiance of a city closure order issued after it was discovered that he regularly employed white waitresses.

"Chinese Restaurant Defies City's Order," the *Vancouver Province* declares. "Legal Battle on License May Yet Be Averted."

The restaurant in question, C.K. Chop Suey Parlor, lost its licence two days earlier on the grounds that Ting's employment of Caucasian women was contrary to an unspoken "agreement between Chinatown restaurant owners and Mayor George C. Miller."

Ting, claiming he was unaware of any such agreement, has continued to operate his business as usual, the paper notes with chagrin, "in defiance of the civic license cancellation order issued on Monday."

"Ting states the waitresses were employed in the café when he took it over last May," the paper explains, "and he was not aware of the agreement."

The employment of white waitresses in Chinatown has been a contentious issue for civic authorities through the 1930s. Following the murder of café server Mary Shaw in 1931 (by an Asian patron), the VPD declared a ban on Caucasian waitresses in the neighbourhood, though it's unclear how regularly the ban was enforced. Similar bans have been in effect, in various forms, throughout BC since 1919, under the guise of safeguarding the morals of white women. However, until the 1930s, when the city granted itself the power to revoke liquor licences, such "offences" were only punished with small fines. Public opinion on the matter has verged on hysteria, with Chinese men derided as corruptors and opium addicts, intent on seducing white women into prostitution or selling them into international sex slavery.

Despite his feigned ignorance, this incident is far from Ting's first clash with civic authorities. The head of the Chinese Benevolent Association, he, along with several other prominent Chinatown restaurateurs, has already been involved in a high-profile battle with City Hall after the VPD revoked the licence for his Hong Kong Café in September 1937. The issue briefly took the spotlight when the waitresses themselves marched on City Hall, defending their employers and demanding an audience with the mayor.

"[Council is] a bunch of fussy old bridge-playing gossips who are self-appointed directors of morals for the girls of Chinatown," an anonymous server complained in the pages of the *Sun*. "They are bound to get us out of here, but what will they do for us then? We must live and heaven knows if a girl is inclined to go wrong, she can do it just as readily on Granville Street as she can down here."

Despite the protestations of servers and restaurant owners, the ban will remain in place into the 1940s. Charlie Ting will continue to battle City Hall until his death in 1939. His funeral, the first public service for a Chinese official in Canada, will be attended by close to 1,000 people.

AUGUST 18, 1945

"To Beard or Not to Beard, That's the Question," reads a lifestyle article in the *Vancouver Province*. "The beard for centuries played an important role. It expressed individual taste or character; it symbolized nations and classes of people. Some of that symbolical character remains today, despite the supremacy of the razor."

The article goes on to discuss various types and styles of beard, tracing their origins through history and linking particular varieties of facial hair with certain fictional and historical personalities.

"Could one imagine Santa Claus clean-shaven, without his luxuriant white mustache and beard? Does not the farmer in the comics still retain his long chin-whiskers? A long white beard seems indispensible to indicate venerable age and wisdom."

However, the biggest question, the article claims, is not what has happened to the beard in recent times, but what will become of it.

"Will the present predominance of the clean-shaven face ever be broken?" the article asks. "Perhaps, as has been suggested, by the influence of homecoming servicemen? That, too, might be in the nature of a symbol of changing taste and of a different slant in our view of life."

Interior of the Steveston Barbershop/Saloon, 1899.
IMAGE COURTESY OF THE VANCOUVER ARCHIVES (OUT P679)

AUGUST 19, 1936

IN FRONT OF 4,000 EAGER FANS, former heavyweight champion and world-famous boxer Max Baer fights James Walsh ("The Alberta Assassin") at the Denman Arena—in a fight that lasts less than five minutes.

Baer, always a colourful character both in and out of the ring, elicits gales of laughter from the crowd with his clownish antics, and, according to the *Vancouver Sun*, Walsh is so terrified of his opponent that the match is over after only a few punches.

"Mr. James J. Walsh, the white hope from Kitscoty, Alberta, was pathetic," writes the paper, "and that is letting the gentleman down a trifle lighter than the fans did. He was in for something tough and he knew it. He stepped into the ring and one look at the towering form of Baer across the ring almost knocked him unconscious even before the first bell. Gathering all his courage, he made a rush at the ex-champ but was tied tighter than a knot. Baer danced about for a minute or so then shoved two or three hammer-like rights into the frightened puss of Mr. Walsh. Moments later, Walsh was sitting squarely on his flabby buttocks wondering what had hit him."

Though Baer's career has already passed its peak (after losing the world heavyweight title to James Braddock in the legendary Cinderella Man match and subsequently losing again to Joe Louis), he will enjoy a fruitful career as an actor, entertainer, and professional wrestler before suddenly dropping dead of a heart attack at age 50.

The Baer/Walsh match will be the final event held inside the Denman Arena. Only a few hours later, it will burn to the ground.

An event inside the Denman Arena, 1919.
IMAGE COURTESY OF THE VANCOUVER ARCHIVES (MIL P100.1, PHOTOGRAPHER STUART THOMSON)

AUGUST 20, 1936

THREE HOURS AFTER AN EXHIBITION bout between former heavy-weight champion Max Baer and "Alberta Assassin" James Walsh, the Denman Arena, a fixture in local sport for 25 years, burns to the ground.

"The Arena presented a terrifying spectacle when it was fully ablaze shortly after 2 a.m.," reports the *Vancouver Sun*. "Great tongues of flame leaped skyward from end to end of the building, and so intense was the heat that firemen were unable to get close to the structure."

The blaze, which began at approximately 1:30 a.m. somewhere within the nearby Fenner and Hood Shipbuilders' building, also wipes out a number of structures in the block nearby, causing an estimated $500,000 in damages. Miraculously, the auditorium next door is only slightly singed. In its time, the Denman Arena played host to everything from bicycle races and boxing matches to dancing and ice hockey. Beneath its rafters, the Vancouver Millionaires won their first—and only—Stanley Cup in 1915.

"The pipes above which swished some of the best hockey players in the world, players who competed since 1911 when the rink was built in a league that set many rules for hockey and provided, later, teams to make up the present NHL, look like spinach as they are strewn in ashes," the paper laments.

"I don't want to talk arenas or hockey or anything," former Millionaire Fred "Cyclone" Taylor says in an interview with the *Province*. "I feel like I've lost an old friend."

Firefighters will battle the flames for the better part of three hours before it is finally subdued. Mercifully, thanks to a lack of wind, the blaze remains contained to a single West End block.

Fire at the Denman Arena, August 20, 1936.
IMAGE COURTESY OF THE VANCOUVER PUBLIC LIBRARY (VPL 6650)

When interviewed regarding the incident, Fire Marshal J.A. Thomas isn't surprised, calling the arena "the worst fire trap in the City of Vancouver ever since it was built," and noting that he was so wary of it, he refused to even enter the building while it was occupied.

Though there will be calls for an improved, fireproof structure, a new arena will never be constructed. Finally, after a failed proposal by council to transform it into a Four Seasons Hotel, the land in the 1970s will be turned into Devonian Harbour Park.

AUGUST 21, 1924

"Point Grey Picks Up Mysterious Signals," declares a headline in the *Daily Province*. "Is It Mars Talking?"

"Mysterious signals picked up at Point Grey wireless station during the past few weeks culminated this morning in a recognized group of sounds which lead the operators to believe that Mars has succeeded in establishing communication with the earth," the paper reports. "Four distinct groups of four dashes came in over the ether at 7:12 a.m. when Mr. W.T. Burford was on duty. These dashes were not in any known code but started on a low note, gradually ascending and concluding with a 'zipp.' The signals were not sent by spark nor continuous wave and the theory that Mars has at last managed to 'get through' is gaining support."

The unusual sounds have been picked up at Point Grey for close to five weeks, reports C.W. Mellish (one of the station's senior operators), and seem to, in the opinion of station employees, be increasing in strength to coincide with Mars's nearness to Earth. Mellish and Burford, described as wireless operators "of long experience," are baffled as to their origin.

"At first he paid no attention to them, but when it was found that the signals could be not tuned out and that they overcame any obstacle, he began to attach importance to the occurrence," the paper reports. "In conversation with Mr. Burford it was decided to keep closer watch on these puzzling 'dashes' and today, with Mars nearer Earth than it has been for a hundred years, it was possible to distinguish a distinct signal."

"The fact that I distinctly got four groups of four dashes convinced me that some intelligible communication force was at work," Burford confesses.

The signals will be monitored for several days, with the paper surmising that within the week "eminent British scientists" will be dispatched to monitor the phenomenon.

No cause for the signals will ever be uncovered.

AUGUST 22, 1964

PARENTS GRIPE, TEENAGERS REJOICE, and thousands of female fans scream themselves hoarse as John, Paul, George, and Ringo—The Beatles—make their first (and only) appearance in Vancouver.

"As a music critic I have had to subject my eardrums to more than a little of the cacophony which currently dominates the hit parade but the stuff shouted by these Liverpudlian tonsorial horrors left me particularly unimpressed," the *Sun*'s William Littler will complain the following day. "That is, what portion of it I could hear between choruses of deafening screams."

The quartet's appearance at Empire Stadium comes on the heels of the phenomenal success of the film *A Hard Day's Night* and just as the band has managed to snag the number one spot in the British and the US charts in both the single and the album category—the first time any artist has ever done so. Unfortunately, security and crowd control at Empire Stadium is woefully inadequate to deal with the 20,000 near-hysterical fans. Before the show has ended, nine people have been taken to hospital for complaints ranging from a broken rib to hysterical exhaustion.

"The first aid posts resembled a disaster area," the *Sun*'s police reporter Stan Shillington will recall. "Dozens of girls slumped in chairs, or corners, or anywhere out of the way, sobbing uncontrollably. Many had been vomiting."

By the time The Beatles take the stage, fan excitement has reached its apex, and police can do little but watch helplessly as thousands of teenagers leave their seats and rush the field. Fearing that audience members may be crushed, Beatles manager Brian Epstein orders radio DJ and event MC Red Robinson onstage to calm the crowd.

Red Robinson attempts to calm the crowd, August 22, 1964.
IMAGE COURTESY OF THE RED ROBINSON COLLECTION.

"So, I get up there and I'm trying to quiet the crowd," Robinson will recall years later, "and suddenly behind my shoulder, over the cacophony of the crowd, I hear John Lennon yelling at me: 'Get the fuck off our stage! What the fuck are you doing on our stage? Nobody interrupts a Beatles performance.' There's a photograph where I'm talking to John—actually screaming at him over the roar of the crowd—and I said, 'John, look down at the edge of the stage. Do you think I want to be here? Your boss and the Chief of Police ordered me up here, to try and settle down the crowd.' At that point, he said: 'Oh, in that case, carry on, mate. But no one has ever done this before. There's never been a need.'"

In total, the performance lasts 29 minutes and 23 seconds.

"They played one more song," Robinson will recall, "and got the hell out of there."

AUGUST 23, 1970

"You'll never know what it's all about until you soak up some sunshine in your birthday suit," a "nude" at Wreck Beach says to a *Vancouver Province* reporter and photographer. "Take off your clothes and I'll talk to you guys."

And, with this, the first official Nude-In begins at Canada's first and largest clothing-optional beach.

"Hundreds of cars clogged Marine Drive," reports the *Province*, "as people, many of whom said they didn't even know where Wreck Beach was, left their cars on the road and clambered down steep cliffs near the University of BC's Totem Park to look or take part in the Nude-In."

Though there are rumours of public nudity at Wreck Beach as early as the 1920s, the beach has only recently become a hotbed of the hippie lifestyle, and the Nude-In—publicized by the *Georgia Straight* and encouraged by staff writer Korky Day (a.k.a. Mr. Natural)—is the beginning of the beach's public status as a clothing-optional location. Day, an advocate of "Free Beaches" (after hearing of similar undertakings in a number of American cities), organized the event (originally intended to take place at Third Beach in Stanley Park) in an effort to create such a place in Vancouver and to protest the August 12 arrest and charge of several other Wreck Beach nudists. While the roads nearby are clogged with thousands of onlookers, the police estimate that the "unclothed" number a mere 200.

"Many of the unclothed lay around, played guitar, read and swam," the paper notes, "apparently oblivious to the throng of onlookers who walked up and down the beach taking in the sights."

Swimmers at Wreck Beach, circa 1970.
Image Courtesy of UBC Rare Books and Special Collections, Georgia Straight Collection.

On the afternoon of the Nude-In, those arrested in the August 12 raid will appeal their charges, and thanks to the efforts of lawyer Don Rosenbloom, all charges will be dropped, paving the way for Wreck's future as the most liberated—and eccentric—beach in the city.

"There were no police evident," the paper reports, "and no arrests were made—seemingly in keeping with the practice that if there's a lot of nudists gathered in one place away from popular beaches, leave them alone."

AUGUST 24, 1997

"BAD BUSKERS, BEWARE," reads a Peter Clough editorial in the *Vancouver Province*. "City Hall will not rest until your racket is quelled. Next target: People who whistle while waiting for the bus."

The editorial, which incorporates quotes from several city councillors, focuses its sights squarely on a report being produced by City Hall, whose aim is to license Vancouver street musicians. Permits, restricted areas, and possibly auditions are discussed by council, with Clough noting: "Licensing has worked well for Granville Island and BC Transit, but we really don't need to turn the entire city into one big Expo '86 site."

"We recognize that these kinds of activities are part of the life and the vitality of the streets of the city," the engineering department's Bob Ross explains. "At the same time we need to get rid of the nuisance aspects."

The report, commissioned after years of complaints by city merchants about "panhandlers with beat-up guitars," will eventually result in the passing of city bylaws requiring a licence for all city buskers.

"[The report] is the surest sign yet that we're regulating ourselves into a state of civic neurosis," the editorial reads. "Before you know it, you'll need a permit to panhandle."

Into the early 2000s, Vancouver's street musicians will maintain that the city's busking bylaws are among the most confusing, misguided, and restrictive in the country.

A street musician of unknown skill, circa 1970.
IMAGE COURTESY OF UBC RARE BOOKS AND SPECIAL COLLECTIONS, GEORGIA STRAIGHT COLLECTION.

AUGUST 25, 1960

AFTER NEARLY FIVE YEARS of construction, $21 million in costs, and one catastrophic collapse, the new Second Narrows Bridge finally opens to the public, providing Vancouver with its first high-volume crossing to the North Shore.

"Decision to build the span next to old Second Narrows rail and traffic bridge was announced by Highways Minister P.A. Gaglardi on May 6, 1955," reports the *Vancouver Sun*. "The cantilever span in the main arch is 1,100 feet long, second only to the world record of 1,800 feet of the famous cantilever bridge at Quebec City."

The construction of the bridge—intended to replace the accident-prone Second Narrows Rail and Traffic Bridge (completed in 1925)—is described by engineer W.G. Swan as "designed on basis of economics . . . Had the cantilever span been required to be a little bit longer, then a suspension bridge (in the style of the Lions Gate Bridge) would have been designed."

Crossings at the Second Narrows have long been plagued by closures and accidents, including multiple ship collisions (such as the *Pacific Gatherer* collision, which closed the span for four years), and the disastrous collapse of 1958 (which occurred during construction and cost 19 workers their lives). As the *Sun* reports, due attention is paid to the tragedy; though Premier W.A.C. Bennett and other dignitaries are on hand, the task of cutting the official ribbon falls to William Wright, "one of 20 workers injured in the bridge's collapse."

The structure itself required more than 15,000 tons of steel to produce (twice that of the Granville Street Bridge and three times that of the Patullo Bridge), and the six 95-ton cords used in its construction are described by the *Sun* as "the largest steel member ever placed in a bridge in Canada."

Construction of the Second Narrows Bridge, 1958.
IMAGE COURTESY OF THE VANCOUVER PUBLIC LIBRARY (WILLIAM CUNNINGHAM, PHOTOGRAPHER)

AUGUST 26, 1893

"A Journalistic Tramp," declares the *Victoria Daily Colonist* as 27-year-old Edward Holmes and his dog, Googuim, arrive in Vancouver, setting a new world record by walking across the continent in 117 days.

Described as "an educated English gentlemen with influential connections" by the *Colonist*, Holmes (who the paper notes "is of athletic appearance and very agreeable manners") has made a name for himself as a world traveller, having walked across both Central America and Japan, and having crossed a number of other countries on the backs of unusual animals (among them a camel, a donkey, and an elephant).

Holmes, who completed the 2,926-mile journey from Montreal to Vancouver in 2,700 hours, arrives feeling "fit" and, surprisingly, 21 days ahead of schedule. The *Colonist*'s representative, who walks the final miles to Hammond Station with Holmes, describes the athlete as "as full of information as an encyclopedia" and estimates his walking speed at approximately 3.5 miles a day.

"Your representative's experience in travelling for miles by the side of the famous walker, as he strode forward at a four-mile gait, light in spirits and nimble as a deer, looking with glad heart to the near realizations of luxurious rest and repose after his tedious tramp of 3,000 miles," continues the paper, "is of sufficient interest for further communication, when your correspondent will air his gratification in being the only newspaper man who acted as a pace maker for the famous traveller, Edward Holmes, on his triumphal home stretch."

AUGUST 27, 1980

Men beside Vancouver Sun sales tents, 1933.
IMAGE COURTESY OF THE VANCOUVER ARCHIVES (CVA 99-2776, PHOTOGRAPHER STUART THOMSON)

"SUN BOUGHT BY SOUTHAM NEWSPAPER GROUP," reads a headline in the *Vancouver Sun* as the 68-year-old daily is purchased by its chief competitor, leading to a total newspaper monopoly in the city and a day known within the industry as "Black Wednesday."

"[The merger is] not only bad for our community, but it's bad for democracy, because the success of democracy relies on an informed public," Mayor Jack Volrich will explain in an interview with the *Sun*. "We would be left with one set of news, one set of reporters, one set of editorial comments with their own particular biases . . . If there were some bylaw we could pass, believe me I would do it."

The move will incite fury city-wide, with the Newspaper Guild demanding action from Justice Minister Jean Chrétien and the immediate launch of a formal inquiry by the Federal Bureau for Competition Policy. Although both papers since 1956 have been part of a media partnership known as Pacific Press—which raised the eyebrows of federal combines investigators—each publication has always retained its own ownership under a holding company designed to share costs. The structure has long proved frustrating for both dailies, resulting in years of friction between their respective owners, Southam Newspapers and F.P. Publications (later bought out by Thomson Newspapers). In addition, management problems and a lack of direction at the dailies were exacerbated by a series of disastrous strikes throughout the 1970s.

Newspaper consolidation has become increasingly widespread throughout the Canada of the 1970s and 1980s. Victoria's *Times* and *Colonist* (both owned by Thomson) merged into a single newspaper earlier in August, and in a 1970 Senate report on mass media, Senator Keith Davey estimated that three newspaper chains controlled 44.7 percent of the country's newspapers.

"They are news monopolies run as corporate enterprises, governed by different considerations from those which influenced papers in the past," asserts Bill McLeman, the Newspaper Guild's Canadian director. "We face the very real danger, no less real because it has yet to materialize, of a vast newspaper chain controlling the news that reaches the largest portion of the nation's population, manipulating power for self-serving political purposes."

Following the merger, the two chains will own a combined total of 59 percent of the country's newspapers. And, even though charges will be laid and the case taken to Federal Court, no one involved with the sale will ever be prosecuted.

By the 1980s, Canada will have the most highly concentrated newspaper ownership in the world.

AUGUST 28, 1966

PASSERSBY GUFFAW AND ELDERLY NEIGHBOURS AVERT their eyes as, sometime in the early morning, unknown vandals (rumoured to be UBC engineering students) apply a coat of red paint to the penis of one of the figures in Jack Harman's controversial *Family Group* sculpture outside the Granville Street headquarters of Pacific Press.

"It had been agreed that a sum not to exceed $50,000 would be set aside to grace the new building with art-work," *Vancouver Sun* publisher Stuart Keate will later recall in his memoirs. "Sculptor Jack Harmon [*sic*] was commissioned and in due course submitted a mock-up which he called *Family Group*. It showed a father and mother and two children, the mother holding a little girl in her arms and the father standing stoically behind his son. With some of the prudery common to medical art-work, Harmon had presented the two males without reproductive equipment. Fair enough. The mock-up was approved by the *Province* publisher at the time, Fred Auger, and by myself, and Harmon proceeded to create a larger-than-life sculpture of considerable power. But with a difference. When the finished work was hoisted into place, in a garden in front of Pacific Press, it was discovered that the young boy had suddenly sprouted a penis."

Harman's impressionist sculpture, which has been highly contentious ever since its installation (as it is technically the city's first "nude" statue), has already been the target of what Keate refers to as "collegiate high-jinks and morality groups."

"After a series of clandestine raids, the offending organ became a sort of hitching-post for a variety of ornaments," Keate will explain, "a glazed doughnut, a garland of buttercups, even a condom."

Despite being caught "red-handed" by *Province* journalist Kathy Tait, the vandals will escape unscathed. Within hours, a workman will be dispatched to remove the paint from the freshly rouged penis, a task he will elect to perform (in the middle of busy Granville Street) using only a Brillo pad and a vigorous rubbing motion. Unfortunately, the Brillo pad will not only remove the paint, but buff the contentious appendage to a brilliant shine, leading Pacific Press staff members to christen it *Le coq d'or*.

The statue (and its penis) will later be placed in front of the Surrey production plant of the Pacific Newspaper Group.

The Family, decorated by pranksters, May 1982.
IMAGE COPYRIGHT VANCOUVER SUN (ROB DRAPER, PHOTOGRAPHER)

AUGUST 29, 1950

"One Vancouverite Is Ready for A-Bomb," reads a front-page headline in the *Vancouver Sun* as construction is completed on the city's first domestic-use bomb shelter.

With nuclear hysteria steadily growing throughout North America, the Shaughnessy resident who commissioned the "atom-proof, blast-proof" structure has been so besieged with phone calls, he has asked *Sun* reporters that he remain anonymous.

"Built of steel-reinforced concrete and equipped with a thick, lead door to keep out gamma rays, the shelter is designed to withstand even a direct hit from a blockbuster," the newspaper reports. "All that shows above ground surface is a curved, white dome, 10 feet long and what looks like a miniature Quonset hut."

The shelter, constructed by the firm of Eccles-Rand Limited, includes a number of helpful features to survive the impending nuclear holocaust, including oxygen tanks, a portable Geiger counter, a pressure valve in case of concussive damage, and a "soda-lime compound to absorb excess carbon dioxide from the breath." Bomb shelters will continue to be a hot discussion topic in Vancouver throughout the 1950s and 1960s, with mail-order, do-it-yourself manuals available from the federal government, demonstration shelters being built on the courthouse lawn, and even recommendations by the city's "civil defence coordinator" that a fallout shelter be constructed below City Hall.

"Inside," the paper explains, "the occupants will enjoy all the comforts of a Second World War air-raid shelter, plus a few new features that the designers and builders, Eccles-Rand Ltd., have thrown in for good measure."

Unfortunately for the anonymous Shaughnessy resident, subsequent research will cast serious doubt on the wisdom of his purchase.

"The likelihood, in the event of a sudden massive attack, using nuclear weapons, is such that the declared Federal policy is total evacuation of the named Target Areas," reads the text of a civil defence report commissioned in 1957. "The power of an H-Bomb is such that virtually no one in the area could survive the effects of the bomb, whether in or out of shelter . . . If in this time the area is devastated by nuclear weapons, there can be little anticipation of return for a very considerable time."

Public Works Canada will continue to publish Home Fallout Protection guides into the mid-1980s.

AUGUST 30, 1958

WITH A LAST-MINUTE SUBSIDY DENIED by the provincial government, ferry service between the North Shore and Vancouver is officially cancelled after 55 years.

"Like the street car, the interurban trains, the steam locomotives, and the lake sternwheelers, the North Vancouver ferries have bowed out to progress," reports the *Vancouver Sun*. "Capt. George Simpson brought Ferry No. 5 in to the north shore ferry slip at 8 o'clock Monday night, and let go a blast of the tubby ship's whistle to mark the end of an era."

The North Vancouver Ferry Service has been in decline for years, and with the construction of both the Lions Gate and the Second Narrows Bridges, a number of vessels have already been decommissioned or sold to keep the company afloat.

Passenger ferries have been running—albeit sporadically—across Burrard Inlet since the *Lily* was first put into service in 1874 (previous crossings are said to have been undertaken by rowboat). However, by 1903, with increased demand for a dependable marine crossing, the seeds for expanded municipal service were sown with the purchase of new, faster, and more efficient boats. The service will grow immensely in popularity as the populations of both Vancouver and North Vancouver increase dramatically, and it will collect large profits up until the end of World War II (with the busiest year being 1943, where an estimated seven million passengers were carried across the inlet).

The final sailings (by North Vancouver No. 4) will take place later in the same day, ending any form of ferry service to the North Shore until the introduction of the SeaBus in 1977.

"They have to take both the losses and the profits, too," an unnamed provincial official is quoted by the *Province* as saying. "Furthermore, it is not a case of a single service. There are still two bridges across Burrard Inlet and it is quite obvious the public prefer those, anyway."

"Red ink on the profit and loss statements, and increasing subsidies finally stilled the ferries," the *Sun* concludes, "which had failed to be stilled by many a foggy night and many a stormy sea."

Ferry landing, 1910.
IMAGE COURTESY OF THE VANCOUVER ARCHIVES (CVA 371-2133)

AUGUST 31, 1957

ONLY A FEW MONTHS AFTER its first taste of rock 'n' roll, Vancouver becomes the third city in Canada to play host to musical royalty as 26,000 fans at Empire Stadium get the chance to experience the King of Rock 'n' Roll himself: Elvis Presley.

"They didn't even have security worth a damn," DJ and event MC Red Robinson will later explain. "They had a few cops—maybe ten . . . They never anticipated it. And the crowd is just unbelievably out-of-control. They didn't sell seats on the ground, so the kids that are back on the ten-yard line at the rear are just running forward, and they're pushing and shoving. And the stage is made out of balsa wood, and it's shaking back and forth. Over the years, I've become friends with D.J. Fontana, Elvis's drummer, and he said: 'Honest to God, I thought we were going to die.'"

Within minutes of Presley's appearance onstage, more than 1,600 fans have already leapt from their seats to rush onto the field for a closer look at their idol. Despite repeated warnings from law enforcement, the performance will be halted on four subsequent occasions in attempts to restore order.

"It was like watching a demented army swarm down the hillside to do battle in the plain when those frenzied teenagers stormed the field," *Vancouver Sun* reporter John Kirkwood will write the following morning. "Elvis and his music played a small part in the dizzy circus. The big show was provided by Vancouver teenagers, transformed into writhing, frenzied idiots of delight by the savage jungle beat music. A hard, bitter core of teenage troublemakers turned Elvis Presley's one-night stand at Empire Stadium into the most disgusting exhibition of mass hysteria and lunacy this city has ever witnessed."

Such reactions have become increasingly common during Presley's North American tour. Less than a year after the release of his debut album (not to mention his first feature film appearance in *Love Me Tender*), the Mississippi-born singer is already a music superstar on an unprecedented scale, an iconic figure as adored by teenagers as he is hated and feared by their parents.

Presley, clad in a gold jacket and black pants, "made love to the microphone," Kirkwood will note, with revulsion, "dropped drunkenly to his knees, and threw himself into more bumps and grinds than the PNE girly show has seen for years."

Then, after only 22 minutes, the King abruptly leaves the building, concealing his exit from overzealous fans through the cunning use of a body double.

"He put the gold jacket on his cousin Gene," Robinson will explain. "Elvis went down a little trapdoor, and he went down below the stage, and Gene, in the gold jacket, gets into a limo, and [the fans] all follow the limo. And when the limo's gone, Elvis gets out and walks across to the Lions' dressing room."

Presley's take for the performance is approximately $21,000.

Elvis Presley in Vancouver, Aug. 1957.
PHOTOGRAPH BY THE PROVINCE NEWSPAPER (VPL 61261)

OFFICIAL
ELVIS
PRESLEY
SHOW

SEPTEMBER 1, 1886

FIVE MONTHS AFTER THE CITY'S INCORPORATION, the Bank of British Columbia—Vancouver's first bank—opens inside the CPR offices on Cordova Street.

"Dan McGillivray made the first deposit," city pioneer George Upham will recall in a conversation with city archivist J.S. Matthews. "I know; I saw him do it. And I made the first withdrawal."

Upham's withdrawal (actually a money order for $100) is presented to bank manager J.C. Keith.

"Mr. Keith handed me in return some bills," Upham will recall. "I counted them; eleven ten dollar bills. I said, looking up from the counting, 'I think you have made a mistake.' Mr. Keith didn't seem pleased, and said quite abruptly, 'Bankers don't make mistakes,' emphasising the word *don't*. So I moved a bit; counted the ten dollar notes again—there was eleven all right—and then went back to the counter, and said to Mr. Keith, 'I think you've made a mistake.' After I said that he was even less pleased."

After a third attempt to return the extra $10 is met with even harsher resistance, Upham leaves the bank, and the matter rests for more than four months.

"Well, about four months afterwards, I was up at the bank again, and there was Mr. Keith again," Upham will recount. "He came over to me, and said, 'You were in here before, weren't you,' quite politely. And then he apologised for what he had said. So I replied, cheery like, 'Oh, that's all right.' Then I added slyly, 'I don't suppose you expect me to give you back that ten dollars after all this long time?' 'I should say not,' ejaculated Mr. Keith, with a smile. 'Would not accept it if you did. Come on across the street; let's have a drink.'"

The Bank of British Columbia in the CPR Depot, 1887.
IMAGE COURTESY OF THE VANCOUVER ARCHIVES (CAN P9)

SEPTEMBER 2, 1976

"'CHARGESEX' CREDIT CARD RACKET ALLEGED," reads a headline in the *Vancouver Province* as following a December 1975 raid, and a lengthy police investigation, the sensational "morality" trial of the Penthouse Nightclub enters its second day in court.

"The first witness Wednesday was a tall woman in dark glasses who said she went to the Penthouse in 1975 with a girlfriend to begin to work for the first time as a professional prostitute," reports the paper. "She told the court she met a man who she thought was a prospective trick who took her to a nearby office. There, she said, he told her he was an owner of the club and wanted to determine if she was talented enough for the club clientel."

The charges, which included conspiring to live off the avails of prostitution and "creating public mischief with intent to corrupt public morals," were laid against Joseph Philliponi, Ross Filippone, Domenick Filippone, cashiers Minerva Kelly and Rose Filippone, and doorman Jan Sedlak, and came as the result of an investigation involving wiretaps, surveillance, and undercover agents posing as both prostitutes and johns. During the 61-day trial, the jury will hear from Vice Squad Detective Norman Elliot (who will testify that the nightclub served as a gathering place for the "local mafia"), undercover officers (one of whom will testify that he was charged a 20 percent fee by Ross Filippone for a credit card cash advance to be used for sex), and Officer Leslie Schulze, who posed as a prostitute on 15 separate occasions, reporting that the club regularly charged her for admission, drinks, and use of tables.

"She said that each time she left the Penthouse with a man—ostensibly to turn a trick—and returned, she was required to pay another $2.95 plus $2 to the cashier and $2 to the doorman-bouncer," the *Province* will report.

In the Vancouver of the 1960s and 1970s, the situation at the Penthouse is far from unusual. Many of the city's high-end prostitutes have taken to operating out of local nightclubs, and by the early 1970s, the Filippones' club in particular will have become a hub for sex-trade workers, with more than 100 estimated to be meeting clients within its walls each night. Cash advances, too, are relatively commonplace in Vancouver nightspots before the advent of the automatic teller machine.

Philliponi will plead ignorance when he takes the stand, denying allegations of "testing" female prostitutes for sex and arguing against the notion that his business ever directly profited from prostitution. Nonetheless, Philliponi and the others will be found guilty on the charge of living off the avails and will be sentenced to fines and jail time. Philliponi will also be found guilty on a separate charge of attempting to bribe a liquor official.

All charges will later be dropped on appeal.

In total, the trial will cost taxpayers upward of $1.5 million.

SEPTEMBER 3, 1929

STATESMAN, AUTHOR, AND SOLDIER Winston Churchill speaks before a crowd of 1,000 at the Vancouver Theatre.

"The speaker drove his points home one after another in a speech clear and direct," reports the *Vancouver Province,* "and yet flashing with brilliant phrases. His wit, his apt illustration and ready delivery carried his audience with him from the time he stepped on the platform, and as he concluded, picturing the greater Empire of the future, he roused the assembly to a high pitch of patriotism."

The former Chancellor of the Exchequer—a fine figure in a cutaway coat, wing collar, and cravat—delivers a 55-minute speech (the longest he's given in some time, the *Province* notes), discussing issues of empire and foreign policy, and warning that "Britain's protecting hand should not yet be withdrawn from Egypt or India."

Winston Churchill, circa 1940.

"Today East and West are buckled together from ocean to ocean by two great transcontinental railway systems," Churchill says of Canada's progress. "The country is growing by every test that can be applied. The movement westward to British Columbia is in full swing, the West is becoming populated, growing and expanding."

The theatre itself is packed for the entirety of the address (which draws hearty cheers throughout), with hundreds turned away and some people even crowding onto the stage. Following his speech, Churchill will depart for Victoria, requesting that all proceeds be donated to furnishing the Canadian Teachers' Hostel in London.

Churchill will be elected prime minister of the United Kingdom in 1940, going on to lead his country through the Second World War and becoming one of Britain's best-known politicians.

SEPTEMBER 4, 1918

THOUSANDS OF ASSEMBLED VANCOUVERITES gasp in horror as a provincial government seaplane, on a test run over the West End, suddenly falls from the sky, inadvertently providing the city with its first plane crash.

"While thousands yesterday watched the flight of the Provincial Government seaplane over Vancouver, the aircraft which had been riding gracefully along on an even keel a thousand feet above the West End of the city, suddenly turned almost a somersault," the *Vancouver Province* will report, "and like a wounded bird dropped impotently towards the earth."

The aircraft, piloted by Lieutenant V.A. Bishop, who has recently returned from the Western Front, falls 1,200 feet and crashes through the roof of the home of Dr. J.C. Farish at the corner of Bute and Alberni. Luckily, no one inside the house is hurt, though the pilot is said to have sustained minor injuries. (The paper notes that he must have lost "considerable blood as a result of his injuries, for the gore mixed with the gasoline from the engine and dripped down the side of the building.") Bishop will later explain that the craft began having engine trouble somewhere above the West End and, despite his attempts to bring the plane down in the waters of English Bay, experienced total engine failure only a moment later.

"The engine started to miss," Bishop will explain in an interview with the *Vancouver Sun*. "It kept up and so I turned her toward Coal Harbour. It was nearer than English Bay, and I wanted to be over the water if I had to come down. Then the engine stopped altogether. The plane started to fall sideways."

The aircraft will remain wedged in the roof of Farish's West End home for hours following the accident, drawing thousands of onlookers and souvenir hunters. The government will foot the bill for repairs and damages, a total of roughly $8,000.

"The airplane, valued by Hoffar Brothers at $7,500, is regarded as practically a total loss," the *Sun* concludes. "The plane proper was smashed to a condition of uselessness, but it is possible that the engine may be saved."

Plane crashed into the roof at 755 Bute, Sept. 4, 1918.
IMAGE COURTESY OF THE VANCOUVER ARCHIVES (AIR P31, PHOTOGRAPHER FRANK GOWEN)

SEPTEMBER 5, 1964

"FAILURE IS IMPOSSIBLE—we haven't even considered it."

Less than a year after uttering these words, ad-executive-turned-publisher William "Val" Warren unveils the first issue of the *Vancouver Times*, the city's only locally owned newspaper since the Pacific Press partnership amalgamated the *Sun* and *Province* into a de facto media monopoly.

"For a long time now there has been some mild concern in Vancouver over the city's general newspaper situation," Warren is quoted as saying in a 1963 interview with *Marketing Magazine*. "There is a feeling around that both papers are the same."

The *Times* will proceed with its decidedly anti–Pacific Press strategy, with Warren recruiting a crew of veteran editors and newsmen, including Victor Odlum, former head of the now defunct *Vancouver Star*. So far, 73,000 subscriptions have been sold, a number that will initially prove too much for the new publication to handle.

"Routes were based on a predicted 50,000," reports trade magazine *Canadian Printer and Publisher*. "Consequently, some areas received first-day editions 24 hours late. To compound the problem, only about 80,000 copies were run and none were available in corner stores. Some were filched from doorsteps, and one carrier lost his entire load of papers when he put his bag down at the side of the road to make a delivery. An antiquated make-shift switchboard couldn't cope with the volume of calls for a week."

Despite the initial success of the paper, the *Times* will be largely ignored by major advertisers, and unable to meet its production costs, it will fold less than a year later.

By the 1980s, 59 percent of the country's newspapers will be owned by only two companies.

SEPTEMBER 6, 1921

SEVEN PEOPLE ARE ARRESTED, and $30,000 in "dope" is seized, as police descend on a Richmond farm and shut down what they believe to be the largest opium operation in the West.

"The police state that the farm was a distribution depot and that opium was sent not only into Vancouver and surrounding towns, but also across the United States border," the *Vancouver Sun* will explain, the following day. "In addition to the opium a complete outfit, alleged to be used in cooking opium, was also seized."

The sale and production of opium has been illegal in Canada since 1908, when then labour minister William Lyon Mackenzie King discovered the city's roaring opium trade while on an unrelated visit to Vancouver. Horrified, he introduced the country's first prohibition legislation. (Before this law, opium manufacture in Vancouver was subject only to a $500 fine.) However, possession and use are still legal. In the years since, the black market on the West Coast has been steadily growing.

After "swooping down" on a barn on the property, police find a large cache of opium hidden in tins under sizable piles of hay. The sting comes after four months of police "suspicion," and observation of property owner Kee Kit.

"Totalling up the seizure the officers found that they had 40 large tins, the retail value of which they estimate at $400 each; 39 smaller tins, of the kind usually retailed in opium dens at $100 each; and a bucket containing enough opium to fill 40 of these smaller tins."

After spending the night in jail, owner Kee Kit and seven others will be released on $1,000 bail.

SEPTEMBER 7, 1907

AT APPROXIMATELY 9 P.M., Vancouver's Chinatown and Japantown neighbourhoods are besieged by a mob of thousands—all of them supporters of the Asiatic Exclusion League, an organization whose stated aim is "to keep Oriental immigrants out of British Columbia" —in the largest and most vicious race riot the city has ever seen.

The crowd (originally numbering 700 or 800, but later swelling to more than 2,000) initially gathers at Main and Hastings, lining the streets with banners reading Stand for a White Canada, before filling City Hall (donated by Mayor Bethune specifically for the occasion). After listening to a number of inflammatory speeches by citizens and members of the local clergy, and burning an effigy of Lieutenant-Governor Robert Dunsmuir (who opposed a recent bill that could have curbed immigration), the mob marches on Chinatown, smashing windows and causing thousands of dollars of damage to homes and storefronts. At the CPR Pier, six Japanese men are thrown into Burrard Inlet by white rioters (though all of them are later rescued).

"When the rioters got through with Chinatown, it looked like a wreck," the Vancouver Daily World will report the following day. "Every Chinese window was broken. Thousands of dollars' worth of plate glass lay in fragments; and then a start was made on Powell Street, where not a Japanese window was spared."

However, before they can advance far into Japantown, the crowd is met with unexpected resistance from members of Vancouver's Japanese community, who have armed themselves with clubs, knives, and guns. Within minutes, the mob is driven from the area under a hail of rocks, bricks, and bottles tossed from the roofs of nearby buildings. Although there will be no fatalities, several people will be seriously injured. Smaller outbreaks of violence will continue for the next two days, but few convictions will ever result. The sole conviction in connection with the riot is against a bookkeeper with the North Vancouver Ferry Company, who will be fined $50 for assaulting a police sergeant.

"Leading Japanese state openly that it is their intention to organize for their own armed defence," the World will report, "the city authorities being evidently powerless to save them from injury to life and property. Last evening the temper of the Japanese was decidedly ugly and the Chinese too are in no frame of mind to stand any more nonsense."

In the days to follow, city, provincial, and federal officials will condemn the violence, and local papers will do their best to separate the "legitimate" protests of the Asiatic Exclusion League from the behaviour of the rioters (described by the World as "20 or 30 undesirables"). Anti-Asian sentiment will continue to increase over the next decade, culminating in the Chinese Immigration Act of 1923, which will ban most forms of Chinese immigration to Canada.

Boarded-up businesses in Chinatown on the morning following the race riot, Sept. 8, 1907.
PHOTOGRAPH BY PHILIP T. TIMMS (VPL 940)

SEPTEMBER 8, 1923

"Woman Driver Is No Longer a Joke," reads a headline in the *Vancouver Sun* as local dailies report on the growth of a shocking new trend: women behind the wheel.

"The woman driver is no longer a stranger on our streets," the paper reports. "The time when the sight of a woman driving a car provoked fear and trembling has gone, for now there are almost as many women drivers as men, and we no longer look askance at them."

The article goes on to praise women on the city's motorways and to commend her involvement in a "broader life, that is, her entrance into business and all sorts of public enterprises." At the same time, the article makes certain to educate female drivers on the finer points of operating an automobile, noting they must learn to "keep a cool head" and to "keep a firm, steady grip on the wheel, and a no less intelligent control of her feet."

"When my wife first endeavoured to drive," says an unnamed Vancouverite, "I was always more or less uneasy as to what was going to happen to us, but as she got experience she seemed to increase her self-confidence and I no longer feel nervous and am quite content to see her at the wheel."

"It gives me a sense of ease," he concludes, "to be on the back seat of our sedan and talk to the boys while Milady drives me home."

Miss Marion E. Meilicke, Vancouver's first female taxi driver, circa 1930.
Image courtesy of the Vancouver Archives (Port P835)

SEPTEMBER 9, 1976

OFFICIALS REJOICE, COMMUTERS GROAN, and congestion is noticeably eased as, following decades of debate, the much-loathed Bylaw Enforcement Officer first appears on Vancouver streets.

"The city's first 10 meter maids went on the job Thursday, patrolling downtown parking meters," the *Vancouver Sun* will report the following day. "The women, complete with badges and uniform, replaced police officers who patrolled meters in the past."

The 10 officers (the first of a proposed 21), paid approximately $750 a month, are the culmination of a public debate that began in the late 1950s when the concept of civilian parking enforcement was first discussed by council. Before the era of the meter maid, parking infractions were dealt with by a team of eight constables, a move that drew considerable public disapproval in the face of rising crime and a pronounced departmental manpower shortage. Although council approved bylaw enforcement on principle in late 1968, the program was scrapped before it could be instituted. By January 1976, parking infractions had become so commonplace that more than half of downtown's parking meters were being illegally occupied for extended periods of time.

"Before, meters were checked every few days and now they will be checked several times a day," explains city engineer Bill Curtis at a press conference. "A lot of people are now using the meters all day. In effect, they're using them for commuter parking, and we'd like to put an end to that."

The bylaw enforcement department will prove so successful that, by the end of October, it will have issued 21,280 tickets, effectively doubling the city's parking revenue.

By 2011, Vancouver will have the highest peak on-street parking rates in North America.

A model demonstrates how to use the city's new parking meters, 1946.
IMAGE COURTESY OF THE VANCOUVER ARCHIVES
(CVA 586-4816, PHOTOGRAPHER DON COLTMAN, STEFFENS COLMER)

SEPTEMBER 10, 1904

AT APPROXIMATELY 9:30 P.M., four miles outside of Mission, CPR Transcontinental Express Train No. 1 falls victim to British Columbia's first train robbery.

"The engineer, Nat Scott, was surprised by a man with a gun," reports the *Vancouver Daily News-Advertiser*, "who was joined by two others, and who forced him to stop the train . . . The small express car was cut off from the rest of the train and run ahead and the car then looted by the robbers, whose booty amounted to about $7,000 in gold dust and cash."

The bandit checks Scott for weapons but, displaying remarkable manners for a thief, leaves the engineer's wallet and watch untouched. The robbers then ransack the express car, stealing $4,000 in gold dust en route to Seattle, as well as $50,000 in US bonds and $250,000 in Australian securities. Upon hearing word of the holdup, the passengers (including millionaire W.H. Malkin) barricade their door and hide their valuables, however, in spite of the passengers' fears, the outlaws never go near their car. The robbery is over in less than 30 minutes, and as the posse departs (tossing the coalman's shovel into the bush to delay the train), their leader good-naturedly advises engineer Scott to be careful backing up so he doesn't "meet with some accident."

In the weeks to follow, the CPR—on the hook for some $300,000 lost in transit—will dispatch Pinkerton agents and expert trackers, and offer an $11,000 reward in an unsuccessful attempt to determine the whereabouts of the gang responsible. Several arrests will be made, with little result. Though unknown to authorities at the time, the group's leader is none other than Bill Miner, a lifelong outlaw nicknamed, owing to his impeccable manners,

Train carrying the Duke and Duchess of Cornwall en route to Vancouver, Sept. 1908.
IMAGE COURTESY OF THE VANCOUVER ARCHIVES (Y P16.3)

"The Gentleman Bandit." Following the heist, Miner will remain at large for a further year and a half, committing another robbery in Oregon and spending time in the interior under the alias George Edwards.

He will be caught by police after a bungled train robbery near Kamloops in 1906.

SEPTEMBER 11, 1898

AT APPROXIMATELY 11:30 P.M., a fire breaks out in the waterfront warehouse of Brackman and Ker, and within hours, it has swelled into an inferno that destroys substantial portions of New Westminster.

"The entire business portion of the city was literally wiped out of existence," the *Vancouver Daily World* will exclaim the following day, "nothing excepting a few remnants of tottering brick being left at daylight to tell the tale of the city's glories, and its handsome business establishments of the previous evening."

The flames, fanned by a strong wind from the waterfront, causes damage estimated at between $2.5 and $3 million, and turns more than 300 buildings to ash, including the post office, the provincial courthouse, and a number of hotels. Despite the valiant efforts of local firefighters, and additional volunteers from Vancouver (the city having purchased a fire engine following its own disastrous fire 12 years earlier), the heat is so intense that no one can access the city hydrants along Front Street.

"With incredible rapidity, the flames spread," the *World* continues. "Front and Columbia Streets went like timber, and the fine brick buildings were consumed as if so much paper. The heat was intense, and a strong wind fanned the furious element, making the streets as light as day."

The blaze will rage until early the following morning, before, thanks to firefighting efforts and a lack of wind, it will burn itself out. In the hours to follow, a relief committee from Vancouver will send 20 tons of supplies to New Westminster residents. A number of deaths are reported after the conflagration, including word of one man burned to death at the docks, a woman said to have died of fright, and another man apparently consumed by flame. While condolences will pour in from each of Vancouver's daily newspapers, the *Province* will offer a less sympathetic conclusion.

"New Westminster is a city of yesterday," the paper declares. "Its dreams of greatness have been scattered to the wandering winds of Heaven. There will always be a community on the old site, but it will never again be the community it was. It is inevitable that the population should rapidly decrease and that most of those who formerly claimed New Westminster as their home should now locate in Vancouver or some other equally advantageous point."

Ruins of New Westminster, after the fire, Sept. 1898.
IMAGE COURTESY OF THE VANCOUVER ARCHIVES (OUT P11, PHOTOGRAPHER BAILEY BROS.)

SEPTEMBER 12, 1907

"THE ASIATIC EXCLUSION LEAGUE has got hold of the right end of the stick," reads an editorial in the *Vancouver Province*, "but it has shown a slight tendency toward an indiscreet though well-meaning zeal."

Five days after the worst race riot in the city's history—one that caused thousands of dollars in damage to Chinatown businesses and resulted in dozens of charges—the Vancouver Police Court heaves a "sigh of relief" as its docket is cleared of the last of its riot-related cases.

"During the hearing of the entire list the counsel for defence have submitted the witnesses to the most savage cross examination," claims the September 13 edition of the *Province*. "And have accomplished their purpose in discovering the strength of the evidence against their respective clients, without hinting that there may be, in reserve, evidence for the defence."

Despite a national public apology by Prime Minister Wilfrid Laurier, strong anti-Asian sentiment continues to pervade the city's public institutions (the newly elected president of the Asiatic Exclusion League is vice-president of the Trades and Labour Council, and the organization itself is supported by Mayor Bethune and the BC Attorney General). Though a number of charges will proceed to trial, only one will result in a conviction: a bookkeeper fined $50 for assaulting a police sergeant.

"It is declared by some that the good name of the city has been injured," a "prominent member" of the Exclusion League is quoted in the paper as saying, "but as no serious damage was done, I think that it is a far-fetched statement."

Three Chinese men reading a newspaper on V.J. Day, Aug. 15, 1945.
IMAGE COURTESY OF THE VANCOUVER ARCHIVES (CVA 586-3960, DON COLTMAN, STEFFENS COLMER)

Less than one year later, a Royal Commission headed by Labour Minister William Lyon Mackenzie King will award the city's Chinese merchants more than $26,000 in damages.

The triumph, though, is short-lived, as it is swiftly followed by increased measures to restrict Asian immigration, culminating in a federal act in 1923 that will effectively ban all Chinese immigration.

SEPTEMBER 13, 1942

WITH THE SECOND WORLD WAR in full swing, and fears of a Japanese invasion reaching their height, the Fort Grey Battery has its first taste of wartime action: a fishing vessel that fails to halt at the examination line.

"It was a hazy Sunday when a fish-packer sailed in across the 'examination line' from Point Atkinson to Point Grey, oblivious to the wartime crisis," historian Peter Moogk will later relate in *The Vancouver Book*. "As the boat chugged on towards the First Narrows, the gunners at the fort received a message to fire a 'stopping round' ahead of the boat to compel the master to come to a stop and to identify himself. It was customary on such occasions to fire a non-explosive, solid shell that would kick up a large splash in front of the offending vessel."

Throughout the summer of 1942, Japanese vessels have attacked several targets along the West Coast, including a lighthouse and radio station on Vancouver Island. The coastal defence guns, hastily installed at Fort Grey (later the site of the UBC Museum of Anthropology), are both a defensive strategy and a way to keep the public feeling secure. However, the soldiers stationed at Fort Grey have seen little action, firing their "stopping round" at such an angle that it accidentally punctures the hull of a nearby freighter.

"The shell hit a wave and started to ricochet across the water at an oblique angle," Moogk will explain, with the round hitting "the freighter above the waterline. As the shell passed through the number 3 hold it turned sideways and punched out a hole below the waterline on the other side. At first this was not noticed. The ship was evidently on its way back to the Burrard Drydocks when the captain received word of flooding in the hold. He beached the freighter on the north shore, just inside the First Narrows. It remained there, on the tidal flats, until it could be patched up and floated off."

An army court of inquiry will later be appointed, but the gunners will be absolved of any blame. Vancouver's coastal defences will be largely closed down by the following year. Because of a publication ban, the event will not be mentioned in any of the local newspapers.

Guns mounted at Stanley Park's Ferguson Point, circa 1914.
IMAGE COURTESY OF THE VANCOUVER ARCHIVES (ST PK P228.1)

SEPTEMBER 14, 1928

THIRTY THOUSAND CHEERING FANS CROWD the streets, the First National Juvenile Band plays "See The Conquering Hero Comes," and parade floats make the journey from the downtown CPR station to Brockton Point as Olympic gold medallist Percy Williams, the "World's Fastest Human," returns home to Vancouver.

"The crowd assembled from the CPR station up Granville to Georgia was about the largest ever packed into that stretch of thoroughfare," reports the *Vancouver Daily Province*. "It was a genuine, wholehearted reception. The demonstration affected spectators in the Fairfield Building to such an extent that they tore up the contents of waste paper baskets and sent the fluttering scraps out over the crowds as confetti."

"This is the best of all," the 20-year-old Williams tells reporters. "I am glad to get back home . . . I have seen a lot of Europe but if you put it all beside Vancouver, I would choose Vancouver."

Following his triumphant return, Williams, winner of two gold medals (for the 100- and 200-metre dash) at the 1928 Amsterdam Olympics, will go on to beat America's best track athletes in 1929, set a world record for speed in 1930, and be made an Officer of the Order of Canada. In 1975, he will be declared the country's all-time greatest Olympic athlete by the Associated Press.

Despite the adulation of the public (including Mayor L.D. Taylor and Premier S.F. Tolmie, who are on hand to present Williams with a brand new Graham-Paige Model Ten-Six Coupe), the painfully shy Williams has never been comfortable in the spotlight. He will appear bewildered and awkward amid the confetti, singing, and cheering of the homecoming parade. His thank-you speech at the Stanley Park grandstand will be a total of 51 words. The celebration

Percy Williams, Sept. 14, 1928.
IMAGE COURTESY OF THE VANCOUVER ARCHIVES (CVA 99-3637, PHOTOGRAPHER STUART THOMSON)

will conclude with Williams donning his now-famous Olympic sprinter's garb and running an exhibition race at Brockton Point. In the months following his triumphant return, Williams will be approached by prominent American universities, athletic associations, and even a film producer keen on a movie deal. His name and likeness will be used to advertise chocolate bars, hats, and even the new Graham-Paige Coupe.

However, a thigh injury incurred while setting his world record will effectively end Williams's running career at the age of 22. He will spend the rest of his life in Vancouver, selling insurance, and living with his mother. By the early 1980s, he will have descended into alcoholism, committing suicide at the age of 74.

SEPTEMBER 15, 1971

The Phyllis Cormack in Vancouver, Sept. 1971. IMAGE COURTESY OF THE UBYSSEY

THE STAGE IS SET FOR THE CREATION of one of the world's largest non-governmental organizations when, in hopes of raising world-wide awareness about a remote US nuclear bomb test on the island of Amchitka, 12 members of the Don't Make a Wave Committee set sail from Vancouver aboard the fishing vessel *Phyllis Cormack*, which has been christened with a new name for the voyage: *Greenpeace*.

Close to 75 people crowd the dock for the send-off, reports the *Vancouver Sun*, "but not to celebrate. They came in good faith, to wish the 12 members of the *Greenpeace* crew a safe and successful journey."

The crew, including Don't Make a Wave co-founder Jim Bohlen, *Georgia Straight* columnist Bob Cummings, and Dr. Lyle Thurston of North Vancouver, are realistic about their mission (some even making out their last will and testament), stating their intention to sail inside the 12-mile prohibited zone around the island.

"What we do when we get there," Bohlen states, "is up to Nixon.'"

"Why?" asks Cummings in a *Straight* piece written on board the vessel. "Why the thousands of dollars squeezed from pockets where they were otherwise needed to make the *Greenpeace* possible? . . . And why the willingness, even eagerness, of the crew to endure six weeks of cold, damp, overcrowded discomfort, seasickness, and the possibility of arrest in order to be present at an exercise in criminal negligence that we know could erupt into a radioactive cataclysm? The immediate answer is that the *Greenpeace* is not designed to slay the AEC [Atomic Energy Commission] Goliath, desirable as that would be, but simply to trip him up long enough for the mass of people, including the Philistines, to realize the terrible dimensions of the threat his games pose to all of us."

Internal strife will dominate the *Greenpeace*'s voyage to Amchitka, and ultimately, the boat will be turned back by the US Coast Guard before it reaches its destination. However, public awareness raised by the *Greenpeace*'s voyage will, five months later, signal the end of the Amchitka nuclear test program. The following year, the Don't Make a Wave Committee will officially change its name to *Greenpeace* and go on to become one of the largest NGOs in the world.

"When I got back from the expedition to Amchitka and sat down to write a book about it, I was convinced we had lost, and I was angry," committee member Bob Hunter will later write. "The best chance ever to actually interfere with nuclear testing, and we had blown it through sheer stupidity . . . As it turned out, all my angst was unnecessary. Time has proven my post-trip despair to be utterly mistaken. The trip was a success beyond anybody's wildest dreams . . . Whatever history decides about the big picture, the legacy of the voyage itself is not just a bunch of guys in a fishing boat, but the *Greenpeace* the entire world has come to love and hate."

SEPTEMBER 16, 1991

VANCOUVERITES AWAKEN to the sight of newsboys in droopy caps, period vests, and cloth shoulder bags as, after close to 80 years, the *Vancouver Sun* makes the switch to morning publication.

"Good morning, British Columbia," reads a sidebar on the front page. "Today *The Sun* shines in the morning around BC. And if the weather office's forecast is correct, even the elements have co-operated. Your four-section morning *Vancouver Sun* is crammed with news, features, business and sports. You'll find some old friends and a few new additions today, and throughout this first week of our rebirth as a morning paper."

The newspaper carriers and the switch to morning publication are the final part of a $700,000 media campaign orchestrated by public relations firm Burson-Marsteller, in an attempt to revamp the *Sun*'s image after months of delays, technical problems, friction with printer's unions, and declining circulation. Unfortunately, the switch to mornings has put the *Sun* in direct competition with the *Vancouver Province*, even though both are owned by Toronto-based Southam, Inc. The switch, according to industry insiders, risks putting undue strain on the company's resources.

"To get both papers on subscribers' doorsteps by 6 a.m., copy deadlines for both papers have shifted to as early as 3 o'clock the previous afternoon," notes an article in the *Globe and Mail*. "Anticipating *Province* readers' concerns, editor-in-chief Brian Butters wrote in a column, 'if a particular story or sports result is not in the edition you get . . . it will be published in the following day's paper.' Critics are calling that delivering yesterday's news tomorrow."

The *Sun*'s choice of Burson-Marsteller is also heavily criticized in the media, as the firm is well-known worldwide for its work with Exxon, Tylenol (following a poisoning scare), and the government of Argentina—where it was once criticized in the pages of the *Sun* itself for "[making] the world think better of a government widely known to be butchering its own citizens."

However, an editorial in the *Prince George Daily News* praises the combination, noting: "After all, the paper has been butchering its readers for years."

SEPTEMBER 17, 1942

LOCAL PAPERS BUZZ and Vancouver mayor J.W. Cornett charges "conspiracy" as, following a strenuous contest, his Worship loses a high-profile cow-milking competition in Chilliwack.

"Mayor J.W. Cornett of Vancouver Wednesday afternoon launched a vigorous protest against the 'unseemly conduct' of two of the other contestants in the cow-milking contest," reports the *Vancouver News-Herald*, "a feature of the annual Chilliwack fair."

The contest, which took place at three o'clock the previous afternoon in front of an audience of approximately 1,200, pitted Cornett against a number of other amateur cow milkers, including first place winner F.T. Paltrey and second place winner George Cruickshank—both of whom, it is charged, joined forces to defeat the mayor.

"Mr. Cornett's resentment and subsequent protest rose out of the claim that the milk in Mr. Cruickshank's bucket was transferred to that of Mr. Palfrey," the paper continues, "thereby giving him enough to put him in the winning brackets. The Mayor declined to state how Cruickshank was able to take second place, after having donated part of his bucket of milk to Palfrey."

Despite Cornett's protestations, the victory will be upheld, though according to reports, the win and the contest itself were relatively unspectacular.

"Fortunately for the contestants, who were given three minutes to milk their allotted cows, the placid Jerseys had already been milked," the paper concludes. "None of the amateur milkers were able to get more than an inch or so in the bottom of the buckets."

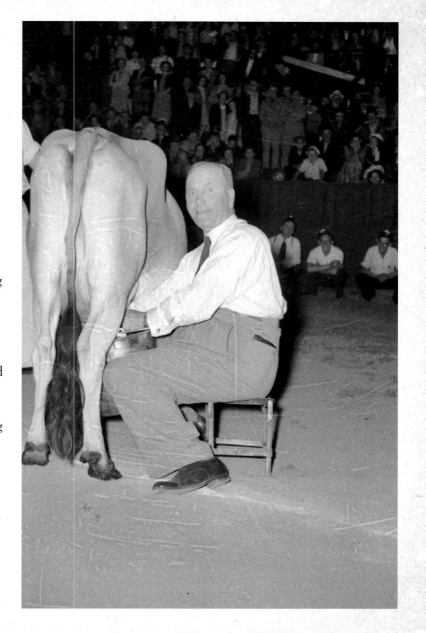

Mayor J.W. Cornett milking a cow.
IMAGE COURTESY OF THE VANCOUVER ARCHIVES (CVA 1184-813, PHOTOGRAPHER JACK LINDSAY)

SEPTEMBER 18, 1983

A LOCAL RUMOUR, A SINISTER PLAN, and dreams of a million-dollar payday end in murder as, following a bungled robbery, Penthouse Nightclub owner Joe Philliponi is shot dead in his Seymour Street office.

"The safe was empty, papers were strewn all over the floor and he was on the floor face down," brother Jimmy Filipponi will explain to the *Vancouver Sun* after discovering the body the following morning. "I don't know if he was shot or if he was knifed, or if he had a heart attack."

The 71-year-old Philiponi (his last name spelled differently from that of his brothers because of a mistake by a customs agent upon the family's arrival from Italy) was a fixture in Vancouver's nightlife for more than half a century, rubbing elbows with high-profile show business personalities such as Duke Ellington, Frank Sinatra, and Sammy Davis Jr. In addition, from the 1950s through the 1970s, the Penthouse was reported to have been the centre of high-end prostitution in the city, with up to 100 women working within its walls each night. The Filipponi's were taken to court in 1977 for living off of the avails of prostitution, but despite a colourful trial, and extensive undercover work by the Vancouver Police Department (thanks to the misplaced zeal of Chief Constable Don Winterton and Vice Squad Inspector "Vic" Lake), all convictions were later overturned on appeal.

Though underworld rumours persist following Philliponi's death, the murder itself will turn out to have been the result of something quite different: plumber Sid Morrisroe and small-time low-life Scott Forsyth (both acquaintances of Philliponi's), believing local rumours of a $1 million bounty kept in the nightclub's safe, set out to rob the aging club owner at gunpoint. Unfortunately for the pair, the safe contained less than $1,200, and panicked and intoxicated, Forsyth shot Philliponi in the temple.

Following a year-long trial, both Forsyth and Morrisroe will be convicted of first-degree murder and sentenced to life in prison.

Philliponi's funeral will later be attended by close to 800 people, including businessmen, exotic dancers, and Supreme Court justices.

Joe Philliponi's body is removed from the scene, Sept. 19, 1983.
IMAGE © VANCOUVER PROVINCE (GERRY KAHRMANN, PHOTOGRAPHER)

SEPTEMBER 19, 1983

"THERE'S NO DOUBT THAT SOME DAY it will be the playground for all those people who live and work downtown."

With these words, uttered by architect Norman Hotson, the *Vancouver Sun* kicks off its look at plans to develop a neighbourhood of "smoke-scarred, empty warehouses" into what may soon become the city's newest "potential character area"—Yaletown.

"I'd like to see it made a historic precinct," says city planner Eric Crickmore, "but not a mandatory one. Right now, we're taking a fairly low-key attitude toward the area."

Ideas for developing the historic neighbourhood, a ramshackle collection of dilapidated warehouses and loading bays, are numerous, the *Sun* notes, with proposals to transform the area into a cultural district tailor-made for artists and creative types, or a "specialty retail area, perhaps like the antique district of Old Montreal."

"Dreams of open-air markets and canals died quickly," the *Sun* reports. "The city has steadfastly resisted the idea of touristy Gastown-style shops in the area."

However, property owners are worried about the future of Yaletown (originally named for Yale, the hometown of the CPR workers who resided there), seeing it as uneconomical and difficult to develop, with its future tied to the construction of nearby BC Place. Despite this, and fears that BC Place's 12,000 residential units will saturate the city's housing market, proposals for lower-rent New York–style warehouse apartments are picked by the paper as a clear favourite for the area.

"There's a lot of talk about it," explains BC Place architect Murray McKinnon. "There are a lot of creative people in the city who would love to live there."

Warehouses in Yaletown, 1970.
IMAGE COURTESY OF THE VANCOUVER ARCHIVES
(CVA 780-811)

SEPTEMBER 20, 1953

A group of Doukhobors in custody, May 1944.
IMAGE COURTESY OF THE VANCOUVER ARCHIVES (CVA 1184-481, PHOTOGRAPHER JACK LINDSAY)

"FANATIC TRIES TO STRIP" exclaims a front-page headline in the *Vancouver Province* as local headlines are dominated by one of BC's most unusual religious groups: The Sons of Freedom.

"Trial of Freedomite Doukhobors was adjourned early, shortly before noon today in Burnaby," reports the paper, "when one woman tried to rip off her clothes as she protested being freed of a charge of parading in the nude at Krestova."

The "fanatic," Dora Soukeroff, one of 148 Doukhobors arrested in the BC Interior for taking part in a nude march protesting compulsory education for their children, shouts: "I am together with my brothers and sisters!" before beginning to strip off her clothing in front of startled spectators.

The Sons of Freedom, in existence since 1903, are a radical sect of the Doukhobor community, a religious group originating in Russia that advocates communal ownership and the rejection of material possessions. Most Doukhobors (the term means "spirit wrestler") are avowedly pacifist, but the Sons of Freedom have taken a more militant stance against the BC government and are responsible for a number of bombings, acts of arson, and mass nude protests over the previous 50 years. They have even, on a number of occasions, burned their own money or belongings (or those of other, more moderate Doukhobors) as a protest against society's ills.

The Doukhobor community's relationship with the BC government has been strained since their arrival in the province in 1908, a battle building from such acts as the Doukhobor refusal to provide data to the Department of Vital Statistics, to participate in compulsory childhood education, or to sign registration for property, even when the property was in the form of a land grant. The province

has convened three commissions of inquiry to address relations with the Doukhobor community, one in 1912, one in 1947, and one in 1956, with little success. A hard-line stance recently taken on the "Doukhobor problem" by Premier W.A.C. Bennett has only exacerbated the situation.

Those convicted of "parading in the nude" will each be sentenced to three years in prison—the standard penalty for such an offence. As a result, their children (101 in all) will be taken from their families and interned in a residential school in New Denver, BC, where they will remain until 1959.

The Sons of Freedom will continue to dominate the headlines into the 1970s, until an accord is signed between Doukhobor sects in 1984 that will put an end to decades of protest, bombings, and arson.

SEPTEMBER 21, 1951

"WHERE IS THE LOW-COST HOME?" asks an editorial in the *Vancouver Sun* as, after a general wartime building lull, a decade-long accommodation shortage, and a steady increase in postwar population, Vancouver's housing crisis once again hits the news.

"It may be, also, that to achieve a truly low-cost home in this high-priced time we will have to spread the repayments over a far longer period than the terms accepted today," the editorial continues. "Housing costs are high, but we can't afford to throw up our hands and say we can't afford to build many more houses until costs come down again. In a city growing as fast as ours this would be the counsel of stupidity and despair. We must have more homes and we must have them at prices people can afford to pay."

For the better part of 80 years, real estate in Vancouver has been more expensive than elsewhere in the country, a real estate boom that began after the arrival of the first CPR passenger train in 1887 and, in spite of a market crash in 1913, has continued to outpace growth elsewhere in Canada. The area has always been popular with land speculators (by 1887, Vancouver had 12 grocery stores and 16 real estate firms), and complaints about high property values have been common since the turn of the century.

"Land prices are high, it is said, higher than anything would warrant," reads an article from the June 1911 issue of *BC Magazine*. "'Why, the workingmen cannot afford to pay at the rate demanded for these tiny outside lots,' asserted one man recently. The same thing was said here twenty years ago, answer the pioneers; others of us know that it was repeated ten years ago and five years ago, and our children and our children's children will hear the same tale of woe decades hence."

A staged photo advertising Vancouver real estate, 1886.
IMAGE COURTESY OF THE VANCOUVER ARCHIVES (LGN 454, PHOTOGRAPHER HARRY T. DEVINE)

Lack of housing has been a major issue in Vancouver since the early 1930s. Rampant overcrowding was common during the Depression years, and during the 1940s, the crisis grew so extreme that the Vancouver Housing Registry was created, with the objective of finding housing for the desperate, potentially by forcing homeowners to rent out extra rooms. The crisis itself will ease somewhat by the 1960s, in large part because of the 1966 *Strata Titles Act*, which allows ownership of apartments for the first time. However, with the average home costing three times the average annual salary, calls for affordable housing will continue throughout the decade and into the next century.

"We live in the land of destiny," *BC Magazine* concludes. "In the land of wealth where, though gold is not idly picked off the rocks or from the pavements in the streets, it is just as surely gained from the platted acres and twenty-footers around us. One day an artisan may put the scanty savings of a lifetime into a tiny holding out among the evergreens, and on the morrow almost, he is building city blocks from the proceeds thereof."

SEPTEMBER 22, 1948

"Isn't it a shame to make money this way, folks?" renowned crooner Bing Crosby chuckles as, before a crowd of roughly 9,000 at the PNE Forum, he sings, tells jokes, and records his world-famous radio show as part of a benefit for the Sunset Community Centre.

Crosby, the top-rated radio entertainer of his generation, sings such hits as "It's Magic," "Side by Side," and "Hair of Gold" (which, as the *Vancouver Province* notes gleefully, contains "a mention of West Vancouver in [its] lyrics") over the course of his two-and-a-half-hour performance—one that also includes the crooner's "riotous" inauguration as "Chief Thunder Voice" of the Squamish Nation.

"The show itself included a half-hour radio program which will be broadcast Oct. 13 by hundreds of American and Canadian stations," the paper continues, "suffered mildly from a few draggy spots, but it still will be fondly remembered as one of the finest benefit entertainments in BC history."

The benefit comes on the heels of several public appearances by Crosby: one where he received the key to the city (and, to the delight of city officials, signed the civic register), another where he sat on the mayor's dais and "presided" over a council meeting, and a third where he drove a tractor around in the mud as part of the earth-turning ceremony at the site of the new centre. Crosby's appearance in Vancouver is the result of efforts by the Sunset Community Association to raise quick money for their new community centre and is due largely to the tireless work of the organization's president, Stan Thomas (who travelled to Hollywood personally in hopes of pitching Crosby on the fundraiser).

The benefit will end up raising close to $26,000 for the Memorial Centre (with the remainder contributed by the city). Although

Bing Crosby, Sept. 21, 1948.
Photograph by William Cunningham (VPL 42600)

the Sunset Community Association had volunteered to pay all of Crosby's costs while in Vancouver, the entertainer will refuse to accept a cent of reimbursement, tearing up the cheque on the train platform, minutes before he is due to leave.

After two years of construction, the Sunset Memorial Centre will open in 1950.

SEPTEMBER 23, 1995

AFTER TWO YEARS OF CONSTRUCTION, $160 million in private financing, and months of anticipation, the Vancouver Canucks play their very first full game at the recently completed facility that is to become their new home: GM Place.

"It's absolutely fantastic. It's better than we expected. It's going to be a great home for us for a long time," gushes general manager Pat Quinn in an interview with the *Vancouver Province*.

"I feel great every time I come here," adds right winger Pavel Bure. "It's great being in this beautiful dressing room and being out on the ice with that big TV screen up there."

More than 15,000 fans attend the exhibition game—a 4 to 3 victory over the Anaheim Mighty Ducks, with many, including former Canuck Robert Dirk, complimenting the arena as a great improvement over their former home at the Pacific Coliseum. GM Place has hosted several other events within its walls before the exhibition game, including a September 19 performance by Bryan Adams. Although the fan response is generally positive, the *Province* is less impressed.

"The highly-paid Canucks hit the ice last night, and the high-paying Canucks fans started shelling out in earnest," reports the paper. "While some said the prices were justified to keep the superstars here, others said the working person can no longer afford to see the working person's game."

The *Province* then goes on to detail its complaints, including the price of soft drinks, coffee, and team memorabilia, contrasting them with the lower prices found in virtually every other arena in the city.

"GM Place coffee will set you back $2.20, almost a buck more than the $1.25 brew just down Pacific Boulevard," the article gripes. "While the $2 small Coke is about half the size of BC Place's 16-oz. $2.25 cup."

"For the average Joe to come and bring the kids, forget it," says Leanne Kemp, a registered nurse. "It's crazy."

However, when questioned by the paper, longshoreman Clayton Eccles is more resigned.

"We've got to help pay Pavel Bure's salary, I guess."

SEPTEMBER 24, 1977

FOLLOWING TWO YEARS of technical challenges, cost overruns, and a marathon 28-hour assembly session by engineers, the Gastown Steam Clock is officially dedicated by Mayor Jack Volrich and hailed as the world's first steam-powered timepiece . . . even though it still runs on electricity.

"When Ray Saunders set out to build the world's first steam-powered clock, skeptics told him he was full of hot air," a 1978 story in the *Vancouver Province* will read. "But he's done it. Almost. The 16-foot clock stands at Cambie and Water Streets in Gastown. But it's still running on electricity."

"There are too many things that can go wrong with a steam engine," Saunders will explain in a December 1977 interview with the *Province*, "that we wanted to get the clock running with an electric motor first."

Saunders, a noted local horologist, was contacted to design the 2.5 ton, 16-foot timepiece, following a suggestion from city planner John Ellis, as part of a widespread Gastown beautification scheme that has been in progress since the early 1970s.

"The initial problem was steam, venting through a manhole at the corner of Cambie and Water Streets," Ellis will explain in a 1978 interview with *Western Living*. "Technical requirements made the steam vent necessary, and it was up to me to make it attractive, or at least a little less ugly . . . Ray Spaxman suggested using the steam to power a kinetic sculpture, and I took it a step further and suggested a clock that would not only tell the time, but would do something entertaining at the same time."

As Saunders recalls, he encountered considerable difficulty having the clock's centrepiece—a hand-built, 12-inch-high steam engine—designed. In fact, four of the five companies he approached told him it couldn't be done.

"I was too stupid to know it couldn't be done," he will explain in a 1978 interview with the *Province*. "I set out to do it anyway and I ran into a lot of opposition."

The cost of the clock has been split between the city and Gastown business owners; however, the project will run into a number of problems during its construction, problems that will drive the price up from its initial $25,000 estimate to more than $57,000. Ellis, for his part, will be unsympathetic, stating in an interview with the *Sun*: "We have a contract for him to provide a clock at a certain date and at a certain cost. The clock was to be up and working. It is in place and it is working, but it's not running on steam."

Installation of the steam engine will be delayed several times throughout 1977 and 1978, and as of 2013, the clock will still be run by three electric motors.

A crowd gathered around the Gastown Steam Clock, Aug. 1978.
PHOTOGRAPH BY ROSE PENZARI (VPL 48694)

SEPTEMBER 25, 1911

AFTER MONTHS OF CONSULTATION, city engineer F.L. Fellowes submits a complete proposal to the Harbour Improvements Committee —a proposal that would allow for the transformation of the False Creek mud flats into an industrial area.

"[The plans] provide for the reclamation of about fifteen acres of mud-flats under the Granville Street Bridge," the *Vancouver Daily World* will report the following day, "and extending east and west in False Creek. They will be raised about five feet above the high water mark, and will provide accommodation for a paving plant, machine and pipe shops, a refuse destructor, creosote and asphalt plants, sand, gravel, brick, cement, sewer and water pipe, and equipment sheds, barns, stables, warehouses and wharves."

The False Creek mud flats, which are so close to the high-water mark that they disappear at high tide, have been discussed as a potential industrial area since 1905; however, it will take a further two years before the federal government (which owns any land below the high-water mark) will grant the city permission to proceed with the project. In 1913, a contract will be awarded to the Pacific Dredging Company to create 34.28 acres of brand new land beneath the Granville Street Bridge, and by 1917, the island will welcome its first tenants. The approximate cost for the entire reclamation (said to be the cheapest in the Harbour Improvement Committee's history), including sewage, water, and a railway line, will work out to $342,000, or approximately $600 per lineal foot.

This will not be the last time dredging is used to fill in portions of False Creek; the same process will later be used to create land under the Georgia Viaduct and in the area that will one day be the site of Pacific Central Station.

While the city's newest industrial area will at first be known locally as "Mud Island," it will eventually be given a more familiar title: Granville Island.

EAST HALF GRANVILLE ISLAND BEFORE FILLING.

The eastern half of Granville Island, prior to filling, 1916.
IMAGE COURTESY OF THE VANCOUVER ARCHIVES (A-8-22.3)

SEPTEMBER 26, 1891

Greer's Beach, 1900.
IMAGE COURTESY OF THE VANCOUVER ARCHIVES (BE P99)

A QUIET BEACHFRONT PROPERTY becomes the scene of a shootout as Samuel "Gritty" Greer, a former Union soldier and noted Vancouver pioneer, exchanges fire with law enforcement officials sent to evict him from his own land.

The skirmish comes after years of work by the CPR to seize control of Greer's property as well as much of the land surrounding what will one day be known as Kitsilano Beach. Early attempts to buy the pioneer out of his lucrative waterfront property were unsuccessful, and, when it became clear that the pioneer would not sell or leave of his own accord, the railroad set in motion plans to remove him.

"They say the CPR wanted title to the land but the government was afraid to give it to them, fearing some after action," city pioneer H.P. McCraney will recall in a conversation with archivist J.S. Matthews, "but [the government] said to the CPR that, if they could get Sam out of the way, or at least if the CPR would guarantee quiet possession for ten years, they would give the company the title."

The struggle has already been lengthy and bitter. Greer has often been seen tearing down telegraph wires in the area and filling in holes dug by the CPR. On one occasion he chased off a sheriff and three deputies with an axe. The posse, led by Sheriff Tom Armstrong, is barely onto the beach when Greer fires several rounds of buckshot, wounding Armstrong and a deputy, and forcing them to retreat. However, a second round of deputies appears later in the afternoon, and Greer is arrested.

"Sam made one terrible mistake," Captain J. Hampton Bole will later explain in a conversation with archivist J.S. Matthews.

"If he had not fired that gun at Tom Armstrong, he would have held his property. That mistake cost him the possession of the part of our city. Public opinion was so strong that the CPR would have had to have given in; the people would have torn up the rails as fast as they laid them."

Greer will later be tried by Judge Matthew Baillie Begbie, found guilty, and sentenced to "one term" in jail. On the day of his arrest, his home and possessions will be burned by law enforcement.

"I think Sam Greer had what we call a 'raw' deal," H.P. McCraney will continue. "He was the only man in Canada who 'held up' the CPR, but they were too strong for him. Alex Henderson told me that he was at the trial, and that Judge Begbie bulldozed the jury into finding Sam guilty, and gave him eighteen months in gaol. Henderson said he never saw a worse case of a judge bulldozing a jury."

Greer will eventually be freed; however, despite more than 30 years of petitioning the government, he will never again regain title to his land. In 1930, thanks to the efforts of Matthews and W.J. Findlay, the northern tip of Kitsilano Beach will be named Greer's Point.

SEPTEMBER 27, 1888

Entrance to Stanley Park, 1906.
IMAGE COURTESY OF THE VANCOUVER ARCHIVES (ST PK P322)

A 20-PIECE MARCHING BAND leads the charge, and a procession of vehicles stretches from Powell Street to Prospect Point, as the city celebrates the official opening of its first public green space: Stanley Park.

The opening ceremonies for the peninsula, simply referred to as "The Park" (it won't be named until October 1889 when it is dedicated by Canada's Governor General, Lord Frederick Stanley), are held at the home of Squamish leader August Jack Khatsalano, whose family has lived at Prospect Point since before 1865. Mayor David Oppenheimer declares that it will be "a place of recreation in the vicinity of a city where its inhabitants can spend some time amid the beauties of nature away from the busy haunts of men." Of little interest to the city is the fact that the park has been used for thousands of years by the West Coast First Nations people as a burial ground and as a site for some of the largest potlatch ceremonies in the Pacific Northwest. In addition, the area has for generations been home to a number of Vancouver families, many of whom have legal claims to their land. However, the pressure brought to bear by local politicians, the CPR, and the widespread support for public parks throughout North America is simply too powerful. Within a decade most of these families will be displaced, many without remuneration.

"The Park road was made around Stanley Park, and ran right through our house," early resident Tim Cummings will recall in a conversation with city archivist J.S. Matthews. "We had to move our house back to let the road go by."

Some, including August Jack himself, will find their gardens, fences, and properties vandalized or destroyed by clearing crews.

"There were two of them," Khatsalano will recount in an interview with Matthews. "They cut off the corner of our house; just a little bit, so they could see where to put their survey line . . . The man said that when the road goes by here, you are going to have lots of money."

Others, in particular many of the park's Asian residents, will not be nearly so fortunate.

"The Park Board ordered the Chinamen to leave the park," Sarah Avison, daughter of the city's first park ranger, will explain, describing an eviction she witnessed, "but the Chinamen would not go, so the Park Board told my father to set fire to the buildings . . . What happened to the Chinese I do not know, but the pigs were set loose and the bull untied, and they got lost in the forest of Stanley Park, and they could not track them down until the snow fell. Then my Dad tracked them down, and they shot them in the bushes, and the bull's head was cut off, and my father had it stuffed and set up in our hallway in our house, the 'Park Cottage.'"

Legal battles for the area will continue into the 20th century. By the late 1920s, all of Stanley Park's residents (with the exception of Cummings) will have been evicted, their homes burned, and their livestock slaughtered. Cummings himself will remain Stanley Park's only official resident until his death in 1958.

"They said 'Pay to go through your place,'" Khatsalano will conclude. "But they have not paid yet."

SEPTEMBER 28, 1967

FOLLOWING ALLEGATIONS OF OBSCENITY, the *Georgia Straight* has its business licence suspended at the request of the mayor.

"It's a filthy, perverted paper," Mayor Tom Campbell announces at a press conference. "It should not be sold to our children."

The suspension, issued by licence inspector Milt Harell, comes after only four months of publication by the controversial alternative weekly, in spite of its impressive circulation (60,000 for the September 22 issue, unusually high for an underground paper). The decision—made at Campbell's behest following "many complaints" —instantly polarizes the city, sparking a demonstration outside of City Hall which will last until 1 a.m.

In the days to follow, editor Dan McLeod will seek a Supreme Court action against the city and the mayor, citing damages for the more than 700 *Straight* vendors affected. A number of vendors will continue to sell the paper anyway, in open defiance of the council order (an infraction that could result in a $100 fine or up to two years in prison). The *Straight* has made a habit of ruffling feathers since it began publication five months earlier, for its frank discussion of sex and drugs, and for the comic strip character Acidman, who regularly appears both high on LSD and with genitals on full display. However, despite McLeod's protests, the suspension is supported by six of council's eight aldermen and will draw more than 600 letters of approval from constituents in the weeks to follow.

Six weeks later, the paper's licence will be reinstated by order of a notice delivered personally by Inspector Harell, albeit with a warning that future issues could result in another cancellation if they don't meet with his approval. While public support will at first be minimal, by 1968 (following a lawsuit launched by McLeod

A protest on behalf of The Georgia Straight, circa 1967.
IMAGE COURTESY OF THE UBYSSEY.

and others against Campbell and city council) the case will become a *cause célèbre* in mainstream newspapers as an example of direct city interference with the freedom of the press.

"They have written articles, citing examples of what they consider to be bad laws or good laws which are misused," Mark Gree of the Vancouver Junior Chamber of Commerce will write in a letter published in the *Straight*'s November 24 issue. "To this the public is indifferent. They write articles condemning the war in Vietnam. To this, again, the public is silent. But dare they mention sex and the public is up in arms."

Though McLeod's lawsuit will ultimately be unsuccessful, the *Straight* will not remain out of the limelight for long; in August 1968, the paper will have been charged with libelling a city magistrate.

SEPTEMBER 29, 1888

AMONG LITTLE FANFARE, the city's media landscape is altered with the introduction of its second daily newspaper, the *Vancouver Daily World*.

"It is always customary in the first issue of a newspaper to define briefly but emphatically the lines upon which it is to be managed," reads the opening editorial, "the policies which it intends to pursue, and the general tone which is to characterize it. The *Vancouver World* will not, in these regards at least, prove an exception to the general rule."

Front-page articles in the first edition include "Our Water Works," "People We Talk About," and "The Manly Arts." Among the paper's goals are to "obtain a truthful record of every day's doings," to "discuss issues from an independent standpoint, giving praise where praise is due, and blame where it is deserved," and to "be thoroughly British Columbian."

"This journal believes that there is an opening on the mainland for a lively evening paper," the editorial continues, "and enters the field with feelings of the sincerest friendship and goodwill towards the contemporary press which has in the past proved itself to be deserving of public sympathy and support."

The paper's circulation will remain modest through the turn of the century; however, following the death of editor John McLagan, it will be bought by businessman (and later Vancouver mayor) Louis D. Taylor, who will transform it from a modest daily into a circulation giant capable of challenging even the rival *Province*. Over the next decade, the *World* will become one of the city's major newspapers, and its headquarters, the World Building, will for two years be the tallest building in the British Empire.

The World Building (later the Bekins Building and the Sun Tower), 1927.
IMAGE COURTESY OF THE VANCOUVER ARCHIVES (STR N164, PHOTOGRAPHER W. J. MOORE)

Unfortunately the paper, once radical for its inclusive nature (former editor Sarah McLagan often used it to campaign for women's suffrage), the *World* under Taylor will often descend into hyperbole and xenophobia, spending years advocating for the exclusion of Chinese, Japanese, and South Asian citizens. By the 1920s, the paper will have fallen on hard times, and in 1924, it will be purchased and shut down by long-time rival the *Vancouver Sun*.

Within weeks of the purchase, the *Sun* will move into the World Building itself, renaming it the Sun Tower.

SEPTEMBER 30, 1867

UNDER A LIGHT DRIZZLE, John "Gassy Jack" Deighton first arrives in Burrard Inlet, bringing with him his wife, his mother-in-law, a cousin by the name of Big William, two chickens, two "weak-backed" chairs, and a dog. They have come in search of a fresh start and, in so doing, inadvertently contribute to the beginnings of the city of Vancouver.

"Jack landed at his destination in the afternoon of the last day of September," an unnamed Vancouver pioneer will remark. "Lookers-on from the mill remarked that it was a doubtful acquisition to the population."

Deighton, a former riverboat captain who will become known as "Gassy Jack" because of his propensity for long-winded stories, arrives in the inlet fleeing bankruptcy. Within 24 hours, he has convinced workers from the nearby Hastings Sawmill to build the city's first bar, The Globe Saloon, in exchange for all the whisky they can drink. The mill workers require little convincing; their only company is currently one another, and the only other saloon in the area is more than 25 kilometres away.

It was "a lonesome place when I came here first, surrounded by Indians," Deighton will later recall in a letter to his brother Tom. "I care not to look outdoors after dark. There was a friend of mine about a mile distant found with his head cut in two."

Despite the rough nature of the area, The Globe will quickly become incredibly successful, and Deighton himself, with his grotesque bulk, mottled complexion, and gift with words, will become a wealthy and respected member of the tiny community. By the time of his death in 1875, the community that grew directly up around his saloon will be on its way to becoming a bustling metropolis. And, although the portion of the city that Deighton helped found will be known as Granville, and later Vancouver on all official maps, locals will continue to call it by another name: Gastown.

"You and I may never see it but this inlet would make the nicest of harbors," Deighton once remarked to miner William Mackie. "It will be a port some day."

OCTOBER 1, 1940

In New Westminster, *Vancouver Province* photographer Claude Detloff inadvertently snaps a photograph that will become the most famous Canadian image of the Second World War. The image, later named *Wait for Me, Daddy*, depicts five-year-old Walter "Whitey" Bernard chasing after his father as the elder Bernard marches with his regiment in preparation to board a troop ship to Nanaimo.

Detloff, a *Province* photographer since 1936, is already notable nationwide, having had his photo coverage of the city's sit-down post-office strike featured in *Life* magazine. When his photograph appears in the following day's edition of the *Province*, *Wait for Me, Daddy* will become an instant sensation, emblematic of the millions of Canadian families separated by war. The photograph will be hung in every school in Vancouver and will receive international exposure when it is purchased by *Life* (for the princely sum of $50). In fact, Detloff's image will soon prove so popular that it will quickly be capitalized upon by the military, who will use the shot—and young "Whitey" himself—to sell war bonds.

"They'd put me up front in my short pants and blue blazer and tell them I hadn't seen my dad for a long time and would they please buy bonds to help him get home sooner," Bernard will recall in a 1978 interview with the *Vancouver Province*. "Then someone would unveil the picture and there'd be a lineup to buy bonds."

Bernard will spend months touring the country as a figurehead at war bond rallies and, following the war, will move to Tofino to manage a Chevron franchise. Jack Bernard, his rifleman father, will return alive.

Life magazine will later declare Detloff's photo one of the 10 Best Images of the 1940s.

Claude Detloff's iconic photograph, Oct. 1, 1940.
Image courtesy of the Vancouver Archives (CVA 371-3183, photographer Claude Detloff)

OCTOBER 2, 1970

"POLITICAL PING PONG" continues between Vancouver and Ottawa, and tensions run high in Point Grey as roughly 300 protesters occupy Jericho Youth Hostel in spite of a federal order closing the facility.

"The summer travellers have long since gone," reports the *Vancouver Province,* "leaving behind the youthful, unemployed, and in many cases the youngsters with 'nowhere else to go.' Many are sick, either physically or mentally, and many more have been pumping drugs into their bodies nightly."

The protesters, in open defiance of the closure order from Ottawa (which runs the summer-only hostel program), have staged noisy demonstrations outside the building, playing instruments, dancing, and stating their willingness to stay until suitable alternative housing is found. Unfortunately, public support for the protest is minimal. With the hostel itself sitting near Jericho Garrison—and surrounded by clusters of military housing—tensions between protesters and those stationed nearby are high.

"I don't want to meet any of those people," an unnamed "Canadian Army Housewife" is quoted as saying. "If any of those people come around my family, I'll use my shotgun."

Inside, facilities are less than adequate. As the *Province* will note, only six toilets and one shower exist to service the 400-bed facility. Within a week, Ottawa will shut off water and electricity to the building, before the city health department will have it restored, citing a "general health bylaw." Some occupants will later be removed to hostel facilities in other portions of the city, and by October 15, in a skirmish later dubbed "The Battle of Jericho," the RCMP will storm the building, forcibly removing all remaining

Protestors at the Jericho Youth Hostel, 1970.
IMAGE COURTESY OF UBC RARE BOOKS AND SPECIAL COLLECTIONS, GEORGIA STRAIGHT COLLECTION

occupants and effectively ending the political embarrassment caused by the Jericho hostel.

In spite of the conflict, less than a year later, a permanent hostel will be established at the site, a hostel that will continue to exist into the new millennium.

OCTOBER 3, 1970

Pilots and city officials sigh with frustration as the federal Department of Transportation rules that the fog dispersal aircraft at Vancouver International Airport is forbidden from taking off in foggy conditions.

"And that," says an airport worker in an interview with the *Vancouver Sun*, "is like telling a water bomber it can't take off until after the forest fire has been put out."

For two days, fog has been wreaking havoc with airline schedules, with cancellations and delays abounding due to the zero visibility conditions that continue to prevail at landing sites in both Vancouver and Abbotsford. Despite high hopes for the specially outfitted DC-3 (the first of its kind in Canada, tested the previous year on Air Canada's dime in Seattle), Ottawa has ruled that the aircraft must remain grounded until visibility increases to a quarter mile. Unfortunately, this distance is identical to the distance required for a commercial jetliner to take off. The $55,000 operation, supported by seven major airlines, is intended to be similar to those that already exist in the United States, where fog-fighting aircraft are permitted even in zero visibility conditions.

"The whole point of the operation, of course, is to go up when the airlines can't," says an unnamed city official. "Good old Ottawa."

An airplane, 1939.
Image courtesy of the Vancouver Archives (CVA 260-1025, photographer James Crookall)

OCTOBER 4, 1946

Debate swirls in the pages of the *Vancouver Sun* as contractors, architects, and the city's planning council sound off on a proposed bylaw banning the "knotty problem" of basement suites.

"Yesterday Town Planning commission urged that all basement dwellings be banned in Vancouver," the story explains. "the present by-law allows one third of basement space to be used for dwelling."

Secondary suites are a contentious issue in the Vancouver of the 1940s, with hundreds of extras added during the Second World War to deal with a city-wide housing shortage. However, the future of these suites—governed by bizarre and draconian bylaws—is far from clear. Many basement suites, the paper notes, are basements "in name only. Contractors heap earth around what is virtually a first floor to circumvent a by-law which only allows frame buildings to stand two storeys high . . . At present, several dozen suites in new apartment houses in the Cambie district are empty because they occupy more than the allowed third of the floor space."

"The present bylaw regarding basement suites is perfectly ridiculous so far as it refers to new buildings," complains architect Ross Lord. "I don't think they realized that new buildings would be built in the present form (with a basement virtually at ground level)."

Basement suites will remain an issue for debate over the coming decades, viewed as a nuisance by many city planners until 1988, when a city-wide referendum will allow for secondary suite rezoning in specific areas. By 2004, prevailing wisdom will have changed drastically, and council will amend all zoning bylaws to allow—and, in fact, encourage—secondary suites in every area of the city.

Teenagers in a basement rec room, Dec. 1942.
Image Courtesy of the Vancouver Archives (CVA 1184-1526, Jack Lindsay, photographer)

OCTOBER 5, 1918

"FIND FIRST CASES SPANISH 'FLU' HERE," reports the *Vancouver Province*, little realizing that these words will mark the beginning of the city's largest—and deadliest—influenza epidemic.

"The first cases of Spanish influenza have appeared in Vancouver," the paper reports. "The city medical health officer, Dr. F.T. Underhill, was notified late Saturday afternoon of doctors identifying two or three cases as the malady which has spread so alarmingly across the continent, but they were described as mild cases so far . . . Dr. Underhill has taken up with the provincial health authorities necessary measures to be taken in the event of an epidemic, but present conditions do not call for extraordinary measures to be taken, such as the closing of theatres or meeting places."

However, fewer than 10 days later, 7 people will be dead, and 180 cases will have been reported city-wide. By October 19, the death toll will have risen to 32, with 900 confirmed cases, and Vancouver will be in the grip of panic. Theatres, churches, and all other public meeting places will be closed (including City Hall) by order of Mayor Gale under the advice of Dr. Underhill. "Ambulance men" will wear gas masks in an attempt to avoid infection, regular citizens will wear cloves of garlic around their necks to combat the disease, and the price of camphor (thought to be an effective deterrent) will rise, in the space of one month, from 40 cents to $6.50 a pound.

Spanish Flu—one of the 20th century's most notorious epidemics—is already spreading elsewhere in the world, having begun in army camps during the First World War before exploding worldwide, causing high death tolls in Europe and North America.

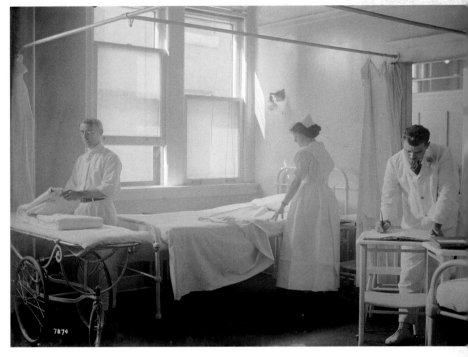

Interior of Vancouver General Hospital, 1919.
IMAGE COURTESY OF THE VANCOUVER ARCHIVES (CVA 99-863, PHOTOGRAPHER STUART THOMSON)

Symptoms will vary wildly from case to case, and bizarrely, the greatest number of deaths in Vancouver will be of people between the ages of 31 and 39.

"The undertaking parlours couldn't handle the bodies as people died," survivor Louise Brooks will recall in a 2008 interview with the Canadian Press. "And I have this vague memory that they were having to use school auditoriums and places like that to store bodies temporarily."

By March of 1919, more than 30 percent of the city's population will have fallen ill, and the epidemic will have claimed the lives of close to 1,200 people.

OCTOBER 6, 1909

An unfortunate day dawns for Vancouver's medical community when, to celebrate the arrival of the city's first motorized ambulance, mechanic Charles Cocking takes the vehicle out for a test drive—and accidentally kills an American tourist.

The ambulance (described by the *Province* as "a very heavy affair") is attempting to pass between two streetcars near Granville and Pender, and fails to stop at the intersection, striking C.F. Keiss of Austin, Texas, as he endeavours to cross the street.

"He was knocked to the ground," the *Province* reports, "the front wheels placing his body in such a position that one of the rear wheels passed over and crushed his head."

Keiss, visiting Vancouver for a hunting expedition, is described as "of middle age, and well dressed," with the paper noting that "his pockets contained cheques and cash to a large amount."

Unfortunately, despite the ambulance's proximity, Keiss will not survive the collision.

"He was immediately placed inside the auto," the paper states, "but was practically dead when picked up."

An ambulance, 1914.
Image courtesy of the Vancouver Archives (A-30-72, photographer A.J. Selset)

OCTOBER 7, 1960

Terror grips the downtown core in the early hours of the morning as John Conroy, a former war hero and "sort of a genius," goes on a shooting rampage in the middle of Granville Street.

"Fusillade on City Street!" reads the headline in the *Vancouver Sun*. "Police are searching for a mysterious letter which could have sparked a wild murder-suicide shooting affray early today."

Conroy, in a walking cast for a broken ankle, inebriated after an estimated 10-hour bender at local nightclubs, and agitated by the contents of a mysterious letter he received, stalks down Granville, firing a high-powered hunting rifle at nearby pedestrians.

"I don't know what was in it," Winnifred Thorne, clerk at the hotel, says of the letter. "He didn't say a word after reading it. He just walked out with a disturbed look on his face."

Conroy fires several shots, killing 26-year-old Arthur Jorgenson from a distance of over 200 metres and narrowly missing other bystanders, who take cover behind cars and buildings. Though Conroy, an unemployed tugboat operator, has a well-known love of guns, he has no history of violence and is described as an intelligent, sensitive man by his close friend John Humphrey. In fact, as Humphrey tells the *Sun*, Conroy had years earlier received the Order of the British Empire for wartime gallantry.

"He'd saved five or six men by pulling them on board a raft," Humphrey will explain in the October 8 edition of the *Sun*. "He was decorated by the late King George."

And though the tugboat mate knows five or six languages and has a propensity for books over television, Humphrey also describes him as "a moody man who could turn vicious when he had too much to drink."

Granville Street, circa 1960.
Image courtesy of the Vancouver Archives (CVA 780-55)

Following the murder of Jorgenson, Conroy staggers back into his hotel and commits suicide. Though the contents of his mystery letter will at first be hotly discussed by local media, it will later be revealed to have merely been a notice from a collection agency, pertaining to a dispute over a TV set.

"I don't think it had anything to do with him shooting anybody," Humphrey will explain, "but it might have been one of the things building up inside him."

OCTOBER 8, 1922

THE MEDIA KICK INTO A FRENZY and racial tensions are polarized city-wide as, following an early-morning traffic stop at the corner of Davie and Granville, Constable Robert McBeath is shot and killed, after a fight with "drink-crazed negro" Fred Deal.

"McBeath and I were standing at the corner of Davie and Granville a little before 2:30 when we saw a car coming north from Drake Street," VPD Detective Quirk (who sustains a gunshot wound to the scalp during the fight) will explain in an interview with the *Vancouver Province*. "The horn was sounding repeatedly and unnecessarily, and the car was zigzagging about the road in such a way that we came to the conclusion that the driver must be under the influence of liquor."

Deal, a driver for and associate of well-known underworld figure Marjorie Earl (who, as every major newspaper will point out in horror, is white), is pulled over under suspicion of intoxication and, according to Quirk's account, immediately goes into a frenzy.

"Just as I had reached the woman [Earl] I heard a yell and looking around I saw the negro had broken loose and was running with McBeath after him," Quirk explains to the *Vancouver Daily World*. "McBeath caught him and when I got there they were scuffling. They were locked pretty tight, so I grabbed the negro by the arm so that he could not do any damage and I had no sooner got hold of his arm when a gun went off and McBeath let go of his grip on the negro who ran up Davie Street to the lane."

Following a brief manhunt, Deal will be arrested and charged with murder. In the days to come, the backlash against the city's black community will be severe. Mayor Tisdall will issue an order to the police department to raid dance halls, pool rooms, and low-

income hotels in an effort to rid the city of "undesirables." Local dailies will dismiss Deal as nothing more than a "crazed negro from the underworld" and will praise McBeath's gallantry and his accomplishments as an athlete, policeman, and war hero.

Deal's first trial will take place within the month and result in a death sentence. However, the case will be overturned on appeal. In 1923, the second trial will cast serious doubt on the official version of the story. In front of a packed courtroom, witnesses will testify to having heard swearing and racial slurs from both Quirk and McBeath, and later evidence will surface indicating that McBeath had a personal vendetta against Marjorie Earl. Photo evidence of Deal following his arrest (including a black eye, a split lip, a broken nose, and multiple lacerations) will lend authenticity to Deal's claims that he was severely beaten by officers on the night of his arrest, and several police witnesses will refute officers' claims that he was intoxicated.

Following a record 10-hour deliberation, Fred Deal will be found guilty of manslaughter, and his sentence will be commuted to life in prison.

Fred Deal, 1922.
IMAGE COURTESY OF THE VANCOUVER POLICE MUSEUM

OCTOBER 9, 1970

AT 8:22 P.M., IN FRONT OF 15,000 FANS, and after months of training and years of waiting, the puck drops on the Vancouver Canucks' very first NHL game—a 3 to 1 loss to the LA Kings.

"There was pomp and ceremony; pipe bands and speeches; red carpets and countless dignitaries to tread on them," reports the *Vancouver Sun*'s Hal Sigurdson. "There was also a small army from the people's television network to record it all for the masses. One small item, however, was missing when the Vancouver Canucks played their first-ever National Hockey League game Friday night . . . Victory."

The pre-game ceremonies involve music, a display of the Stanley Cup, a parade of Vancouver hockey players from years past (including 87-year-old legend Fred "Cyclone" Taylor), a telegram from Prime Minister Pierre Trudeau, and dignitaries such as Premier W.A.C. Bennett, League President Clarence Campbell, Chief Dan George, and Vancouver mayor Tom Campbell (who is heartily booed by the crowd).

Vancouver's quest to obtain an NHL franchise has been a lengthy one, with the city being passed over in 1965 in favour of six American cities. With the ardent support of local politicians and businessmen (including former mayor Fred Hume and White Spot owner Nat Bailey), the team was finally awarded the 14th NHL franchise earlier in the year.

The team's first official league fight takes place five minutes into the game, and its first league goal is scored roughly two minutes into the third period by defenceman Barry Wilkins, a move that draws deafening cheers from the crowd.

Not all fans are as enthusiastic, the *Sun* reports. Remarks from the stands, as recorded by the paper, include "The Western League was better!" and "Come on, you're in the big leagues now!"

The Canucks will continue to play at the Pacific Coliseum until 1995, when they will be moved to a brand new facility at GM Place.

OCTOBER 10, 1920

"City Hall More Lively as Election Gossip Starts," reads a headline in the *Vancouver Sun* as, for the first time since 1886, a city election will be held without the traditional ward system.

"Although civic election day seems to the 'man in the street' a long way off, the corridors of the City Hall are already beginning to buzz with rumours," the paper reports. "Those who intend entering the contests have to be far-seeing and, with a new factor to be considered in the Proportional Representation system of voting, interest has begun to be manifested earlier than usual."

Ever since its first council meeting, Vancouver has used a ward system for electing civic government, with the wards increasing in size and in number over the years from five to 12. However, early in 1920, a referendum was held on election policy, with the result being a city-wide switch to proportional representation.

"All the present Aldermen are likely to try their luck again in the 'free-for-all' scramble which the PR system of 'Aldermen-at-Large' will create," the paper reports, "and many of the hardy annuals who have been only occasionally successful under the ward system are likely to make the experiment of appealing to the voters of the whole city."

Unfortunately, the experiment will prove unpopular with voters, and a return to wards will take place only three years later. The city will change its municipal election particulars a number of times in the ensuing years, adding wards and changing the length of terms. In 1936 (following another referendum), it will again adopt the at-large system—unusual for a city of its size. Despite a number of proposals, studies, debates, public hearings, and civic plebiscites, Vancouver will ultimately retain its at-large system into the new millennium.

A referendum in 1988 to reinstitute city wards will fall short by 4 percent.

By the year 2000, the city will have held no fewer than eight referendums on the ward/at-large question.

L.D. Taylor campaign poster, circa 1930.
Image courtesy of the Vancouver Archives (CVA 677-807, photographer Philip T. Timms)

OCTOBER 11, 1957

"Court Upholds *Lord's Day Act,*" reports a headline in the *Vancouver Sun* as, following an appeal of charges laid four months previously, the Vancouver Mounties are found guilty of playing professional baseball on a Sunday.

"Magistrate N.J. Bartman fined the club $50 on each of three charges laid four months ago under *Lord's Day Act*," the paper explains. "The judgement could mean an end to Sunday ball in Vancouver."

The team stands convicted of contravening a number of provisions of the act, including "unlawfully for gain employing persons to work (on Sunday)," "unlawfully providing a performance for which either a direct or indirect fee was charged for admission," and "unlawfully engaging in a public game for gain."

Sunday sports have been a contentious and heavily discussed issue in Vancouver since 1949 when the first city plebiscite on the issue was conducted. However, according to the *Sun*, "stiff opposition" has been encountered, both from the provincial government and from local organizations such as the Lord's Day Alliance—a group opposed to Sunday entertainment of any kind.

"It is time the Act was revised to bring it abreast of modern thinking," complains Mounties director Harold Merilees. "Until then, I sincerely hope the symphony isn't pestered."

Reverend Stanley Higgs, president of the Lord's Day Alliance (whose complaints led to the team's prosecution in the first place), is reportedly pleased with the outcome of the trial, "but didn't want to appear smug about it."

"The *Lord's Day Act,* presumably modelled imperfectly on the divine precept, by its very nature touches questions both of physical

Baseball, 1919.
Image courtesy of the Vancouver Archives (CVA 99-723, photographer Stuart Thomson)

and moral order, and has, in this instance, excited public opinion for and against the introduction of sports into Sunday," reads the text of the judgment prepared by Magistrate Bartman. "It is not for the court to criticize the legislation itself. In construction of statutes their words must be interpreted in their ordinary grammatical sense, unless there is something to indicate otherwise. If the words are clear, they must be followed to their manifest conclusion."

A second city plebiscite on the issue will be conducted in the wake of the decision, leading to a high-profile battle that will go all the way to the BC Supreme Court. The decision will ultimately be upheld, and beginning in 1959, Sunday sport will at last be permitted in the city of Vancouver. However, entertainment venues and other businesses (including the CBC) will continue to be prosecuted under the *Lord's Day Act* well into the 1970s.

OCTOBER 12, 1962

NEON SIGNS ARE TORN LOOSE on Granville Street, trees are ripped from their roots, and, at close to midnight, the Stanley Park causeway becomes the scene of mass panic as Hurricane Freda hits Vancouver.

"Stanley Park causeway became a scene of terror and death Friday midnight as the violent wind flung giant fir trees across the road," reports the *Vancouver Province*. "Joseph Plag described how he watched with horror as a giant tree toppled with a roar and smashed a car in front of his."

The city has been ravaged by powerful storms since early morning, with reports of winds reaching 129 miles per hour, destroying property, felling electrical wires, and causing widespread damage. Telephones and lights are out in vast sections of the city, radio stations have gone off the air, and looting is reported in the downtown core.

"The hurricane force winds were accompanied by driving rain and strange flashes of white light," the *Province* continues. "The weather forecaster said it was a form of lightning."

One person has already been killed as a result of the high winds, and a second is crushed to death on the causeway when a falling tree lands on top of her car. Before the end of the day, the storm will have felled nearly 3,000 trees in Stanley Park and will require more than $150,000 in cleanup.

OCTOBER 13, 1962

LITERATI QUAKE IN FEAR as the RCMP Morality Squad raids two bookstores and the public library after receiving word that they may be circulating "obscene material."

"Royal Canadian Mounted Police swooped down on bookstores and the Vancouver Public Library Friday in a hunt for copies of author Henry Miller's sex-in-Paris novel, *Tropic of Cancer*," reports the *Vancouver Sun*. "Two plain-clothes officers seized one volume at Duthie Books, and learned three other volumes were in circulation from the public library."

Using a writ of assistance, which allows the police to enter public buildings, commercial establishments, and private residences without notification, they will ultimately confiscate three copies of Miller's book, which has been banned in Canada since 1958.

Raids, confiscation, and censorship by the police and Canada Customs are not unusual in British Columbia. In the past, works such as D.H. Lawrence's *Lady Chatterley's Lover*, James Joyce's *Ulysses*, and Norman Mailer's *The Naked and the Dead* have been subject to provincial or nationwide bans, with airport luggage searches, criminal trials, and heavy fines levied against people seen to be distributors.

"We've been instructed to find and seize the books wherever possible," a spokesman for the RCMP tells reporters. "When books are on the banned list, customs men are always watching for them."

"Personally, I can't see why the book can't be allowed into Canada," VPL assistant director Morton Jordan retorts in the pages of the *Sun*. "Miller is pretty highly regarded, his book is well written and although a little spicy in places, is considered a good literary work."

"If the customs or police would only send us a list of books they have on the banned list we would know what books to stock and what not," complains an employee of Duthie Books. "As it is, the banned books list is somewhat secret and we are in the dark."

Tropic of Cancer will come to be widely regarded as one of the great literary works of the 20th century.

Vancouver Public Library, circa 1960s.

OCTOBER 14, 1959

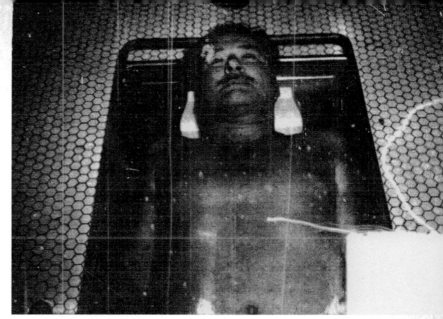

Errol Flynn, Oct. 14, 1959

"Mac. We've got a beauty for you."

Several minutes after hearing these words, Vancouver coroner Glen McDonald receives the most famous cadaver of his career: Errol Flynn.

"I was about to leave [the] office when the telephone rang," McDonald will recall. "I was looking forward to a gin and tonic."

Flynn—one of Hollywood's most notorious stars, well known for his heavy drinking, drug use, and insatiable sexual appetite—had fallen ill on his way to the airport after a week in Vancouver with his 16-year-old lover, Beverly Aadland. Despite being brought to the Burnaby Street apartment of Dr. Grant Gould, Flynn's hard-living ways had finally caught up with him; he was pronounced dead less than two hours later. The autopsy concludes that the movie star's death was due to a number of factors associated with his flamboyant lifestyle, including heart disease, diverticulosis, and cirrhosis of the liver. However, during the final moments of the examination, McDonald and chief pathologist Tom Harmon make another interesting discovery: a number of sizable venereal warts on the end of Flynn's penis.

"Tom seemed fascinated," McDonald will recall, "[and said,] 'Look, I'm going to be lecturing at the Institute of Pathology and I just thought it might be of interest if I could remove these things and fix them in formaldehyde and use them as a visual aid.' 'No way!' I said. 'We're not going to do that. I don't want anything done that isn't relevant to the case because we're really in the limelight tonight. We're on the hot seat. How can we send Mr. Flynn back to his wife with part of his bloody endowment missing?'

However, when McDonald returns to the observation room after a brief absence, he discovers that the venereal warts have disappeared.

"The first thing I noticed was that the VD warts had gone—vanished from the end of Mr. Flynn's penis," McDonald will continue. "Then I spotted a jar of formaldehyde on a shelf that looked suspiciously like it might contain VD warts."

Following a heated argument, McDonald manages to convince Harmon to return the warts, which they reattach to the cadaver using "the good offices of scotch tape."

"Maybe the Doc had never seen warts of that enormity," McDonald will conclude. "Maybe he wanted a souvenir. I never did figure out why the temptation had been too great . . . And I was relieved to learn later, talking with the Chief Coroner in Los Angeles, that a further autopsy was performed and the results concurred in every respect with what we had found."

The scotch tape is never mentioned.

OCTOBER 15, 1970

At two in the afternoon, following their repeated refusal to comply with an October 2 federal eviction order, close to 100 protesters are cleared from the Jericho Youth Hostel by a storm of police officers in a skirmish later dubbed "The Battle of Jericho."

The operation begins peacefully enough, with a small contingent of military police officers handing out eviction notices and a troop of chartered buses on the scene to transport protesters to temporary housing elsewhere in the city. A number of the hostel's inhabitants depart peacefully, while others remain defiant, refusing to leave the premises and chanting slogans including "All we want is a place to sleep."

"During the earlier part of the night the transients—calling themselves the Jericho Family—danced to drums, laughed and clowned," the *Sun* reports. "A few smoked marijuana, many conducted small and vociferous meetings and some held impromptu karate classes."

However, following their forced removal from the building (many with their possessions still inside) by a team of 150 armed officers, the mood of the hostel's former inhabitants turns ugly, with youths staging a dramatic sit-down protest in the middle of Fourth Avenue.

"Realizing that they had been decisively turfed out of the only place they had to live, the crowd's mood began to change," an October 21 article in the *Georgia Straight* will report. "In desperation about 100 Jericho people took over the street in front of the base, blocking traffic."

Unfortunately for the protesters, police are not in a charitable mood. After declaring the gathering an unlawful assembly, officers (in full riot gear and with badge numbers covered) charge the crowd, dispersing them with boots and riot sticks. Protesters respond by hurling rocks at police, and the battle continues to rage across Point Grey until the Jericho Family takes refuge in the UBC Student Union Building. There they will remain until the following morning when, owing to their hostile reception by UBC students and staff, they will agree to be taken to shelter facilities elsewhere.

"Most of them are now on the street or crashing at private houses," the *Straight* will claim. "But no one who was in the Jericho march will ever forget it."

Following the protest, eight people will be arrested, and an estimated 25 protesters will have been injured.

In 1973, a permanent hostel will be established on the Jericho site.

OCTOBER 16, 1983

LOCAL PAPERS REPORT ON THE OPENING of the Vancouver Art Gallery at its new home on Georgia and Hornby, an act that officially took place at 11:30 a.m. the previous day following a speech by Governor General Ed Schreyer.

"The steps of the gallery are shaded by the blank bulk of the Eaton's building," writes the *Vancouver Sun*. "Up on the platform by the sculpture garden, the North Vancouver Youth Band strikes up the military version of 'Joshua Fit the Battle of Jericho.' On the stairs, women in hats and dresses, women with kid gloves and men with sportscoats and ties, await Governor General Ed Schreyer."

"I think you have made an excellent start here," Schreyer said to the 2,500-person crowd. "It bodes well for the future."

The crowd milling about at the opening was a diverse one, from dignitaries (including Schreyer, Mayor Mike Harcourt, and Premier Bill Bennett) to Solidarity movement protesters demanding a general strike, to people on their way to the city's second annual Chocolate Extravaganza. For the first three hours, lineups are said to have extended out the front doors as people clamoured to get their very own $15 annual membership. The Art Gallery, relocated from its original facility on Georgia (between Bute and Thurlow where it has been since the mid-1930s), is the final step in a downtown revitalization program that has been moving steadily forward for close to a decade and which includes Robson Square, the law courts, and even an outdoor skating rink. The building, formerly the city courthouse, has undergone extensive renovations (courtesy of noted architect Arthur Erickson), and features a sophisticated climate-control system to preserve the gallery's more delicate works. It even boasts a new entranceway, a decision that caused a media frenzy and so upset Alderman Warnett Kennedy that he resigned from the VAG board of directors.

Vancouver's first art society was formed as early as 1887; however, it wasn't until 1931 that a site was purchased by the city to house its growing collection of artwork. Admission was first charged in 1963 (a decision that caused a local uproar). By the early 1970s, it was recognized that the original facility was no longer adequate for the gallery's expanding needs, and after years of financial wrangling between the city, province, and Ottawa, the courthouse site was selected as the gallery's new permanent home, and construction began in early 1980.

In his address, Schreyer praised the work done by Vancouver Art Gallery staff in bringing the project to fruition and urges the gallery (and galleries nationwide) to include more First Nations Art—an oversight the VAG has been criticized for before.

"While there has been impressive evolution of indigenous art in Canada and while we've managed to avoid the chauvinism that is a sign of cultural immaturity," Schreyer noted, "there is a problem that indigenous art doesn't merit permanent exhibition space in our galleries."

"We may have a deficiency in terms of what's in our collection," former gallery president Ron Longstaffe retorts in the pages of the *Sun*, "but there's no bias against Indian art. We don't have any French Impressionists either."

OCTOBER 17, 1980

Twenty policemen, two paddy wagons, two dog teams, and several motorcycle units descend on a South Vancouver neighbourhood after receiving word of a cross-burning ceremony taking place, presided over by the Ku Klux Klan—the first public action the group has taken in Vancouver in nearly 50 years.

"Police seized two rifles and a shotgun after searching the Klan members' vehicles and took the names of the 30 Klan members who assembled for the Saturday night ceremony," reports the *Vancouver Sun*. "The cross-burning took place only a few hours after an anti-racism rally in a South Vancouver park was disrupted by a stick-swinging group of demonstrators."

The burning ceremony, held to celebrate the assassination of Egyptian president Anwar Sadat, was, according to VPD Sergeant Koos Dykstra, "a well-publicized fact—more than one person knew about it." In fact, in the days preceding the ceremony, local papers such as the *Sun* and the *Province* were invited, though all declined the chance to attend. Despite the publicity and the allegiance of the Klan members, police are unsure if charges can be laid.

"There are certain laws against this sort of thing," explains VPD Inspector Ron Foyle, "but I am not sure what will be done at this time."

The Klan flourished briefly in the Vancouver of the 1920s, planning and executing a number of public actions from their "Imperial Palace"; however, their membership quickly dwindled following a city bylaw which prohibited the wearing of masks. However, the Klan has remained active, albeit in extremely small numbers, across the country, attempting several unsuccessful resurgences through the decades, even going so far as to attempt

The Ku Klux Klan outside their headquarters at Glen Brae (later Canuck Place), Nov. 1925.
Image courtesy of the Vancouver Archives (CVA 99-1496, photographer Stuart Thomson)

a recruiting drive in Vancouver during the weekend of the cross-burning ceremony.

National Grand Wizard Alexander McQuirter praises the ceremony as well as the violence against anti-racism protesters, calling them an aid to "the Klan's promotion of an all-white country."

McQuirter will later be arrested several times for Klan-related activities. After spending a number of years in prison, he will eventually renounce and apologize for his racist past.

"I was a different person 25 years ago," he will tell Stewart Bell of the *National Post*. "I have learned something important over the many years since 1980—that it was not possible for me to change my past, but it was possible for me to change."

The Imperial Palace, headquarters of the 1920s Vancouver Klan, would later go on to become Canuck Place.

OCTOBER 18, 1928

"New Traffic Signals Work without Hitch," announces a headline in the *Vancouver Sun*, heralding the arrival of the city's first automated traffic light.

"At noon today the first automatic traffic signal went into operation at Main and Hastings streets," reads the paper. "The signal is the first of several which will be demonstrated and tested before any one type is accepted as standard. Chief of Police H.W.

Long and Inspector George Hood point out that the installation is to primarily protect life and property, and secondarily, the speeding up of traffic."

The new system, the paper remarks, is exceedingly simple, allowing traffic through in seven-second intervals, controlled by red, green, and amber lights, and, helpfully, containing semaphore arms which feature the words "STOP" and "GO." During the afternoon, the city takes film of the new system, refining the details of its operation, in hopes that it will eventually be able to handle "traffic without delay."

"It will be necessary, however," the paper cautions, "for autoists to educate themselves in the matter of right and left-hand turns so long as these are permissible at busy corners . . . It is pointed out by those responsible for the installation that when the signals are placed on a number of intersections throughout a city, a central control can be synchronized and signals at the various points along a line of traffic can be so set that an auto driven at a given rate of speed, will suffer no delay, each consecutive signal being at the 'Go' by the time the car reaches that point."

Directing traffic at Abbott and Hastings, 1925.
Image courtesy of the Vancouver Archives (CVA 99-2390, photographer Stuart Thomson)

OCTOBER 19, 1966

VANCOUVERITES BREATHE A COLLECTIVE SIGH of relief as, after a protracted battle with city council, and the suspension of his business licence, proprietor Les Stork agrees to "cover up" the staff at The Bunkhouse, the city's first—and last—topless restaurant.

"Stork said he will, in future, concentrate on his evening folk-singing entertainment and its youthful audiences," reports the *Vancouver Province*, "and is doing away with the noon luncheons where waitresses were bare bosomed. Council earlier defined the topless waitresses as offensive and in bad taste and ordered Stork to cover the girls up or show cause why his license shouldn't be revoked. Stork agreed to cover up the waitresses, then uncovered them after seeking legal advice and maintaining he was being discriminated against by Council."

Stork's lawyer, Lorne Montaine, will meet with city council, arguing that the restaurant is being operated "in a sophisticated manner," noting that all male patrons are required to wear shirts, ties, and jackets.

"Today the waitresses are covered with nets," Montaine will tell the council. "They are covered and no bylaw has been offended."

Stork's restaurant has been open for less than a month and during that time has drawn heavy fire from city council, who have invoked special powers to suspend the Bunkhouse's licence. However, licence inspector Milt Harrell maintains that, once the waitresses are "covered up," the licence will quickly be reinstated. Harrell is quoted by the *Province* as saying that "a number of chorus girls appear at night clubs in the city in topless attire except that they wear 'pasties.'"

"He said," the paper concludes, indignant, "he doesn't class these shows as obscene or offensive to the community."

Stork will go on to be named as a suspected pimp during the high-profile Penthouse "morality" trial of 1977, though no official charges will ever be laid.

OCTOBER 20, 1928

AUDIENCES PACK THE CAPITOL THEATRE on Granville Street, eager for their chance to experience a new brand of cinema with *Mother Knows Best*, the city's first exposure to talking pictures.

"Although not a 'talkie' for its entire footage, *Mother Knows Best*, the feature film at the Capitol Theatre this week gave its viewers a taste of the screen presentation of the future," gushes

the *Vancouver Sun*. "In this entertaining story of the stage and the great war there are numerous talking sequences in addition to the musical synchronization."

The Capitol Theatre, first opened in 1921, has long enjoyed a reputation as one of Granville Street's more luxurious movie houses. There, patrons—attired in evening dress and waited on by ushers in tailcoats and pillbox hats—sit in the 2,500-seat auditorium, thrilling to films accompanied by the live orchestra of Calvin Winter and his Capitolians. The Capitol is the first movie house in Vancouver to show a "talkie," bowing to an increasing demand for the technology since the 1927 release of *The Jazz Singer*, the world's first widely released talking picture.

"As for the story itself," the paper continues, "it commands closest attention throughout. Louise Dresser gives a great performance as the mother, while Madge Bellamy and Barry Norton are also seen and heard to advantage . . . The picture possesses appealing heart interest, supplemented by the fact that in parts of the film, the spoken word synchronizes with the visualisation."

The Capitol will remain one of the city's most popular movie houses before eventually being sold to Famous Players, which, in the mid-1970s, will transform it into the Lower Mainland's first multiplex.

The theatre will finally be closed in 2006 to make way for a condominium development.

Interior of the Capitol Theatre, circa 1940.
IMAGE COURTESY OF THE VANCOUVER ARCHIVES (CVA 1184-3587, PHOTOGRAPHER JACK LINDSAY)

OCTOBER 21, 1897

A CAPACITY CROWD PACKS the Homer Street Methodist Church as Vancouverites clamour to get a chance to hear the poetry of Pauline Johnson.

"The evening's entertainment could hardly have been more interesting," reports the *Vancouver Daily World.* "Miss Johnson possesses a strong personality and her wonderful elocutionary and dramatic powers combined to give a perfect rendering of her graphic descriptions of Indian life. She appeared in the picturesque costume of a Mohawk Indian woman which added greatly to the effectiveness of her selections."

Johnson, daughter of a Mohawk chief, is already a well-known Canadian poet. Her work celebrates her First Nations heritage and has led to nationwide fame as a writer and orator. In the years to come, she will speak before audiences in Canada, the United States, and Europe —always in the buckskin costume she designed for herself, garnering worldwide acclaim before retiring from touring in 1909. She will then retire to Vancouver's West End, with the remainder of that year spent composing stories for her 1910 anthology *Legends of Vancouver,* written in collaboration with her friend Chief Joe Capilano of the Squamish Nation.

Though *Legends of Vancouver* (first published in the *Vancouver Province*) will become an instant sensation, Johnson will by this time be sick with breast cancer, and her finances will have deteriorated drastically. Following her death in Victoria in 1913, the city will hold its own funeral ceremony, reportedly the largest in its history.

Pauline Johnson, 1902.
IMAGE COURTESY OF THE VANCOUVER ARCHIVES (PORT P1633, PHOTOGRAPHER EDWARDS BROS.)

Johnson's ashes will be buried near Siwash Rock, making her the only person to have been officially buried in Stanley Park.

Though there will be some debate regarding Johnson's reputation and writings in the years to follow, *Legends of Vancouver* will continue to be widely read into the 21st century.

OCTOBER 22, 1969

WITH A ROYAL COMMISSION CONVENED to examine and revamp BC's archaic liquor laws, the *Vancouver Sun* and Prince George brewer Ben Ginter set out to challenge one of the province's more unusual beer parlour bans: standing while drinking.

"He was refused [service while standing]—as he was to be in four more beer parlors during the impromptu pub crawl," the article explains. "After three more stops during which time he had been mistaken for a professional wrestler by a patron and asked for an autograph, Ginter had to settle for a table. At the St. Regis he had been told it was 'the law in Canada that people sit while drinking beer' and at the Marble Arch the bartender explained the rules and asked 'where are you guys from anyway?'"

At four different establishments, Ginter and the *Sun* reporter will be refused service while standing, told unequivocally that the practice is against the law.

"It isn't a law," Ginter protests. "But these people are scared out of their wits by the Liquor Control Board and they have no alternative. They either do as they're told or they get closed down."

Ginter, head of the Prince George–based Tartan Brewing, is in town to testify before the Royal Commission (headed by Judge William Morrow), alleging collusion between the province's three largest breweries (Molson, Carling, and Labatt), a monopoly on drinking establishments by the hotel industry, and bribery of liquor board officials.

British Columbia has, for decades, been host to a number of unusual liquor laws, such as a ban on female servers in beer parlours, a provision against listing vodka for sale (given that its colourless, odourless nature could contribute to juvenile delinquency),

Beer parlour, June 30, 1944. Note the separate "Ladies" area in the rear.
IMAGE COURTESY OF THE VANCOUVER ARCHIVES (CVA 586-2866, DON COLTMAN, STEFFENS COLMER)

a government-mandated beer price of 10 cents, a total ban on recommendations by liquor store employees (even if asked), and a moratorium on windows, music, and food in licensed premises. In addition, establishments also enforce Liquor Control Board rules that have no basis in law (such as the ban on standing). The Liquor Control Board is itself a bizarre institution, with the bulk of its decisions made by a single man, Colonel Donald McGugan. McGugan (known as "the Liquor Czar" by the local dailies) is notorious for his bullheadedness, inexplicable decisions, and unwillingness to provide explanation (a trait that led even notoriously megalomaniacal Mayor Tom Campbell to label him "a dictator"). His rulings remain absolute—no appeal is possible, despite a previous Royal Commission's recommendation to institute a more flexible three-member board.

Following Ginter's experiment, Judge Morrow himself will visit several local beer parlours to test the standing ban, with identical results. Although the Morrow Report, released in 1970, will recommend sweeping changes to the province's liquor regulations, calling for sidewalk cafés, extended licences, female servers, and even drinking in parks, few of the committee's suggestions will ever be implemented by government.

OCTOBER 23, 1977

WEST END RESIDENTS CLICK THEIR TONGUES in disapproval and mallards city-wide quake in fear as both local papers report on a chilling trend that has recently descended on Lost Lagoon: duck rape.

"Gangs of bossy male mallards, the dominant variety in Lost Lagoon and Beaver Lake, are bullying other birds," reports the *Vancouver Sun*, "committing homosexual acts and even raping female ducks at an alarming rate."

"Part of the problem is that we are so close to the West End," Stanley Park zoo curator Larry LeSage says in an interview with the paper. "People with pet domestic ducks who want to get rid of them leave them at Stanley Park where they breed with the wild ducks. The cross-breeding produces an aggressive type of duck that attacks the other birds, sometimes killing them."

For decades, Lost Lagoon has had a reputation as a duck preserve, with thousands of the winged creatures calling the area home each fall. But for the past three years, LeSage notes with alarm, he has seen a dramatic change in the character of the area's ducks— and, he notes with particular alarm, there has also been a growing trend toward homosexual behaviour.

"I first noticed that the mallards were gay," LeSage confides in an interview with the *Vancouver Province*. "Now it has spread to the wood ducks."

Baffled, and convinced that the creatures' behaviour is the result of an overabundance of male ducks, LeSage has even asked Canadian Wildlife Services to step in and balance the genders.

"If they are gay, it's not because the ducks are becoming decadent," LeSage tells the *Province*. "Ducks have aggressive tendencies and a lack of females could make them turn to each other."

Despite LeSage's alarm, worldwide research conducted into the mid-1990s will reveal that homosexuality, rape, and even necrophilia are in fact common among duck populations, particularly in areas with high population density, with male homosexuality observed in two to 19 percent of all mallard pairs.

As for the exact reason behind the "growing homosexual tendencies" of Lost Lagoon's ducks, LeSage is at a loss.

"I can't blame that on the West End."

OCTOBER 24, 1968

CHAOS DESCENDS ON THE UNIVERSITY OF BRITISH COLUMBIA AS, following an address by activist and Youth International Party leader Jerry Rubin, more than 500 students (and a pig) enter and occupy the university's faculty club.

"At the end of his hour-long talk, 500 students marched into the club which is officially restricted to faculty members," explains the *Vancouver Province*. "The students were later joined by others from Simon Fraser University and Vancouver City College."

Rubin, on a continent-wide university speaking tour (arranged to coincide with the upcoming American presidential election), spends the majority of his address telling stories, burning dollar bills, and encouraging students to vote for the pig (christened "Pigasus") for the next president of the United States.

"It's a typical Jerry Rubin stunt—sort of show business," complains Dave Zirnhelt, the president of the UBC student council. "He's directing his efforts against the wrong people."

Shaun Sullivan, former council president, voices his agreement in an interview with the *Province*.

"This is a real setback for academic reform at UBC. These people are getting all mixed up in an American cause which is not applicable to the Canadian university structure."

The club management, who, the paper notes, "was able to lock up most of the liquor supplies before the takeover," admits that the occupiers are mostly well behaved, and at the behest of the faculty itself, they have refrained from calling the police. However, the occupation polarizes the student body, with close to 200 students massing outside, with the intent to storm the building, and several groups of students elsewhere on campus burning dollar bills "In defiance," they said, "of a society which holds money all-important."

The sit-in will last only 23 hours before students will vote to vacate the premises in favour of attending an outdoor peace rally.

"The crowd of students in the Faculty Club dropped to about 60 early Friday morning, following a late-night party," reports the *Province*. "There were reports that some openly smoked marijuana at the party."

The pig will be returned unharmed.

OCTOBER 25, 1918

"For God's sake, hurry. The water is coming in my room."

These desperate words, relayed by wireless operator David Robinson, are among the last to be received from the Vancouver-bound CPR steamship *Princess Sophia* before the vessel sinks into the icy waters of the Pacific. All 356 on board are lost in what will become known as the worst marine disaster in West Coast history.

"With her wireless frantically crying for the help that could not reach her and a blinding snowstorm driving across her stricken bows, the CPR steamship *Princess Sophia* slipped into deep water off the ledge in Lynn Canal last night and every soul aboard was lost," reports the *Vancouver Sun*. "The vessels which had been standing by were powerless to render aid. The ship, apparently, was hurled right across the reef and those aboard her were precipitated into the raging waters."

The *Princess Sophia*, which has been lodged against Vanderbilt reef since running aground in bad weather more than 24 hours earlier, has been unable to evacuate due to the storm and the structure of the reef itself, which prevents lifeboats from being launched or rescue vessels from approaching.

Captain Leonard Locke, an experienced navigator, has advised other ships to stay clear of the *Sophia*, in hopes that the storm will abate. Passengers have since waited on board in terror, many making out their final will and testament, or composing letters to loved ones. Though a number of rescue attempts were undertaken on the afternoon of October 24, none have been successful. Finally, late in the afternoon of October 25, rescue vessels receive a frantic radio transmission that the ship is, at last, sinking.

"Instantly, the *Cedar*, under a full head of steam, fought her way back through the darkness and the snow to where she had last seen the *Sophia*," the *Sun* explains. "There was no sign of the *Princess Sophia*; only the blinding snow-storm and a wilderness of mad waters."

The only survivor of the disaster will be a small dog, which manages to swim its way to a small island nearby and will recover in the days to follow. Bodies will continue to wash up on shore for months, sometimes as far as 30 miles away, dead of exposure or covered and suffocated by engine oil. Two lifeboats will be recovered near the reef, both empty, speaking to the speed with which the *Sophia* sunk to the bottom of the ocean. In fact, many of the watches of the bodies recovered will have stopped at 5:50 p.m., less than half an hour after Robinson's final transmission.

"There is no hope that any of the *Sophia*'s passengers might be clinging to rocks or ledges or to bits of wreckage," the paper concludes, "for long before they would have been pounded to pulp by the heavy seas that break on those stern rocks. All are lost of that crowd who joyfully departed from Skagway late on Wednesday night, counting themselves fortunate that they had escaped a long winter in the northern port."

The Princess Sophia *in happier times, circa 1914.*
Image courtesy of the Vancouver Archives (CVA 99-1185, photographer Stuart Thomson)

OCTOBER 26, 1968

AT A MORNING CEREMONY before a crowd of approximately 1,500, federal Consumer Affairs Minister Ron Basford opens the city's $3.5 million planetarium and museum complex, a facility made possible by a sizable grant from local millionaire H.R. MacMillan.

"I do not know what to say," the 83-year-old MacMillan remarks. "But I am very pleased that it was possible to provide this planetarium to the city of Vancouver."

Following the official opening ceremony, MacMillan and Mayor Tom Campbell take the public on a tour of the planetarium facility and theatre, which features 265 seats, a 25-channel sound system (designed in Vancouver), a three-ton Zeiss projector with hundreds of lenses inside, and in front of the building a $44,000 stainless steel crab statue designed by Vancouver sculptor George Norris and built by a team of local welders.

The facility was in heavy discussion for several years following MacMillan's original grant, delayed by debates over location (Little Mountain was at one point a contender) and staffing (27-year-old director David Rodger was viewed as a bold choice, having no education in science and a background largely in radio and entertainment). By 1966, a decision was made to combine MacMillan's planetarium with a museum, archives building, and observatory as part of a centennial project facility at the Vanier Park site.

In the months to come, the planetarium will go on to become immensely popular with locals, and within the first two weeks more than 30,000 people will have paid their $1 admission fee to walk through its doors. Director David Rodger will go on to write and produce more than 40 shows for the planetarium, resigning in 1980 after years of cutbacks and administrative conflicts. The archives building will open in 1972 and the observatory in 1980.

"The MacMillan Planetarium, a most popular addition to Vancouver's entertainment life, could probably run the same show for six months or a year and still attract sell-out crowds," a 1969 *Province* article will declare. "The stars are spectacular after many looks; and the sound system, piping extra amounts of majesty into the sky, gives the audience a sample of how it feels to be a god."

OCTOBER 27, 1911

AFTER NEARLY A MONTH OF FRUITLESS SEARCHING, the *Vancouver Province* joyously reports on the capture and destruction of the city's most recent animal menace: the Stanley Park cougar.

"This cougar hunt has been so remarkable as to be almost without parallel in Canada," the paper exclaims. "It has not been the case of chasing up some cowed animal temporarily absent from his usual quarters in a travelling circus, but one of hunting absolutely wild, big game within the limits of a big city. Think of the park as it was yesterday morning. Engirdling it were automobiles, every type of latest civilization, while within its wooded depths slunk the cougar, even as its like might have in the dawning of the world's history."

The eight-foot, 137-pound cougar, which had for the previous three weeks made its home in the park, was the subject of public discussion and newspaper coverage after it was discovered, having devoured three goats and two deer in the Stanley Park zoo. Since then, it has been the target of dozens of local hunters, with the blessing of both the *Province* (which has offered a $50 reward) and the Park Board superintendent, Adrian Balmer.

"Probably the happiest man in Vancouver last night was Mr. Balmer," says the paper. "One may guess the relief with which he saw the long vigil of the past three weeks come to an end. His fears that were the animal not soon destroyed it might transfer its attention to the elk, or even schoolchildren were not without foundation."

The cougar, which was finally tracked down and shot the previous afternoon (after a furious chase) was subsequently displayed in the *Province*'s front window, with the paper noting that it "at once attracted a large crowd, and the pressure without was at

The slain cougar and hunters in the Hastings Street office of the Province, Oct. 26, 1911.
IMAGE COURTESY OF THE VANCOUVER ARCHIVES (ST PK P271.2)

times so great that it looked as though many would be treated to a shower bath—of glass."

Hunters Max Michaud, George Shannon, and Henry Hornby of Cloverdale collect the reward, as well as having their faces featured on the front page of the *Province*, and for many years, the cougar will be displayed in the Stanley Park Pavilion.

"Looking savage and cruel just as she was in life, the animal is to be seen stuffed, in a case above the mantelpiece, in the Park Pavilion," Robert Allison Hood will later recall in his memoirs. "Thus were the deer avenged."

OCTOBER 28, 1922

TRAFFIC IS DISRUPTED along a number of major downtown routes, including the Georgia Viaduct, and streetcars are filled to capacity for hours as a parade staged by close to 1,200 UBC students surges through the city in a dramatic demand for better facilities.

"The students of UBC have more than 48,000 signatures to their petition for the removal of the University to Point Grey," reports the *Vancouver Sun.* "And the committee reports that the forms are still coming in. Before the students send the petition to the government they expect to have more than 60,000 names."

The parade, part of a student council "Build the University" campaign, begins at 12:30 p.m. and departs from the Georgia Viaduct before marching down Main, Hastings, and Granville, then boarding streetcars on Davie Street. Once at the university grounds, students will surge onto the steps of the unfinished (for eight years) science building and hang class banners.

"From these points," the paper continues, "they will march to the site of the University in Point Grey. Here, they will form the letters UBC under the eye of the moving picture camera."

Agitation for a move to Point Grey has been ongoing since September of 1910, when two million acres were set aside (over a nine-year period) as the grounds for a provincial university. Although initial construction began on a science building in 1914, the intervention of the First World War effectively halted all further development of the site. Although BC's first provincial university act was passed in 1890, the move toward higher education has been slow; before the creation of UBC, students were educated by a satellite of McGill University and housed in a series of decrepit facilities (one being condemned by the city building inspector in

The Main Library Building at UBC, 1925.
IMAGE COURTESY OF THE VANCOUVER ARCHIVES (CVA 447-265, PHOTOGRAPHER WALTER E. FROST)

1911). Since its first lectures officially began in September 1915, UBC students have been housed in a pair of cramped shacks near Vancouver General Hospital. And although university president Frank Wesbrook has continued to push for the move to Point Grey into the 1920s, little progress has been made with the provincial government, leading protesters to take to the streets.

"We're thru with tents and hovels, we're done with shingle stain," they chant.

"That's why we want you to join us and carry our campaign!
The government can't refuse us, no matter what they say,
For we'll get people voting for our new home in Point Grey."

In the days to follow, a petition drafted by the campaign committee will be brought to Victoria and presented to the Speaker of the House. Less than a week later, the premier will agree to a loan of $1.5 million to begin immediate construction on the Point Grey facility.

The first of UBC's buildings will open its doors in March 1925.

OCTOBER 29, 1960

FOLLOWING A DRAMATIC RAID on his West End apartment, police arrest one of the FBI's Ten Most Wanted—32-year-old Joseph Corbett—in connection with the murder of Adolph Coors, heir to the Coors Brewing empire.

"Joseph Corbett, the most wanted US killer since the days of John Dillinger, was captured today in Vancouver," the *Vancouver Sun* exclaims. "Six carloads of city police and Federal Bureau of Investigation officers moved in on a West End apartment hotel and arrested him without a struggle."

The six-foot-two Corbett, who has been on the run from the law since an escape from a California prison in 1955 (where he was serving five years to life for the second-degree murder of an American serviceman), is suspected to have killed Coors during a bungled kidnap attempt in February 1960. Following the brewery heir's disappearance, a number of ransom notes were sent to the family before his battered body was recovered in Colorado in September. Since the incident, Corbett—with police and the FBI on his trail—has escaped to Canada, slowly making his way west, stopping for several months in Toronto and several more in Winnipeg. The raid, during which Corbett surrenders without incident, comes after VPD Constable Jack Marshall recognizes the murderer's vehicle outside the Maxine Hotel near Beach and Bidwell.

"And the raiding cars moved in," the *Sun* continues. "They showed a wanted poster to Mrs. Mary Bell, 61, manager of the apartments. She recognized Corbett immediately. He had made no effort at disguise."

"The FBI men said I had a desperate criminal here and there might be some shooting," Bell tells the paper. "I asked them couldn't I go around and give him his linen. I didn't know then he was a murderer."

Corbett will be held in the city jail for several days and visited by his father (a resident of Seattle) before being extradited to the United States, where he will be charged with Coors's murder and sentenced to 18 years in prison.

OCTOBER 30, 1956

"Illness forced sale of complete herd of 37 Chinchillas and all equipment," reads an advertisement in the *Vancouver News-Herald*'s Want Ads section. "No reas. offers refused."

Other items in the paper's two-and-a-half pages of classified ads (available at rates of $1 a week for two lines and $2 a week for four lines) include sides of Calgary beef (29 cents each), a 1952 Chevrolet Sedan (priced at $1,095), a "roll-rimmed bathtub" ($20), a two-man cross-cut saw, and "1 squirrel monkey, very tame."

Furnished suites listed in the paper are priced variously at $20 a month (for a suite on East Eighth without its own stove), $40 per month (on Arbutus Street), and $65 per month (for a "working man" suite in Kitsilano described only as "warm").

Jobs advertised include "Boys and Girls to Deliver Telegrams," power machine operators, and "Real Estate Salesmen. Experience not necessary."

Newspaper delivery boy, circa 1940.
Image Courtesy of the Vancouver Archives (CVA 1184-862, Jack Lindsay, photographer)

OCTOBER 31, 1918

THOUSANDS OF ASSEMBLED VANCOUVERITES gape in awe as, at 12:15 p.m. and using only his bare hands, Harry Gardiner, also known as "The Human Fly," scales the outside of the World Tower in a publicity stunt organized as part of a Victory Loan Drive.

"It will be the most thrilling and spectacular stunt ever seen in Vancouver," reports the morning edition of the *Sun*, printed hours before Gardiner's ascent, "for the Tower building is about as easy to climb as the side of an iceberg. Thousands saw him climb the sheer face of the Hotel Vancouver and held their breath at the sight, but today's feat is much more difficult and dangerous."

The 47-year-old Gardiner, who received his nickname from President Grover Cleveland, makes his way up the 340-foot structure dressed in his trademark white canvas clothes and horn-rimmed spectacles. (Gardiner never uses special equipment or apparel; all of his climbs are accomplished in ordinary street clothes.) At one point, he even stands on one foot, bringing cheers and gasps from the crowd below.

"As each ledge was reached he first mopped his forehead then urged the cheering crowd to be sure to buy Victory Bonds," reports the *Province*. "The difficulties of the climb are manifold for the building has none of the ornate decorations which abound on the front of the Hotel Vancouver. For the most part it is climbing plain bricks and mortar with a cornice or two breaking the journey and adding to its difficulties. But nothing that has been erected around Vancouver appears to present any real obstacle to this exalted 'second storey man.'"

Human Fly acts are a popular form of entertainment at the time, and Gardiner, among the most famous of them, will entertain throughout the 1920s and 1930s, reportedly climbing close to 700 buildings and man-made structures. In the years to come, a number of imitators will emerge, before cities will begin to pass ordinances banning the climbing of public buildings.

Crowd observing Harry Gardiner's ascent of the World Building, Oct. 31, 1918.
IMAGE COURTESY OF THE VANCOUVER ARCHIVES (BU P550, PHOTOGRAPHER STUART THOMSON)

NOVEMBER 1, 1892

"The Night o' the Season," declares the *Vancouver Daily World* as the paper gives its post-mortem on the "ways in which the traditional Hallowe'en was spent in the city."

"Wm. McCraney, ex MP, assisted by Mrs. McCraney, entertained a number of members of the Burrard Literary Club and others at his residence, 511 Howe Street, on Monday evening," the paper explains. "Mr. and Mrs. McCraney, who have always been noted for their hospitality, were at their best and succeeded in making their guests feel thoroughly at home . . . Needless to say, justice was done to the abundance of good things provided by the amiable hostess, while the parlor games were so enjoyable that it would be difficult to imagine how to spend a more pleasant evening. It was a late hour before the party broke up and judging from the unanimous expressions of approval as to the evening's pleasure, the members of the club and others who were present will cherish for a long time to come delightful recollections of the affair."

Halloween celebrations occurred city-wide, held by diverse groups of Vancouverites, including the Scottish Society, the St. Andrew's Church Literary Society, the Sons of England, and the Ladies of the First Presbyterian Church. In addition, the paper notes: "There were several fashionable dances in commemoration of the day which were participated in by the youth and beauty of the city."

However, as the *World* explains, not all of the Hallow's Eve celebrations were of the most savoury persuasion.

"The usual number of pranks were played around town," the article explains, disapprovingly, "among them being puttying up keyholes, placing a lot of barrels around the Princess Street Methodist church, placarding the Congregational church as 'To Let,' cutting down billboards on Westminster Avenue, removing signs of Cordova Street merchants, unhinging gates, tearing down fences, and many others, which, while they might afford amusement for the time being, have the effect of eliciting from some of the victims unparliamentary expressions."

People dressed in Halloween costume, circa 1940.
Image courtesy of the Vancouver Archives (CVA 1184-1085)

NOVEMBER 2, 1974

VANCOUVER AUDIENCES SCRATCH THEIR HEADS, and local critics sharpen their claws, as George Harrison kicks off his disastrous 30-date North American *Dark Horse* tour with a performance at the Pacific Coliseum.

"A slight percentage of the knowledgeable did enjoy it," complains *Vancouver Sun* music critic Don Stanley, "a slightly larger percentage attempted to look intelligent, and the rest of us suffered. It's either to the credit or the shame of Vancouver audiences that only a few people yelled 'Boogie,' and that one girl cried 'Unbutton your overalls, George!'"

Harrison does himself few favours with the audience by refusing to play all but four Beatles numbers, tampering with the lyrics of those he chooses to retain ("While My Guitar Gently Weeps," for example, is changed to "While My Guitar Tries to Smile"), and the tour itself (known derisively by critics as the Dark Hoarse tour because of Harrison's thrashed vocals) will meet with poor reception—and sometimes open hostility—throughout North America.

"[The band] couldn't adequately cover up for Harrison's vocals," Stanley continues. "He attempted to storm through the material, à la Dylan's recent magnificent tour, and ended up agonizingly hoarse. As a showman, he was utterly eclipsed by Billy Preston—'I see I'll have to pay him more money,' Harrison said weakly, after Preston's 'Outta Space' finally released the audience's frustrated energy."

And, in a move that further alienates concertgoers, Harrison decides to supplement his own material with two sets performed by a 16-piece Indian orchestra fronted by sitar virtuoso Ravi Shankar.

"This will be educational," Harrison declares. "I'd die for Indian music, but I wouldn't die for this [tapping his electric guitar]. Don't have preconceived ideas, and maybe you'll like it."

Thus far, 1974 has been a tumultuous year for Harrison; it has marked the formation of his own record label, and after years of friction, the end of his relationship with wife Patti Boyd (who subsequently became involved with his good friend Eric Clapton). The reviews of Harrison's tour, his lingering laryngitis, and the critically loathed *Dark Horse* album that follows will prove so discouraging for the guitarist that he will make only rare live appearances throughout the remainder of his career, and he will never again embark on a solo tour of North America.

NOVEMBER 3, 1942

PEDESTRIANS DUCK FOR COVER, and fears of an Axis attack seem momentarily plausible, as at 9:37 p.m. in downtown Vancouver one of the two Courthouse Lions is damaged by a bomb.

"The lion on the right of a person facing the Court House was shattered," explains the *Vancouver Sun*. "The hind quarters were blown away from the rest of the body and three blocks of granite at least a foot in diameter, were blown on to a nearby parking space. Smaller chunks were scattered over the roadway and lawn."

Damage to the 10-ton lion—the lions carved over a period of three months and put in place in 1910—is estimated to be minimal; however, a number of witnesses on the scene narrowly avoid being injured by flying granite and debris, including janitor Frederick Brown, who was within 25 feet of the explosion. Though police have no leads on the identity of the perpetrator (the *Province* will dismiss him as a "crackpot"), it is assumed that the blast was caused by two sticks of dynamite, wired together by two to three feet of fuse.

"There were two blasts, about five seconds apart," witness Sergeant P.E.J. Tomey will tell the *Sun*. "The second was the loudest. Right after the first, I saw a short man dash from the steps. I saw him in the light of the explosion as he started to run across the grounds toward Georgia and Hornby."

This is not the first time the Courthouse Lions have been vandalized, the *Sun* notes. In November 1939, they were both defaced with green swastikas. And, although police will follow up on Sergeant Tomey's report of "a short man," and even make an arrest several days later, the suspect will be released, with no charges laid. Luckily, the damage to the statue will not be permanent; in fact, stonecutters John Whitworth and Herbert Ede, who first carved the lions back in 1910 still work in the city.

"We could cut off his hind quarters and fit on a new piece, just as nice as you please," Whitworth explains in an interview with the *Vancouver Province*. "He'd be as good as new and you'd never know, except for a very faint line where the join is, that anything had ever happened."

Damage to the Courthouse Lion, Nov. 1942.
IMAGE COURTESY OF THE VANCOUVER ARCHIVES (CVA 1184-3631)

NOVEMBER 4, 1970

LOCAL MARINE BIOLOGISTS redouble their efforts, and animal lovers city-wide mourn, as the Vancouver Aquarium announces the loss of one of its most unusual species—the narwhal.

"Pathologists found bacteria in the blood in the culture they were studying," reports Dr. Murray Newman, director of the aquarium, in an interview with the *Vancouver Sun*, "but they're not absolutely certain the bacteria were present before the narwhal's death. It is possible that a scratch or minor injury led to an infection. But the animal did not have any major injuries when she died."

Of the six narwhal calves originally captured for display at the Vancouver Aquarium, only two remain, the rest having succumbed to a variety of illnesses.

"Three narwhal calves died of pneumonia within the first two weeks they were held in the research pool at the aquarium," the paper continues. "Of the six captured in the Arctic last summer, only two—a young male and an older female—are left now."

The Vancouver Aquarium, the first public aquarium in Canada, has gained a reputation for exhibiting exotic sea mammals since it became, in 1964, among the first facilities in the world to capture and display an orca (in an improvised pen at Jericho Beach). In fact, the aquarium's study of the creatures is credited with completely transforming science's view of killer whales; previously thought to be vicious and bloodthirsty, they were instead proven to be docile, easily handled, and highly trainable. Following the purchase of the facility's first orca, and the construction of a 500,000-litre pool (a decision that deadlocked the aquarium board for hours), mammals have been a regular feature at the aquarium, and whale shows will remain a popular attraction for close to 30 years.

In 1992 the Park Board will vote to halt the capture of cetaceans for display purposes, and in 2001, with the transfer of Bjossa, the last remaining orca, the Vancouver Aquarium will end its association with the species.

NOVEMBER 5, 1942

FIREFIGHTERS ASSEMBLE, and close to 4,000 spectators line the Granville Street Bridge, as a dramatic midnight fire consumes two large industrial plants on Granville Island.

"The blaze was spectacular," reports the *Vancouver Sun*. "Spectators by the thousands crowded Granville Bridge—at times obstructing auto and street car traffic—and flowed over Granville Island roadways where firemen and 30 police officers were battling the flames."

The three-alarm fire, which begins at approximately 11:45 p.m. and rages for more than an hour, is thought to have broken out in the boiler room of Overseas Wood Products, a sawmill, before spreading to the nearby Tyee Machinery Company. With the assistance of firefighters from five different fire halls and of the False Creek fireboat *J.H. Carlisle* (all of which are on the scene within minutes), the blaze is swiftly subdued, but not before destroying Overseas Wood Products, consuming much of Tyee Machinery (heavily involved in war production), and causing an estimated $200,000 in damage.

"It's all a mystery to me," sawmill night watchman R.J. Statham tells the *Sun*. "It all happened so suddenly."

All of the Tyee and Overseas employees manage to escape the blaze unharmed. Though the flames briefly threaten nearby buildings and cause a power outage for all 12 manufacturers in the area, the fire will not adversely affect the operation of any other Granville Island businesses.

View of Granville Island from the Granville Street Bridge, 1932.
IMAGE COURTESY OF THE VANCOUVER ARCHIVES (CVA 20-67)

NOVEMBER 6, 1941

Men moving their shack beneath the Georgia Viaduct, circa 1930.
IMAGE COURTESY OF THE VANCOUVER ARCHIVES (CVA 260-297)

FOLLOWING YEARS OF PETITIONING by ex-alderman Helena Gutteridge, a city inspector's report, and a standard of housing bylaw that has been before council for close to a year, the *Vancouver News-Herald* launches a series detailing the disastrous state of city housing conditions.

"Vancouver is facing a housing crisis," the paper warns. "Real Estate Agents have difficulty finding apartments, and houses to accommodate hundreds of people seeking new quarters every day—soldiers' families, war workers and the like who are swelling the city's population."

In addition, the paper warns, slum-like conditions abound in various parts of the city, notably in a number of decrepit shacks on the shore of False Creek and in a series of run-down cabins and rooming houses in the West End, some of which contain only one bathroom for up to 20 people.

"They are jampacked in dreary rows," the report explains, "Many of the houses list grotesquely up to a yard of difference in height of opposite corners. Over the district hangs the reek of low tide and sooty smoke of False Creek. And on listing porches, around broken down fences on the sidewalk and in the gutter, scores of grubby-faced children play."

"This is not a new condition," Gutteridge will write in a letter published the following day, "and is not a surprise to persons and groups that have been endeavouring to get some action thereon for some time . . . What has happened to the Standard of Housing bylaw reposing on the table at the City Hall for the past 18 months? Has Alderman Corey forgotten it?"

Gutteridge, during her single term as an alderman (the first woman in city history to hold the position), was instrumental in drafting Vancouver's first standard of housing bylaw. Composed after six months of surveying, it calls for buildings to be maintained in good working order, with yards free of garbage and floors to be carpeted, and for all buildings to be well ventilated. Unfortunately, as Alderman Hugh Corey explains, the proposal has yet to be favourably received by either the public or the council, with the nation at war and the city already affected by a severe housing shortage.

"We received a great deal of opposition in the city and the other members of the council thought that the time was inopportune while the nation was at war," Corey will protest in the following day's paper. "In the meantime, I thought that there was no possibility of the thing being passed and it was left in abeyance because there was neither public nor council demand for it."

Despite Gutteridge's protestations, the city's housing shortage will continue throughout the 1940s and well into the 1960s, until the drafting of the 1966 *Strata Titles Act* will allow for the creation of the condominium.

NOVEMBER 7, 1949

FOLLOWING A GLUT OF HALLOWEEN VANDALISM, Mayor Charles E. Thompson speaks before a crowd at Dunbar United Church, advocating a new approach to dealing with the problem of "juvenile terrorists": vigilante justice.

"As your chief Magistrate it is not my intention to sit idly by and allow buildings to be burned, hydrants and street lights wrecked, false alarms to be sent into the police and fire stations, stabbing affrays and personal injuries to continue under the guise of Halloween pranks," Thompson thunders. "If this vicious tendency is allowed to go unchecked it can easily spread to gigantic proportions."

Thompson goes on to denounce the many evils of the recent "Halloween depredations," likening them to the danger caused by fires, earthquakes, and floods. And further, he states, the city as a whole must re-examine its commitment to "our machinery of good and wholesome community living."

"It may be necessary for us to call out a citizen's voluntary group to patrol each block in its own area in such times as Halloween," Thompson concludes. "If there are more young people on the golf links on Sunday mornings, or away on weekend drives, or doing a host of other things, except going to church, there is an answer to that condition if we have the courage to find it."

As it turns out, Thompson is hardly alone in his condemnation of youth vandalism, nor in the hard-line tactics he advocates.

"Perhaps we should buy a few policemen's nightsticks," Alderman George Miller will comment in the November 8 edition of the *Vancouver News-Herald*, "and give some of these rowdies a good cut across the backside."

Child with military cap and swagger, 1943.
IMAGE COURTESY OF THE VANCOUVER ARCHIVES
(CVA 586-1335, DON COLTMAN AND STEFFANS COLMER, PHOTOGRAPHERS)

NOVEMBER 8, 1927

CELEBRATIONS ARE HELD and the *Vancouver Sun* announces "an important milestone" in the city's theatrical history as Vancouver heralds the grand opening of its newest entertainment venue: the Orpheum.

"Holiday crowds filled the vast auditorium from 1:30 p.m., when the doors were opened, until nearly midnight," reports the *Vancouver Sun*, "showing keen appreciation of the luxurious appointments of the magnificent playhouse and of an entertainment program featuring the best in vaudeville, and an intriguing movie drama."

The 3,000-seat theatre—actually known as the "New Orpheum" (the original Orpheum will later surrender its name and be re-christened the Vancouver Theatre)—is dedicated by Mayor L.D. Taylor, with an additional speech made by Mary Ellen Smith, the country's first female MLA, there to "voice an appreciation from the women of British Columbia."

The interior of the building is elaborately decorated, including rose-coloured rugs, panelled walls hung with silk tapestries, and a multitude of oil paintings, mostly of landscapes.

"In the main auditorium an atmosphere of spaciousness is the keynote," the paper continues, "yet no section of the great hall seems distant from the stage. A wealth of luxurious draperies and chandeliers glittering with myriads of cut crystals harmonize with the Spanish Renaissance design."

Acts in the first day's program include Toto, a clown renowned countrywide as a "master at the art of convulsing his audiences with laughter without the aid of language," the comedy stylings of Pat Henning, and dancing numbers by a pair known as Chaney and Fox.

The "New" Orpheum, 1946.
IMAGE COURTESY OF THE VANCOUVER ARCHIVES (CVA 1184-2290)

The film *The Wise Wife* is, by the *Sun*'s account, the story of a lady "confronted with the problem of how to hold on to her husband, when a younger woman seeks to steal him away."

The Orpheum will remain one of the city's premiere vaudeville and movie houses for close to 40 years. Following an attempt by Famous Players to gut the building and turn it into a multiplex, it will eventually be purchased by the City of Vancouver for continued use as a live venue.

The theatre will be designated a National Historic Site in 1979.

NOVEMBER 9, 1949

At approximately 7:30 a.m., the body of "attractive 45-year-old spinster" Ferne Blanche Fisher is pulled from the waters of False Creek, and the discovery of her bruised, partially stripped (and partially shaved) corpse touches off one of Vancouver's most notorious murder investigations.

"One feature of the case which is definitely puzzling investigators is the fact that the body hair had been shaven from the woman," reports the *Vancouver Sun*. "The hair on her head had not been touched. Police believe that she had not been dead long before the body was seen floating in the water . . . When she was

discovered this morning, she was not wearing any underwear, shoes, or stockings. There was a cut on her forehead which was bleeding when Constables Richard Begley and Jack Eaton took her body from the water."

Though police consider Fisher's death suspicious and likely the result of foul play, few leads present themselves, even after Woodward's Department Store (Fisher's former employer) offers a $2,000 reward for information.

However, a break in the case will occur in late December when some of Fisher's belongings are discovered inside the filthy waterfront hut of a 28-year-old labourer named Frederick Ducharme. Ducharme, arrested for vagrancy after police spot him wearing nothing but a raincoat and running shoes, will confess to the murder later in the same day after a number of Fisher's belongings are discovered in his home. Ducharme's history of indecent exposure and bizarre rituals (including tying a string to what the *Sun* will refer to as his "lower person" and using it to steer himself around the city) will be well reported during his trial, which will commence before a courtroom packed with spectators in March 1950.

Seventeen days of testimony will be heard at the trial—at that time the longest in BC history—and on the strength of the evidence, Ducharme will be convicted of Fisher's abduction, rape, and murder. On July 14, 1958, he will be hanged at Oakalla Prison, with *Sun* reporter Mac Reynolds remarking that he "died without a flicker of emotion crossing his pale face."

Crowd awaiting the appearance of Frederick Ducharme after his murder trial, March 1950.
Image Courtesy of the Vancouver Public Library

NOVEMBER 10, 1927

HEALTH-CONSCIOUS VANCOUVERITES are given a glimpse of the newest health craze out of LA, courtesy of Dr. Frank McCoy: the orange fast.

"Many who have been reading my daily health articles have been sufficiently interested to wish to try the orange fast which I so often recommend," McCoy states, syndicated in the pages of the *Sun*. "In today's article I am going to lay down some simple rules which anyone can follow without any possibility of harmful consequences. No matter what disorder you may be suffering from I can assure you that you will be benefited by taking a few days of the orange fast followed by a restricted, cleansing diet."

The fast, McCoy explains, must be undertaken for five days, and requires nothing more than an eight-ounce glass of orange juice to be taken every two hours. Keeping to a regular schedule is essential, the doctor explains, to avoid any unpleasant symptoms, "unless, perhaps, when you may have a slight headache due to the stirring up of systemic toxins."

"Every day you must take one or two enemas," McCoy continues, "using plain warm water, and not over a quart at a time. Also take two sponge or shower baths daily to keep the pores of the skin open and to assist in elimination. This fast will give your alimentary canal a rest, and you will eliminate vast quantities of impurities which will relieve the body of accumulated poisons and help you in every way to overcome any disorder from which you may be suffering."

Throughout the mid-1920s, McCoy (whose doctorate is actually in chiropractic and "physical culture") will enjoy some time in the spotlight after the publication of his 1926 book *The Fast Way to Health*, in which he advocates the use of diet to treat a number of disorders, among them "torpid liver," "biliousness," "genital derangement," and even deafness. However, after a brief period of celebrity, during which he will write for the *LA Times* and have his work syndicated in Canada and the US, McCoy's reputation will take a serious nosedive after a 1934 editorial in the *Journal of the American Medical Association* dismisses his theories as "the apotheosis of nonsense" in an editorial entitled "A Dietary Quack Discusses Dysentery" (following McCoy's claim that amoebic dysentery can be cured through "the use of two or three enemas, taken one hour apart").

His association with the *LA Times* having ended in 1932, McCoy will vanish from the "medical" landscape soon afterward.

NOVEMBER 11, 1918

Even though it's nearly midnight, steamships blow their horns, Stanley Park's Nine O'Clock Gun fires more than a dozen times, and jubilant Vancouverites fill the streets as news reaches the city that, after four gruelling years, the First World War has come to an end.

"Armistice Signed; No two words that ever came over the wire caused such a magical transformation and spontaneously joyful outburst in this staid, young Western city as did these," reports the *Vancouver Sun*. "In less time than it takes to tell it, the half-deserted streets were teeming with hastily aroused but wildly enthusiastic citizens, who gave vent to their long pent-up feelings with hearty cheers, innumerable congratulations, and soon amassed a remarkable collection of noise-making devices."

Celebrations continue well into the early hours of the morning, with thousands of Vancouverites calling the *Sun*'s offices to verify the news, the Point Grey wireless station broadcasting developments to nearby ships at sea, and a handful of "red-blooded enthusiasts" randomly pulling fire alarms in celebration.

"The spontaneous and unofficial celebration was kept up fair into the morning hours," the *Sun* concludes, "when the majority of the celebrators regretfully retired to get a few hours' rest in preparation for the greater celebration that will ensue this afternoon and evening."

Close to 65,000 Canadians are said to have died during the four years of fighting.

Crowds at Granville and Georgia on Armistice Day, Nov. 11, 1918.
Image courtesy of the Vancouver Archives (Mil P14.2)

COLUMBIA GRAFONOLAS
PIANOS
FLETCHER BROS LTD

BUY TILL IT HURTS

SINKS U. BOATS

HUDSONS BAY C.

FLAGS OF FREE

Stuart Thomson.
501 Georgia St.
Vancouver
B.C.

NOVEMBER 12, 1954

FROM CJOR HEADQUARTERS in the basement of the Grosvenor Hotel, 16-year-old Robert Gordon "Red" Robinson officially begins his broadcast career, launching the first radio program in the country dedicated to rock 'n' roll. Though still a student at King Edward Secondary, Robinson has been working behind the scenes as a writer and operator at the station for the better part of the year as part of Al Jordan's afternoon program *Theme for Teens*, work that eventually brings him to the attention of station manager and disc jockey Vic Waters.

"I'm running down after school, down the stairs, as I always did, and Vic comes up to me and says: 'Red, I don't think we're going to continue with the teen show,'" Robinson will later recall. "And I was crushed. But he said, 'You know, the sales manager and I have been talking this over, and what we'd like to do is have you do the show all by yourself today, and when you're finished with it, come down to the lobby, and we'll tell you what we're going to do. So, I went on there, just hyper as you can imagine. I went on, I blasted rock 'n' roll, and the first record I ever played there on my own was 'Maria' by The Four Tunes—the old Tommy Dorsey tune, but done doo-wop style. It was fantastic. And afterward, I came out into the lobby, and Vic Waters said: 'The show's yours, kid.'"

Though his association with CJOR began only the previous year, Robinson has been a long-time fan of radio in general (in particular Jack Cullen's *Owl Prowl*), an interest that led to his first (unofficial) on-air experience: calling *Theme for Teens* posing as movie star Jimmy Stewart.

"[Stewart]'s here going hunting," Robinson will explain. "They had a picture of him on the front page of the *Sun* holding a hunting knife. So, I phoned up Al Jordan's show and said, 'Oh, hi Al, it's Jimmy Stewart.' The next day, Jack Wasserman of the *Vancouver Sun* wrote, 'Oh, wasn't that nice of Jimmy Stewart to call a kids' show?'"

Robinson's antics (after several days, he got up the courage to call again, this time as Peter Lorre) quickly led to an invitation to visit the station and, following that, a job offer from Jordan himself.

"I guess I slipped a bit in the impersonation, because he said: 'Did you call in the other day as Jimmy Stewart?'" Robinson will explain. "And I said, 'Uh, yes sir.' He said: 'I want you to come down to the show.' Long story short, I go down, I start appearing on there, I started writing skits."

The Robinson-hosted *Theme for Teens* will become an instant sensation with local teenagers, as part of a nationwide interest in the burgeoning rock 'n' roll genre, though, as Robinson will note, the show is not without its detractors.

"There were black radio stations, and you didn't play black music," Robinson will explain. "Even in Canada, I'd have people calling me saying: 'Nigger lover.' I'm not kidding you. Or going: 'Why are you playing that devil's music?' I took it from all sides."

Nonetheless, by the time he graduates from high school, Red Robinson will be on the air 50 hours a week and go on to become one of the best-known disc jockeys of his generation, MCing for acts such as Little Richard, The Beatles, and Elvis Presley.

NOVEMBER 13, 1937

LOCALS SCRATCH THEIR HEADS and city bakers prepare for war as MLA Dr. Lyle Telford asserts that the city is run by a nefarious "bread racket."

"Appointment of a special legislative committee to investigate alleged unfair 'spreads' in bread prices and a flour combine, and other startling charges in connection with the baking industry, will be requested shortly by Dr. Lyle Telford, CCF MLA," reports the *Vancouver Province*.

"If it's the last thing I do, I'll break the flour combine," Telford tells council during an hour-long speech denouncing the evils of the bread industry. "These gentlemen have overplayed their hand and I'm going to fight them with every means in my power."

Telford's speech, which comes after the industry's second price increase in under a year (from seven cents the previous November to a whopping nine cents), urges a provincial inquiry into financial mismanagement, wasteful distribution methods, and underweight loaves. Telford also alleges that a syndicate of flour milling companies controls all local bakeries. And this isn't the first time that bread has made local headlines; in the early 1920s, the Vancouver Police launched an investigation into underweight bread, which, while ultimately unsuccessful, gave rise to a city bread bylaw enacted in April 1921. City Bylaw 2148, which includes provisions for 13-, 15-, and 16-ounce loaves, stipulates that all bread products must be labelled as "bread."

"All bread sold or offered for sale shall be in loaves of not less than sixteen ounces avoirdupois weight for each loaf of pan-baked bread," states the text of the bylaw, "and of not less than fourteen ounces avoirdupois weight for each loaf of hearth-baked bread, and

Baker placing bread in the oven, 1945.
IMAGE COURTESY OF THE VANCOUVER ARCHIVES (CVA 1184-1817)

shall in all other respects conform to the provisions of this bylaw; and it shall be unlawful for any person to manufacture on any premises, or to sell or offer for sale, any bread or flour confection that does not conform to the provisions of this By-law in that behalf."

While Telford's allegations will ultimately go nowhere, his charges will be far from the end of the headaches for Vancouver's bread industry; in 1958, following another series of price increases, the city will call on the attorney general to launch a provincial inquiry. A revision to the city's bread bylaw will take place in 1959, notable for allowing loaves of 7, 16, 20, 22.5, 24, 28, 30, 32, and 48 ounces—with 7-ounce loaves, the bylaw states, being sold specifically for members of the public living alone.

Between 1887 and 1972, the city will have passed a total of 14 different bread bylaws.

NOVEMBER 14, 2007

AFTER CLOSE TO A MONTH, and the launch of legal proceedings against the RCMP, Victoria native Paul Pritchard is finally able to recover his home video of the Robert Dziekanski taser incident from police and release it to the mainstream media.

"On the video you will see some things that I didn't talk about before because I didn't see them until I reviewed the tape," Pritchard says in the *Vancouver Sun*. "It's really brutal."

Pritchard, 25, was returning from China when he witnessed and recorded the incident, in which four Mounted Police officers administered multiple Taser shocks to Dziekanski after he began to grow agitated at Vancouver International Airport.

"They are all standing around him and they all look like they should be having coffee and a cigarette," Pritchard continues. "[Dziekanski]'s giving up. He's shrugging his shoulders and walking away. He is making no dangerous moves or threatening mannerisms towards them and he kind of puts his back to them and that's when they shoot him with the Taser."

Following a public outcry, the BC Civil Liberties Association will file a formal complaint against the RCMP, alleging that the force actively misrepresented the facts surrounding Dziekanski's death and suppressed Pritchard's video without due cause.

"The RCMP sought to suppress a video that will likely cast their officers' actions in a very negative light," BC Civil Liberties president Jason Gratl says in an interview with the *Sun*. "This kind of public manipulation is not appropriate nor dignified for Canada's national police force."

Three years later, a report into the incident published by retired BC Court of Appeal Justice Thomas Braidwood will conclude that the officers were not justified in their use of a conducted energy weapon and that they deliberately misled investigators in the weeks that followed.

All four officers involved in the case will be charged with perjury; however, no assault charges will be laid.

NOVEMBER 15, 1937

AFTER FIVE MONTHS OF INTERVIEWS and data collection, a special committee led by Helena Gutteridge, Frank Buck, and Albert J. Harrison files a disastrous interim housing report with council, revealing a city rife with accommodation shortages and substandard housing.

"Apart from overcrowding, a very unfortunate condition is being perpetuated in connection with dilapidated and, in some cases, condemned dwellings," the report states. "Under ordinary circumstances, these buildings would stand vacant, or be demolished, but the great lack of suitable accommodation has forced people to occupy these premises to the detriment of their health and well-being. The rentals obtained are small and, therefore, the landlords will carry out no repairs, nor make any improvements; thus, damp and cold add their toll to the misery of the occupants."

Buck, Harrison, and Gutteridge were appointed by the city in late June to survey the city's housing situation, with the hopes of drawing up a comprehensive plan. What the committee has discovered is a lack of construction, hundreds of people living in "some 210 boat houses and 110 dwellings on piles, or on the foreshore" of Burrard Inlet, homes without electricity, running water, or sewage.

"When the tide is out they settle into mud, slime and filthy water," the report states. "Water full of drifting waste and fouled with human excrement. One area reeks with the stench of decaying things, another with the gases arising from the fountain-like discharge from a sewage outlet just beyond the shacks, a fountain of continuous pollution, and of eternal shame so long as it poisons the waters on which float the huts of human beings."

Overcrowding is also a serious issue, thanks to a Depression-era building lull; in one instance, the committee finds two adults and 11 children living in a four-room house with no interior toilet or bathtub, and in another, 30 people (14 of them children) packed into a 14-room, two-bathroom house on Cambie Street.

Helena Gutteridge will continue to push for new and affordable housing for the remainder of her term in office. City-wide, the demand for available accommodation will continue to grow, exacerbated after the Second World War by thousands of returning servicemen, and climax in 1946 with the occupation of the Hotel Vancouver by veterans in a dramatic demand for housing.

Vancouver's housing shortage will continue to be an issue throughout the 1940s and 50s. However, it will ease following the enactment of the 1966 Strata Titles Act, which will, for the first time, allow for modern condominium living.

NOVEMBER 16, 1900

A STEADY RAIN FALLS on an assembled crowd, as at 8:15 in the morning, convicted thief and murderer Yip Luck dies at the end of a hangman's rope, becoming the 14th person to be hanged in New Westminster since Confederation.

"At 6 o'clock Yip Luck breakfasted heartily on pork chops, coffee and bread," the *Vancouver Province* reports in a lengthy article on the front page. "As the time drew near for the execution, the missionary earnestly prayed for Yip Luck to see the divine forgiveness, but met with unwilling responses. [Missionary] Thom states that in his own mind the man died in the Christian faith so far as his ignorant mind was capable of grasping the truth."

Luck, who was convicted earlier in the year of murdering Steveston police chief Alexander Main with an axe, has also confessed to two other murders in BC and that he was "the author of several robberies in town." His hanging is sparsely attended, numbering "about forty people, the majority of them members of the police force."

According to the paper, Luck shows no fear as he is escorted to the platform by the sheriff, with "no sign of a break-down" even as the noose is fitted around his neck. However, due to the rain, there is a rather sizable hitch in the proceedings; with constant rainfall hitting the scaffold for several days, the wood of the trapdoor has swelled to a point where it refuses to open.

"A murmur of surprise broke from the onlookers," the *Province* explains, "which was increased a moment later as a second attempt was made to spring the trap. Again the body of the condemned man settled perceptibly, but the trap remained in position . . . The strain on the nerves of the man must have been fearful, as twice the door beneath his feet was jarred, but failed to act, but with all this he uttered no sound."

On the third attempt, the trap opens, and Luck dies instantly of a broken neck. Over the history of the region, a total of 77 people will be executed in New Westminster and Burnaby. Though capital punishment will be on Canada's official books until 1976, the last actual hanging in British Columbia will take place at Burnaby's Oakalla Prison in 1959.

NOVEMBER 17, 2001

SHOCK REVERBERATES through Vancouver's gay community as, at close to 2:30 in the morning, the severely beaten body of Aaron Webster is discovered near Second Beach, touching off a year-long investigation into one of the city's most notorious hate crimes.

"This has all the earmarks of an attack that was prompted by the man's sexual orientation," Detective Scott Driemel tells the *Vancouver Province*, confirming that the police intend to investigate the incident as a gay bashing.

Found by friend Tim Chisholm, Webster, 41, is naked except for a pair of hiking boots, having been struck repeatedly by what police suppose was "a baseball bat or a pool cue."

"Trails in that area of the park," the paper notes, "are well-known gay strolls, where homosexuals go for anonymous sex in the bushes at night with partners they meet there."

Despite extensive media coverage, and a memorial march on the day following the attack, the case will remain unsolved for more than a year. However, in 2003, the first of four arrests will be made, culminating in the prosecution of Danny Rao and Ryan Cran, a trial that will acquit Rao but put Cran behind bars for six years on the charge of manslaughter. Cran will eventually be released on parole in 2009.

"This is horrible. Truly horrible," says Jim Deva, head of Little Sister's Bookstore on Davie. "The violence of this just goes to show how dangerous it is to be gay."

A 1995 survey of Vancouver's gay community revealed that close to one-third of respondents have reported having experienced physical assault in their lifetimes.

NOVEMBER 18, 1922

"Life Is a Joyous Affair at the Friday Dances," reports the *Vancouver Sun*'s society page on the city enjoying its weekend with "gay abandon."

"The week of work had ended," the paper continues, "and there was in view a glorious weekend of golfing, dancing and tea-ing. The weather promised to be fine, although the weather is a fickle dame, and likely, at the slightest provocation, to change her whimsical mind."

The paper mentions a number of the goings-on about town, calling them "more than delightful" and taking nearly two columns to list every single attendee at each.

Other "society" items include "Miss Gertrude McInnis, York Street, entertained last evening at a jolly dance for a number of her friends," "Dr. B.D. Gillies is spending a few weeks in Penticton," and "the ladies in charge of the tea room for the Kiwanis Advertising Show, to be held next week in the Manufacturer's Building, met yesterday to complete plans for serving tea both afternoon and evening during the week."

Bayview telephone operators at a dance, circa 1920.
Image courtesy of the Vancouver Archives (CVA 99-3246)

NOVEMBER 19, 2005

Tears flow and conspiracy theories abound as, following a close civic election, Vision Vancouver mayoral candidate Jim Green loses to the Non-Partisan Association's Sam Sullivan by only 3,747 votes—a slim margin turned suspicious when it is revealed that 4,273 votes were collected by a complete political unknown: James Green.

"Vancouver mayoral candidate James Green says it's nonsense to think Jim Green lost the mayoralty because of confusion over their names," the *Vancouver Sun* will report the following day. "However, had all of James Green's 4,273 votes gone to Jim Green, who got 57,796, Green would have won the mayor's chair with 526 votes."

"I really wanted to be your mayor with all my heart and soul," Green says in his concession speech before breaking down in tears. "We had a good time. We built a lot of support."

Green, who grew up in the Deep South and immigrated to Canada to avoid serving in Vietnam, has for decades been a tireless advocate for the poor and disenfranchised, in particular those on the Downtown Eastside. His achievements include co-founding the Portland Hotel Society (which also operates the supervised injection site InSite), founding United We Can (a street charity bottle depot), establishing Blade Runners (a group dedicated to providing low-income kids and teenagers with job skills), and serving as chairman of Four Corners Community Savings (a community bank that paid union wages and served 6,000 low-income customers before closing in 2004). This is Green's second attempt to secure the mayoralty, having first run against Gordon Campbell in 1990

(he would also run unsuccessfully against Campbell in 1996 as MLA for Vancouver–Point Grey), and it is the first election for Vision Vancouver, a party Green co-founded along with former Coalition of Progressive Electors councillors Larry Campbell, Raymond Louie, and Tim Stevenson.

"I did not enter this race to be a spoiler," James Green tells the *Sun*, attempting to dismiss allegations of a conspiracy. "That was not my motivation. I didn't spend hours and hours walking the streets, talking to people just to spoil the ballot for Jim Green."

Despite the defeat, Jim Green (who has been an alderman since 2002, when Vision's forerunner COPE all but decimated the NPA) will continue to work with the people of the Downtown Eastside for the remainder of his career, drawing adulation and ire for his dedication to the Woodward's redevelopment and being presented with the Freedom of the City in 2012 by Gregor Robertson, the city's first Vision mayor.

Thirty-six hours after receiving the award, Green will die of lung cancer in his Vancouver home.

"Mr. Green is not charm personified," the *Globe*'s Rod Mickleburgh will write. "He can bruise feelings. Not everyone on the small, tough turf of the DTES is a fan. Yet few would deny his heartfelt desire for social change, to make Vancouver a more decent place to live."

NOVEMBER 20, 1982

Nearly a century after the passage of the federal *Lord's Day Act* and after 12 years of serious city-wide debate, Sunday shopping is approved by Vancouver voters by a majority of 58.2 percent.

"It has struck a blow for freedom of choice," London Drugs senior vice-president Mark Nussbaum beams in a November 22 interview with the *Vancouver Sun*. "Nobody forces you to shop on Sunday but you can choose."

Although the plebiscite (part of the civic election) is merely a statement of opinion, council and the local dailies expect a bylaw to be drafted and implemented almost immediately. The referendum comes on the heels of the provincial *Holiday Shopping Regulation Act*, implemented in 1980, which set a minimum number of shopping hours throughout British Columbia unless specifically approved by local voters. Previous to this, Sunday hours were governed by a federal statute, the *Lord's Day Act*, passed in 1906, which stipulated that no business was permitted "to sell or offer for sale or purchase any goods, chattels, or other personal property, or to carry on or transact any business of his ordinary calling, or in connection with such calling." Prosecutions under the act (which could only be undertaken by the provincial Attorney General) were widespread as early as 1932, when 12 store managers, 12 florists, and two vegetable dealers were charged for making sales on a Sunday, for items such as lead pencils and thermos bottles.

The debate became even more heated in the 1970s when Attorney General Leslie Peterson began threatening Gastown merchants with fines, closure, and the revoking of licences for operating their businesses on the Sabbath. And, by 1978, Vancouver mayor Jack Volrich, who was decidedly in favour of Sunday closures, threatened to prosecute 16 stores who refused to close their doors. By 1979, Vancouver was the only city in the Lower Mainland still attempting to implement Sunday closure restrictions; Richmond, Burnaby, Delta, North Vancouver, and New Westminster had all chosen to leave operating hours in the hands of merchants, and even Calgary had removed its Sunday restrictions back in 1972. Despite Volrich's zeal, Attorney General Garde Gardom would refuse to prosecute, calling the *Lord's Day Act* "archaic, unworkable, and ineffective." In 1979, the BC Supreme Court would overturn the city's attempt to revoke the business licence of one Bernie Cobin, whose furniture store (known as The Warehouse) remained open in defiance of city closure orders.

Despite the victory, some people, including some merchants, are not enthusiastic about the change.

"All we can do is get public opinion interested in the fact that it is destroying our way of living," John Wallace, manager of the BC Retail Merchants Association of Canada, will declare. "BC has always been a place where families could be together on Sundays—where people could go to the beach or go skiing."

NOVEMBER 21, 1979

AFTER 45 YEARS, MILLIONS OF PICTURES, and outlasting every one of his competitors, a chapter of Vancouver's history draws to a close with the retirement of Alphonso "Foncie" Pulice, the city's last remaining street photographer.

"I'm the last of the street photographers," Pulice beams in an interview with the *Vancouver Province*'s Chuck Davis. "It's the end of an era. All the rest are dead . . . I said I'd retire at 65 and I kept my word. When I started back in 1934 there were six companies in Vancouver but when we really started to go was during the war. The public couldn't get film, you see, so the street photographers were all they had."

Street photography was once extremely common in most major cities before the advent of affordable personal cameras. At the trend's height, Pulice was one of nine photographers offering the same service, and was, by his own estimate, taking between 4,000 and 5,000 pictures per day. Having formed his own business after his return from World War II, Pulice plied his trade all over Vancouver, his distinctive "Foncie's Fotos" cart

popping up along Granville Street, at the PNE, and in Stanley Park. His candid photographs of thousands of Vancouverites (after Pulice snapped a photo, the subject would be presented with a ticket redeemable in 24 hours) became so widely known that families would often telephone ahead to make an appointment. However, as he notes with a grin, not everyone was a fan of his work.

"I've had a few people angry I took their picture," he says. "They'd demand the negatives. I always gave the negatives to them if they insisted. One fellow threatened to beat me up. I told him: 'Please . . . don't touch the camera. You can punch me— but don't hit the camera.'"

Following his retirement, Foncie's camera rig will be donated to the Museum of Vancouver. And, in 2013 (10 years after his death at the age of 88), he will be the subject of both a MOV exhibit and a documentary film.

By the end of his career, Pulice will have taken an estimated 15 million photographs.

Foncie Pulice with an early version of his distinctive camera, circa 1950.
(MUSEUM OF VANCOUVER COLLECTION; H2004.76.1)

NOVEMBER 22, 1965

As local parents throw up their hands in despair, the *Province*'s Alan Morley bemoans the poor attitude, lax work ethic, and "scraggly" appearance of the city's newest youth subculture: the Beatnik.

"The girl I passed on the street looked positively scraggly," Morley says with horror, "no makeup, dirty fingernails, wrinkled, tight pants on thin legs, run-down shoes and so on. A so-called 'beatnik' type, of course . . . I grew up in this city and this province when a substantial portion of their inhabitants were scraggly by necessity, not by choice. Lean, scrawny, undernourished, beat, bulldozed, hopeless, dirty, ragged, overworked and despised. Despised not only by those better off, but by themselves, and seeing no way out of it."

Morley, in his editorial (which takes up nearly a quarter of the paper's front page), muses on the declining state of the city's youth and reflects on his own early adulthood, working 10-hour days in the mines of British Columbia as part of a generation that aspired to flush toilets and bathtubs and "a change of decent clothes to wear on Sundays."

However, he reasons, the beatnik's appearance is merely an elaborate ruse, an "enforced scraggliness of which the beatnik has neither knowledge nor experience nor even theoretical comprehension," likening the subculture's unkempt appearance to a woman's makeup, "or a man who insists on wearing a lampshade for a hat at a lively party."

Morley concludes his editorial having, in his mind, made peace with the city's youth, and the Beatnik in particular.

"I'm sure by far the most of them will grow up to be charming and intelligent young adults," he declares, secure in his benevolence, "I was probably a bigger fool myself at that age."

NOVEMBER 23, 1967

FOLLOWING A NUMBER OF PROPOSALS and more than a year of community outrage, a meeting regarding City Hall's $340 million plan to bulldoze large portions of Strathcona for an interurban freeway degenerates into chaos.

"A public meeting on freeways was turned into a shouting, arm-waving melee and was adjourned by Mayor Tom Campbell Thursday night when he felt it had reached near-riot proportions," reports the *Vancouver Sun*. "A crowd of 500 jamming the council chamber and overflowing into the committee rooms heaped scorn on members of council and hurled abuse at city officials."

During the proceedings, Aldermen Ernie Broome and Peter Graham are booed off the floor, and Mayor Campbell (who voted against having the meeting and stressed that it would be an occasion for information, "not reconsideration") endures non-stop volleys of abuse from those gathered. The proposed freeway project, contentious since its introduction, includes a waterfront parkway along English Bay, freeway routes along Main and Venables, an eight-lane, 10-metre deep trench running through downtown, and connecting overpasses along Gore and Carrall that would level large portions of Chinatown and Gastown. Opposition has been fierce from Chinatown businesses and a number of community groups, including the Strathcona Property Owners and Tenants Association. The controversy has already resulted in the resignation of at least one city official.

Campbell, a former developer himself (his plan to construct a Four Seasons Hotel at the foot of Georgia Street will meet with similar resistance), is characteristically unsympathetic.

A protest against the Chinatown freeway, circa 1967.
(IMAGE COURTESY OF THE UBYSSEY, BOB BROWN, PHOTOGRAPHER)

"This wasn't public reaction," Campbell snarls. "This was university reaction."

However, according to the *Sun*'s estimates, the crowd is predominantly middle-aged, with roughly 30 "university-aged persons" and the remainder of the attendees being "citizens at large."

"[Community needs] are apparently being sacrificed for the sake of a straight line on a theoretical plan for the benefit of non-residents," reads a dispatch from the Carnegie Ratepayers' Association, "whose only concern with the community is going through it as fast as possible, and a public-be-damned attitude on the part of the engineering staff."

Eventually, following sustained public outrage and the inability of the federal and provincial governments to settle on who should pay for the freeway system, the project will be abandoned—but not before the construction of the new Dunsmuir and Georgia Viaducts, and the levelling of 15 blocks in the area, including Hogan's Alley, once the city's only predominantly black neighbourhood.

NOVEMBER 24, 1934

"Eight Arrivals for Each Departure!" screams the front page of the *Vancouver Sun*, as, following a prolonged Depression-related building lull and a sudden influx of new arrivals, Vancouver is faced with an acute housing shortage.

"This growing movement toward Vancouver has been felt markedly during the past 10 months, several cartage companies in the city reporting increases in the Vancouver-bound traffic," the paper reports. "A direct result of the inflow of new residents has been the heavy demands for rentals for modern houses. There is a distinct shortage of this type of house, real estate men report, and soon scarcely any will be available."

The shortage is the result of a number of factors, notably a concentrated push for population growth which has been taking place since the early 1900s—a plan exemplified by the popular turn-of-the-century slogan "In 1910, Vancouver then will have 100,000 men!" Now, new arrivals are at an all-time high, with building costs on the rise, homes and apartments becoming increasingly difficult to come by, Depression-era incomes perilously low, and land and material costs increasing exponentially. Vancouver's housing shortfall will shortly become a provincial and city-wide concern, leading to the creation of a civic housing committee in 1937.

"As soon as financial conditions ease up a bit and money becomes cheaper there should be quite a building boom," says John Waller, a local real estate agent. "There is quite a shortage of more modern homes in Vancouver due, largely, to the increasing numbers coming into the city from the prairies. The demand for rentals is greater than the supply. There is not nearly the selection offering that there was in the summer."

The city's housing crunch will result in severe overcrowding, particularly in the West End, and will climax with the dramatic occupation of the Hotel Vancouver in 1946 by homeless Second World War veterans. While the occupation will receive widespread public support, the changes effected by it will be minimal. Housing will remain in short supply citywide throughout the 30s, 40s, and 50s. However, in 1966, the era of modern apartment living will begin with the implementation of the Strata Titles Act, legislation which allows for the creation of condominiums.

Unemployed men in one of the city's "Hobo Jungles" near Dunlevy Avenue, 1931.
Image courtesy of the Vancouver Archives (Re N10.02)

NOVEMBER 25, 2005

REPRESENTATIVES FROM ALL THREE LEVELS OF GOVERNMENT gather at the Vancouver International Airport as, before the assembled media, the name of Vancouver's newest rapid transit system is announced: the Canada Line.

"Formerly known as the RAV line, the newly-dubbed Canada Line will feature sleek grey trains that will be able to travel at a maximum speed of 80 kilometres per hour," reports the *Vancouver Sun*, "and carry up to 334 passengers between Waterfront Station, the airport, and Richmond."

The design of the train cars is also unveiled at the ceremony, and it is announced that work on the 16-station, $1.9 billion project has begun.

"It's been a long process to get it to this point," former Surrey mayor Doug McCallum says, "and now it is actually physically being constructed, and it's on time, on budget, and we hope to be able to open it in 2009."

The project is funded by the federal government, TransLink, and the BC Airport Authority. In an exuberant address, Transportation Minister Kevin Falcon praises the project as a "generational investment."

"One hundred years from now people will still be riding the [Canada Line]," Falcon declares, "and we will still be receiving the environmental benefits and sustainability this line represents."

By 2009, the cost projection for the line will be more than $2 billion, though the system will open on time in August 2009.

NOVEMBER 26, 1963

AT 12:30 P.M. IN THE University of British Columbia's Armoury building, a memorial service is held for assassinated United States president John Fitzgerald Kennedy.

"It was a simple and moving symbol of the meaning of the youthful, courageous US president held for UBC students," the *Ubyssey* will report in its November 28 edition. "For many students it was the first time they had attended a religious service in years."

The service, which takes place a day after the state funeral in Washington, will include speeches by university president John B. MacDonald and chancellor Phyllis Ross, and feature prayers led by the principals of St. Mark's College. Mourning has been widespread throughout Vancouver since Kennedy's assassination in Dallas three days earlier, with local dailies printing lengthy eulogies and memorial services springing up in churches city-wide.

This is not the first time Vancouverites have gathered to mourn an American head of state; in April 1865, as the *Vancouver Sun* notes, news of the death of Abraham Lincoln was greeted with "tears in the streets."

"John Fitzgerald Kennedy was an American public servant with courage and conviction," President MacDonald concludes in an address to the gathered students. "A gallant soldier in a righteous cause, a scholar blessed with wisdom, a graduate with honor in the school of practical politics, a man of wealth with a passion to help the underprivileged, a strong young American with confidence in his strong young country."

NOVEMBER 27, 1953

THE BC AUTO ASSOCIATION and the *Vancouver News-Herald* are unanimous in their denunciation of the latest sneaky tactic employed by VPD officers behind the wheel of ghost cars: ordinary clothes.

"Members of the board of directors meeting in the Hotel Georgia heartily commended the present work and objective of the traffic department," the paper reports, "but took exception to the officers 'who are impersonating citizens' by working in sports clothes."

"Vancouver's traffic is of common interest to both the BCAA and city police enforcement," Alderman Halford Wilson charges at the association meeting, "but I think that police officers should be dressed as officers."

"As a salesman in the downtown area I frequently carry a considerable sum of money and goods in my car for business purposes," reads a letter addressed to the BCAA from a concerned salesman. "If I am forced to stop by an unmarked car and two men approach me, I would be in a position of not knowing whether I was going to be held up and robbed of my goods, money and possibly my car or given a traffic ticket."

The BCAA also opposes raising speeding tickets from $2 to $5.

VPD Traffic Officer and patrol car, 1948. IMAGE COPYRIGHT VANCOUVER PUBLIC LIBRARY

NOVEMBER 28, 1956

AFTER CLOSE TO 25 YEARS OF PUBLIC SERVICE, politician and philanthropist "Friendly" Fred Hume is elected to his fourth term as Vancouver's mayor, marking the first time a chief magistrate has been elected by acclamation since 1921.

"Mayor Hume was high in praise of Mrs. Hume for the help and support she has given him throughout the years," reports the *Vancouver Province*. "He was elected by acclamation at City Hall at noon today when nominations closed with no other candidates for mayor."

"I didn't know I had so many friends," the affable Hume beams as he is renamed to his post by city clerk Ronald Thompson. "Actually, I had seriously thought this year of dropping out, but so many of my friends urged me to carry on and I was flattered by this and felt I would like to continue if I could for the next two years."

Hume, already a millionaire as the head of Hume and Rumble (an electrical contracting firm), served for 18 years in New Westminster (nine as an alderman and nine as mayor). Upon first taking office in Vancouver in 1950, he caused an uproar among aldermen by insisting that all but $1 of his $7,500 annual salary be donated to charity.

Hume is also the owner of the WHL Vancouver Canucks and, in the years to come, will be a driving force behind pushing the National Hockey League to grant Vancouver a franchise. His funeral in 1967 will be attended by more than 2,000 people, and when the Vancouver Canucks create an award for the team's unsung heroes, it will be named in Hume's honour.

Fred Hume speaks before a crowd at City Hall, Sept. 4, 1951.
IMAGE COURTESY OF THE VANCOUVER ARCHIVES (PORT P1226)

NOVEMBER 29, 1974

Two POLICEMEN ARE HOSPITALIZED with stab wounds, a bystander suffers a gunshot to the shoulder, and one inmate remains at large after a dramatic lunch-hour jailbreak from the Main Street police station unleashes four convicted felons on downtown Vancouver.

"Police said the four—all inmates of BC Penitentiary—overpowered the deputy and the officer in the third floor jail, seizing the officer's gun," the *Vancouver Sun* reports. "They then fled along an alley on to Hastings Street, one waving the officer's .38 calibre revolver."

The inmates are Larry Marshall (charged with possession of a dangerous weapon), Robert Hume and Gordon Andrews (charged with robbery), and Vincent Fitzgerald (charged with hashish possession). Although the prisoners had been "searched to the skin" before their court appearance, one of them manages to obtain a razor before being returned to the third-floor jail cell and subsequently uses it to stab the unsuspecting deputy. In the course of their escape, they slash the throat of Police Constable Rick Robinson and knock a third officer unconscious before fleeing into the alley behind the station.

A witness, Romeo Thomas, reports seeing the inmates in the alleyway, one brandishing a revolver, and recounts their unsuccessful attempt to steal a car.

"One had a gun," Thomas recounts. "They stopped this poor fellow. He was sitting in his car, waiting for a red light. They tried to pull the car door open. He refused and they shot him."

Three of the inmates escape in another car but are immediately pursued by police. They are recaptured less than five minutes later.

The fourth, Fitzgerald, boards a bus at Second and Main, and despite an extensive police search, no trace of him is found.

"He has two tattoos on his left arm," reports the *Sun*, appealing to readers to identify the escaped felon. "One reading 'Uncle' and the other 'Angel of Death.'"

NOVEMBER 30, 1926

CITIZENRY, POLITICIANS, and business interests are sharply divided as a government commission convenes to argue the merits of the most contentious civic issue of the year: whether or not to build the Lions Gate Bridge.

"Argument pro and con on the proposal to build a bridge across the Lions Gate was heard at the opening session this morning of the commission appointed by the government to receive representations from all parties whose interests may be affected by the construction of the bridge," reads the *Vancouver Sun*.

The idea of a bridge across the First Narrows has been circulating since at least the 1890s (suggested by George Grant Mackay, who went on to build the original Capilano Suspension Bridge); however, public discussion of the idea has only recently become widespread, thanks to the efforts of the Greater Vancouver Publicity Bureau. The bureau includes representatives from the City of Vancouver, the Cities of North and West Vancouver, the Harbour Board, and the Department of Indian Affairs, and has been involved in an extensive publicity push in favour of the idea (responsible in early May for renaming the span "Lions' Gate"). It faces strong opposition to the proposal, both from park commissioner C.E. Tisdall and the Vancouver Board of Trade (who are said to be "unanimously opposed"). Opponents to the bridge proposal have existed since the idea was introduced, with concerns including interference with navigation, destruction of land in Stanley Park, and worries about competition for toll money with the Second Narrows Bridge.

However, the remainder of the commission is in support of the idea, having received proposals and plans from a number of architectural firms and having given the city approval to request Stanley Park lands from the Department of Defence. While the *Sun* is in full support of the bridge, the rival *Province* is bitterly opposed, claiming that the structure would "constitute a hindrance to harbour travel and ruin Stanley Park."

A plebiscite will be held by the city later in 1926 and will be soundly defeated. A second plebiscite, held in 1933, will approve construction of the bridge by a margin of two to one. Following some financial wrangling, the necessary land on the opposite side of Burrard Inlet will be purchased by the Guinness Brewing family (of the Irish beer fame) through a syndicate known as British Properties Ltd.

Guinness will own the bridge until 1955, charging each car a toll of 25 cents.

Construction of the Lions Gate Bridge, 1937.
IMAGE COURTESY OF THE VANCOUVER ARCHIVES (CVA 260-773)

DECEMBER 1, 1939

THE SIDEWALK OUTSIDE CITY HALL is packed with eager vendors, many of whom have waited close to 12 hours hoping to receive that most lucrative of holiday honours: Christmas tree street-vending permits.

"Permits to sell Christmas trees at 'preferred' street intersections were the prizes which kept nearly thirty men waiting outside the City Hall all night Thursday," reports the *Vancouver Province* on the all-night vigil held by prospective salespeople. "Some of them had waited there since Wednesday afternoon, and when the hall opened nearly 100 had gathered to receive civic sanction for their tree-sales programme."

The "biggest 'plums,'" according to the paper, are the corner of 41st and West Boulevard, 25th and Granville, First and Commercial, and Nanaimo and Hastings. And, while there is some disappointment surrounding the fact that 150 of the 250 vending corners have been awarded to returning soldiers, there is little complaint amongst the early arrivals. Civic regulations state that vendors are forbidden from selling their wares before December 1 and after December 24, with assistant licence inspector Donald MacDonald insisting "this year that the salesmen leave their corners clean and tidy when they go out of business Christmas night."

"Some have been known," the paper notes sourly, "to leave their unsold stock standing forlornly on the pavement."

BC Tel employees by their company Christmas tree, circa 1940.
IMAGE COURTESY OF THE VANCOUVER ARCHIVES (CVA 1184-2799, JACK LINDSAY, PHOTOGRAPHER)

DECEMBER 2, 1986

"Trash the ash or be prepared to part with some cash," reads an article in the *Vancouver Province*, reporting on the news that, one day earlier, Vancouver's first clean air bylaw came into effect, banning smoking in the workplace.

According to bylaw author Geoff Rowlands, the "vast majority [of workplaces] butted out yesterday," including Vancouver General Hospital, where smoking is now permitted only in the east cafeteria. The ban, reported by local dailies to be the strictest in the country, comes on the heels of other anti-smoking bylaws passed elsewhere in Canada, including one in North York, Ontario, in 1976 (banning smoking in supermarkets) and others passed in Ottawa and Toronto in 1977 (credited as the country's first comprehensive anti-smoking legislation).

Among Canadians, Vancouver boasts some of the lowest smoking rates in the country (26 percent compared with 31 percent elsewhere); however, as Rowlands notes, his office had received roughly 30 complaints by mid-afternoon of the ban's first day.

"They are mainly from employees whose management is perhaps not quite as sensitive to the issue as it should be," Rowlands explains. "We've asked them to take it up with their bosses. But if they are afraid to do so, we will write to the company, outlining their responsibility. It will be a 'nice' letter. We are not looking for confrontation here."

Despite some scrutiny and continued debate in the media, many other cities in Canada will follow suit throughout the 1980s, and a dramatic decline in per capita spending on cigarettes (a decline that began in 1983) will continue into the millennium.

As of September 2010, smoking will be banned in all of Vancouver's public spaces.

Cigarette display in the window of Owl Drugs, Main and Hastings, 1934.
Image courtesy of the Vancouver Archives (CVA 99-4618)

DECEMBER 3, 1970

HISTORIANS AND MERCHANTS breathe a collective sigh of relief as, after having been missing for two months, the head of Gastown's Gassy Jack statue is recovered from a city parking garage.

"Gassy Jack is getting his head back," reports the *Vancouver Province*. "Sometime next week, the copper-and-concrete statue of Gassy Jack Deighton, standing at Maple Tree Square, will once again have a head on its shoulders, after exactly two months of decapitude. The severed head was found in an East End parking garage by Gastown clown W.H. Stonehouse, who was looking for a pad for the night. He now stands to collect the $50 reward offered by Larry Killam's Town Group Company."

The theft, which took place in early October, is thought to have been the work of vandals, with few leads for the police department. The statue has been in place in Maple Tree Square since early 1970, when it was installed without city approval by four local businessmen (including Killam), as part of a Gastown revitalization project that also includes cobblestone streets, new lampposts, and the Gastown Steam Clock. Although initially unenthused (Mayor Tom Campbell originally planned to have it shipped to the city dump), city council later put their support behind the statue, allowing it to stay provided merchants had it properly anchored and maintained.

No suspects will ever be charged in the theft.

The statue (and its head) will remain in Maple Tree Square into the next millennium.

Gastown, 1970.
IMAGE COURTESY OF THE VANCOUVER ARCHIVES (CVA 780-770)

DECEMBER 4, 1947

LOCAL PAPERS REPORT ON THE NEWS that "with a thunderous crash" Stanley Park's famed Lumbermen's Arch has been destroyed by a city bulldozer.

"Like an old sick horse that had to be put out of its misery, Vancouver's famed Lumbermen's Arch was torn down Wednesday," reports the *Vancouver Province*'s Clyde Gilmour, "but a new one is almost certain to take its place."

Lumbermen's Arch—the first of two to share that name—was originally constructed in 1912 at the corner of Hamilton and Pender as one of 10 festive arches built for a civic holiday to honour the visiting Duke of Connaught. Following the celebrations, it was disassembled and floated by barge to Stanley Park, where it has stood for 34 years, held together without the use of nails, screws, or fasteners of any kind.

Unfortunately, the arch is now in such an advanced state of decay that it is considered a hazard to tourists (despite an offer by Bloedel, Stewart and Welch Ltd. to replace all of its logs free of charge). However, as Park Board chairman R. Rowe Holland declares, a new monument will likely be erected by the BC Lumber Manufacturers' Association, though no timeline on the construction is given.

"Thousands of visitors approaching Vancouver by sea or strolling through its best-known outing ground admired the monument and spread its fame abroad," the paper explains. "Hundreds of lovers carved their initials on its walls encircled by sculptured hearts."

The second Lumbermen's Arch will be dedicated in 1952 with little civic fanfare.

Lumbermen's Arch, 1940.
IMAGE COURTESY OF THE VANCOUVER ARCHIVES (ARCH P43)

DECEMBER 5, 1975

"OUGHT WE TO ASK FOR THE RESIGNATION of homosexual politicians?" asks an editorial in the *Vancouver Sun*. "The answer is 'yes.' Although the civilized citizen believes in sexual freedom between any two or more consenting adults, only the imprudent citizen knowingly elects a homosexual to Parliament."

The article's author, former *Maclean's* journalist and war hero McKenzie Porter, is already well known to readers and editors countrywide for his vitriolic, provocative columns. He has described decorated First Nations war hero Tommy Prince as "irritating," claimed South African blacks had "but a veneer of civilization" (in an article arguing for the continuation of apartheid), and condemned the use of workplace washrooms to defecate (a theft of an employer's time as well as an "offence to the eyes, ears and nose of one's colleagues"). In fact, his racist, sexist tirades have already resulted in a libel suit for a previous employer, the *Toronto Telegram*.

"It is true that homosexuality often coincides with genius," Porter allows. "But genius, which sometimes is akin to madness, is not a political asset. What a politician needs more than any other intellectual virtue is common sense. And common sense, as we shall see, rarely occurs in homosexuals. During my 40 years in journalism, on both sides of the Atlantic, I have acquired many male and female homosexual friends. All make delightful, mentally stimulating company. But I cannot think of one who is suited to political office."

Porter goes on to cite a number of "scientific" studies with which he is familiar, building a case for the "frailties" of the homosexual population. Among Porter's complaints are excessive stinginess or excessive extravagance, extreme tidiness, a propensity toward sadism or a propensity toward masochism, a love of fashionable furniture and draperies, and a general interest in fashion ("not so much for a comely appearance," he warns, "as for astonishment and the excitement of gossip").

"Homosexuals may make engaging guests at house parties," the article concludes. "But they are inimical to the interests of all political parties. When a politician finds himself yielding to homosexual temptations, he knows in his inner heart, that he is no longer fitted for office. Then, if he has any sense of obligation to his constituents, he will resign."

Three years later, Robert Douglas Cook will run for provincial office in West Vancouver–Howe Sound as Canada's first openly gay political candidate. In the years to follow, Greater Vancouver will also furnish the country with its first openly gay MP and cabinet minister, Svend Robinson, who will serve the government for 25 years over seven consecutive terms.

DECEMBER 6, 1952

"I NOW CONVOKE, on this tenth day of February, nineteen hundred and whatever-it-is-plus-five, in the Metropolis of Vancouver, a Public Hearing to consider any objections to the proposal to eliminate the said metropolis."

At the official opening of UBC's Frederic Wood Theatre, Vancouver audiences get their first chance to experience a dramatic staged reading of celebrated writer Earle Birney's surrealist masterpiece *Trial of a City (The Damnation of Vancouver)*, courtesy of the Graduate Players Club.

Originally written and produced as a radio play for CBC in spring 1952, the production (set "five years from now" in the basement of the city courthouse) concerns a public hearing around whether or not to completely annihilate Vancouver and replace it with a dam site. Featured characters include Legion, the counsel for the city, and Mr. Gabriel Powers, counsel for the "Office of the Future," who speaks the gibberish of "future's language" and is intent on destroying every living person in the city. Other characters include Skuh-wath-kwuh-tlath-kyootl of the Coast Salish Nation, and Gassy Jack, who speaks in a broad brogue and never stops talking.

Birney, a UBC professor of creative writing (and responsible for the establishment of the country's first university creative writing program), is also a successful novelist and two-time recipient of the Governor General's Award for Poetry. He has been called by Northrop Frye one of Canada's "leading poets."

The play will be produced a second time at UBC in 1954. It will also have several brushes with success in the years to come, being adapted into a television drama by CBC, considered for Stratford, and commissioned for a 10-day engagement at the Vancouver Centennial. However, because of allegations of "highbrowism" at the CBC, the television production will be shelved, and soon afterward, under similar circumstances, both the Stratford and Centennial productions will be quietly shut down.

"What [the Centennial Committee chairman] did say was that Gassy Jack would have to be dematerialized even before the play started, and replaced by Centennial Sam," Birney will recall years later. "The latter was a cartoon line-drawing of a winsome old prospector, used on Centennial promotional material. I was requested to write Jack out and Sam in. When I refused I lost my last chance, it seems, to watch my play on Canadian boards."

DECEMBER 7, 1930

WITH AN ESTIMATED 55,000 already in use about the city and gaining popularity among "small boys and old men," the *Vancouver Province* writes on the state of "the newest sport of sports" to hit the city, that "cruel weapon of savage combat": the yo-yo.

"A yo-yo, it might be well to make clear," explains the paper, "is the national weapon of the 100 per cent Philippino. It is as simple as it is effective: merely a piece of heavy, polished wood at the end of a short grass rope—a sort of club with a rope handle. The Philippine Island natives are said to be able to whip a yo-yo into action at startling speed . . . But, proficient as the Philippino may be as a yo-yoist, the fact remains that now, today, in Vancouver, there are thousands of yo-yoists who can outperform the originators of this strange and historic instrument."

Though yo-yos have come to enjoy worldwide popularity throughout the mid-1920s, the toy itself has existed since ancient Greece. Manufactured as a "bandalore" in the United States of the mid-1800s and taking its name from the northern Philippine Ilokano word *yóyo*, the modern yo-yo first gained popularity in the 1920s when Filipino American Pedro Flores started his own manufacturing company. By 1929, Flores's factories were producing 300,000 units daily, and the device was known worldwide. (Later the company and all its assets would be purchased by American entrepreneur Donald F. Duncan, who marketed the device and patented its name.) Within the previous week, the paper explains, department stores city-wide have reported phenomenal sales of yo-yos.

The article then goes on to carefully describe the shape and size of a yo-yo, giving some handy tips on its operation, including instructions on "side-slips, nose dives, and the tricky Immelman turn." The yo-yo itself will continue to enjoy widespread popularity, both in Vancouver and elsewhere, for the better part of the 20th century and will be inducted in 1999 into the National Toy Hall of Fame.

"Thus has the newest toy—the newest novelty device for bringing happiness to the hearts of small boys—come to us," the *Province* concludes. "A direct descendant of cruel primitive weapons."

No proof will be produced that the device was ever used in combat.

Man atop a Sun *vehicle, advertising the newspaper's $100 Yo-Yo Contest, March 28, 1933.*
IMAGE COURTESY OF THE VANCOUVER ARCHIVES (CVA 371-1922)

DECEMBER 8, 1918

"THE STARS INCLINE BUT DO NOT COMPEL," warns the *Vancouver Sun*'s daily horoscope. "Although the Sun is in benefic aspect today, it is not a very lucky rule, as Uranus, Neptune and Saturn are all adverse. While the sun is in a kindly sway it is an auspicious time to seek the companionship of persons of influence. Visits to relatives are well directed, for out of social intercourse under this planetary rule great benefits may accrue."

Horoscopes are still a relatively new addition to local newspapers, coinciding with a general increase in interest in astrology across North America. Before mid-1918, none of Vancouver's dailies even carried regular daily horoscopes, instead filling their leisure sections with acrostic puzzles, short stories, social news, and series such as "The Gospel as Preached in Vancouver Pulpits." In fact, the *Sun* is the first Vancouver paper to carry a horoscope (the rival *World* will fold in 1924 without ever having printed them and the *Province* won't incorporate them for at least another 15 years).

"Agriculture is not well-directed during this government of the stars, and there may be heavy losses of livestock," the horoscope warns. "Organizers, managers, secret service employees, brokers and bankers should delay making any plans, as under this direction of the stars, the judgement is not likely to be trustworthy."

Among the paper's other predictions are a warning that "Neptune is held to encourage superstition," that "the stars seem to presage outbreaks of intolerance and uncharitableness," and most dire of all, that "Uranus is in a place unfriendly to orthodox faiths."

DECEMBER 9, 1926

"I HAVE NEVER HAD AS MUCH REASON to be gratified as I have at the result of the present contest," declares Louis Denison Taylor as, for the sixth time in his lengthy political career, he is elected mayor of Vancouver.

"A majority in every ward in the city shows that after all I still retain the confidence of the people as a whole," Taylor beams.

L.D. Taylor preparing for a dive in the First Narrows, June 1926.
IMAGE COURTESY OF THE VANCOUVER ARCHIVES (CVA 1477-30)

"I can hardly express an appreciation of this wonderful show of confidence."

Taylor, easily recognizable in his horn-rimmed glasses and trademark red tie, will remain Vancouver's longest-serving mayor, being elected eight separate times. Before and during his time in politics, he has been involved in all manner of other enterprises, including owning the *Vancouver World* newspaper, working as a banker, and spending time as a fugitive from justice (allegations that caused him to flee to Vancouver, a secret he kept all his life). In the years to come, Taylor will continue to be at the centre of civic controversy for his "Open Town" policies, which focus police attention on violent crime and away from vice crimes such as prostitution and gambling. He will have few friends in the media, with the *Province* even going so far as to label him a "socialist."

"If a Socialist is a man who stands by what he thinks right and does not fear to express his opinions irrespective of monopolies, corporations, and other similar influences," Taylor would declare in rebuttal, "who dares to speak on behalf of the masses of the people, then I am a Socialist."

Taylor's policies, along with long-standing allegations of nepotism, will often put him at odds with moral reformers, culminating in a high-profile investigation into corruption in the police department and the mayor's office in 1928. Though Taylor will ultimately be cleared of all charges, the inquiry will eventually prove a disaster to his political career—he will lose to Gerry McGeer in 1934 by the largest margin in city history.

DECEMBER 10, 1942

"Gas Masks to Go on Sale Here Monday" reports the *Vancouver News-Herald* as wartime Vancouver receives word that it will be the first city in the province to provide commercially available respirators.

"Monday is the day, 9 to 5 is the time, and downtown is the place where the distribution of Vancouver's 100,000 respirators (gas masks to you) will start," reports the paper. "For the cost price of $1.25, the people of Vancouver may buy their protection from death-carrying gases that the enemy is liable to drop upon the city any day."

While only 100,000 will initially be in stock, the paper assures its readers that an adequate supply will soon be available for the entire population. Proper fitting, the article continues, is essential. Two expert mask fitters will be available at the as yet undisclosed retail location. Masks are available in sizes for both adults and children. "It is expected," the paper explains, "that the masks for babies will be available shortly."

"Even your best friends won't recognize you when you appear in your respirator," the article concludes. "If you are particularly anxious to avoid detection, just wait until next Monday, when you may go downtown and for $1.25 buy yourself not only protection from death-bringing gases, but also from creditors, mothers-in-law, and would-be touch-makers."

Child in a gas mask, 1943.

DECEMBER 11, 1954

Public hysteria over juvenile delinquency reaches a fever pitch in Vancouver as, following a day of collection, 8,000 comic books are burned in a public bonfire at False Creek Park, making history as the first public burning of its kind in Canada.

"Despite heated public criticism, more than 200 adults braved rain and wind to see 8,000 crime comics burned in a public bonfire Saturday night," the *Province* will report in its December 13 edition. "And about 500 city youngsters are now reading hard-cover children's classics instead of the lurid thrillers."

"We have no apologies for the bonfire," says event organizer Jaycee Len Wynne in an interview with the paper, "despite all the public criticism of 'book burning.' It was only a symbolic torch, and the fuel was utter trash. We owe a lot of publicity to the idea—it was talked about all across Canada. Now more people may take up the lead from us, join the PTA and other groups in fighting this trash."

Public hysteria over comic books has been growing throughout 1954, largely as a result of the work of German-born psychiatrist Fredric Wertham, whose book *Seduction of the Innocent*, published earlier in the year, uses anecdotal evidence to link comics with juvenile delinquency. Among Wertham's assertions are that Batman and Robin are homosexual partners, that Wonder Woman is a lesbian, that female genitalia is present in drawings of trees or muscles, and that "Crime Comics," such as those published by giant E.C. Comics, encourage criminal behaviour in children.

"Some of the kiddies brought as many as 25 or 30 of the comic books to Enniskillen Hall, Seventh and Ontario," the paper continues, "to exchange them for such works as *Robinson Crusoe* and *Tom Brown's School Days*."

Wertham's work, and the moral panic it will cause, will become so widespread that it will result in a number of similar comic book burnings throughout the United States and ultimately lead to a series of senate subcommittee hearings on violence in the medium. The committee's findings, though concluding that comic books themselves don't cause crime, will result in the creation of the highly restrictive Comics Code Authority, which will destroy E.C. Comics and lead to a severe decline in the comic book industry for nearly two years.

DECEMBER 12, 1985

LOCAL DAILIES BUZZ WITH THE NEWS THAT, one day earlier, after years of construction and decades of discussion, Metro Vancouver's SkyTrain system began its first day of service.

"The opening of the SkyTrain writes a new and exciting chapter in the history of transportation in British Columbia," Premier W.R. Bennett will write in a self-congratulatory address composed for the *SkyTrain Commemorative Magazine*. "The development of this project—the most significant development in transportation in British Columbia since the arrival of the first CPR train 100 years ago—gives the Lower Mainland Region and its people the world's finest rapid transit system."

"When we first raised the idea, I was astonished by the overwhelming degree of public support," Transit Minister Grace McCarthy will beam on a subsequent page. "Work is underway on the Parkway's 7-Eleven Trail, the John Molson Way, the International Mile of Flags, the Variety Club Park, the Dutch Mile, the Filipino Plaza, and the Royal Canadian Legion's Tulip Mile."

The trains, which will operate free of charge for eight days, are only the first part of a larger, regional rapid transit strategy, with the intention being to expand beyond the original 15 stations, with lines extending into Surrey and Coquitlam. Rapid transit options have been discussed throughout the city of Vancouver for the better part of a decade. Although a combination underground/elevated system was initially favoured, it was only the 1982 acquisition of the CPR's Dunsmuir rail tunnel (a 1.4-kilometre tunnel under downtown) that ultimately made such a system economically feasible (other options included road-level trains throughout the downtown core).

Construction of the SkyTrain line, Feb. 1983.
IMAGE COURTESY OF THE VANCOUVER ARCHIVES (CVA 800-3073)

The system opens on time and under budget and, within the first day, transports 9,000 guests.

Following the initial eight days of service, the SkyTrain line will be closed for the remainder of 1985. It will welcome its first paying customers on January 3, 1986.

"Millions of Expo visitors will ride the SkyTrain next year," McCarthy will conclude, "and we want to let them know that there's a big, wide British Columbia out there and that they should get out and see it."

DECEMBER 13, 1933

"BRIDGE PASSES!" reads the jubilant front page of the *Vancouver Daily News-Herald* as, following years of debate, a failed plebiscite, and an exhaustive advertising campaign, Vancouverites vote four to one in favour of constructing the single longest suspension span in the British Empire—the Lions Gate Bridge.

"Vancouver on Wednesday gave its emphatic endorsement to more work and more wages for its citizens when it voted overwhelmingly in favour of construction of the First Narrows bridge," reports the *News-Herald*. "It was Vancouver's answer to the arguments that had been raised against acceptance of the $6,000,000 of British capital, as well as to the earnest efforts put forward by the *News-Herald* and leading citizens on behalf of the proposal."

The idea of a bridge across the First Narrows has been debated since the 1890s when West Vancouver civil engineer and wealthy landowner George Grant Mackay first suggested it as a way of increasing his own property value; however, it wasn't until the mid-1920s, with backing from the Greater Vancouver Publicity Bureau (responsible for renaming it "Lions' Gate"), that the idea first came to civic plebiscite—a proposal that was soundly defeated in 1926.

"Probably never before has an idea been debated so strenuously as the First Narrows bridge process," the article notes.

Although it is never mentioned in the paper, the land on the opposite side of Burrard Inlet has actually been purchased by the Guinness Brewing family (through a company known as British Properties), who have also agreed to shoulder the cost of construction in exchange for ownership of the bridge. Whether Guinness is also responsible for the weeks of advertising in local newspapers is unclear; however, unlike the 1926 plebiscite, public

The Lions Gate Bridge under construction, circa 1938.
IMAGE COURTESY OF THE VANCOUVER ARCHIVES (CVA 260-816)

opinion has already been swayed strongly in favour of the crossing, with a majority in favour returned in every one of the 47 polling stations city-wide.

"Just how much interest had been aroused was amply evidenced at the polls Wednesday, more particularly by what is usually termed the working class," reports the paper. "They endorsed the plan to give work and wages to Vancouver workmen and many of them didn't hesitate to make plain their views when they entered the polls and demanded 'Where do we vote for the First Narrows Bridge?'"

The Lions Gate Bridge will open on November 12, 1938 (having cost approximately $6 million), and motorists will be charged a toll of 25 cents.

Guinness will later sell the bridge to the province, and in April 1963, all tolls will be removed.

DECEMBER 14, 1934

VANCOUVERITES MAKE A DECISIVE VOTE for change as "colourful reformer" Gerry G. McGeer unseats long-time mayor Louis D. Taylor, winning the largest civic majority in Vancouver history.

"McGeer was awarded a four-to-one mandate to carry out his policy of aggressive civic reform in the field of finance and City Hall and Police Department administration," reports the *Vancouver Sun.* "Rolling up a smashing majority of 25,543, the victorious candidate practically obliterated his opponent in the heaviest day's polling the city has ever known."

An exuberant McGeer is joined by thousands of cheering supporters on his victory parade from the offices of the *Sun* to the crystal ballroom at the Hotel Vancouver. Backed by the Kitsilano Boys' Band, McGeer speaks to his supporters, declaring that his victory means "a new deal for Vancouver."

"The old order has changed and a new spirit is abroad," McGeer shouts before the assembled crowd.

McGeer, who has succeeded in painting his op-

ponent as outdated and corrupt, ran on a platform of aggressive civic reform, vowing to cut back city expenditures and, above all, to ferret out corruption in the police force. By contrast, Taylor's "Open Town" policy—whereby police resources were committed to violent crime and away from vice crime—has in recent years led to outrage by moral reformists and allegations of widespread police and political corruption. A public inquiry held in 1928 revealed that the Vancouver Police Department was indeed taking bribes from underworld figures in exchange for protection. Although Taylor was never directly linked to any criminal activity, his opponents in the media and at City Hall capitalized on this finding, which proved disastrous for his civic career.

"A man with youth, vigor, and vision had captured the popular imagination," the *Sun* gushes. "His program of action had an irresistible appeal to nearly every class in the community. Mayor Taylor, linked to the past, was hopelessly overwhelmed by public discontent."

McGeer's tenure as mayor will be characterized by his aggressive attitude toward union mobilization (which he will treat as "Bolshevik uprisings"), his extravagant spending (he will finance construction of a new City Hall in the middle of the Depression), and his appointment of Police Chief Walter Mulligan, who will go on to be involved in the largest corruption scandal in the history of the VPD.

McGeer will return to office in 1946 but will die in his sleep before his term is up.

Mayor McGeer visits Charles Jones's "Bird Paradise" on Hoy Street, Jan. 1936.
IMAGE COURTESY OF THE VANCOUVER ARCHIVES (PORT P138)

DECEMBER 15, 1966

"Bubble, bubble, toil and trouble," reads an article in the *Vancouver Sun* as, thanks to the work of an unknown prankster, the city's brand new courthouse fountain begins overflowing with bubbles, only hours after it is first turned on.

"For months, workmen as far away as Italy have toiled on Vancouver's courthouse fountain," the paper declares. "Thursday night, Premier W.A.C. Bennett went to the trouble of unveiling it in a rainstorm. And then, two hours and twenty minutes later came the bubbles. A prankster dumped in a packet of detergent and the bubbles came thick and fast as foaming suds flew in every direction, and thick foam covered the cloverleaf surface of the water at the bottom of the fountain."

The plans for the "controversial" courthouse fountain (known officially as the BC Centennial Fountain) have been kept secret throughout the construction process, and the fountain itself has cost the provincial government roughly $250,000 to build. According to official reports, the "symbolic twin-pillar centrepiece" is "meant to represent mankind rising from the sea and depicts gods of Celtic mythology." It is also said to include special built-in filters, designed to remove any additives, including dyes.

According to the paper, only a small crowd gathers to watch the unveiling, owing to the torrential rainstorm beating down upon them, and, thoroughly soaked, Premier Bennett refrains from making a speech.

"Give it a cheer!" shouts Mayor Bill Rathie. "It's one of the wonders of the western world."

"Haven't we got enough water already?" retorts a woman under an umbrella.

Her male companion nods.

"It would be better if they'd put in a big fireplace and held a wiener roast."

The fountain will continue to "lather" until it is shut off later in the evening.

The original courthouse fountain, circa 1920.
Image courtesy of the Vancouver Archives (Mon P35)

DECEMBER 16, 1979

ONE HOME IS DESTROYED, several others are damaged, and a number of roads in Vancouver, Burnaby, and Port Moody are washed out by rain and mudslides as, in a 30-hour period, 40 millimetres of rain hit the Lower Mainland.

"I'm afraid it's going to get a hell of a lot worse," claims an RCMP spokesman in Burnaby in an interview with the *Vancouver Sun*.

The weather report calls for further rain in the days to come, with floods closing portions of Fourth Avenue, Marine Drive, and Yukon Street. Secondary schools in Port Moody are evacuated, and one apartment building's ground-floor kitchen is filled nearly to the top with mud. The provincial government, while unwilling to label the city an official disaster area, has nonetheless sent members of the Provincial Emergency Measures Program to conduct surveys and find temporary housing for the displaced.

"Residents interviewed on the weekend were wondering if their damage was covered by insurance or if they would be losers because the disaster may be classified as an 'act of God,'" the *Sun* continues. "Emergency coordinator Frank Clegg surveyed the area Sunday and ordered provincial work crews and engineers into the area to clean up the mess."

"[Provincial authorities] will assess the damage and give us an overview and we will respond to that," states Deputy Premier Grace McCarthy upon surveying the damage. "We will advise the government to give all the assistance that the provincial government can give."

The flooding will continue for several more days.

Heavy rain at Hastings and Richards, circa 1907.
IMAGE COURTESY OF THE VANCOUVER ARCHIVES (CVA 677-584, PHILLIP TIMMS, PHOTOGRAPHER)

DECEMBER 17, 1958

FOLLOWING A STRENUOUS DEBATE, the *Vancouver Sun* reports that city council has voted to defer the most contentious public issue of the year: meter maids.

"Aldermen Tuesday deferred action on the idea first proposed by Ald. Evelyn Caldwell until it could be considered in terms of the 1959 budget because of costs involved," the paper explains. "Ald. George Miller pointed out that the police department, if men are relieved from parking meter duty by women, will want to maintain its established strength."

The program, discussed after the success of similar programs in Seattle and Portland, is favoured by the local dailies, owing to a city-wide manpower shortage in the police department and the potential for the program to free officers for "more important duties." Since parking meters were first installed in 1947, tickets have been issued by a team of eight male constables, totalling 96 man-hours of work a week. While council initially intends to rule on the issue by February 1959, the debate over civilian bylaw enforcement will continue for the better part of 20 years. Although Alderman Earle Adams will dismiss the idea as "ridiculous" in November 1959, a subsequent study will reveal that 58 percent of Vancouverites are in favour of meter maids. Alderman Halford Wilson will be in favour of hiring "war veterans rather than women to do the job."

Opinion will remain divided until September 1976 when the first of the city's bylaw enforcement officers will take to the streets, to be loathed by motorists into the new millennium.

Parking Attendant in the lot of the Hudson's Bay Company, 1943.
IMAGE COURTESY OF THE VANCOUVER ARCHIVES
(CVA 586-1781, DON COLTMAN AND STEFFANS COLMER, PHOTOGRAPHERS)

DECEMBER 18, 1918

LOCAL PAPERS BUZZ WITH THE NEWS THAT, following the issue of a warrant for his arrest, former prohibition commissioner Walter Findlay has failed to appear in a Victoria courtroom on charges of trafficking in bootleg liquor.

"W.C. Findlay, ex-prohibition commissioner, is being sought on a warrant charging him with breach of trust in the performance of his duties as a public official," writes the *Vancouver Province*. "The maximum penalty on conviction is five years imprisonment in the penitentiary."

Findlay, who rose to prominence as a member of the People's Prohibition Association (and who was awarded his position in late 1917 for his dedicated crusade against liquor), stands charged with the import and sale of illegal alcohol, some of it rerouted from other destinations, and some simply stolen from government warehouses. As the Royal Commission convened on the matter will quickly learn, Findlay was not particularly careful when it came to his criminal activities: the warehouse used to store alcohol was rented in his name, and a subsequent seizure of 109 cases of whisky will be found to have his initials inscribed on them. In fact, one day before the issue of his arrest warrant, Findlay appeared in Victoria, pleaded guilty, and was fined $1,000 for importing liquor.

"It is believed in police circles here that following the payment of his fine the ex-commissioner went right through on the boat to Seattle," the *Province* continues, "fearing that the Police Court proceedings might be followed by an investigation by a commission."

As the paper notes, this is hardly the first time Findlay has disappeared in the face of legal action.

"It will be recalled that the local inquiry was called towards the end of August last," points out the *Province*, dryly, "when it developed that the then Commissioner had been 'obliged' to go to a conference at Ottawa."

Findlay will be found by police almost immediately and one week later will appear before the Royal Commission, refusing to testify or answer any questions. Despite his refusal to talk, the packed courtroom will hear startling testimony from a number of witnesses, alleging the existence of a city-wide storage and distribution network (even pointing to liquor delivery by the Hudson's Bay Company).

At the close of the Royal Commission, Findlay will be sentenced to two years in prison. Though a new prohibition commissioner has already been appointed, Prohibition itself will be repealed by late 1920.

DECEMBER 19, 1964

"Dance-Hall Fad Comes to Town," reads a headline in the *Vancouver Sun* as the paper examines the newest sensation to sweep through town: the discotheque.

"Chances are that several thousand Vancouver teenagers will soon be digging [discotheques]—with the frantic intensity that only teen-agers seem to be capable of producing," the paper declares. "Because seven (7, count 'em 7) discotheque rooms are within a couple of months of being born in our area."

The discotheque "movement," the paper explains, started in France (as a result of the Nazi ban on jazz music during the Second World War) but was popularized only after the opening of Paris's Whisky a Go-Go in the late 1940s and by American venues such as New York's Peppermint Lounge. BC's first discotheque was opened in Victoria in September 1963 and within months was playing host to more than 2,000 people a day.

"So, what's a discotheque room?" the paper asks. "Basically, it's a place where people go to dance to recorded music. Usually, there's a great big old juke box in a discotheque room, playing whatever you want, free. That is to say you don't put any dimes in the machine. What you do is pay at the door. By the hour. In the more sophisti-cated discotheques, they have a sort of musical czar, who is the logical extension of the Guy Lombardo syndrome. This fellow's job is to sense the mood of the crowd, and play appropriate records, in order to mold the crowd into appropriate emotional shape."

Though the Victoria clubs have already met with great success, club owners are wary of opening their doors in Vancouver, where city bylaws state that teenagers are only permitted to dance on Friday and Saturday nights, must be between 14 and 18 years old, and need to be part of a couple.

Despite these restrictions, discotheques will quickly grow in popularity, replacing the jukebox with a set of turntables. Coinciding with the birth of disco music in America, they will eventually be the genesis of the modern nightclub.

The *Sun*, however, is not impressed.

"At some of them today," it notes with disdain, "it's entirely possible to spend $10 for a drink."

DECEMBER 20, 1955

THE CHRISTMAS SEASON BECOMES decidedly less jolly as the *Vancouver Sun*'s Jack Scott attempts to bring some practicality to the holidays' most dangerous "adult conspiracy": Santa Claus.

Scott, in a short piece entitled "Santa Without Tears," takes a cue from Canadian Dr. Brock Chisholm (whose fiery orations and anti-Santa statements in the 1940s led to calls for his resignation as deputy health minister), aiming to protect local children from "the disillusionment of the eventual discovery that Daddy and Mommy are great, big, bald-faced liars, and, of course, the suspicion that everything else they've said is liable to be just as unreliable."

According to Scott, his "modified" Chisholm routine appears to have met with "some success."

"To the question 'Is there a Santa?' I reply in this fashion," he explains. "'There's a Santa like there are fairies in the garden or mermaids in the sea or elves in the woods. The fun is in the make-believe. Santa is like the star on the top of the Christmas tree. It isn't a real star, but it's easy to pretend it is.' This is every bit as appealing to kids as the sometimes elaborate business of trying to fabricate a flesh-and-blood Santa on our own adult terms."

"The older youngsters—those who, you can bet your life, know all about the masquerade—hop onto Santa's knee with a cynical pleasure," Scott continues, pausing only momentarily to defend Chisholm's ideas. "They are wise to the choreography of the annual gavotte and they enjoy it as a part of the whole dance. But a great many of the younger children react between mild fright and pure terror, torn between a very natural fear of this strange apparition and the knowledge that in some way he's the key to the Christmas loot."

Santa Claus at a Hudson's Bay Company Christmas Party, circa 1943.
IMAGE COURTESY OF THE VANCOUVER ARCHIVES
(CVA 586-1750, DON COLTMAN AND STEFFANS COLMER, PHOTOGRAPHERS)

Chisholm, known for years to follow as "Canada's most famously articulate angry man," will serve as the president of the World Federation of Mental Health in 1957, and will be made in 1967 a Companion of the Order of Canada.

Vancouver children will continue to believe in Santa Claus well into the next century.

DECEMBER 21, 1952

JUST IN TIME FOR THE HOLIDAYS, the *Vancouver Sun* prints a story on "Hiram," the stuffed monkey who has become the unofficial mascot of the BC Children's Hospital.

"He was sitting quietly in the nurse's station, minding his own business, just looking as blue as a stuffed monkey can look," the paper reports. "Some perched their hat on his head. A nurse looked at what appeared to be a change of expression on Hiram's face, laughed, and dashed out. She returned with the clothing stripped from a doll in the children's toy cupboard. As Hiram donned the clothes, he acquired a new character."

The 24-inch-high stuffed monkey, given to the hospital as a Christmas gift, has since become a quiet celebrity among younger patients, thanks to Nurse Kathleen Stewart, who provided the doll with his first tailor-made outfit, that of an "Indian rajah". As the article notes, Hiram has amassed a large number of outfits in subsequent years, sewed by nursing staff, including Santa Claus, St Patrick, a Spanish dancer, a prima ballerina, the Easter Bunny, Hiawatha, and even a bridal gown.

"Now, the children beg to go by the nurses' station in Lower East on their way to the treatment room 'just to see Hiram,'" the paper continues. "Those returning to hospital for treatment ask first: 'Is Hiram still here? What is he wearing?'"

"Right now Hiram is dressed in satin and gold to represent the Christmas Angel," the *Sun* explains, adding "Whatever the garb of the occasion, BC's sick and crippled children know Hiram and love him."

DECEMBER 22, 1980

FOLLOWING NEARLY 30 YEARS OF DEBATE, Vancouver takes its first major steps toward urban rapid transit as the *Sun* reports on a plan to adapt the CPR's old Dunsmuir rail tunnel and include it in a downtown light-rail network.

"At the moment, it is not an urban planner's dream," reads the article. "It's dark, damp, and smoky. And it has rats. But, according to Clive Rock, Urban Transit Authority transportation planner, the Dunsmuir tunnel will be transformed when rapid transit comes to Vancouver."

"I imagine we will be paying a lot of attention to esthetics because we're going to have to live with it for a long time," Rock says during a guided tour with *Sun* reporter Maureen McEvoy.

The 1.4-kilometre tunnel, originally built in 1932 for a little over a million dollars, has for decades served as a connection between CPR railyards at Burrard Inlet and False Creek, and has been suggested as the ideal candidate for integration into the proposed transit system due to its location—away from power lines, water mains, and natural gas lines.

"From the warmth of a CPR yard engine, the diesel's powerful headlight illuminates the tunnel's grey-walled gloom," the *Sun* continues. "It is hard to imagine that by 1983 the snaking tunnel could be part of a subway system, complete with colorful murals decorating the walls of three proposed station stops."

A comprehensive report on the tunnel's feasibility is expected from the GVRD by January, with the plan being to unveil a downtown transit system to coincide with the opening of BC Place in 1983.

"The tunnel has one major disadvantage, however," the paper cautions. "It is not very big. Measuring just over 6.70 metres high and 4.87 metres wide, renovations would be necessary whether the Canadian-designed automated light rapid-transit system or conventional light rapid transit is used."

Options include deepening the tunnel, boring a second tunnel beside the original (at a cost of over $8 million), or widening the tunnel (which Rock dismisses as "very time-consuming and dangerous").

While the Dunsmuir tunnel won't be ready in time for the opening of BC Place, it will later be integrated into the SkyTrain Line in time for Expo 86. The existing tunnel will be deepened (allowing for two rail lines going in opposite directions to be stacked on top of one another) and will eventually form the portion of track between Stadium–Chinatown and Burrard stations.

Construction on the Dunsmuir tunnel, circa 1930.
IMAGE COURTESY OF THE VANCOUVER ARCHIVES (CVA 152-6.04)

DECEMBER 23, 1952

A FOUR TO FOUR SPLIT VOTE IN CITY COUNCIL is ended by Mayor Fred Hume, upholding a council prohibition on City Hall Christmas parties.

"A last-minute bid Monday to lift the ban on office parties Christmas Eve at City Hall failed Monday when aldermen upheld the prohibition in a split vote," reports the *Vancouver Sun*. "The vote, taken at a closed city council meeting, came after many civic employees had expressed sharp criticism of the plan to close the building at noon."

While the *Sun* remains cryptic around the exact reason for banning City Hall festivities, the implication is that civic employees have been known to engage in more than their share of holiday cheer.

"Last week, aldermen said the move was aimed at giving workers an extra half-day to complete Christmas shopping," the article continues, "but the staff said it was an implied criticism of conduct at past parties. At Monday's meeting, a proposal was advanced that the ruling be changed to give employees the option of quitting at noon or staying in the building until 3 p.m. for departmental parties."

Aldermen will be evenly divided, with Mayor Fred Hume breaking the tie and voting to uphold the out-by-noon ruling.

A Christmas party, 1942.
IMAGE COURTESY OF THE VANCOUVER ARCHIVES (CVA 1184-1552)

DECEMBER 24, 1975

Joe Philliponi. IMAGE © VANCOUVER PROVINCE (JOHN DENNISTON, PHOTOGRAPHER)

"CABARET FACING 'MUSIC,'" reports a headline in the *Vancouver Province* as, after a lengthy police investigation, "morality" charges are laid against the owners of the Penthouse Nightclub.

Facing charges of conspiring to live off of the avails of prostitution, "conspiring to corrupt public morals," and keeping a common bawdy house are operators Joseph Philliponi and Ross Filippone, as well as Domenick Filippone, doorman Jan Sedlak, and cashiers Rose Filippone and Minerva Kelly. The charges are laid following a December 19 raid and an undercover investigation by both male and female officers (posing as prostitutes and johns) ongoing throughout 1975.

The Penthouse has had a reputation as the centre of high-end prostitution in Vancouver for the better part of a decade, with allegations that the club housed more than 100 prostitutes on any given evening—all of whom are alleged to have paid fees to use the building as a headquarters. The sensational 61-day trial to follow will include allegations of exploitation, attempted bribery of liquor officials, and mafia connections, and focuses on testimony that the Filippones gave credit card cash advances that customers would then use on prostitutes. At the same time charges are laid, the Penthouse is informed that its liquor licence will not be renewed, which will force the business to shut its doors for three years.

"It's like being hanged today and tried in June," Philliponi complains.

However, despite a lengthy trial, and an initial guilty verdict that will include fines and jail time for all involved, the case (as well as a separate charge against Philliponi involving bribery of a liquor official), the Court of Appeal of British Columbia will overturn the conviction, finding no evidence that the Filippones either encouraged or directly profited from the prostitutes who operated within their walls.

The Penthouse Nightclub will reopen in 1978, but not before Philliponi announces his retirement.

He will continue to work behind the scenes at the club until he is found murdered in his office in 1983.

DECEMBER 25, 1886

FESTIVITIES AND GOOD CHEER ABOUND as the inhabitants of the city of Vancouver celebrate their first Christmas since incorporation.

"Did we have a busy day?" former chief of police John McLaren will ask in an interview with archivist J.S. Matthews. "Well, yes, we did, but it was not in the matter of making arrests. The late M.A. MacLean was mayor then, and he thought the duty of the police force on that day was to ensure that everyone had his share of happiness rather than bother about making arrests. It was close to our duty that day to find anyone who was moping alone in a shack or tent, and see that he got out and enjoyed himself. On that day in Vancouver crimes were not even thought of, much less committed. We did not have much of a jail to put anyone in anyway, and no one would have been cruel enough to chain a man up to a stump just because he had had a drink or two."

"There were, I think, three Protestant and one Roman Catholic place of worship," Mrs. George Eldon will add in her own conversation with Matthews. "I think they all had services on Christmas morning, but, bless you, when the services were over pastors and priest and all members of all denominations shook hands and wished each other a Merry Christmas. If there was a tent or shack where anyone thought there lacked Christmas cheer there was no question as to what church the occupants belonged. They were visited, and if the shack was bare they were genially forced to come somewhere where good cheer prevailed."

"There were only three hotels worthy of a name in the city then," McLaren will conclude. "They were all crowded, but there was no quarrelling or fighting on that Christmas day. It was a case of, 'Drink hearty, but behave yourselves, and let the spirit of the day prevail and forget your troubles.' Vancouver has had many happy Christmas days since then, but none more genuinely jolly than that one."

A Christmas party, circa 1938.
IMAGE COURTESY OF THE VANCOUVER ARCHIVES (MIL P211)

DECEMBER 26, 1961

A PARADE OF OLD-TIME AUTOMOBILES MAKES ITS WAY through Stanley Park as the Vancouver chapter of the Vintage Car Club of Canada embarks upon its fourth annual Boxing Day Vintage Car Rally.

"Twenty-three shining cars dating from the early 1900s circled Stanley Park and toured Vancouver Tuesday in the fourth annual Boxing Day Rally," reports the *Vancouver Province*. "Best car trophy went to Bob Spence driving an immaculate, bright green 1926 Model T Ford pickup."

The parade, which has been held since 1958, runs from Stanley Park to the land in Kitsilano that will later be home to the planetarium. It features an ever-changing roster of vintage automobiles, such as a 1938 Rolls-Royce Phantom V-12, a newly restored 1930 Packard Super 8 (which takes home a trophy for Most Desirable Car), and a 1923 Buick Touring. A number of other trophies are awarded throughout the course of the event, including the grand prize (given to Douglas Jordan, whose car required the most extensive restoration) and a "Hard Luck" trophy (presented to Lorne Finlay, whose 1928 Auburn Sedan is said to have had the "thirstiest radiator" at the rally).

The Vintage Car Club was formed in Vancouver in February 1958 to organize a tour of vintage cars from Fernie to Victoria as part of BC's centennial celebration. While preceded by similar associations south of the border (such as Seattle–Tacoma's Horseless Carriage Club), the club boasts of being the first of its kind in the province.

The organization's membership will grow steadily in the years to come and, in the late 1960s, will be instrumental in lobbying for provincial government registration of collector vehicles.

"Most of our cars have lights that can't be dimmed," one member tells the *Province*. "The majority have only 2-wheel brakes, most have no windshield wipers and turning signals. Our cars are in top-notch mechanical condition and the authorities should revise the regulations to consider vintage cars."

By the late 1960s, the Vintage Car Club will have chapters in Victoria and the Okanagan, and will eventually grow to include a total of 23 chapters province-wide. They will continue to host the annual Boxing Day Rally (as well as other events year-round) into the new millennium.

DECEMBER 27, 1965

A Vancouver Sun *delivery vehicle, Jan. 22, 1934.*
IMAGE COURTESY OF THE VANCOUVER ARCHIVES (CVA 99-4593)

THE CITY TAKES ONE SMALL STEP CLOSER to a total newspaper monopoly as, for the first time, the *Vancouver Sun* and *Vancouver Province* begin publishing from within the same facility—the newly completed Pacific Press building at Seventh and Granville.

"Despite the weather and treacherous road conditions, one of the most gigantic moves in Vancouver history came off without a major hitch and slightly ahead of schedule," reports the *Vancouver Province*'s Tom Hazlitt. "Officials said the operation was completed successfully, thanks mainly to the efforts of 200 employees and movers who worked through Christmas Eve and Christmas Day."

The $14 million, 350,000-square-foot site—initially intended to cost approximately $5 million—was not the preferred choice for Southam (which owns the *Province*) or F.P. Publications (which owns the *Sun*), both of which had purchased land in different areas of the city to modernize their facilities. Construction has been fraught with delays, owing to the decision to build the entire structure out of lightweight concrete rather than structural steel. Despite these difficulties, the Pacific Press building will be replete with modern conveniences, being one of the first newsrooms in the country to use air conditioning.

The rival dailies' decision to move to a single facility comes as a surprise to very few. In 1956, the *Sun* joined with the rival *Province* to create a partnership known as Pacific Press, which, although owned 50–50 by Southam and the Cromie family (previous owners of the *Sun*), tied the two publications together economically, creating a de facto newspaper monopoly in Vancouver. However, despite an inquiry by the Restrictive Trade Practices Commission, no legal action was ever taken, paving the way for the papers to invest in a shared publishing facility.

"Each paper has assured us that it will retain its former character," wrote Scott Young in a 1957 *Globe and Mail* article. "Since the chief characteristic of each paper was its bitter competitive spirit toward the other, this character-retention will be quite a trick, something like watching a wrestling match between Siamese twins."

While the papers will operate quasi-independently within the same building for another 15 years, the seeds of a media monopoly have already been sown. In 1980, the *Sun* too will be acquired by the Southam chain, ultimately being sold to CanWest Global Communications, a company that owns the *National Post*, Global TV, the *Vancouver Courier*, and sizable interests in the Food Network, HGTV, Showcase, and History Television as well as dozens of other media properties.

DECEMBER 28, 1918

LOCALS HOLD THEIR BREATH, and a Victoria courtroom overflows with spectators, as the Royal Commission investigating Walter Findlay enters its second day, investigating allegations that the former prohibition commissioner has been trafficking in bootleg liquor.

"W.C. Findlay, the former Prohibition commissioner, has exchanged the amenities of 'the bridal suite' at the city bastile for the rigors of Oakalla," the *Vancouver Daily World* will report in its December 30 edition. "Findlay obtained bail on Saturday and so was released from the custody of police, who were holding him on the charge preferred in reference to the disappearance of part of the liquor stock belonging to the government."

Findlay, who was relegated to Oakalla for refusing to testify before the Royal Commission, stands charged with using confiscated liquor stock and alcohol destined for other destinations for monetary gain, as part of a vast city-wide network trafficking in intoxicants. In the days to follow, startling evidence will emerge in the courtroom: "a complete delivery system existed by which liquor found its way to private addresses," "a special tariff was paid for transportation," and "a very large consignment went up to a Shaughnessy Heights address." There will even be allegations by several drivers that the Hudson's Bay Company was involved in the operation.

For the better part of six months, the Findlay case has gripped public attention; the former commissioner, a prominent member of the People's Prohibition Association (a group which has subsequently denounced him) made his reputation crusading against the evils of alcohol, and demonizing the city's hotel industry, which retains

Stills impounded during Prohibition, 1917.
IMAGE COURTESY OF THE VANCOUVER ARCHIVES (CVA 480-215)

a monopoly on the sale of beer and spirits. Findlay has already pleaded guilty in a Victoria courtroom to the import of alcohol (an offence with a $1,000 fine), and the hearing, originally scheduled to begin in August, has already been delayed several times by Findlay's lack of co-operation. Before it's over, the Royal Commission expects to hear the testimony of more than 120 witnesses.

In spite of his refusal to testify, Findlay will be sentenced to two years in prison (for "breach of trust"). Just in time for the appointment of a new prohibition commissioner, the act will be officially repealed in 1920.

The scope of the city's bootleg liquor traffic will never be fully explored.

DECEMBER 29, 1910

After a year of searching, and a further 12 months of delay, a letter is finally sent to the Vancouver Park Board, informing it of the imminent arrival of Stanley Park's newest non-native species: the eastern grey squirrel.

"We received word this morning that one of our trappers had shipped to you one dozen of grey squirrels," reads the letter from Pennsylvania naturalist firm Wenz & Mackensen. "A long time ago we placed this order with the trapper and we had no idea that he would fill it after such a long delay without first consulting us. He, however, has shipped the squirrels, and the fact cannot be altered. Since it is practically impossible to get these squirrels at any time than in the winter, and since they can take care of themselves if liberated now, we do not think that there will be such great objection on your part to receive these squirrels, and we would ask you to kindly accept them, if you can possibly make use of them."

The Park Board has been looking to add grey squirrels to the grounds since at least the spring of 1909, with chairman Charles Tisdall having sent letters to New York Parks commissioner Henry Smith and to Baltimore Parks superintendent William Manning in hopes of acquiring the elusive creatures. Unfortunately for Tisdall, neither Smith nor Manning were willing to part with their respective squirrels, referring him instead to breeders and trappers throughout the United States.

"Although we have a good many grey squirrels in Druid Hill Park, it is unwise for us to sell any because their numbers are not increasing," Manning replied in his April 1910 letter, "and they are a great attraction to the public who feed them from their hands in the most frequented parts of the park."

The introduction of non-native species is a popular idea in the parks of North America's early 20th century, in keeping with the popular notion of a "modernized wilderness," tamed and improved by human intervention. In fact, a number of other species have already been introduced to Stanley Park (among them, swans, which will prove easy targets for predators), selected expressly for their pleasant appearance and potential entertainment value. The squirrels (which cost only $16 because "they were shipped to you without an order") will be released in the early part of 1911.

By the early 2000s, they will have spread across the province, with their population within Stanley Park estimated at more than 1,000.

DECEMBER 30, 1972

"MATTHEWS ARCHIVES OPENS," writes *The Vancouver Sun* as, after years of civic combat, the Vancouver Archives opens in its new permanent home in Vanier Park, named for the man who made its existence possible: Major James Skit Matthews.

"[Matthews was] the man most responsible for this building and the archives it contains," Mayor Tom Campbell tells the *Sun* during a ribbon-cutting ceremony which is also attended by Matthews's 73-year-old son, James. "It was during the years when most other men his age are in retirement that he built up his collection. It was he who single-handedly ruled council with an iron fist and got what he wanted."

The $1.2 million, 30,000-square-foot structure (built mostly underground so as not to distract from the planetarium) is the first municipal building in Canada constructed specifically to house archives and, in keeping with its idyllic surroundings, contains a grass roof for public use. During its decades of existence, the Vancouver Archives (and its irascible curator) has found itself housed in a number of different facilities. Matthews had kept his collection, including interviews with dozens of city pioneers, in his Kitsilano home before being given its first official space in a decrepit attic room at City Hall. In the years to follow, the major and his materials were variously shuffled to the Vancouver Public Library's basement, the ninth floor of City Hall, and the third floor of the library (before leaving the building altogether in 1964) as the major clashed with city officials on all levels.

"I don't want any part of the city," Matthews once declared in an interview with the *Province*. "It has made nothing but a mess of the archives."

The Vancouver Archives' first home above City Hall, 1931.
IMAGE COURTESY OF THE VANCOUVER ARCHIVES (CITY N11)

Notorious for his tenacity, Matthews (who once threw a Swiss post-graduate student out of the building for dropping a file folder, and who kidnapped his first wife in a failed attempt to reconcile) fought years of forced retirement and indifference from council, suggesting a permanent home for his archival holdings as early as 1959. Though the project languished for more than a decade, it later became part of a series of centennial projects, a series that also included the Vancouver Museum facility.

Although the major didn't live to see the project reach fruition (dying in 1970 at the age of 91), the J.S. Matthews building will continue to serve researchers and locals into the next millennium.

DECEMBER 31, 1897

THE CITY MOURNS AS BUSINESSMAN, landowner, and former mayor David Oppenheimer passes away one day before his 66th birthday.

"David Oppenheimer was a born organizer and leader of men," the *Vancouver Daily World* will write in its January 3 edition. "Not a brilliant public speaker he had yet the ability to imbue others with a conception of his plans and a desire to carry them out. The truth of this is exemplified by his four terms in the mayoralty chair and the general goodness of his character was shown by the fact that even his bitterest opponents had nothing to say against him personally."

The Bavarian-born Oppenheimer, who immigrated to North America in 1848, has been an influential part of city and provincial history for more than a decade. A businessman of diverse interests, his holdings by 1877 included a steamship line, an electric company, a number of mining operations, a smelter, and a popular local grocery store—all operated as part of Oppenheimer Brothers, a company formed with his brother, Isaac. Oppenheimer was also a major shareholder in the Vancouver Improvement Company, a syndicate of wealthy businessmen formed at the urging of realtor Arthur Wellington Ross, acting on an insider tip from railroad president W.C. Van Horne. The syndicate purchased sizable tracts of land in the then tiny logging village of Granville, capitalizing on soaring land values brought about by its designation as the CPR's western rail terminus. Though his broken English made him a poor public speaker, Oppenheimer possessed an uncanny ability to influence others. In fact, it was he who virtually single-handedly convinced private landowners to grant their property to the CPR in the mid-1880s (a feat that guaranteed an astronomical increase in the syndicate's land values). As a result, by the time they became aldermen in 1887, the Oppenheimer brothers were already (as part of the syndicate) the second-biggest landowners in town, owning virtually everything east of Carrall Street. When the time came to name certain of the East End's streets, surveyor L.A. Hamilton will honour him by naming a prominent east-west thoroughfare Oppenheimer Street.

"He was not all things to all men," the *World* will continue, "he was the same thing to all men, genial, honest, and kind-hearted to a fault . . . He saw into the future further than the ordinary eye could reach and he planned and builded accordingly."

Oppenheimer served four consecutive terms as Vancouver's mayor before resigning because of ill health in 1891, working closely with the railroad to construct the Hotel Vancouver, the Vancouver Opera House, a train station, a new post office, and a CPR wharf. His remains will lie in state at the city Masonic Temple for several days before being transported to the Hebrew Cemetery in Brooklyn. In 1909, a statue will be dedicated to the late mayor in Stanley Park. In 1959, Oppenheimer Elementary will open its doors on Scarboro Avenue.

Oppenheimer Street will remain a prominent city thoroughfare, though by the time of the former mayor's death, it will have been given a new name: Cordova.

Portrait of David Oppenheimer, 1891.
IMAGE COURTESY OF THE VANCOUVER ARCHIVES (PORT P662)

NOTES

JANUARY

Jan. 1: The history of amalgamation in Vancouver is from Daniel Francis, *L.D: Mayor Louis Taylor and the Rise of Vancouver* (Arsenal Pulp Press, 2004).

Jan. 4: All of the specifications of the first Granville Street Bridge are from the *Vancouver Daily News-Advertiser* (Jan. 4, 1889). Details of the demolition of the original bridge can be found in the *Vancouver Sun* (March 24, 1939), and information on the cost of the bridges is located in the Vancouver Public Library's Pacific Press Clippings.

Jan. 5: Details on the early history of organized hockey are from Malcolm G. Kelly and Mark Askin, *The Complete Idiot's Guide to the History of Hockey* (Alpha Books, 2000).

Jan. 7: The quote regarding the shark "of the genuine Hawaiian man-eating variety" is from the *Vancouver Daily World* (July 7, 1905).

Jan. 8: Background on John Robson, the Incorporation Committee, and the CPR, as well as related quotes by MLAs, is from Derek Pethick, *Vancouver: The Pioneer Years 1774–1886* (Sunfire Publications, 1984), and Pierre Berton's *The Last Spike* (McClelland and Stewart, 1971).

Jan. 18: Useful background information on and context for the Walter Mulligan Scandal can be found in Ian MacDonald and Betty O'Keefe, *Top Cop on the Take: The Walter Mulligan Affair* (Heritage House Publishing, 1997).

Jan. 19: The history of the Vancouver Public Library is from Gwen Hayball, "A History of the Vancouver Public Library, *British Columbia Historical News*, 10(3), April 1977. The conversation with J.S. Matthews is from Matthews, *Early Vancouver*, Vol. 3, p. 114 (City of Vancouver Archives), and H.P. McCraney's remarks are part of the CVA McCraney File (Major Matthews Collection).

Jan. 20: The interview with Rick McGrath describing the economic basis for the *Straight* occupation is from an interview with the author conducted for *The Dependent Magazine* in spring 2010.

Jan. 21: Statistics on Vancouver's precipitation and snowfall records are from the Weather Network. The "local dailies" mentioned are the *Sun*, *Province*, and *News-Herald*.

Jan. 22: Information on the Granville Street Mall, including all references to "Concept Five" and the aims of transforming downtown can be found in the Vancouver Public Library's "Granville Mall" Pacific Press Clippings. Alderman Volrich's comments about liquor licences and the "better quality" of establishments can be found in the *Vancouver Sun* (Jan. 31, 1974). Mayor Phillips' plans to make downtown "a really pleasant place" are taken from a May 1973 interview with the *Vancouver Sun*. Context surrounding the Granville Mall's decline can be found in Nicholas Fyfe, *Images of the Street: Planning, Identity and Control in Public Space* (Psychology Press, 1998), and the police statistics

regarding the rise of the drug trade in the early 1980s are from the *Vancouver Sun* (Feb. 18, 1982).

Jan. 23: Specifics on the English Bay Pier, including blueprints and proposal letters, are from the Vancouver Archives' English Bay Pier files. The proposal itself comes from a letter by T.H. Eslick, addressed to the Vancouver Park Board, Jan. 19, 1931. The text of W.S. Rawling's letter of April 9, 1931, can also be found in the English Bay Pier files.

Jan. 26: Useful context for the occupation of the Hotel Vancouver comes from Jill Wade, "A Palace for the Public: Housing Reform and the 1946 Occupation of the Old Hotel Vancouver," *BC Studies*, 69–70, 1986.

Jan. 28: Information regarding the BC Penitentiary's history of hostage situations comes from multiple sources, among them the *Vancouver Sun* (Jan. 30, 1978) and Michael Barnholden's *Reading the Riot Act: A Brief History of Riots in Vancouver* (Anvil Press, 2005). Details of the resolution of the incident are from the Vancouver Public Library's Pacific Press Clippings (*Vancouver Sun* and *Province*, Jan. 28 to Feb. 4, 1978).

Jan. 29: Useful context for the plight of the Wobblies also comes from Barnholden, *Reading the Riot Act*. The assertion that the police were "compelled" to charge the mob comes from the *Daily News-Advertiser* (Jan. 30, 1912). R.P. Pettipiece's party affiliation is from Wayne D. Madden, "Vancouver's Elected Representatives" (W.D. Madden, 2003).

FEBRUARY

Feb. 4: Useful information on Joe Fortes's life and legacy are from Lisa Anne Smith and Barb Rogers, *Our Friend Joe: The Joe Fortes Story* (Ronsdale Press, 2012).

Feb. 6: Relevant information on the drug panic of the 1920s is from Catherine Carstairs, *Hop Heads and Hypes: Drug Use, Regulation and Resistance in Canada 1920–1961* (University of Toronto, PhD dissertation, Library of Canada, 2001).

Feb. 7: The newspaper report of "several days later" is the *Vancouver Sun* (Feb. 9, 1925).

Feb. 8: Biographical information on Marie Lloyd can be found in the *Oxford Dictionary of National Biography* (Oxford University Press, 2004). The detail surrounding Lloyd's "objectionable" showing of an ankle (as part of her number "The Ankle Watch") is from an interview in Ivan Ackery, *Fifty Years on Theatre Row* (Hancock House, 1980)

Feb. 9: All pertinent information regarding the Vancouver Opera House is from Ivan Ackery, *Fifty Years on Theatre Row* (Hancock House, 1980), and *The Chuck Davis History of Metropolitan Vancouver* (Harbour Publishing, 2012).

Feb. 10: The history of BC's liquor laws and the evolution of the beer parlour are from Robert A. Campbell, *Demon Rum and Easy Money: Government Control of Liquor in British Columbia from Prohibition to Privatization* (Carleton University Press, 1991), and Robert A. Campbell, "Ladies and Escorts: Gender Segregation and Public Policy in British Columbia Beer Parlours 1925-1945", *BC Studies*, 105–106, 1995.

Feb. 14: Useful context surrounding the selection of Queenborough as the capital of BC can be found in Margaret A. Ormsby, *British Columbia: A History* (Macmillan, 1958). The quotes excerpted from Moody's letters of March 17, 1859, can be found in the Provincial Archives of British Columbia's Lands and Works Department Correspondence (F485). J.S. Helmcken's recollections are from his book *The Reminiscences of Doctor John Sebastian Helmcken* (University of British Columbia Press, 1975).

Feb. 15: The text of Lester Pearson's speech is from "Text of the Address by the Right Honourable Lester B. Pearson, Prime Minister of Canada, on the Occasion of the Inauguration of the Flag of Canada" (Ottawa: Office of the Prime Minister, 1965).

Feb. 17: The Asiatic Exclusion League pamphlet is circa 1921, was published in Vancouver, and can be found at the Vancouver Archives.

Feb. 24: The conversation with W.H. Gallagher is from J.S. Matthews, *Early Vancouver*, Vol. 1 (City of Vancouver Archives). Useful historical context surrounding the city's first race riot is provided by Patricia Roy's exemplary "The Preservation of the Peace in Vancouver: The Aftermath of the Anti-Chinese Riot of 1887," *BC Studies*, April 1976.

Feb. 25: A wealth of information on the history of drug prohibition in Canada was provided by Catherine Carstairs, *Hop Heads and Hypes: Drug Use, Regulation and Resistance in Canada 1920–1961* (University of Toronto, PhD dissertation, Library of Canada, 2001). Statistics on Vancouver's current standing were from Colin Kenny and Pierre Claude Nolin, *Cannabis: Report of the Special Senate Committee on Illegal Drugs* (University of Toronto Press, 2003), a United Nations report published in the *Vancouver Sun* (April 12, 2007), and Stephen T. Easton, *Marijuana Growth in British Columbia* (Fraser Institute, 2004).

Feb. 26: Pertinent history and background on Japanese internment, and Minister Ian Mackenzie comes from a number of sources, among them Ann G. Sunahara, *The Politics of Racism: The Uprooting of Japanese Canadians during World War II* (James Lorimer, 1981), and Judith Roberts-Moore, "The Office of the Custodian of Enemy Property: An Overview of the Office and its Records, 1920–1952," Archivaria, Summer 1986. Mackenzie's "No Japs from the Rockies to the Seas" quote is from the text of his nomination speech, Sept. 18, 1944. The quote from the Vancouver Real Estate Exchange is from the *Vancouver Sun* (Feb. 25, 1942).

Feb. 27: Information on licences for "body-rub" parlours are current as of 2012 from the city licensing department. In Christopher Dafoe's editorial, it is unclear whether "Jock McSporran" is real or simply a character invented by Dafoe for comedic effect. Alderman Harry Rankin's comment about the exploitation of women is drawn from the *Vancouver Sun* (Feb. 25, 1976).

MARCH

March 2: The election results are from Elections Canada.

March 6: Context surrounding the explosion of the Greenhill Park, and its aftermath can be found in John Stanton's "The Green Hill Park Disaster," *The Northern Mariner*, January 1991. The text of Justice Smith's report is excerpted from Report of the Inquiry Commission (May 1945).

March 7: Biographical data on E. Pauline Johnson is from Charlotte Gray, *Flint and Feather: The Life and Times of E. Pauline Johnson, Tekahionwake* (HarperCollins, 2002), and from Robin Laurence's introduction to the 1997 edition of *Legends of Vancouver* (Douglas & McIntyre).

March 8: The assessment of Andrew Carnegie's personal donations is from the *New York Times* (Aug. 12, 1919). The interview with Mayor T.O. Townley is from the Vancouver *Province* (March 8, 1901).

March 9: Relevant background on Terry Fox's amputation and legacy can be found in Leslie Scrivener, *Terry Fox: His Story* (Terry Fox Foundation, 1981). The excerpt from the letter is from correspondence between Terry Fox and Canadian Cancer Society executive director Blair MacKenzie.

March 10: Information on the history of the Second Narrows Bridge is from Eric Jamieson, *Tragedy at Second Narrows* (Harbour Publishing. 2008).

March 12: The history of Granville Island is drawn from multiple sources, among them the *Vancouver Sun* (March 9, 1968, and Feb. 21, 1978), and a column by Chuck Davis in the Vancouver *Province* (Nov. 18, 1979). The phrase "somewhat dishevelled industrial area" is from a quote attributed to Ron Basford in the *Vancouver Sun* (March 12, 1977).

March 14: Information on Howard Hughes's stay in Vancouver is drawn from multiple sources, among them the *Vancouver Courier* (Dec. 16, 2004) and James Phelan, *Howard Hughes: The Hidden Years (Collins*, 1977). The interviews with Stan Yip are from the *Winnipeg Free Press* (June 21, 2003) and the *Vancouver Courier* (Dec. 16, 2004).

March 16: Useful information on the CPR's Empress ships can be found in Donald E. Waite, *Vancouver Exposed: A History in Photographs* (Waite Bird Photos, 2010).

March 17: The history of the English Bay Pier is from the Vancouver Archives' English Bay and English Bay Pier files. The quote from W.H. Roberts is excerpted from the *Vancouver Sun* (Feb. 7, 1939).

March 19: The history of the Orpheum Theatre is from Ackery, *Fifty Years on Theatre Row*. Its designation as a National Historic Site of Canada is from the Historic Sites and Monuments Board of Canada's minutes, November 1979 (Screening Paper, 1979).

March 20: All relevant information on the Janet Smith murder is from Ed Starkins, *Who Killed Janet Smith?* (Anvil Press, 1985).

March 21: Details on Rick Hansen's Man in Motion tour are from Hansen and Jim Taylor, *Rick Hansen, Man in Motion* (Douglas & McIntyre, 1987). Specifics on the funds raised by the tour are from the *Vancouver Sun* (May 22, 2007).

March 24: Information on the history of butter and margarine in Canada is from W.H. Heick, *A Propensity to Protect: Butter, Margarine, and the Rise of Urban Culture in Canada* (Wilfrid Laurier University Press, 1991).

March 25: Details on Helena Gutteridge's life and work are from Irene Howard, *The Struggle for Social Justice in British Columbia: Helena Gutteridge, the Unknown Reformer* (UBC Press, 1992).

March 26: The history of the Stanley Cup is from Jack Falla et al., *Quest for the Cup* (Key Porter Books, 2001).

March 28: Relevant data on poliomyelitis is from J.I. Cohen, "Enteroviruses and Reoviruses," in *Harrison's Principles of Internal Medicine*, 16th ed. (McGraw-Hill Professional). Additional information is from Louis P. Cain, "Water and Sanitation Services in Vancouver: An Historical Perspective," *BC Studies*, 30, 1976.

March 29: The history of the Klondike Gold Rush and its economic effect on Vancouver is from Pierre Berton, *Klondike: The Last Great Gold Rush 1896–1899* (Doubleday Canada, 2001). News of a "ton of gold" is from the *Seattle Post-Intelligencer* (July 17, 1897).

March 30: The text of the *Georgia Straight* manifesto is from a copy of the document provided to the author by Pierre Coupey. Useful context for Vancouver's "Summer of Love" can be found in Lawrence Aronsen, *City of Love and Revolution: Vancouver in the Sixties* (New Star Books, 2010). Tom Campbell's reference to hippies as "scum" is from *Vancouver Life* (May 1968).

March 31: Additional information surrounding the case of George Walkem and Blanche Bond is from the Vancouver *Province* (April 11, 1908) and the *Vancouver Daily News-Advertiser* (April 11, 1908). Background on the Supreme Court decision to strike down Canada's abortion law is from the text of Regina v. Morgentaler (1988).

APRIL

April 1: Joachim Foikis's remarks on fooldom are from Patrick Nagel, "Vancouver's Fool: Is He or Isn't He?" *Vancouver Sun Weekend Magazine* (June 22, 1968) and *Vancouver Sun* (April 2, 1968).

April 2: J.S. Helmcken's reminiscences on the capital debate are from *The Reminiscences of Doctor John Sebastian Helmcken*.

April 7: A wealth of information on the sterilization act, its intentions, and its legacy can be found in Gail van Heeswijk's thesis, *An Act Respecting Sexual Sterilization: Reasons for Enacting and Repealing the Act* (University of Waterloo, 1984).

April 8: Context for the life and career of Ray Woods are from the *Cass City Chronicle* (Jan. 6, 1939).

April 12: F.C. Wade's letter and Swaine's reports can be found among the Vancouver Archives' collection of Park Board Correspondence (CVA 48-C-1-file 4, and CVA 48-C-5 files 2 and 3, respectively). Invaluable context for the environmental history of Stanley Park, and forestry philosophy in general, was provided by Sean Kheraj, "Improving Nature: Remaking Stanley Park's Forest," *BC Studies*, Summer 2008.

April 13: Information on the life and legacy of Frank Rogers and the stevedores, as well as the quote from Mike Vidulich, is from Janet Mary Nichol's article on Rogers in *BC Historical News*, 36(22), 2003.

April 14: Information on the North American patent medicine industry is from James Harvey Young, *The Toadstool Millionaires: A Social History of Patent Medicines in America before Federal Regulation* (Princeton University Press, 1961).

April 16: The final fate of the Frances Street squats is from the *Ubyssey* (Nov. 30, 1990).

April 18: The history of violence in the NHL, as well as the quote from the *Toronto Star*, is from Jack Falla et al., *Quest for the Cup*.

April 19: Information on the history and consequences of the Indian Act and the potlatch ban can be found in Christopher Bracken's *The Potlatch Papers: A Colonial Case History* (University of Chicago Press, 1997), and William Halliday, *Potlatch and Totem: The Recollections of an Indian Agent* (J.M. Dent, 1935).

April 20: The history of Vancouver's 4/20 celebration is from Chris Goodwin, "4/20: Smoke Out the Globe," *Cannabis Culture* (April 1, 2010); Marc Emery, "Origins of 4/20 as a Day of Celebration and Protests," *Huffington Post* (April 20, 2012); and Maria Alicia Gaura, "Stoner Chic Traces Origin to San Rafael," *San Francisco Chronicle* (April 20, 2000).

April 25: The interview with Mrs. Theodore Ludgate is from J.S. Matthews, *Early Vancouver*, Vol. 5, p. 149. Deadman's Island's history as a smallpox burial ground is from Mike Steele, *Vancouver's*

Famous Stanley Park: A Year-Round Playground (Heritage House, 1993).

April 26: Information on residential school health experiments can be found in Megan Sproule-Jones, "Crusading for the Forgotten: Dr. Peter Bryce, Public Health, and Prairie Native Residential Schools," *Canadian Bulletin of Medical History*, 13, 1996, and David Napier, "Ottawa Experimented on Native Kids", *Anglican Journal*, May 1, 2000.

April 29: The history of Oakalla Prison and capital punishment are from Earl Andersen, *Hard Place to Do Time: The History of Oakalla Prison 1919–1991* (Hillpoint Publications, 1993).

MAY

May 2: Information on Expo 86's operating expenses, revenues, and other general statistics is from the fair's *General Report on the 1986 World Exposition, May 2–October 13, 1986* (Department of External Affairs, 1986).

May 3: Quotes from J.T. Abray and George Schetky concerning the city's first election are from J.S. Matthews, *Early Vancouver*, Vol. 3, p. 235, and Vol. 5, p. 189). The conversation with V.W. Haywood is also from *Early Vancouver*, Vol. 4, p. 210.

May 5: Pierre Coupey's reminiscences regarding the founding of the *Georgia Straight*, as well as the remarks surrounding the printing of the second issue, come from an interview with the author conducted for *The Dependent Magazine* in spring 2010.

May 9: Additional information surrounding the Bank of British Columbia can be found in Chuck Davis', *The Chuck Davis History of Metropolitan Vancouver* (Harbour Publishing, 2011).

May 10: W.H. Gallagher's recollection of the first council meeting is from the *Vancouver Historical Journal* (CVA, Oct. 3, 1958).

May 11: Fred Hume's legacy is from his obituary in the *Sun* and *Province* (Feb. 18, 1967). The quotes from aldermen concerning Hume's plan to fill False Creek with concrete are from the *Vancouver Daily Province* (May 10, 1951). (Outrage about the proposal was significant enough to be covered in two successive editions.)

May 12: Information surrounding the second city council meeting, Stanley Park, and CPR manoeuvring is from Jean Barman, *Stanley Park's Secret: The Forgotten Families of Whoi Whoi, Kanaka Ranch, and Brockton Point* (Harbour Publishing, 2005).

May 13: The history of District Lot 301 is from Lisa Smedman's "Vancouver: Stories of a City" (CanWest Publishing, 2008).

May 15: Background on the Arthur Laing Bridge and its troublesome commuter lanes is from the *Vancouver Courier* (May 2, 1984), *Vancouver Sun* (Dec. 9, 1975), and Vancouver *Province* (May 17, 1976). The quote from Mayor Art Phillips is from

the Vancouver *Province* (May 17, 1976).

May 19: Vancouver's dubious honour as the bank robbery capital of North America is from the *Vancouver Sun* (Nov. 17, 2008).

May 20: Discussion of horse-drawn traffic on the Granville Street Bridge is from the *Vancouver Star* (May 18, 1929). (Discussion was ongoing for several days.)

May 22: Context surrounding the Vancouver Canucks' entry into the NHL is from Stephen Drake, *The Vancouver Canucks: The Best Players and the Greatest Games* (Overtime Books, 2007), and Norm Jewison, *Vancouver Canucks: The First Twenty Years* (Polestar Publications, 1990).

May 23: Information and context surrounding the Komagata Maru comes from multiple sources, among them Ali Kazimi, *Undesirables: White Canada and the Komagata Maru* (Douglas & McIntyre, 2011), and the text of Order-in-Council 1255 (approved June 3, 1908).

May 24: Canada's current drug enforcement expenditures are from J. Rehm et al., *The Costs of Substance Abuse in Canada* (Canadian Centre on Substance Abuse, 2006).

May 25: The history of Lost Lagoon is from Mike Steele, *Vancouver's Famous Stanley Park: A Year-Round Playground* (Heritage House, 1993).

May 26: The history of the Vancouver Public Library is from Stanley Read, R.V. Cardin, Morton Jordan, and Margaret Brunette, *Vancouver Public Library: A Capsule History* (Vancouver Public Library, 1975)

May 27: The life and legacy of Harry Jerome are from Fil Fraser, *Running Uphill: The Short, Fast Life of Canadian Champion Harry Jerome* (Dragon Hill Publications, 2006), and Tom Hawthorn, "Fame Was Fleeting: Vancouver's Williams and Jerome Raced on through Tragedy and Triumph," Vancouver *Province* (July 14, 1996).

May 28: The history of the Vancouver Fire Department, and all associated quotes are from Alex Matches, *Vancouver's Bravest: A Firefighting History* (Hancock House, 2007).

May 29: Information on the life of Jack Deighton comes from multiple sources, including Jill Foran, *Vancouver's Old-Time Scoundrels: Gassy Jack's Exploits and Other Skulduggery* (Altitude Publications, 2003); Raymond Hull and Olga Ruskin, *Gastown's Gassy Jack* (Gordon Soules Economic Research, 1971); and Deighton's obituary in the *Mainland Guardian* (June 9, 1875).

May 30: Information on Steve Fonyo's life and career is from the Vancouver *Province* (Sept. 13, 2006) and the text of the "Termination of Appointment to the Order of Canada," *Canadian Gazette,* 144(4), Jan. 23, 2010.

JUNE

June 3: Background on the Clark Park gang is from Aaron Chapman, "Gangs of Vancouver," *Vancouver Courier* (Feb. 4, 2011).

June 4: Many of the details of L.D. Taylor's life and achievements, as well as the "personal correspondence," are from Daniel Francis, *L.D: Mayor Louis Taylor and the Rise of Vancouver* (Arsenal Pulp Press, 2004).

June 5: Context for the English Bay and waterfront beautification plans are from the Vancouver *Province* (May 18, 1961).

June 7: Career details for Pavel Bure are from Greg Douglas and Grant Kerr, *Canucks at Forty: Our Game, Our Stories, Our Passion* (John Wiley, 2010).

June 12: The history of the Vancouver Archives is from multiple sources, including Daphne Sleigh, *The Man Who Saved Vancouver* (Heritage House, 2008). J.S. Matthews's recollections of the Vancouver Archives' beginnings are from a photo annotation in *Early Vancouver*, Vol. 7, p. 9. The quote from Matthews's key-to-the-city celebration is from the Vancouver *Province* (Nov. 17, 1953). The interaction between Matthews and Mayor L.D. Taylor is also from *Early Vancouver*, Vol. 7, p. 12. The quote regarding Matthews's sanity is from an interview with an anonymous "historian" in the *Vancouver Sun* (Dec. 29, 1970).

June 13: W.F. Findlay's recollections of the Great Fire of 1886 are from J.S. Matthews, *Early Vancouver*, Vol. 1, pp. 199, 203.

June 16: The history of White Spot is from Constance Brissenden, *Triple-O: The White Spot Story* (Opus Books, 1993). The quotes are from Bailey's eulogies in the *Sun* and *Province* (March 28, 1978).

June 19: The history of the Vancouver Police Department's first female constables is from the Vancouver Police Museum and from the Vancouver *Province* (Jan. 21, 1976).

June 21: The institution of sales of beer by the glass in British Columbia is from the *Daily Province* (Feb. 2, 1925).

June 26: The history of the electric streetcar is from Heather Conn and Henry Ewart, *Vancouver's Glory Years: Public Transit 1890–1915* (Whitecap Books, 2003).

June 27: Background details on Bill Haley and the Comets are from Greg Potter and Red Robinson, *Backstage Vancouver: A Century of Entertainment Legends* (Harbour Publishing, 2004), and from an interview with Robinson conducted by the author in December of 2012.

June 29: The details of Daniel Fry's polygraph experience are from Fry, "My Experience with the Lie Detector," Saucers, 2(3), Sept. 1954. The term "West Coast saucerpeople" is from a review of Fry's book by Jacqueline Sanders in *Saucerian*, 5, 1955. Fry's doctorate of Cosmism was awarded on April 26, 1960, by St. Andrew's Ecumenical University, an institution that advertised heavily in science fiction publications and conferred "honorary" degrees based solely on the submission of a resume.

June 30: The text of the Chinese exclusion act is from An Act Respecting Chinese Immigration (Ottawa, F.A. Acland, 1923). Statistics regarding British Columbia's Chinese population is from a 1921 survey (6,484 out of a total population of 117,217), and additional background information is from James Morton, *In the Sea of Sterile Mountains: The Chinese in British Columbia* (J.J. Douglas, 1974), and "Anti-Chinese Immigration Laws in Canada, 1885–1967" (pamphlet, Citizenship and Immigration Canada).

JULY

July 1: The history of the Georgia Viaduct is from the *Vancouver Express* (April 16, 1970) and Pacific Press Georgia Viaduct Clippings File.

July 2: Pertinent details on Gerry McGeer, and his tenure as mayor are from David Ricardo Williams, *Mayor Gerry: The Remarkable Gerald Grattan McGeer* (Douglas & McIntyre, 1986).

July 4: Quotes from W.H. Evans regarding the first passenger train are from J.S. Matthews, *Early Vancouver*, Vol. 5, p. 125.

July 7: The history of BC's health care system is from Nancy Scrambler et al., *The History and Present Status of the Health Insurance System in British Columbia* (Health Promotion Directorate, Health and Welfare Canada, 1981).

July 9: Statistics on Vancouver animal control are from the city's Open Data Catalogue.

July 10: The "slime-covered, sewage-infected bog" quote is from the *Vancouver Sun* (March 31, 1954). The history of the city's waste-disposal system is from the Vancouver Public Library Sewers—BC—Vancouver Clippings File, in particular the *Province* (Sept. 19, 1953).

July 11: The history of Vancouver's civic motto is from the Vancouver *Province* (July 12, 1961).

July 12: The history of the sex trade and Vancouver's red light districts is from Daniel Francis, *Red Light Neon: A History of Vancouver's Sex Trade* (Subway Books, 2006).

July 13: The quotes regarding Vancouver's bicycle craze are from J.S. Matthews, *Early Vancouver*, Vol. 1, p. 80. Text of the bylaw itself is from "Bylaws of the City of Vancouver, Consolidated up to the 31st Day of March, 1898."

July 16: The history of Lumbermen's Arch is from the *Vancouver Sun* (March 15, 1952; May 9, 1952; June 16, 1988) and the Vancouver *Province* (Sept. 21, 1940). Discussion of replacing

the arch is from the *Vancouver Courier* (Sept. 14, 1997).

July 17: Pertinent information and context surrounding Moby Doll and Vancouver's association with whales is from Murray Newman, *People, Fish and Whales: The Vancouver Aquarium Story* (Harbour Publishing, 2006), and Murray Newman, *Life in a Fishbowl: Confessions of an Aquarium Director* (Douglas & McIntyre, 1994), as well as Mark T. Werner, *What the Whale Was: Orca Cultural Histories in British Columbia since 1964* (University of British Columbia, 2010).

July 19: The history of sliced bread is from multiple sources, in particular Paul Wenske, "History of Sliced Bread Little Known on Its 75th Anniversary," *Kansas City Star* (July 29, 2003), and Don Vorhees, *Why Do Donuts Have Holes? Fascinating Facts about What We Eat and Drink* (Citadel Press, 2004).

July 20: The text of the 1885 and 1900 head tax bills (An Act Respecting Chinese Immigration and An Act Respecting and Restricting Chinese Immigration is from the Canada Department of Trade and Commerce. Additional information on the Chinese in BC is from James Morton, *In the Sea of Sterile Mountains: The Chinese in British Columbia* (J.J. Douglas, 1973), the text of the Conservative Party's "Address by the Prime Minister on the Chinese Head Tax Redress" (Ottawa, June 22, 2006), and "No Direct Cash In Head Tax Redress," *Vancouver Sun* (Nov. 24, 2005).

July 22: Context surrounding the fishermen's strike is from Janet Mary Nichol's article on Frank Rogers in *BC Historical News*, 36(22), 2003.

July 24: The letter to the mayor's office is from the Vancouver Archives' Park Board Correspondence.

July 25: The history of SkyTrain is from "SkyTrain: Transportation the World Looks Up To," Commemorative Magazine Guide (Martin Communications, 1986).

July 26: The quotes from William H. Evans regarding the SS Beaver are from J.S. Matthews, *Early Vancouver*, Vol. 6, p. 49). Useful history on the Beaver can be found in Derek Pethick, *SS Beaver: The Ship That Saved the West* (Mitchell Press, 1970).

AUGUST

Aug. 1: Background on the life of Percy Williams is from Tom Hawthorn, "Fame Was Fleeting: Vancouver's Williams and Jerome Raced on through Tragedy and Triumph, Vancouver *Province* (July 14, 1996), and Samuel Hawley, *I Just Ran: Percy Williams, World's Fastest Human* (Ronsdale Press, 2011).

Aug. 2: The history of "Ginger" Goodwin and the fight for organized labour is from Roger Stonebanks, *Fighting for Dignity: The Ginger Goodwin Story* (Canadian Committee on Labour History, 2004).

Aug. 3: All correspondence between the Park Board and the Electric Railway Construction Company is from the Vancouver Archives' Park Board Correspondence. The history of tramways in Stanley Park is from the Vancouver *Province* (Oct. 27, 1910).

Aug. 4: Background for the Gay Games, in particular the USOC lawsuit, is from the *San Francisco Bay Chronicle* (Sept. 5, 2001).

Aug. 5: Useful information and context regarding the *Vancouver Times* is from the text of Marc Edge, "Failure Is Impossible: The Short Life and Slow Death of the Vancouver Times," presented to the Western Journalism Historians' Conference at Berkeley (2001).

Aug. 6: Pertinent history and context for the CPR's dealings with Port Moody are from Berton, *The Last Spike*. The quote regarding the British Columbian's "cast iron lies" is from the *Port Moody Gazette* (Aug. 9, 1884).

Aug. 7: Allan Fotheringham's quotes regarding the Gastown riot are from the *Vancouver Sun* (Aug. 9, 1971).

Aug. 8: Quotes from on Vancouver's first electric light are from J.S. Matthews, *Early Vancouver*, Vol. 1, p. 95, and Vol. 7, p. 214. Relevant history of the B.C. Electric Light Company is from Conn and Ewart, *Vancouver's Glory Years*.

Aug. 11: Munro's comment about "big boobies," as well as other details of the Lover's Lane incident, are taken from his autobiography *The Sky's No Limit* (Key Porter Books, 1985).

Aug. 13: The history of pollution in English Bay is from the Vancouver Public Library Sewers—BC—Vancouver Clippings File, in particular the *Province* (Sept. 19, 1953). Discussion surrounding the chlorination of English Bay is from the *Vancouver Sun* (May 22, 1959).

Aug. 14: Property values are from J.P. Nicholls, *Real Estate Values in Vancouver: A Reminiscence* (City Archives, 1954). Bertrand Sinclair's observations on Vancouver are from his novel, *The Inverted Pyramid* (Ronsdale Press, 2011 edition).

Aug. 17: A wealth of research on Vancouver's ban on white waitresses is provided by Rosanne Sia in her thesis, *Making and Defending Intimate Spaces: White Waitresses Policed in Vancouver's Chinatown Cafés* (University of British Columbia, 2010). The anonymous white waitress's description of City Hall is from the *Vancouver Sun* (Sept. 17, 1937).

Aug. 23: Much of the context and history surrounding Wreck Beach, as well as the quote from Don Rosenbloom, can be found in Carellin Brooks, *Wreck Beach* (New Star Books, 2007). The estimates on numbers of "unclothed" come from the *Vancouver Sun* (Aug. 23, 1970).

Aug. 24: City buskers' comments on the restrictive nature of local bylaws are from interviews conducted by the author in September 2011 for an unpublished article in *The Dependent Magazine*.

Aug. 27: Useful background on the Pacific Press merger is from Marc Edge, *Pacific Press: The Unauthorized Story of Vancouver's Newspaper Monopoly* (New Star Books, 2001). The quote from Jack Volrich is from the *Vancouver Sun* (Sept. 3, 1980), the quote from Guild director Bill McLeman is from the *Vancouver Sun* (Aug. 28, 1980), and Senator Keith Davey's data on newspaper ownership is from his report *The Uncertain Mirror*, Vol. 1 (Information Canada, 1970).

Aug. 28: Mention of the Harman statue (and its penis) comes from multiple sources: the date is from Marc Edge, *Pacific Press*. The remaining information comes from Stuart Keate's *Paper Boy* (Clarke, Irwin, 1980).

Aug. 29: The text of the civic defence committee report on nuclear attack is from the Federal Civil Defence Group's Greater Vancouver Target Area (April 1957). The timeline on Public Works Canada's Home Fallout Protection guide is from *Home Fallout Protection* (Public Works Canada, 1986).

Aug. 31: Red Robinson's recollection of the Elvis Presley performance at Empire Stadium is from an interview conducted by the author in January 2013.

SEPTEMBER

Sept. 1: Quotes are from J.S. Matthews, *Early Vancouver*, Vol. 6, p. 13.

Sept. 2: Officer Leslie Schulze's explanation of the Penthouse's door policy is from the Vancouver *Province* (Sept. 24, 1976). All pertinent background on the nightclub's operations is from Aaron Chapman, *Liquor, Lust and the Law: The Story of Vancouver's Legendary Penthouse Nightclub* (Arsenal Pulp Press, 2012).

Sept. 5: Background on the *Vancouver Times* and all related quotes are from Marc Edge, "Failure Is Impossible: The Short Life and Slow Death of the Vancouver Times," presented to the Western Journalism Historians' Conference at Berkeley (2001).

Sept. 9: Information on Vancouver's on-street parking rates is from the *Vancouver Sun* (April 12, 2012).

Sept. 14: Background on the life of Percy Williams is from Tom Hawthorn, "Fame Was Fleeting: Vancouver's Williams and Jerome Raced on Through Tragedy and Triumph," Vancouver *Province* (July 14, 1996), and Samuel Hawley, *I Just Ran: Percy Williams, World's Fastest Human* (Ronsdale Press, 2011).

Sept. 15: Bob Hunter's quotes regarding the Greenpeace are from his book *The Greenpeace to Amchitka* (Arsenal Pulp Press, 2004).

Sept. 19: Useful context for land values in Vancouver can be found in multiple sources, among them J.P. Nicholls, *Real Estate Values in Vancouver: A Reminiscence* (City Archives, 1954), and John Weaver, "The Property Industry and Land Use Controls:

The Vancouver Experience 1910–1945," *BC Historical Readings* (Douglas & McIntyre, 1981). Quotes regarding affordability in early Vancouver are from R.J. McDougal, "Vancouver Real Estate," *BC Magazine* (June 1911).

Sept. 20: History of the Doukhobors and the Sons of Freedom is from Gregory J. Cran, *Negotiating Buck Naked: Doukhobors, Public Policy, and Conflict Resolution* (UBC Press, 2006).

Sept. 22: All quotes regarding Bing Crosby's benefit for the Sunset Memorial Centre are from the Vancouver *Province* (Sept. 22 and 23, 1948).

Sept. 24: Quotes from Ray Saunders regarding the Gastown Steam Clock are from the Vancouver *Province* (March 27, 1978), *Vancouver Sun* (Dec. 30, 1977), and *Western Living* (March 1978)

Sept. 26: Quotes are from J.S. Matthews, *Early Vancouver*, Vol. 1, p. 179.

Sept. 27: A large amount of detailed information and historical context surrounding the opening of Stanley Park, and the families displaced by it, can be found in Jean Barman, *Stanley Park's Secret: The Forgotten Families of Whoi Whoi, Kanaka Ranch and Brockton Point* (Harbour Publishing, 2005). Conversations with J.S. Matthews are recorded in the Archives' Early Vancouver collection, and Sarah Avison's story regarding the eviction of Asian settlers can be found in the Archives' Major Matthews Collection, Topical and Categorical Files—Henry Avison.

Sept. 28: The *Straight*'s 1967 circulation numbers are from Allan Fotheringham's column in the *Vancouver Sun* (Oct. 12, 1967). Context for the *Straight*'s licence battle is from the wealth of material present in the Vancouver Public Library *Georgia Straight* Clippings File.

Sept. 30: The unnamed Vancouver pioneer's comments regarding Jack Deighton can be found in Alan Morley, *Vancouver: Milltown to Metropolis* (Mitchell Press, 1961). Useful context and history of Deighton's life were found in Raymond Hull and Olga Ruskin, *Gastown's Gassy Jack: The Life and Times of Captain John Deighton of England, California, and British Columbia* (Gordon Soules Economic Research, 1971).

OCTOBER

Oct. 1: The history and legacy of Claude Detloff's Wait for Me, Daddy photograph are from the *Vancouver Sun* (July 19, 1978) and Vancouver *Province* (July 19, 1978, and Oct. 2, 1940).

Oct. 5: The history and legacy of the Spanish Flu is from Betty O'Keefe and Ian MacDonald, *Dr. Fred and the Spanish Lady: Fighting the Killer Flu* (Heritage House, 2004). Statistics regarding influenza deaths are from Sarah Buchanan, *Spanish Influenza in the City of Vancouver 1918–1919* (University of Victoria, 2012).

Oct. 8: Relevant context for the trial of Fred Deal is from Lani Russwurm, "Black and Blue, Life and Death," *Republic of East Vancouver* (Feb. 2008).

Oct. 10: Pertinent statistics and the history of the city's electoral system is from Thomas R. Berger, *A City of Neighbourhoods: Report of the 2004 Vancouver Electoral Reform Commission,* and Vancouver Public Library Pacific Press Ward System Clippings File.

Oct. 14: All of McDonald's quotes regarding the autopsy of Errol Flynn are excerpted from his book *How Come I'm Dead?* (Hancock House, 1985).

Oct. 20: Information on the history of the Capitol Theatre is from *The Chuck Davis History of Metropolitan Vancouver,* an article in the Vancouver Sun (Feb. 23, 2012), and Ackery, *Fifty Years on Theatre Row.* The opening of Mother Knows Best has been erroneously reported by several sources to have been on Oct. 18.

Oct. 22: Information on the Liquor Control Board, the Morrow Commission, and Colonel Donald McGugan are from Campbell, *Demon Rum and Easy Money.*

Oct. 23: Information on the duck rapists of Stanley Park is from "Lost Lagoon's Queer Ducks," *Vancouver Sun* (Oct. 25, 1977); "Ducks! What Would Anita Say?" Vancouver *Province* (Oct. 23, 1977); B. Bagemihl, *Biological Exuberance, Animal Homosexuality and Natural Diversity* (Profile Books, 1999); and T. Lebret, "The Pair Formation in the Annual Cycle of the Mallard," Anas platyrhynchos (1961).

Oct. 26: The 1969 article is from the Vancouver *Province* (May 31, 1969).

Oct. 27: Useful context for the case of the Stanley Park Cougar was found in Sean Kheraj, "Demonstrating Wildlife: Negotiating the Animal Landscape of Vancouver's Stanley Park 1888–1996," Environment and History, 18, 2012. The quote regarding the reward offer is from the Vancouver *Province* (Oct. 25, 1911). Robert Allison Hood's recollection is from his book *By Shore and Trail in Stanley Park: Legends and Reminiscences of Vancouver's Beauty-spot and Region of Romance, with Historical and Natural History Details* (McClelland & Stewart, 1929).

Oct. 28: The history of UBC is from Harry T. Logan, *Tuum Est: A History of the University of British Columbia* (Mitchell Press, 1958).

Oct. 29: Background on the Joseph Corbett case is from the Vancouver *Province* (Oct. 31, 1960) and the Douglas County History Research Center's Adolph Coors III murder investigation collection, 1960–1961 (Douglas County Libraries, Castle Rock, Colorado)

Oct. 31: Certain details regarding Harry Gardiner are from "The Adventures of the Human Fly," *Detroit News* (Feb. 4, 1996).

NOVEMBER

Nov. 9: Details surrounding the case of Frederick Ducharme are from Jack Webster, *Webster!* (Douglas & McIntyre, 1990).

Nov. 10: Background on Frank McCoy is from *Frank McCoy, The Fast Way to Health* (Kessinger Publishing, 1926), and Alan Scherstuhl, "Healing 'Female Genital Derangement': 12 Deeply Crazy Discoveries at the Last Bookstore's Warehouse Sale," *LA Weekly* (Feb. 28, 2011). "A Dietary Quack Discusses Dysentery" and the record of McCoy's dismissal from the *LA Times* are from the *Journal of the American Medical Association* (Aug. 4, 1934, and Aug. 23, 1934).

Nov. 11: Estimate provided by the Commonwealth War Graves Commission.

Nov. 12: Details of Red Robinson's career on CJOR is from an interview conducted by the author in January 2013.

Nov. 13: History of the city's bread bylaws is from the Vancouver Archives and the text of civic bylaw 2148.

Nov. 15: All quotes are from Buck, Gutteridge, et al., Interim Report of the Special Housing Committee (City of Vancouver, 1937).

Nov. 19: The life and career of Jim Green is from multiple sources, among them Rod Mickleburgh, "Jim Green Is A Dreamer and a Doer," *Globe and Mail* (Feb. 16, 2012); Tom Hawthorn, "A Boisterous Voice for Vancouver's Poor Falls Silent," *Globe and Mail* (Feb. 28, 2012); David Beers, "A Last Conversation with Jim Green," *The Tyee* (March 1, 2012); and Rex Wyler, "Jim Green, *The Tyee* Interview," The Tyee (Nov. 17, 2005).

Nov. 20: History of the city's Sunday closure order is from the *Vancouver Express* (Jan. 22, 1979), Vancouver *Province* (May 14, 1932), *Vancouver Sun* (June 8, 1957), and the Vancouver Public Library Pacific Press Lord's Day Act Clippings File.

Nov. 28: Fred Hume's legacy is from his obituary in the February 18th, 1967 editions of the *Sun* and *Province*. The quote regarding Hume's annual salary is from remarks recorded in the Feb 13th, 1931 edition of *The Vancouver Sun*.

Nov. 30: The history of the bridge is from the Lions' Gate Bridge promotional pamphlet (Vancouver Sun Publishing, 1939), as well as the Vancouver *Province* (May 8, 1926) and the *Vancouver Sun* (January 11, 1955; January 21, 1955; April 1, 1963).

DECEMBER

Dec. 2: The history of anti-smoking legislation in Canada is from The History of Smoke-Free Spaces (Canadian Public Health Association, online resource), and "Vancouver Bans Smoking in Parks" (CBC News, April 20, 2010).

Dec. 3: Mayor Campbell's reaction to the Gassy Jack statue is from an interview with Larry Killam in the Vancouver *Province* (Sept. 23, 1978).

Dec. 5: The history of LGBT politicians in Canada is from the *Seattle Post-Intelligencer* (Aug. 9, 2003) and Karen Fulcher, "We've Come a Long Way, Baby!" *PinkPlayMags* (Autumn 2010). Porter's assessment of Tommy Prince is from *Maclean's* (Sept. 1, 1952), his thoughts on apartheid are from the *Toronto Sun* (July 24, 1985), and his tirade against workplace bathroom usage is from the *Toronto Sun* (Nov. 12, 1976). Additional context is from "I Sing the Body Hygienic," *Torontoist* (Oct. 15, 2011).

Dec. 6: History of the life and career of Earle Birney are from Neil Besner, "Birney, Alfred Earle" (The Canadian Encyclopedia), and Earle Birney's introduction to *Trial of a City and Other Verse* (Ryerson, 1952).

Dec. 7: The history of the yo-yo comes from multiple sources, among them the text of U.S. Patent 59,745 (North America's first yo-yo patent, dated Nov. 20, 1866), and Charles Panati, *Extraordinary Origins of Everyday Things* (Avon, 1987).

Dec. 11: Background on North America's comic book hysteria is from Fredric Wertham's *Seduction of the Innocent* (Reinhardt and Company, 1954); Carol L. Tilley, "Seducing the Innocent: Fredric Wertham and the Falsifications that Helped Condemn Comics," *Information & Culture: A Journal of History* (2012); and Bart Beaty, *Fredric Wertham and the Critique of Mass Culture* (University Press of Mississippi, 2005).

Dec. 12: Pertinent information on the history of the SkyTrain is from the SkyTrain Commemorative Magazine (January 1986).

Dec. 13: The history of the bridge is from the Lions' Gate Bridge promotional pamphlet (Vancouver Sun Publishing, 1939), as well as the Vancouver *Province* (May 8, 1926) and the *Vancouver Sun* (January 11, 1955; January 21, 1955; April 1, 1963).

Dec. 17: History of city parking enforcement comes from multiple sources. Discussion of "more important duties" is from the *Province* (Aug. 15, 1958). Mention of the birth of the city's parking meters is from the Vancouver *Province* (Jan. 2, 1953). Earle Adams's dismissal of meter maids is from the *Province* (Nov. 20, 1959). The survey referenced is from the *Vancouver Sun* (Jan. 29, 1959).

Dec. 18: History of the Walter Findlay affair is from *Demon Rum and Easy Money* and the Vancouver *Province* (Dec. 30, 1918). News of Findlay's appointment as liquor commissioner is from the *Vancouver Daily Province* (Sept. 1, 1917).

Dec. 26: The history of the Vintage Car Club of Canada is from the *Vancouver Sun* (Dec. 26, 1980) and the official history of the Vintage Car Club of Canada.

Dec. 27: Additional context for the Pacific Press/Southam merger, as well as all pertinent info on the history of the Southam chain, can be found in Marc Edge, *Pacific Press: The Untold Story of Vancouver's Media Monopoly* (New Star Books, 2001).

Dec. 28: History of the Walter Findlay affair is from *Demon Rum and Easy Money* and the Vancouver *Province* (Dec. 30, 1918). News of Findlay's appointment as liquor commissioner is from the *Vancouver Daily Province* (Sept. 1, 1917).

Dec. 29: All of the letters can be found in the Vancouver Archives' collection of Park Board Correspondence 1909–1910. Invaluable context for the history of Stanley Park's animals was provided by Sean Kheraj, "Demonstrating Wildlife: Negotiating the Animal Landscape of Vancouver's Stanley Park 1888–1996, Environment and History," 2009. The phrase "modernized wilderness" comes from Tina Loo, "Making Modern Wilderness: Conserving Wildlife in Twentieth-Century Canada," *Canadian Historical Review*, 2001. Additional information on current eastern grey squirrel populations comes from Yeen Ten Hwang and Serge Lariviere, "A Test of Interspecific Effects of Introduced Eastern Grey Squirrels on Douglas's in Vancouver, British Columbia," Canadian Field Naturalist, 2006.

Dec. 30: The quote from J.S. Matthews is from "Get Out? It's Major's Pleasure" in the Vancouver *Province* (June 25, 1964). Information on the history of the archives and the life of Major Matthews is from Daphne Sleig, *The Man Who Saved Vancouver* (Heritage House, 2008).

Dec. 31: Relevant details on the life of David Oppenheimer are from Lisa Smedman, *Vancouver: Stories of a City* (CanWest Publishing, 2008). Information on Oppenheimer Street is from Elizabeth Walker, *Street Names of Vancouver* (Vancouver Historical Society, 1999).

INDEX